CONTROL AND DYNAMIC SYSTEMS

Advances in Theory and Applications

Volume 28

CONTROL AND DYNAMIC SYSTEMS

ADVANCES IN THEORY AND APPLICATIONS

Edited by
C. T. LEONDES

School of Engineering and Applied Science
University of California, Los Angeles
Los Angeles, California

VOLUME 28: ADVANCES IN ALGORITHMS
AND COMPUTATIONAL TECHNIQUES
IN DYNAMIC SYSTEMS CONTROL
Part 1 of 3

ACADEMIC PRESS, INC.
Harcourt Brace Jovanovich, Publishers
San Diego   New York   Berkeley   Boston
London   Sydney   Tokyo   Toronto

ACADEMIC PRESS RAPID MANUSCRIPT REPRODUCTION

ACADEMIC PRESS, INC.
San Diego, California 92101

United Kingdom Edition published by
ACADEMIC PRESS LIMITED
24-28 Oval Road, London NW1 7DX

LIBRARY OF CONGRESS CATALOG CARD NUMBER: 64-8027

ISBN 0-12-012728-8 (alk. paper)

PRINTED IN THE UNITED STATES OF AMERICA
88 89 90 91   9 8 7 6 5 4 3 2 1

CONTENTS

Algorithms and Computational Techniques in
Stochastic Optimal Control

Hagop V. Panossian

Computational Techniques for the Matrix Pseudoinverse in
Minimum Variance Reduced-Order Filtering and Control

Thomas H. Kerr

Decomposition Technique in Multiobjective Discrete-Time Dynamic
Problems: The Envelope Approach

Duan Li and Yacov Y. Haimes

Algorithms and Computational Techniques in Robotic Systems

Shiuh-Jer Huang

A Methodology Based on Reduced Complexity Algorithm
for System Applications Using Microprocessors

T. Y. Yan and K. Yao

Algorithms for Image-Based Trackers of Maneuvering Targets

D. D. Sworder and R. G. Hutchins

Modeling and Simplification of Linear and Nonlinear Systems

Alan A. Desrochers

PREFACE

Developments in algorithms and computational techniques for control and dynamic systems have matured to such an extent over the past 25–30 years that it is now quite appropriate to devote a volume of *Control and Dynamic Systems* to this subject. However, the proliferation of significant published material and new research in this field has been so great that adequate coverage could not be encompassed in one volume: thus, this volume is the first of a trilogy to be devoted to this subject.

The first contribution in this volume, "Algorithms and Computational Techniques in Stochastic Optimal Control," by H. V. Panossian, presents a remarkably comprehensive treatment of the state of the art of the algorithms and numerical techniques that are required for the analysis and control design of stochastic linear systems with multiplicative and additive noise. Both the discrete-time and the continuous-time cases are treated in a general setting, and important developments are presented. A unified approach to the linear stochastic optimal control and estimation problems with multiplicative and additive noise are presented, and new results that extend the existing theory are presented. The next contribution, "Computational Techniques for the Matrix Pseudoinverse in Minimum Variance Reduced-Order Filtering and Control," by T. H. Kerr, constitutes a uniquely comprehensive treatment of pseudoinverse matrix calculation in estimation theory for various significant applications and explores in depth the minimum variance reduced-order design methodology for selecting reduced-order filters. Numerous outputs are developed in this contribution, and various cautions in Kalman filter analysis and applications are presented. The next contribution, "Decomposition Technique in Multiobjective Discrete-Time Dynamic Problems: The Envelope Approach," by D. Li and Y. Y. Haimes, constitutes a presentation of a significant new, unified approach to the decomposition–coordination problem of large-scale multiobjective systems. In addition, the solution procedure presented gives a great deal of insight into large-scale multiobjective optimization problems. Haimes is, perhaps, the single most important contributor on the international scene to this broadly complex and most significant area, and so this contribution by him and a coauthor is a significant addition to this volume. The next contribution, "Algorithms and

Computational Techniques in Robotic Systems," by S.-J. Huang, is a comprehensive treatment of these issues in the major area of activity of robotic systems on the international scene, and many significant and highly useful techniques are presented in this article.

The fifth contribution to this volume, "A Methodology Based on Reduced Complexity Algorithm for System Applications Using Microprocessors," by T. Y. Yan and K. Yao, presents significant analytical and practical results on the implementation of linear data equalizers. It is generally recognized by practitioners in the field that the replacement of high-precision multipliers by optimized binary shifts is an importantly useful technique for fast processing, which is applicable to many various signal-processing problems. In addition, the techniques presented are particularly attractive in low-cost microprocessor implementations. In the following contribution, "Algorithms for Image-Based Trackers of Maneuvering Targets," by D. D. Sworder and R. G. Hutchins, salient features of image-based pointing and tracking system are presented. This is a particularly interesting example of algorithm development for systems of interest in the aerospace, as well as the industrial arena, and, incidentally, an interesting and significant applied example of what is now popularly referred to as artificial intelligence. The final contribution to this volume, "Modeling and Simplification of Linear and Nonlinear Systems," by A. A. Desrochers, is particularly important to the theme of this volume, for not only are important algorithms for this process presented here, but the application of algorithms and computational techniques are to models which describe the dynamics of systems to an adequate degree. The powerful method introduced in this contribution for modeling both linear and nonlinear dynamic systems is that of the group method of data handling. Basically, this is a multilayer decision scheme for fitting a function with a polynomial. Each layer of this technique consists of a bank of quadratic polynomial functions with inputs from the previous layer having been passed through a selection layer.

This volume is a particularly appropriate volume with which to begin this trilogy. The authors of this volume are all to be commended for their superb contributions to this volume, which will most certainly be a significant reference source for workers on the international scene for many years to come.

ALGORITHMS AND COMPUTATIONAL TECHNIQUES IN STOCHASTIC OPTIMAL CONTROL

HAGOP V. PANOSSIAN

Rocketdyne Division
Rockwell International
Canoga Park, California 91304

I. INTRODUCTION

In stochastic optimal control applications, numerical algorithms and computational techniques are the fundamental tools necessary for solution of complex systems. Thus, filtering, prediction, identification, optimization, and control are essential entities in the overall solution process of complex dynamic problems. In the filtering process, signals are extracted from noisy observations. Prediction deals with projecting future values by extrapolation of a given time history of signals. As in the case of filtering, when the mathematical model of the system under consideration is known, it is theoretically possible to achieve optimal prediction of the future values of the system states. Even when the model is only partially known, it is plausible to generate an estimate of the model via utilization of past data [1]. Identification is the process of obtaining an analytical model of complex dynamic systems from noisy observations. Moreover, parameters within a prescribed model are estimated, and the accuracy of the system representation is analyzed through identification [2]. Optimization, on the other hand, is concerned with selection of an appropriate model (or concept or design) from a range of possibilities [3]. The basic concern in dynamic systems is the stability and control of the states of the plant under consideration, especially when random disturbances or loads act upon it. The normal approach is to manipulate the input to the system plant so that the outputs attain a set of predetermined performance requirements. The overall problem of optimal stochastic control then encompasses all the various aspects that were mentioned above. When uncertainties and random effects influence the decision, the performance, or the accuracy of the mathematical model at hand, then probabilistic measures are necessary to deal with the system [4].

1

Analysis and design of complex systems requires *a priori* knowledge regarding overall performance, characteristics of the plant and the controller, and mutual interactions of the controller with the system. Moreover, the accuracy of the analytical representation of the system depends upon the assumptions made, the approximations used, the nonlinearities present, the unmodeled dynamics of the system, the parameters involved, and the random disturbances that could affect the plant. Thus, modeling and control of modern complex systems entail an appreciable degree of uncertainty. One very good example of modern complex control systems that is the subject of extensive research is the problem of modeling and control design of large flexible space structures to be deployed in space. Inherent in such systems is the high degree of uncertainty involved in the modeling process due to various factors. The uncertainties are mainly due to modeling approximations, noise and tolerances in components, random disturbances, parametric errors, configurational and random changes (that are often a function of time), and many other factors that cannot be accounted for with absolute accuracy. Statistical data regarding these uncertainties can play an important role in creating stochastic models for the control system under consideration. These models will be more realistic and close to the real plant on an average basis.

Various authors have addressed the issue of controlling linear/nonlinear systems with uncertainty in the model dynamics and control system. Most of the work done in the past, however, deals with system models with only additive noise to compensate for all uncertainties mentioned above; a large portion of the literature deals with linear models in the discrete- or continuous-time domains. For a list of references on the subject see Kwakernaak and Sivan [4] and Mendel and Gieseking [5].

Optimal control theory for deterministic systems is at a respectable level of maturity, thanks to recent mathematical developments such as the maximum principle, dynamic programming, stability theory, functional analysis, and filtering and estimation theory. However, stochastic optimal control theory for systems with multiplicative and additive noise needs further developments for practical implementation and meaningful applications. The present article is concerned with research and theory in the optimal control of stochastic systems with multiplicative and additive noise that are represented by linear/bilinear models. Specifically, the algorithms and numerical techniques that are utilized in solving such systems will be briefly surveyed and discussed appropriately.

BACKGROUND

Methods for the optimal modeling and control of complex dynamic systems have been quite thoroughly investigated under deterministic conditions. However, when the plant to be controlled is subject to uncertainties (that are functions of the states and the controls and are random in nature with known statistics), then we have a stochastic problem at hand [6]. Analysis and synthesis of the problem of optimal control under multiplicative noise has been of great interest in the past few years. For even though the general problem with stochastic variations is encountered in numerous references, starting with the well-known works of Wiener and Kalman, the optimal control of systems with state-dependence and control-dependence noise was not treated until the early part of the 1960s [7].

According to the published literature, the first authors in the U. S. who solved a simple case of a control problem with random coefficients were Drenick and Shaw in 1964 [8]. A similar problem was considered in a discrete-time setting of Gunkel and Franklin]9]. The stability of control systems was not addressed until 1965 by Krasovskii [10]. Aoki [11] and others followed with various papers on the subject.

The optimal control problem for infinite-dimensional linear systems in Hilbert spaces is solved, both for deterministic and for stochastic systems with only additive noise [12]. Similarly, linear quadratic Gaussian (LQG) theory is well established and is at a high level of maturity [4, 13]. However, stochastic control, and even deterministic control for nonlinear systems, is a field that is still open for research. The controllers that have to act under conditions of stochastic indeterminacy can only be functions of the observed data, and thus of the "feedback" or "closed-loop" type. In situations of linear systems with only additive white Gaussian noise and quadratic performance indices, the certainty equivalence principle is directly applicable. The certainty equivalence (or separation) principle states the the optimal stochastic feedback control is equivalent to the deterministic case with the state vector replaced by its estimate. When multiplicative noise is present, the above-mentioned separability does not hold true. This aspect of the stochastic optimal control problem has been treated by various authors [3, 11].

The stochastic linear quadratic Gaussian problem has a number of limitations. One major drawback is the fact that there is no systematic procedure for selecting appropriate weighting matrices in the performance index, nor for choosing the covariances of the noise vectors of the measurement and the state equations [14].

All the limitations notwithstanding, LQG control is applied to a wide variety of systems ranging from large-scale integrated systems with multiple sensor-actuator loops to computer-controlled systems with filters, adaptation, failure detection, reconfiguration, and redundancy management. Moreover, the advent of very large flexible space antennas, and structures such as the space station, require new approaches to modeling under uncertainties because it is virtually impossible to test these large structures under appropriate and realistic conditions. The need for more effective control and system integration, and more accurate modeling techniques, dictate the use of stochastic modeling and control methodology as a viable approach for systems with complexities, uncertainty, and high performance requirements.

In control theory the mathematical modeling and control design of complex dynamic systems and maintaining a set of variables within definite bounds are the underlying objectives. In the operation of complex physical systems, disturbances and external effects, which cannot be exactly predicted, subject the states of the system to strains and stresses and create the need to utilize stochastic models.

Various concepts of stochastic stability arise as a natural consequence of the study of the qualitative behavior of a system that is subject to random disturbances. Admissible controls for specific applications are determined, *a priori*, by establishing effective stability criteria. The criteria chosen often lead to quantitative performance indices on the basis of which admissible control strategies can be meaningfully compared. The latter, in turn, leads to the well-known problem of optimization, i.e., determination of an optimal control function within an admissible class of controls [15].

The disturbances that we are concerned with herein are of three types: control-dependent noise, state-dependent noise, and purely additive noise. Control-dependent noise arises from fluctuations in system structure, or of system energy content. The errors and disturbances during application of the controller can be modeled as multiplicative noise in the control matrix in a linear system. Other causes of multiplicative noise that are control-dependent are modeling of system parameters as idealized white Gaussian noise processes. Control-dependent noise tends to increase errors by diminishing the useful effect of the controller. Stabilization, especially by linear feedback, may not be possible in such cases when the noise levels are high.

State-dependent noise, on the other hand, could be considered as an internal dynamic disturbance which may be due to unmodeled dynamics, especially in systems with stringent performance requirements. Additive noise is considered as an environmental disturbance which, together with the control, acts on the basic dynamics of a system and affects it characteristic behavior. Large state-dependent noise has a destabilizing effect on the dynamics of the system and tends to increase the magnitude of the optimal gain.

Stability may not be achieved even with a deterministic control input if the state-dependent noise is of large magnitude. Moreover, stabilization of an uncertain system may only be achieved through nonlinear state feedback [16]. Uncertain linear systems containing time-dependent, unknown but bounded parameters, have recently attracted a considerable amount of interest [17–22]. The quadratic Lyapunov function approach is utilized in the above articles for the development of the stability theory of uncertain systems.

II.   REVIEW OF STOCHASTIC
OPTIMAL CONTROL

A relatively new accomplishment in modern control theory is the introduction of the concept of state-space representation of a system. The optimal reconstruction of the state from observed data and the unification between the "state-space" theory and the classical transfer function theory have created opportunities for further research and understanding of complex practical issues, which has led to new approaches in systems control. In the present section we will state the general problem that is under consideration, the important relations between modeling and control, and the stochastic nature of modeling under uncertainty (specifically, the uncertainties that are state- and control-dependent and additive in nature). We will discuss both discrete-time and continuous-time stochastic models. It should be noted that, while the minimal state-space in deterministic control theory is almost unique, there are many solutions to the stochastic problem [23].

The most general representation of a complex dynamic control system with high performance requirements is, of course, a set of nonlinear, perhaps infinite-dimensional, stochastic differential or difference equations [24]. However, for all practical purposes, approximations and simplifications are carried out in order to render the problem tractable and to obtain meaningful solutions.

A. LINEAR QUADRATIC GAUSSIAN SYSTEMS

Optimal control theory and estimation for the so-called LQG problem provides the control engineer and the system designer a unified procedure. The LQG approach to optimal control has been praised [25] and criticized [26, 27] by prominent control scientists. The arguments for the LQG approach primarily stress the advantages of this design process in terms of the ease of solution of the equations involved on digital computers. The fundamental criticism, on the other hand, is the absence of a formal procedure for the choice of the weighting matrices in the quadratic performance criterion.

A generalized model for a control system with disturbances can be represented by a stochastic differential equation with an additive noise term (due to errors in the deterministic model, errors in the parameters, and other random effects), as follows:

$$\dot{x}(t) = f(x(t), u(t), t) + \xi(t) \tag{1}$$

where $x(t) \in R^n$ is the state vector, $u(t) \in R^m$ is the control vector, ($\dot{x}$) indicates the time derivative of x, $f(\cdot)$ is the plant nonlinearity and is an n-vector-valued function of $x(t)$ and $u(t)$, and $\xi(t) \in R^n$ is a zero-mean white Gaussian noise vector with $cov[\xi(t), \xi^T(\tau)] = Q(t) \delta(t - \tau)$ for all $t \geq 0$.

A measurement system is assumed given that has an analytical representation of the form:

$$z(t) = y(t) + \gamma(t) \tag{2}$$
$$= g(x(t)) + \gamma(t),$$

where g is the vector-valued nonlinear function due to the output and $\gamma(t) \in R^r$ is a zero-mean white Gaussian noise vector with a covariance of $E[\gamma(t)\gamma^T(\tau)] = R(t) \delta(t - \tau)$. The noise elements are assumed to be independent of each other and the initial state.

The uncertainty in the overall physical process can be modeled in three parts, as follows:

1) The initial state at time $t = 0$, $x(0) = x_0$ is considered a random variable with mean value $E[x_0] = x_0$ and $E[(x_0 - x_0)(x_0 - x_0)^T] = \varepsilon_0 \geq 0$.

2) The uncertainty in the plant dynamic model is expressed by $\xi(t)$.

3) The uncertainty in the measurements is represented by $\gamma(t)$.

The normal approach is to generate simple linear models from 1) and 2) in the following form:

$$\dot{x}(t) = Ax(t) + Bu(t) + \xi(t) \tag{3}$$

$$z(t) = Hx(t) + \gamma(t). \tag{4}$$

The problem of generating estimates of the state variable from the noisy measurements in (4) is of fundamental importance to LQG problems. The linear Gaussian nature of the above problem allows the definition of various optimization criteria (least squares, maximum likelihood, minimum variance, etc.), all of which lead to the same solution. It has been shown [28] that the optimal estimate of x(t) represented by $\hat{x}(t)$ is generated by the following equation:

$$\dot{\hat{x}}(t) = A\hat{x}(t) + Bu(t) + K(t)[z(t) - C\hat{x}(t)] \tag{5}$$

with $\hat{x}(t_0) = \bar{x}_0 - x_0(t_0)$.

The problem of finding the matrix function $K(\tau)$, $t_0 \leq \tau \geq t$, and the initial condition $\hat{x}(t_0)$ for the minimization of the average weighted quadratic error is given by

$$J = E[e^T(t)W(t)e(t)] \tag{6}$$

where

$$e(t) = x(t) - \hat{x}(t) \tag{7}$$

and W(t) is a positive-definite symmetric weighting matrix, is known as the optimal observer problem in (5). It can be shown that

$$\bar{e}(t) = [A - K(t)C]\bar{e}(t), \quad t \geq t_0 \tag{8}$$

where $\bar{e}(t) = E[e(t)]$. Moreover, if $\hat{x}(t_0) = x_0$, then $E[e(t_0)] = 0$. Then the following Riccati equation should be solved:

$$\dot{S} = A(t)S(t) + S(t)A^T(t) + Q(t) - S(t)C^T(t)R^{-1}(t)C(t)S(t), \tag{9}$$

with $S(t_0) = S_0$ and

$$S(t) = E[[x(t) - \bar{x}(t)][x(t) - \bar{x}(t)]^T]. \tag{10}$$

The solution to the optimal observer problem defined above is independent of the error-weighting matrix W(t), and it is known as the Kalman–Bucy filter. It is proved [28] that this filter is a minimum mean-square linear estimator.

In the steady-state situation, (9) reduces to an algebraic Riccati equation that can easily be solved with modern personal computers.

B.   STOCHASTIC SYSTEMS WITH STATE-
        AND CONTROL-DEPENDENT NOISE

In modeling and designing a control system the important factors that need careful consideration are: 1) performance requirements, 2) uncertainties, 3) constraints, and 4) available measurement/information system. The level of performance dictates the degree of accuracy of the model, for the higher the performance requirements, the more effective a controller is needed, thus creating the need for accuracy. Uncertainties in parameters may be left as they are, and a "robust" control system may be designed that is essentially insensitive to parameter variations. Alternately, the levels of uncertainties can be reduced through extensive testing and verification (whenever possible) or by means of real-time, on-line (or non-real-time) system identification. It is the former approach that is advocated and surveyed herein. The main reason for such an approach is twofold. First, system identification of complex control systems is often costly and practically not feasible. Second, a "robust" control system has some advantages that make it more desirable [29]. Moreover, it is not always possible to generate an optimal (even a suboptimal) closed-loop system from an open-loop one, and it could be very involved. There does not seem to be a general approach to approximating nonlinear, stochastic models with linear ones.

Various fields of application have motivated research in the analysis and control design of systems with multiplicative and additive noise. Thus, control systems that involve human operators [30–39], complex econometric systems with stochastically varying delays [33, 34], mechanical systems with random vibrations, aerospace systems with high performance requirements (e.g., momentum exchange for regulating the angular precision of rotating spacecraft [31]), can all be cast into linear mathematical models with multiplicative noise. In addition, problems associated with reflections of transmitted signals from the ionosphere, as well as certain processes that involve random sampling errors, can be formulated in the above-mentioned fashion [9].

Further examples of systems with multiplicative noise models are: nuclear fission and heat-transfer processes; migrations of people; migration of biological cells (as a consequence of the stochastic nature of cell divisions and separation), and noisy measurements on input and output variables. Furthermore, in pursuit–evasion game theory, the response trajectories of the pursuer and the evader may deviate from their nominal paths due to random parameter variations, thus resulting in a situation whereby state-dependence and control-dependent noise is realistically included in the system dynamic model [37]. Modeling of process disturbances with Gaussian white noise often results in multiplicative noise models as well [36].

The control and the stability characteristics of systems with the above-mentioned formulations are rather different from deterministic systems, or systems with only additive noise elements [39–41]. The formulation of stochastic models should be carried out with caution since optimal control laws that are derived from incorrectly specified stochastic disturbances may lead to instability [35, 37–42].

The monumental works of Feldbaum, Bellman, and Pontryagin dealt with a wide range of control problems: stochastic, deterministic, linear, and nonlinear. They were among the first researchers to realize the statistical nature of the problem and the need for stochastic modeling of control systems under high performance requirements and uncertainties [41].

1.   The Continuous-Time Case

Consider the system given by Eqs. (10)–(12), given below. The control analysis of this system has created worldwide interest. Florentin [42–45] (especially in Ref. [44]), Gersch and Kozin [46], Drenick and Shaw [8], Krasovskii [9], and Krasovskii [47], seem to be the first researchers to analyze the above-mentioned control system in the early 1960s. Even though their considerations were basically in the scalar, or single-input/single-output situation, they all realized the complex nature of the system and did not fail to point out that the random variations could result in nonexistence of an optimal control input under multiplicative noise. During the latter part of the 1960s, interest increased in control systems with multiplicative noise. Thus, Wonham [48], Gorman and Zaborski [49], Kleinman [50], Tou [51], and McLane [30] considered multivariable systems and derived their optimal control characteristics.

Kleinman, Gorman, and Zaborskii considered the case with control-dependent noise, while Wonham and McLane treated state-dependent noise situations. The stability of stochastic systems was reviewed by Kozin [52], who brought to light several practical issues.

Consider the following ordinary differential equations with multiplicative and additive noise, representing a linear control system:

$$\frac{dx(t)}{dt} = A(t)x(t) + B(t)u(t) + \sum_{i=1}^{n_1} F_i(t)x(t)\xi_i(t)$$

$$+ \sum_{j=1}^{n_2} G_j(t)u(t)\gamma_j(t) + E(t)\omega(t), \tag{11}$$

where $x(t) \sim \dim(n)$, $u(t) \sim \dim(m)$ are the state and the control vectors, respectively. ξ_i, $i = 1, \ldots, n_1$, γ_j, $j = 1, \ldots, n_2$, and $\omega(t) \sim \dim(n)$ are zero-mean white Gaussian independent random processes with given statistics (realistically these could be nonwhite and non-Gaussian; however, for convenience quite often they are taken as Gaussian white processes). $A(t) \sim \dim(n \times n)$, $B(t) \sim \dim(n \times m)$, $F_i \sim$

$\dim(m \times n)$, $i = 1, ..., n_1$, $G_j \sim \dim(n \times m)$, $j = 1, ..., n_2$, and $E(t) \sim \dim(n \times n)$ are matrix functions, all defined and bounded in the time interval of interest. $E(t)$ is of full rank.

The measurement system that provides noisy information is given as follows:

$$y(t) = C(t)x(t) + D(t)v(t), \tag{12}$$

where $y(t) \sim \dim(p)$ is the measurement vector, and $v(t) \sim \dim(p)$ is the zero-mean white Gaussian measurement noise vector with given statistics. $C(t) \sim \dim(p \times n)$ and $D(t) \sim \dim(p \times n)$ are matrix functions that are of full rank, bounded, and defined over the interval under consideration.

The performance functional that normally accompanies systems like (11) and (12) is given by the following quadratic measure:

$$J = E\left[x^T(t_f)H(t_f)x(t_f) + \int_{t_0}^{t_f} [x^T(t)Q(t)x(t) + u^T(t)R(t)u(t)] \right] \tag{13}$$

where $H(t)$, $Q(t)$ are positive-semidefinite and $R(t)$ is a positive-definite matrix function defined and bounded over the time interval $[t_0, t_f]$. In (13), $E[\cdot]$ is the statistical expectation operator. The optimal stochastic control problem is then to determine the admissible control input $u(t)$ [that normally satisfies a given constraint, such as $u(t)\varepsilon\Xi$] such that J is minimized.

Under additive noise only the system above has an optimal control that feeds back the estimates, $\hat{x}(t)$ of the state $x(t)$ and the "certainty equivalence" principle [3] holds true. However, under the present conditions it turns out that a set of nonlinear matrix differential equations have to be solved and the separation principle mentioned above does not apply. Thus, the estimation and control problem have to be addressed simultaneously.

2. The Discrete-Time Case

Similar to the continuous case, the control system in the discrete-time domain is given by:

$$x(k + 1) = \Phi(k)x(k) + \Gamma(k)u(k) + \sum_{i=1}^{r_1} \zeta_i(k)\theta_i(k)x(k) \tag{14}$$

$$+ \sum_{j=1}^{r_2} \rho_j(k)\Psi_j(k)u(k) + \Lambda(k)\alpha(k),$$

where $x \sim \dim(n)$ is the state vector, $u \sim \dim(m)$ is the control vector, ζ_i, $i = 1$, ..., r_1, and ρ_j, $j = 1$, ..., r_2, are zero-mean white Gaussian, independent, noise elements with given statistics, and $\alpha \sim \dim(n)$ is an additive, zero-mean white Gaussian noise vector with given statistical data and independent from the other noise elements. $\Phi \sim \dim(n \times n)$ and $\Gamma \sim \dim(n \times m)$ are the state-transition and the control matrices, respectively, of appropriate characteristics. Also, $\theta_i \sim \dim(n \times n)$, $i = 1$, ..., r_1 are coefficient matrices, and so is $\Lambda \sim \dim(n \times n)$, all of full rank.

The measurement system for (14) is

$$y(k) = H(k)x(k) + E(k)\lambda(k), \tag{15}$$

where $y(k) \sim \dim(p)$ is the measurement vector at time k, and $\lambda(k) \sim \dim(p)$ is the zero-mean white Gaussian noise vector with given statistics and independent from the rest of the noise vectors. H and E are coefficient matrices of full rank and appropriate dimensions.

The performance criterion for such a system is normally given by:

$$J_d = E\left[x^T(N)Sx(N) + \sum_{i=1}^{N-1} [x^T(i)Q(i)x(i) + u^T(i)R(i)u(i)] \right] \tag{16}$$

where N is the final time step (in the infinite-time situation $N \to \infty$), S and Q are matrices of appropriate dimensions and positive semidefinite, while R is a positive-definite matrix of compatible dimensions. The discrete-time optimal stochastic control problem is to determine the control law that will minimize J_d using the information from (15). Thus, as in the continuous-time case, there could be some constraint on u. Moreover, the separation principle being inapplicable, the filtering and control have to be solved simultaneously.

C.   STOCHASTIC OPTIMIZATION

Numerical optimization entails minimizing a function subject to constraints. Aircraft-structure design is one field where stress and strain energy considerations lead to nonlinear optimization problems. Mostly local optimization problems are considered in practice due to the difficulty in handling global optimization problems. Various approaches exist to reduce the computational requirement in global optimization via parallel processing techniques [53]. It is a widely accepted fact that regular deterministic partial or ordinary differential equation representation of complex control systems is only a limiting simplified model of the real system. In mathematical physics, and in mathematical modeling in general, the identification of some characteristics of a model, such as the initial conditions, parameters, or external effects, can only be realized in a probabilistic sense. In a similar argument, the linear differential equations representations of systems are only mathematical approximations to a real nonlinear system. Moreover, the limited accuracy of parameters, dimensions, etc., available to the modeler, as well as other unpredictable effects, lead to nonlinear stochastic differential equation representations of complex control systems. Major contributions to the analytical solution of complex nonlinear stochastic systems are due to Adomian [24]. Approximate numerical and analytical solutions of linear and nonlinear, stochastic and deterministic systems are generated by means of series approximations. Thus, equations that are solved are of the following general form:

$$L[y] + N(y, \dot{y}, \ddot{y}, \ldots) = x(t), \tag{17}$$

where L is a linear stochastic operator and N is a stochastic nonlinear term with x(t) as a stochastic forcing function. The technique developed by Adomian consists of dividing L into the sum of a deterministic operator, whose Green's function can be easily determined, and a random operator. Under such transformations, (17) becomes a nonlinear stochastic Volterra equation that can be solved via an appropriate iterative algorithm. The iterative method, with the polynomial expansion that Adomian developed, offer significant advantages over existing methods [54]. Separation of statistical averages occurs naturally in this procedure, making closure approximation and "smallness" and white-noise assumptions unnecessary. First- and second-order statistics can be calculated directly in terms of input statistics and a "stochastic Green's function" [24].

For a linear stochastic control system

$$\dot{x} = Ax + Bu + \xi, \tag{18}$$

where $x(t, \omega)\epsilon R^n$ is a stochastic process with $\omega\epsilon(\Omega, F, \mu)$ a random variable in an appropriate probability space and with known statistics, $A = [a_{ij}(t, \omega)]$ [tϵT and $\omega\epsilon(\Omega, F, \mu)$] is an n × n state matrix, $B = [b_{ij}(t, \omega)]$ is an m × n stochastic control matrix, $u(t)\epsilon R^n$ is a control vector, and $\xi\epsilon R^n$ is a random vector with known statistics. Then (18) can be represented in operator notation as follows: let

$$\dot{x} - Ax = \mathscr{L} x \tag{19}$$

then $\mathscr{L}$ is a linear stochastic differential operator in the form of

$$\mathscr{L}x = y, \tag{20}$$

where $y = Bu + \xi$.

Suppose $\mathscr{L}$ can be decomposed into a linear deterministic operator L whose inverse exists plus a perturbation term R such that

$$x = L^{-1}y - L^{-1}Rx. \tag{21}$$

Then

$$x = z(t, \omega) + \int_0^t K(t, \tau, \omega)x(\tau, \omega) \, d\tau, \tag{22}$$

where x and z are n-dimensional vectors and K is an n × n matrix given by K = $\Phi(t, \tau)\alpha(\tau, \omega)$, where Φ is the Green's matrix of L (or the state transition matrix) and $\alpha(\cdot, \cdot)$ represents the stochastic elements of the matrix A in (18). Now, (22) is a Volterra integral equation that can be solved via a Neumann series of the form:

$$x(t, \omega) = \sum_{n=0}^{\infty} x_n(t, \omega) \tag{23}$$

iteratively, such as:

$$x_0(t, \omega) = z(t, \omega)$$
$$x_1(t, \omega) = \int_0^t \Phi(t, \tau)\alpha(\tau, \omega)x_0(\tau, \omega) \, d\tau \tag{24}$$

$$\cdot$$
$$\cdot$$
$$\cdot$$

$$x_n(t, \omega) = \int_0^t \Phi(t, \tau)\alpha(\tau, \omega)x_{n-1}(t, \omega) \, d\tau.$$

For details of the above development and examples, the reader is referred to Refs. [24] and [25].

In a functional analytic setting [12], stochastic optimization is carried out in a measure theoretic structure integrated with the natural topological structure. The measures involved are only finitely additive on the field of cylinder sets (such as the Gauss measure). Important tools for the optimization process turn out to be the Krein factorization theorem and the infinite-dimensional Riccati equation.

Suppose ξ is a weak random variable in a Hilbert space H with known finite statistical measures. Then there is a bounded linear self-adjoint nonnegative operator R (the covariance) defined by

$$E[(\xi - E[\xi]) \, [\xi - E(\xi)]^T] = R_\xi,$$

where E[•] is the statistical bilinear and continuous expectation operator defined on H. If L is a Hilbert–Schmidt operator mapping H into H and η is another random variable like ξ with covariance of R, and such that $E[\xi\eta^*] = S$, then $E[(\xi, \xi)(\eta, y)]$ = Q(x, y) for every x, y ∈ H defines a continuous bilinear map. Hence, S is a bounded linear operator such that $Q(x, y) = [Sx, y]$, where $(\cdot, \cdot)$ is an inner product and the asterisk indicates the complex conjugate transpose. Then

$$E[\|\xi - L\|^2] = tr(R_\xi + LR_\eta L^* - 2LS^*)$$

$$= Q(L).$$

(25)

Here, $Q(L)$ is a quadratic form in L in the Hilbert space of all Hilbert–Schmidt operators. The minimization of $Q(L)$ can be viewed as the simplest linear estimation problem in Hilbert spaces. For further details, see [12].

III.   MODELING, OPTIMAL CONTROL, ESTIMATION, IDENTIFICATION, AND DESIGN OF STOCHASTIC SYSTEMS

The uniqueness of a stochastic differential equation that represents a control system is a very important aspect of stochastic modeling and control. Under high degrees of uncertainty there is an entire spectrum of stochastic models corresponding to a single deterministic control system, each of which will reduce to the given deterministic model when the uncertainties are removed [55]. Once the statistical information is determined, then a unique stochastic model is chosen and the statistical expectation of a performance functional is optimized.

A.   MODELING AND CONTROL OF LARGE FLEXIBLE – SPACE STRUCTURES UNDER UNCERTAINTY

The mathematical modeling and control design of large flexible-space structures (LFSS) is currently a topic of extensive research. The theory of elasticity forms the core of modeling of the flexible body dynamics of such systems. Thus, stresses and strains created by various effects result in deformations and displacements that can mathematically be approximated by partial differential equations with forcing functions and random disturbances. Engineering structures generally consist of discrete parts of finite length fastened together into a complete, integrated system [56–58]. The idealized representation of each of these parts is by infinite-dimensional distributed parameter systems, given by partial differential equations (linear or nonlinear, depending on the specific structure and the performance requirements at hand). The derivation of a finite-dimensional model is normally carried out by approximations that reduce the partial differential equation models to ordinary differential equation models via various techniques. These methods essentially project the infinite-dimensional space into a finite-dimensional one. The most commonly used of these techniques are the finite element, the Rayleigh–Ritz–Galerkin, and the lumped-parameter methods [59]. The rigid-body dynamics, on the other hand, are described by ordinary differential equations. Thus, LFSS are coupled systems of elastically deformable and rigid bodies whose behavior is characterized by nonhomogeneous, hybrid equations with uncertain parameters and random disturbances [60].

There are some fundamental assumptions inherent in generating finite-dimensional models for LFSS. Namely, the existence of:

1) An "accurate" finite-dimensional model arbitrarily close to the ideal infinite system;

2) A maximum fundamental natural frequency of vibrations such that all the modes with higher fundamental frequencies can be neglected;

3) Interaction of various modes, either stable or unstable, that can be modeled;

4) A finite control bandwidth *vis a vis* expected disturbances and desired performance specifications; and

5) A finite amount of structural damping.

The inherent reason for the analytical representation of the dynamics of LFSS is to design a control system in order to

1) Stabilize the system with reference to a given set of coordinates,

2) Point the instrumentation with some *a priori* constraint on accuracy and performance; and

3) Control shape variations.

While only an inertial model with six degrees of freedom is required in the rigid-body dynamics situation, a consideration of control of elastic modes (as well as the standard rigid-body coordinates) must be made whenever the structural configurations are very large, or when stringent performance specifications dictate robust maneuverability requirements. The above-mentioned unified approach to the active control of flexible-body responses, in addition to rigid-body responses, is often referred to as control/structure interaction [61].

The traditional and widely accepted approach to LFSS modeling is by the finite element (FE) method. There are various computer programs that can generate large-order FE models for complex control systems. Examples of these codes include NASTRAN and DISCOS. The FE technique will normally generate large-dimensional models that have relatively good accuracy in the lower frequencies and their corresponding modes, and the uncertainties and errors increase drastically as higher frequencies are included. Furthermore, for every new parametric value, a new model has to be generated, which rules out any insight into the physical behavior of the system relative to parameter variations. Recently, a great deal of interest was focused on distributed parameter modeling of LFSS [62]. This latter approach is definitely more concise in mathematical notation, provides some insight relative to physical behavior and design variations, and renders parametric studies possible. However, all the above-mentioned facts notwithstanding, uncertainties inherent to LFSS are so large that any approach to their mathematical modeling will still be inadequate for designing robust control systems without addressing the stochastic nature of the problem or performing on-line identification (which is very costly). Thus, theoretically, it is possible to develop a "best" deterministic model for LFSS. Then one can incorporate all uncertainties that can statistically be identified into this model for a realistic stochastic model that is closer to the real system, in an average sense [63–66].

There is extensive literature on modeling and control design of LFSS. Two quite comprehensive surveys related to dynamics and control of LFSS were published recently [67, 68]. Most of the existing literature deals with methods of generating deterministic analytical models. In the best case, authors discuss stochastic models with some additive white Gaussian noise vector in the linear dynamic model. This additive random vector is supposed to account for all uncertainties due to modeling approximations, noise and tolerances in components, random effects, parametric errors, etc. Nevertheless, several authors [69–71] pointed out, in the early 1960s, that there are various uncertainties that have to be accounted for in modeling of flexible structures. Hoshiya and Shah [71], in particular, considered the free vibration of a beam that has random material and dimensional parameters with given statistics, and they generated the general stochastic equations relative to the n-th natural frequency. Moreover, they performed sensitivity analyses between random input and output parameters of the stochastic system under consideration. Collins and Thomson [72] also investigated the statistical eigenvalue–eigenvector problem under random mass and stiffness perturbations. Several other authors continued this trend by addressing uncertainty in eigenvalues and eigenvectors due to randomness in structural properties and inputs [73–79]. Hyland [65, 66] and Bernstein and Hyland [80] were the first to address the stochastic closed-loop problem for LFSS. They presented the analytical model of structures with uncertainties in the frequencies and analyzed the optimal control problem under a maximum entropy setting. The author has presented another approach to stochastic modeling of LFSS [63, 64] by incorporating statistical data into the best system dynamic model available. The frequency, damping, and mode shape parameters are considered to be stochastic processes with known statistics, and their closed-loop stability characteristics, under various considerations, were analyzed. A stochastic control strategy is then developed under a given performance criterion.

1.   The Modeling Problem

Modeling of a control system is a direct function of the performance requirements and the size and complexity of the system. However, accuracy requirements and the degree of detailed modeling are related to performance specifications and expected disturbances more than anything else [68]. The control-system model may be generated through simple procedures if accuracy requirements permit leniency, or complicated FE or distributed parameter models may be necessary for high accuracy and stringent performance requirements. However, it is the balance between analysis and testing that renders the derivation of acceptable analytical models possible. Knowledge of structural characteristics can further improve the model and thus result in a better control system.

There are many problems that face the designer/dynamicist which include data acquisition, excitation, hardware, and testing limitations, and many other constraints. Currently there are two basic testing techniques, namely

1) multiexciter normal mode method, and

2) single excitation source frequency response matrix approach.

Each of these approaches has its advantages and disadvantages. One underlying problem with all testing methods is relating the number of measurements, the number of identified mode shapes, and the order of the mathematical model of the system [81].

Determination of modal characteristics of structures is the main object of experimental testing. Thus, natural frequencies, damping ratios, and modes are very important, physically meaningful elements for applications in stability and control, prediction of response and loads, vibration, and modeling, among others [82]. In the above-mentioned parameters, damping is the hardest to identify and model, especially in the case of LFSS, since these have inherently very low damping [83].

One should realize that, in the final analysis, a dynamical system model is a mathematical abstraction that represents the input–output relationship of a "state" vector (which, in turn, represents some internal characteristics) with respect to an ordered set, time. Furthermore, a system model is a finite-dimensional realization on a given interval and with known input–output characteristics, if it is completely reachable and completely observable. These conditions are in general very hard to meet, and thus the realization issue of dynamic control systems remains a nontrivial one [84].

2.   Infinite-Dimensional
   Distributed Parameter Method

There are many advocates of distributed parameter modeling and control design of LFSS [62]. Several authors assess the theoretical and practical advantages of partial differential equation representation of LFSS in terms of suitability for analysis, conciseness, and provision for physical understanding [85]. The usual procedure followed for modeling of distributed structures is the extended Hamilton principle, whereby expressions are derived for the kinetic and potential energy and for the virtual work of the system, and then the mathematical model is generated using the variational approach [86]. For any virtual displacement from the system's trajectory, the following is true:

$$\delta \int_{t_1}^{t_2} (T - V)\, dt = \delta \int_{t_1}^{t_2} FU{\cdot}r\, dt = 0, \forall\, t_1, t_2 \tag{26}$$

where T and V are the kinetic and the potential energies, respectively, and FU·r is the virtual work of the applied forces during the displacement. The modeling problem is now reduced to the computation of the differential terms in (26) and their variations [87]. Furthermore, application of the variation principle and some manipulations yield the following:

$$L[x(s, t)] = [M(s)]\ddot{x}(t) + [D(s) + G(s)]\dot{x}(t) + [K(s) + H(s)]x(t) = F(s)u(t), \qquad (27)$$

where $x(t)$ is the spacial displacement vector, L is a linear transformation, [M], [D], [G], [S], [H] are matrices whose elements are scalars and functions of spacial variables. Also, the latter matrices are bounded operators with domains in appropriate spaces. In (27), [M] is known as the mass or inertia matrix, [D] is called the damping matrix, and [K] is the stiffness matrix. [G] is often referred to as the gyroscopic or coriolis matrix, and [H] is referred to as the circulatory matrix. Appropriate transformations will transform (27) into the state–space representation. Thus, by taking $y = (x, \dot{x})^T$, we have:

$$\dot{y} = Ay + Bu, \qquad (28)$$

where

$$A = \begin{bmatrix} 0 & I \\ -[M]^{-1} & [K+H] \end{bmatrix} - \begin{bmatrix} I & \\ [M]^{-1} & [D+G] \end{bmatrix}$$

$$B = \begin{bmatrix} 0 \\ [M]^{-1} & F \end{bmatrix}$$

In the above equations, $(\cdot)^{-1}$ is the inversion operator, $(\cdot)^T$ is the transportation operator, t is time, and s is the spacial variable. For a stable system $[D + G]$ is a positive-definite matrix operator. In most cases it is also self-adjoint [88]. Moreover, [M] and $[K + H]$ are real, positive, self-adjoint operators in most applications.

In general, s will be a stochastic process, thus making [M], $[D + G]$, $[K + H]$, and [F] random operators. Hence, (28) is a stochastic system with multiplicative and additive noise in the infinite-dimensional space [89]. The above-mentioned stochastic modeling and control problem in infinite-dimensional spaces for LFSS is still an open field for research.

3.   Finite-Dimensional Models: Model Reduction

For implementation and controller design purposes, any infinite-dimensional system model will have to be reduced, somehow, to a finite-dimensional system model. There are various approximation techniques to this end, all of which essentially project the infinite-dimensional spaces onto finite-dimensional ones and thus reduce partial differential equations to ordinary differential equations [89], or large-order models to smaller ones [90].

For structural response analysis, accurate expressions for the most significant (in some sense) normal modes are required. However, most real-life structures (especially the futuristic LFSS) have very complex geometries, attachments, and boundary conditions, thus making it almost impossible to derive exact expressions for the normal modes [91]. Herein lies the need for approximation. Model reduction is accomplished by utilizing separation of variables and reducing (28) to a set of ordinary differential equations, which have to at least satisfy the rigid boundary conditions [87]. Three basic approaches widely used in the industry are Rayleigh–Ritz, Galerkin, and the FE methods. The first method performs the approximations from the variational statement of the equilibrium conditions and involves choosing an appropriate sequence of shape functions that converge to a solution. The second method, on the other hand, requires minimization of the approximation error with the right sequence of admissible functions that converge to a solution. The third approach is more direct and general, in that it treats the system as an assemblage of discrete elements that have balanced displacements and internal forces at the nodal locations. Thus a sequence of approximation functions are chosen that converge to a solution for each discrete element. Furthermore, the selected structural elements must be sufficiently simple in order to match the overall repertoire. Otherwise, submodels should be developed and boundary conditions carefully matched [68].

The capabilities and wide use of the above-mentioned approaches notwithstanding, accurate modeling is still an art that is learned from experience and perfected by personal ingenuity. Moreover, even when accurate large-dimensional models are developed, the issue of reducing the model down to a practically implementable order is of paramount importance in control design. There is a great deal of research interest in this particular area [92]. Thus, several model order-reduction techniques have been proposed by various authors, most of which deal with the problem as a mode-selection process based on an appropriate error criterion [90, 93, 94].

LFSS control design and analysis entails development of a very large-order finite-dimensional model which is followed by a large-order (50 or more) evaluation model. However, the evaluation model is usually reduced further for control synthesis. Moreover, for practical on-board implementation purposes, a reduced-order (<10 modes) controller model has to be generated with special consideration for spillover, i.e., the effect of sensor-actuator locations on the unmodeled or truncated modes of the structure [95]. Thus, (28) is now a large-order, finite-dimensional model, and it can be represented by the following:

$$
\begin{bmatrix} \dot{y}_c \\ \dot{y}_R \\ \dot{y}_s \end{bmatrix} = \begin{bmatrix} A_c & 0 & 0 \\ 0 & A_R & 0 \\ 0 & 0 & A_s \end{bmatrix} \begin{bmatrix} y_c \\ y_R \\ y_s \end{bmatrix} + \begin{bmatrix} B_c u \\ 0 \\ 0 \end{bmatrix} \tag{29}
$$

where y_c is the controlled, y_R is the reduced, and y_s is the suppressed state vector components (similarly for A_c, A_R, A_s, B_c). A part of the large dynamic model is considered absolutely insignificant and, hence, it is suppressed. Another part, which is considered for spillover effects and evaluation purposes represented by y_R, are eventually truncated, and all that remains for the control design is y_c. Most of the approaches used in dynamics and control analysis are normally performed through model truncation, whereby modes that have fundamental natural frequencies above an *a priori* chosen frequency are simply discarded. For LFSS, however, the frequency criterion for structural control is not sufficient in general, and specialized selective removal of modes is more appropriate [96, 97].

4.   Uncertainty Management in Modeling and Control of Large-Space Structures

A very important consideration in controller design for LFSS aims at ensuring stability under modeling and parametric errors, and unmodeled or truncated modes. The simplest approach to the solution of the above-mentioned robustness condition involves direct output feedback, which requires actuators and sensors to be collocated and placed appropriately. There are various other approaches which, in the presence of uncertainties and realistic actuators and sensors, have their respective limitations. All these techniques have disadvantages that could most often lead to serious stability problems [98].

Uncertainty in modeling and control design of LFSS may arise either from randomness in the properties of the structure itself or from modeling approximations and process idealization [64]. Experimentation and testing is one way of reducing uncertainty in the analytical model, or in verifying and modifying it. However, LFSSs are intended to be deployed in space under near-zero gravitational force and testing of such systems on earth is virtually impossible [99]. Moreover, the modal characteristics of LFSS are very dense, and some of their eigenvalues are very low and nearly identical. To overcome the above-mentioned difficulties, several authors have presented various nonconventional approaches to testing and data acquisition techniques, one of which is called the multiple boundary condition test (MBCT) [100]. In this approach, a flexible beam is tested and analyzed with a variety of constraint conditions and constraint locations, and the test results are used to modify parameters that are in error. All the recent developments in techniques of testing LFSS notwithstanding, some underlying requirements still remain and must be addressed. Namely, treatment of nonlinearities and randomness, design growth and complexity, coupling, and transformation of test results from scaled-down microstructures to derive characteristics of LFSS [68].

5.   Uncertainties: Occurrence and Management

Modeling and control design of LFSS entail three basic types of randomness. Namely, uncertainties in the dynamic model, uncertainties in the control system, and random disturbances which have a diverse effect on the performance of the system. The first of the above-mentioned stochastic phenomena is due to modeling nonlinear effects by approximate linear functions, model parameter errors, configuration growth and change, as well as internal and external disturbances. Uncertainties in the control system are due to errors in positioning and actuating of controllers, as well as to internal and external control-dependent noise. The purely stochastic phenomena of the random disturbances are very hard to account for, since information relative to their statistical characteristics is often limited [64].

In situations of very high performance requirements for large and complex control systems under uncertainty, the problem of initial data for modeling purposes is a nontrivial and serious one [101]. Moreover, modeling of LFSS with appropriate consideration of all important uncertainties comprises a stochastic problem of high complexity. Two issues are of paramount importance. First, the objective of the control system should be identified. Second, the initial data, with consistent probability distributions, should be specified. Moreover, an appropriate measurement system should be selected based on the control performance and objective. Even with the best modeling and model reduction, however, it is conceivable that better and more robust control performance can be achieved when uncertainties are modeled through stochastic multiplicative and additive noise elements; optimal control strategies derived under a wide range of parameter variations and random disturbances will result in robust control systems under controllability and observability assumptions [37].

For uncertainty management purposes, consider (28) in a finite-dimensional setting. Under appropriate conditions of stability, symmetry, and positivity, (28) can be transformed, such that

$$A = \begin{bmatrix} [0] & I \\ -[\omega^2] & -[2\zeta\omega] \end{bmatrix}; \quad B = \begin{bmatrix} 0 \\ [\Phi^T] & [M]^{-1}F \end{bmatrix},$$

where ω is the frequency, ζ is the damping ratio, Φ is the modal matrix of the system, and $[\omega^2]$ and $[2\zeta\omega]$ are diagonal matrices with entries shown in brackets. Formulation of the mathematical model in such a "modal" setting reduces the problem of uncertainties to three different sets, namely, uncertainties in the frequencies, uncertainties in the damping ratios, and uncertainties in the mode shapes. Moreover, if the Vandermonde matrix [102] is utilized, then the uncertainties of the modes can be deduced from uncertainties of the frequencies and damping ratios. A similar modeling approach with only uncertainties in the frequencies was presented by Hyland [65]. However, his approach to control design is based on minimum entropy, while Ref. [63] treats the optimal control problem via dynamic programming.

There are other approaches to treatment of uncertainties in modal parameters of structural systems that were mentioned earlier. The basis for all these, however, is quantifying and reducing uncertainty via testing and experience. Structural uncertainty is taken as the difference between prediction and measurement, and statistical correlation analysis is utilized to generate the "true" values of the modal characteristics. In essence, the final model is still deterministic. However, the model suggested in Refs. [63] and [65] will take the best available model, incorporate statistical data into the uncertain elements, and thus generate a stochastic model that is closer to the real structural system, on an average basis.

6. Control Design and Uncertainties

Development of control design under stochastic indeterminacy is a relatively new approach to the control problem dictated by the high performance and stringent accuracy requirements of modern-day spacecraft. The controller under such circumstances influences the system dynamics in two ways:

1) Through the dynamics of the control system, and
2) Through its dependence on the conditional distributions and their respective moments [103].

This "duality" is a very important consideration in any stochastic control problem [104]. Furthermore, the analysis of a control system and the synthesis of its corresponding regulating member can be regarded as stochastic problems, for the fundamental disturbances and stochastic uncertainty of control systems often cannot be neutralized by simple regulation; their direct measurement is not, in general, possible. Indirect determination is possible, however. Thus, measuring inputs and outputs and analyzing their characteristics furnishes valuable information. The lack of complete information on the stochastic uncertainties leads to *a posteriori* probability distributions of their parameters. Although the latter do not provide exact values of the parameters, it is more accurate than *a priori* distributions. *A posteriori* probability distributions reflect the real characteristics of the uncertainties. In general, the controllers whose regulation procedures encompass investigating and directing simultaneously through their feedback processes, are referred to as "dual" controllers [103]. This duality is a significant feature of stochastic control systems.

The stochastic problem described above can be represented via several different approaches. The most common of these approaches is the Bayesian method, whereby *a priori* distributions of all random variables are available. Another approach is the minimax method. There are several other non-Bayesian approaches as well (the interested reader can consult [104]).

7. Characteristic Features of Future LFSS

The most significant features of LFSS are related to their vibrational modes. The vibrational modes of such structures are numerous, very densely populated, and have very low frequencies, often coinciding with the on-board controller bandwidth. Moreover, the difficulty associated with the uncertainty involved in predicting these characteristics renders its analysis and design a difficult problem [105].

The special features relative to control design of LFSS are many, a few important ones of which will be mentioned below. The first and foremost of these is that, "theoretically," there exist an infinite number of elastic modes (in addition to the rigid-body modes) that have low and uncertain natural damping. The controller bandwidth, and usually a significant number of the system modes, have an overlapping region. This latter feature is the underlying characteristic for the accurate formulation of the structural, vibrational, and attitude control problem for LFSS.

The interaction and coupling that exist between the flexible modes of LFSS and the controller of both the attitude and the shape control systems contribute to the complexity of such inherently complex problems [106]. Consequently, a well-posed control problem for LFSS entails a precise formulation of the performance criteria, careful modeling of couplings, inclusion of disturbances and statistical data in the dynamic model, and selection of a practical and appropriate measurement system. Another important complication in generating reliable dynamic models for LFSS is the fact that not only the higher frequencies of the flexible modes are in error, but the lowest ones, being very close to each other, are also very difficult to predict with high accuracy [107].

The enormous size and number of geometrical attachments, as well as the new materials that are currently being designed and tested for use in LFSS, create a large-scale problem of complexity. Moreover, the need for such structures to be transported by the space shuttle and deployed in space is even a more formidable source of uncertainty and complexity. Thus, consideration of all the above-mentioned salient features of LFSS render its modeling, analysis, and control design a formidable task.

8. Model Verification and Validation Problems and the Need for Advancement in Technology

There are numerous approaches to validation and verification of dynamic models of spacecraft, all of which deal with experimentation and/or on-board identification techniques [107]. However, it is widely believed that current techniques that are used to treat dynamic problems in LFSS properly are inadequate, and that technological innovations and advancement are necessary in the areas of efficient modeling, nonlinear analysis, model verification and validation, as well as other areas [61, 68, 108]. Normally, bround tests are structured and performed to provide correlation with the analysis and thus lead to necessary modifications and refinement of the analytical model. Nevertheless, in-orbit tests are crucial in the case of LFSS because they could reveal unexpected nonlinearities, couplings, and other interactions, as well as provide some means of validating ground test results and verifying analytical models. In-orbit tests are, however, costly and harder to design and implement. Scaled testing is another approach to validation and verification. However, the technology involved in scaled testing is not thoroughly adequate for LFSS for the same reason as mentioned above. Furthermore, technology advancement is needed in adapting scaling experimentation techniques to LFSS in order to address all the different features and uncertainties involved [82].

System identification for LFSS in orbit is a difficult task as yet unresolved. Because of modeling uncertainties and the high performance requirements of LFSS control systems, it is necessary to design identification systems that start performing as soon as the structure is deployed, since fine modifications of the control laws might be required before the LFSS goes into orbit. Moreover, identification routines will be required that can handle any system and parameter variations while in orbit. However, systems identification, and even parameter identification, are difficult to achieve in orbit because of instrumentation constraints, cost, and various other aspects. Thus, alternate approaches should be developed to tackle all the problems involved in LFSS modeling for control [67].

The modeling issue of LFSS still remains a very important one, and a unified approach is required that can generate a realistic model that is close to the real system under consideration, in some predetermined sense. Moreover, uncertainties in LFSS modeling and control design being so high, it is essential to treat the problem in a stochastic setting for accuracy and robustness.

B.   OPTIMAL CONTROL OF LINEAR
STOCHASTIC SYSTEMS

It is a widely known fact that the optimal control law for linear stochastic systems with only additive, Gaussian noise and a quadratic performance criterion is of the feedback type and is accomplished by cascading the optimal state estimate with the deterministic optimal controller in (5). Thus, two Riccati equations are solved, and the appropriate estimates and the optimal feedback gains are derived, which furnish the engineer with the optimal controller. We underscore the fact that, by virtue of the separation principle (certainty equivalence), the two above-mentioned Riccati equations are independent [109].

During the 1970s, the control problem with multiplicative noise was expanded further. It was McLane [32] who determined a linear feedback controller for systems with multiplicative and additive noise through the Hamiltonian approach. In his analysis, the measurement system was assumed perfect.

Simultaneously, Haussmann [110] studied the same problem using Lyapunov methods, and derived conditions under which an optimal control law exists. The above researchers concluded that, in the use of control-dependent noise, the control is cautious (small gains), while for state-dependent noise more active controls are required (large gains). Feedback stabilizability in the mean-square sense was taken up by Willems and Willems [35], and necessary and sufficient conditions were presented.

During the latter part of the 1970s, several authors tackled the control problem with multiplicative noise [111]. Timofeev and Chernyavskii [112] considered a worst-case situation in which the statistics of the random variables are not known, but only an admissible set for their distributions is given, while Bismut [113] derived existence results for an optimal control in a random feedback form, using functional analysis. Moreover, he showed that a unique solution to the matrix Riccati equation exists under assumptions of independence of the coefficients of the equation and the criteria from the noise parameters.

1. Problem Statement and Solution, Continuous-Time Case

Consider a linear stochastic control system given as follows:

$$\dot{x}(t) = Ax(t) + Bu(t) + C(\xi)x(t) + D(\gamma)u(t) + E\omega(t), \tag{30}$$

where $x \in R^n$, $u \in R^m$ are the state and the control vectors, respectively; ξ, γ, ω are independent zero-mean Gaussian white noise processes with known covariances of Σ_ξ, Σ_γ, and Σ_ω and of appropriate dimensions. (A, B) is assumed stabilizable. The optimal control problem is to derive a feedback controller $u = \phi(x)$ that minimizes, in the steady state, the expected value of the following cost functional:

$$J_t = \lim_{t \to 0} E\left[\frac{1}{t}\int_0^t [x^T(t)Qx(t) + u^T(t)Ru(t)]\, dt\right] \tag{31}$$

where Q and R are positive-semidefinite and positive-definite matrices, respectively, each of appropriate dimensions. It is well known [47] that when EE^T is positive definite then an optimal control exists given that the control- and state-dependent noises are "sufficiently" small. Moreover, Haussmann [110] has shown that when the above-mentioned noises affect only the stable modes, independent of the magnitudes of the control- and state-dependent noise vectors, an optimal control exists.

Assume a linear feedback control law of the following form:

$$u = -Kx(t). \tag{32}$$

Then an optimal K can be chosen if (A, B) is stabilizable, subject to the following:

$$\inf_K \left\| \int_0^\infty e^{t(A-BK)^T}\left[K^T\Gamma(I)K + \Delta(I)\right] e^{t(A-BK)}\, dt \right\| < 1, \tag{33}$$

where

$$\Delta(S) = \text{Tr}\{E[C^T(\xi)SC(\xi)]\} \tag{34}$$

and

$$\Gamma(S) = \text{tr}\{E[D^T(\gamma)SD(\gamma)]\}. \tag{35}$$

Tr is the matrix trace operator to be defined later, and S is any positive semidefinite matrix of appropriate dimensions. Thus,

$$K = [\Gamma(P) + R]^{-1}B^T P \tag{36}$$

and P is the unique positive-definite solution of the following Riccati-like matrix algebraic equation:

$$Q + A^T P + PA + \Delta(P)[\Gamma(P) + R]^{-1} B^T P = 0. \tag{37}$$

Remark 1. We will need to establish certain rules regarding the expected value of products of matrices that appear in (35) and (36). We will thus need to evaluate quantities of the following form:

$$E[ABA^T],$$

where A and B are random matrices with stochastic Gaussian elements. To this end, we propose the following lemma, that is proved in (37).

Lemma 1. Let A and B be stochastic matrices with random Gaussian white elements and given statistics of:

$$E[A] = \overline{A}, \ E[B] = \overline{B}$$

$$E[(A - \overline{A})(A - \overline{A})^T] = \Sigma^{AA}, E[(B - \overline{B})(B - \overline{B})^T] = \Sigma^{BB}$$

$$E[(A - \overline{A})(B - \overline{B})^T] = \Sigma^{AB}.$$

Then,

$$E[ABA^T] = \overline{A}\,\overline{B}\,\overline{A}^T + \text{Tr}\,(\Sigma^{AA}\,\overline{B}),$$

where Tr represents the matrix trace operator to be given below, and A^T is the transpose of A.

$$Tr(\Sigma^{AA}\overline{B}) = \begin{bmatrix} tr(\Sigma^{A_1 A_1}\overline{B}) & tr(\Sigma^{A_1 A_2}\overline{B}^T) & ... & tr(\Sigma^{A_1 A_k}\overline{B}^T) \\ tr(\Sigma^{A_2 A_1}\overline{B})^T & tr(\Sigma^{A_2 A_2}\overline{B}) & ... & tr(\Sigma^{A_2 A_k}\overline{B}^T) \\ tr(\Sigma^{A_n A_1}\overline{B}^T) & tr(\Sigma^{A_n A_2}\overline{B}^T) & \vdots & tr(\Sigma^{A_k A_k}\overline{B}) \end{bmatrix}$$
(38)

where A_i is the i-th column of A.

The minimum cost of such a system is given by:

$tr(E^T PE)$.
(39)

2.   The Discrete-Time Case

There is definitely a richer literature for the discrete-time problem. The first article on the subject was published by Gunkel and Franklin [9], in which the effect of random sampling in sampled-data control systems was presented in the form of multiplicative noise. Tou [51] followed by advocating the concept of adaptive and learning control under large parameter fluctuations, and used statistical decision theory and dynamic programming. Aoki [11] pointed out that the certainty equivalence principle does not result in optimal control laws under multiplicative noise situations. Controllability of stochastic linear systems was taken up by Connors [114]. His analysis utilizes dynamic programming and derives necessary and sufficient conditions of controllability for systems with multiplicative noise and perfect measurements. Murphy [115] and Grammaticos and Horowitz [116] considered linear systems with unknown gains, while Ku and Athans [117] showed that the open-loop feedback optimal adaptive gains are functions of current and future uncertainty of the parameter estimates. Bar-Shalom and Sivan [118] studied linear systems with random parameters and derived optimal open-loop and open-loop feedback controllers under a quadratic criterion. Stability characteristics for stochastic nonlinear difference systems perturbed by random disturbances were treated for the first time by Konstantinov [119] and Mishra and Mahalanabis [120]. Kendrick [121], Shupp [122], and Aoki [3, 11] presented applications of linear stochastic systems to macroeconomic and economic systems. Katayama [123] treated the asymptotic properties of the matrix Riccati equation with random coefficients, while Athans, Ku, and Gershwin [124] and Ku and

Athans [125] studied the limitations and conditions under which the infinite horizon solution of the optimal stochastic control problem does not exist. Wittenmark [126] presented a survey of stochastic self-organizing, self-optimizing control methods, whereby he also mentioned some aspects of multiplicative noise.

It was Zabczyk [89] who studied the general, infinite-dimensional stochastic control problem of linear systems with multiplicative and additive noise in Hilbert spaces. His analysis contributes significantly to discrete-time systems' stochastic observability, controllability, existence, and uniqueness of solutions, as well as the characteristics of the Riccati equation, both under finite- and infinite-time situations.

Existence and uniqueness issues are also tackled in Zabczyk's article and so are stabilizability and detectability conditions. Stochastic observability is introduced for the discrete-time stochastic system considered, and novel results related to the finite-dimensional applications are discussed. Joshi [127] and Harris [128] also treated the same problem. The latter presented results on controllability for discrete stochastic systems with the random variables in the state and control matrices drawn from different distributions. Pakshin [129–131] analyzed the estimation and control synthesis of discrete-time linear systems by deriving a filter and a controller that are optimal in the class of linear systems. Furthermore, he derived a suboptimal solution for systems with nonquadratic criteria. Tugnait [132] presented results on uniform asymptotic stability of linear stochastic estimators with white multiplicative noise (as well as additive) contaminating the measurement system.

Panossian [37] and Panossian and Leondes [133, 134] studied various aspects of multivariable linear stochastic, discrete-time systems that are partly deterministic, and partly stochastic with multiplicative and additive noise. Furthermore, they analyzed the estimation problem under partly exactly and partly noisy measurements (the latter having multiplicative and additive components as well). Results on a reduced-order linear stochastic observer were also presented that will produce estimates that are optimal in the subclass of linear reduced-order stochastic systems. De Koning [38, 135, 136], on the other hand, reported results on linear discrete-time systems with stochastic parameters having models whereby the state and control matrices are sequences of random matrices with fixed statistics. These articles dealt with the behavior of the first and second moments of the random variables, and through the characteristics of these moments De Koning addressed the issues of stability, detectability, stability in the mean and mean-square sense, and optimal estimation. The subject of systems with random coefficients is still of current research interest. Moreover, design and control of uncertain linear systems was last considered by Petersen [137].

3. Problem Statement and Solution

Consider a dynamical system represented by the following vector difference equation:

$$x(k + 1) = \begin{bmatrix} x_1(k + 1) \\ x_2(k + 1) \end{bmatrix} = \begin{bmatrix} A(k) & 0_{n_1 \times n_2} \\ 0_{n_2 \times n_1} & \theta(k) \end{bmatrix} x(k)$$

$$\tag{40}$$

$$+ \begin{bmatrix} B(k) \\ \Gamma(k) \end{bmatrix} u(k) + \begin{bmatrix} 0 \\ \xi_0(k) \end{bmatrix}$$

for $k = 0, 1, \ldots, N$. For brevity, we can write (40) as

$$x(k + 1) = \Phi(k)x(k) + \Psi(k)u(k) + \xi(k), \tag{41}$$

where:

1) x is an n-dimensional state vector composed of $x_1(k + 1)$, an n_1-dimensional vector, and $x_2(k + 1)$, an n_2-dimensional random vector.
2) $u(k)$ is the m-dimensional control vector.
3) $\theta(k)$ and $\Gamma(k)$ are $n_2 \times n_2$- and $n_2 \times m$-dimensional matrices of randomly varying parameters, which are assumed to be Gaussian and white (uncorrelated in time), with known means of:

$$E[\theta(k)] = \bar{\theta}(k); \quad E[\Gamma(k)] = \bar{\Gamma}(k) \tag{42}$$

and covariances of:

$$E[(\theta(k) - \bar{\theta}(k)) (\theta(j) - \bar{\theta}(j))^T] = \Sigma^{\theta\theta}(k)\delta_{kj} \tag{43}$$

$$E\{(\Gamma(k) - \bar{\Gamma}(k)) (\Gamma(j) - \bar{\Gamma}(j))^T] = \Sigma^{\Gamma\Gamma}(k)\delta_{kj} \tag{44}$$

and cross-covariance matrix given by:

$$E[(\theta(k) - \bar{\theta}(k)) (\Gamma(j) - \bar{\Gamma}(j))^T] = \Sigma^{\theta\Gamma}(k)\delta_{kj} \tag{45}$$

4) $A(k)$ and $B(k)$ are $n_1 \times n_1$- and $n_1 \times m$-dimensional deterministic matrices, respectively.

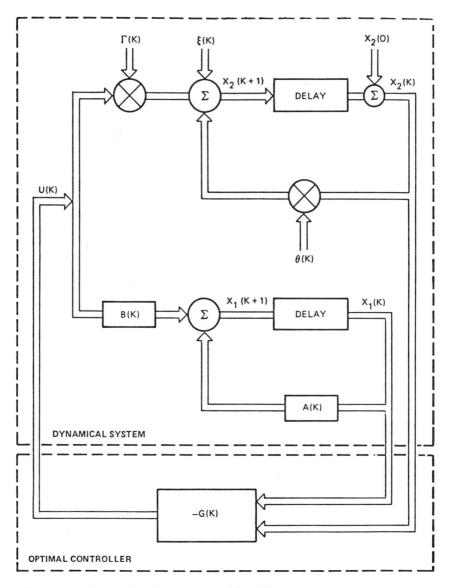

Fig. 1. Optimal controller for the system of Eq. (40).

5) $\xi_0(k)$ is an n_2-dimensional zero-mean white Gaussian noise vector which is assumed to be independent of all the other random variables of the control system, and

$$E[(\xi_0(k)\xi_0^T(j)] = \Sigma_0^\xi(k)\delta_{kj}.$$ (46)

6) $0_{n_1 \times n_2}$ is the $n_1 \times n_2$ null matrix

7) $\Phi(k) = \begin{bmatrix} A(k) & 0_{n_1 \times n_2} \\ 0_{n_2 \times n_1} & \theta(k) \end{bmatrix}$ and $\Gamma(k) = \begin{bmatrix} B(k) \\ \Gamma(k) \end{bmatrix}$

8) $x(0)$ is deterministic (for convenience).

We note that δ_{kj} is the Kronecker delta operator.

The scalar index of performance for the above control system is defined by the following quadratic cost functional:

$$J(u) = E \frac{1}{2} x^T(n)Fx(N) + \frac{1}{2} \sum_{k=0}^{N-1} [x^T(k)Q(k)x(k) + u^T(k)R(k)u(k)],$$ (47)

where F and Q are positive-semidefinite and R positive-definite matrices of appropriate dimensions.

The stochastic optimal control problem now is to determine a control sequence $\{u_i\}_{i=0}^{k-1}$, such that the functional $J(u)$ in (47) is minimized.

Under the circumstance of a general linear stochastic system of the form of (41), where $\xi(k)$ is a vector of correlated noise, it is possible, by means of (37), to model the additive colored noise by a system of first-order equations driven by Gaussian white noise. Thus, if

$$\xi(k + 1) = \theta(k)\xi(k) + \xi_0(k),$$ (48)

then (41) augmented with (48) would take the shape given in (40). Hence, the reason for the particular diagonal matrix-type form that appears in (40) is due to the above-mentioned generalizations. See Fig. 1 for a block diagram of the system.

We make the assumption that all the state variables can be measured exactly. That is, the information set consists of the following:

$$I(k) = \{x(0), x(1), ..., x(k), u(0), u(1), ..., u(k - 1)\}$$ (49)

The optimal control for the system given by (40) minimizing $J(u)$ in (47) is (37).

$$u^*(k) = -G^*(k)x^*(k), \tag{50}$$

where

$$G^*(k) = \left(R(k) + E\left\{ \begin{bmatrix} B(k) \\ \Gamma(k) \end{bmatrix}^T K(k+1) \begin{bmatrix} B(k) \\ \Gamma(k) \end{bmatrix} \right\} \right)^{-1} \tag{52}$$

$$\times E\left\{ \begin{bmatrix} B(k) \\ \Gamma(k) \end{bmatrix}^T K(k+1) \begin{bmatrix} A(k) & 0 \\ 0 & \theta(k) \end{bmatrix} \right\}$$

and where $K(k)$ is given by the following Riccati-like matrix difference equation:

$$K(k) = Q(k) + E\left\{ \begin{bmatrix} A(k) & 0 \\ 0 & \theta(k) \end{bmatrix}^T K(k+1) \begin{bmatrix} A(k) & 0 \\ 0 & \theta(k) \end{bmatrix} \right\}$$

$$- E\left\{ \begin{bmatrix} A(k) & 0 \\ 0 & \theta(k) \end{bmatrix}^T K(k+1) \begin{bmatrix} B(k) \\ \Gamma(k) \end{bmatrix} \right\}$$

$$\tag{52}$$

$$\times \left(R(k) + E\left\{ \begin{bmatrix} B(k) \\ \Gamma(k) \end{bmatrix}^T K(k+1) \begin{bmatrix} B(k) \\ \Gamma(k) \end{bmatrix} \right\} \right)^{-1}$$

$$\times E\left\{ \begin{bmatrix} B(k) \\ \Gamma(k) \end{bmatrix}^T K(k+1) \begin{bmatrix} A(k) & 0 \\ 0 & \theta(k) \end{bmatrix} \right\}$$

with

$$K(N) = F. \tag{53}$$

The optimal state trajectory can now be derived from the solution of the following difference equation:

$$x(k + 1) = [\Phi(k) - \Psi(k)G^*(k)]x(k), \quad x(0) = x_0, \tag{54}$$

where $\Phi(k)$ and $\Psi(k)$ are obvious in terms of A, B, and the other matrices in (1).

Clearly, the optimal control vector given by (50) is a random vector since $x(k)$ is itself a random variable. Due to the uncertainties within the system and the control, we note that the state and the control vectors are both weighted by the covariances and the means of the random parameters, and that the Riccati-like equation (52) cannot be reduced to coupled linear equations.

The extremal control of a stochastic multivariable discrete time dynamical system is not necessarily the unique optimal control; we must establish that the second-order partial derivative of the Hamiltonian function of our problem with respect to u is positive definite [129]. The Hamiltonian function is given by:

$$H_d = \frac{1}{2}x^T(k)K(k)x(k) + \sum_{i=k}^{N-1} Tr(K(i + 1)\Sigma_\xi^\xi \xi)$$

$$+ P^T[\Phi(k)x(k) + \Psi(k)u(k) + \xi(k)]. \tag{55}$$

Hence, $\partial^2 d/\partial u^2$ is given by:

$$\frac{\partial^2 H_d}{\partial^2 u} = R(k) + E[\Psi(k)^T K(k + 1)\Psi(k)] > 0. \tag{56}$$

The solution $K(k)$ to the Riccati-like equation (39) is non-negative-definite and unique for $N < \infty$. For a proof see Ref. [76].

C.   OPTIMAL ESTIMATION, IDENTIFICATION, AND DESIGN OF STOCHASTIC SYSTEMS

For the first time in the published literature, the problem of estimation under uncertainty was studied by Bondaros and Konstantinov [138] through a Hamiltonian procedure. In this model, multiplicative and additive noise contaminated not only the state equation, but also the measurement equation. The analysis proved that the uncorrelated additive perturbations in the dynamics and observation equations increase the estimation error. A similar increase in the estimation error occurs if the additive and multiplicative noises of the measurement system are correlated. Milshtein [139–141] derived stabilizing controllers for the steady-state problem with both perfect and noisy measurements by reducing it to a constrained minimization problem, while Katayama [123] considered the related problem of asymptotic stability properties of the Riccati equation with constant but unknown coefficients.

1. Control with Incomplete Information, the Continuous-Time Case

Consider the more general problem of a control system with incomplete information. Thus, the system equation is given by (30) and a linear measurement system is given by:

$$y(t) = Fx(t) + G(t). \tag{57}$$

where H is a positive definite symmetric matrix of appropriate dimensions.

Let $\hat{x}(t)$ denote the unbiased estimate of $x(t)$ which minimizes the following performance index:

$$J_e = E[\tilde{x}^T(t)U\tilde{x}(t)] \tag{59}$$

$$= tr(UE[\tilde{x}(t)\tilde{x}^T(t)],$$

where $\tilde{x} = x(t) - \hat{x}(t)$ is the error in estimation and U is an $n \times n$ positive definite symmetric matrix. Once again, suppose the control law is of the linear feedback type given by

$$u(t) = -M(t)x(t), \tag{60}$$

and let us choose a filter of the form:

$$\hat{x}(t) = L(t)\hat{x}(t) + K(t)y(t). \tag{61}$$

Use of the unbiasedness property $E[x(t) - \hat{x}(t)] = 0$ and some manipulations yield:

$$L = A - BM - KF. \tag{62}$$

Thus

$$\hat{x}(t) = A\hat{x}(t) + Bu(t) + K(t) [y(t) - F\hat{x}(t)], \tag{63}$$

where the gain matrix K is of $n \times p$ dimensions.

The error dynamic equation for the above system is given by:

$$\dot{\tilde{x}}(t) = [A - KF]\tilde{x}(t) + C(\xi)x(t) - D(\gamma)M(t)x(t)$$

$$+ D(\gamma)M(t)\tilde{x}(t) + E\omega(t) + K(t)Gv(t). \tag{64}$$

Define:

$$X = \begin{bmatrix} x \\ \tilde{x} \end{bmatrix} \quad \zeta = \begin{bmatrix} \omega \\ \upsilon \end{bmatrix}$$

$$\bar{A} = \begin{bmatrix} A - BM(t) & BM(t) \\ 0 & A - K(t)F \end{bmatrix} \tag{65}$$

$$\bar{C} = \begin{bmatrix} C & 0 \\ C & 0 \end{bmatrix}, \quad \bar{D} = \begin{bmatrix} -DM & DM \\ -DM & DM \end{bmatrix}, \quad \bar{E} = \begin{bmatrix} E & 0 \\ E & -KG \end{bmatrix}$$

$$\dot{X} = (\bar{A} + \bar{C} + \bar{D})X + \bar{G}\zeta.$$

Define:

$$\bar{H} = \begin{bmatrix} H & 0 \\ 0 & U \end{bmatrix}, \quad \bar{Q} = \begin{bmatrix} Q + M^T RM & -M^T RM \\ -M^T RM & M^T RM \end{bmatrix},$$

and the cost functional for the system X can be written as:

$$J_X = E\left[X^T(T)HX(T) + \int_0^T X^T \bar{Q}X \, dt \right]. \tag{66}$$

Let

$$P = E[XX^T] = \begin{bmatrix} P_{11} & P_{12} \\ P_{12}^T & P_{22} \end{bmatrix}. \tag{67}$$

Then

$$J_X = \text{tr}[\overline{H}P(T)] + \int_0^T \text{tr}(\overline{Q}P) \, dt. \tag{68}$$

Using the equation for $\dot{X}$ we obtain

$$\dot{P} = \overline{A}P + P\overline{A}^T + \overline{C}P\overline{C}^T + \overline{D}P\overline{D}^T + \overline{E}\overline{E}^T. \tag{69}$$

The optimal stochastic control problem is now reduced to the optimal deterministic control problem of minimizing J_X subject to the dynamic constraint of P.

Use of the matrix maximum principle is one way of deriving a solution. Thus, let the Hamiltonian of the system be given by:

$$H = \text{tr}(\overline{Q}P) + \text{tr}(\overline{A}P + P\overline{A}^T + \overline{C}P\overline{C}^T + \overline{D}P\overline{D}^T + \overline{E}\overline{E}^T)S, \tag{70}$$

where S is the $n \times n$ symmetric costate matrix.

$$S = \begin{bmatrix} S_{11} & S_{12} \\ S_{12}^T & S_{22} \end{bmatrix}.$$

Then

$$\dot{S} = -\frac{\partial H}{\partial P} = -(\overline{Q} + \overline{A}^T S + S\overline{A} + \overline{C}^T S\overline{C} + \overline{D}^T S\overline{D}) \tag{71}$$

with

$$F(T) = \frac{\partial \, \text{tr}[\overline{H}P(T)]}{\partial P(T)} = \overline{H}$$

$$P(0) = P_0.$$

From the necessary condition we obtain

$$K = P_{22}S^T + S_{22}^{-1}S_{12}^T P_{12}. \tag{72}$$

$\partial H / \partial M = 0$ yields

$$DM(P_{11} - P_{12}^T - P_{12} + P_{22}) - B^T(S_{11}P_{11} - S_{11}P_{12} + S_{12}P_{12}^T - S_{12}P_{22})$$

$$\tag{73}$$

$$+ D^T(F_{11} + F_{12}^T + F_{12} + F_{22}) M (P_{11} - P_{12} - P_{12}^T + P_{22}) = 0.$$

Under certain simplifying assumptions it is possible to generate easily computable solutions of this system [142, 143].

2.   The Estimation Problem:
          The Discrete-Time Case

In the following we assume (for convenience) that

$E[x(0)\xi^T(k)] = 0$, for $k = 0, 1, ..., N$.

Similarly, $\xi(k)$ is independent of all the elements of $\theta(k)$ and $\Gamma(k)$ for all $k = 0, 1, ..., N$. The system measurements are given by

$$y(k) = \begin{bmatrix} y_1(k) \\ y_2(k) \end{bmatrix} = \begin{bmatrix} C(k) \\ \Omega(k) \end{bmatrix} \begin{bmatrix} x_1(k) \\ x_2(k) \end{bmatrix} + \begin{bmatrix} 0 \\ v(k) \end{bmatrix} \tag{74}$$

where $y_1(k)$ is the l-dimensional vector of exact measurements, $y_2(k)$ is the q-dimensional vector of noisy measurements, $C(k)$ is the $l \times n$ deterministic (rank l) matrix and $\Omega(k)$ the $q \times n$ stochastic matrix of Gaussian elements having

$E[\Omega(k)] = \overline{\Omega}(k)$

$E[(\Omega(k) - \overline{\Omega}(k)) (\Omega(r) - \overline{\Omega}(r))^T] = \Sigma^{\Omega\Omega}(k)\delta_{kr}.$

Finally, $v(k)$ is a vector of Gaussian white noise with dimension $q \times l$ and statistics of

$E[(\Omega(k) - \overline{\Omega}(k)) (\Omega(r) - \overline{\Omega}(r))^T] = \Sigma^{\Omega\Omega}(k)\delta_{kr}.$

$$E[v(k)v^T(r)] = \Sigma^{vv}(k)\delta_{kr}$$

$$E[v(k)\xi^T(r)] = \Sigma^{v\xi(k)}\delta_{kr}.$$

3.   Reformulation of the Problem

The solution to the stochastic optimal control problem with multiplicative and additive random parameters shows the effects of uncertainties in the performance of the control system. Here the control gain will be a function of the unconditional means and covariances of the uncertainties. Hence the suboptimal stochastic control is considered based upon the open-loop feedback method [57]. Thus a control of the form

$$u(k) = -L(k)x(k) \tag{75}$$

is assumed, and x(k) is found by means of the Kalman–Bucy type filtering algorithms. Here we construct an algorithm of lower dimension than that of the Kalman–Bucy filter [namely $(n - l)$]. A similar lowering of dimension is possible with the noiseless measurements $y_1(k)$ in (74). A system is constructed whereby the optimal mean-square estimate x(k) of the state vector x(k) is derived by a lesser amount of calculation [roughly $(n - l)^3$ multiplications] than in the Kalman–Bucy filter, which requires roughly n^3 multiplications [11]. Let us select a vector z(k) of dimension $(n - l)$ such that the augmented vector

$$\begin{bmatrix} z(k) \\ y_1(k) \end{bmatrix}$$

will be connected with x(k) by a nondegenerate transformation M(k) by

$$\begin{bmatrix} z(k) \\ y_1(k) \end{bmatrix} = M(k)x(k), \tag{76}$$

where det $M(k) \neq 0$ and

$$M(k) = \begin{bmatrix} M_1(k) \\ C(k) \end{bmatrix}$$

and $M_1(k)$ is an $(n - l) \times n$-dimensional matrix.
  Hence,

$$x(k) = M^{-1}(k) \begin{bmatrix} z(k) \\ y_1(k) \end{bmatrix}. \tag{77}$$

Substituting (77) into (40) we get

$$x(k+1) = M^{-1}(k+1) \begin{bmatrix} z(k+1) \\ y_1(k+1) \end{bmatrix}$$

$$= \begin{bmatrix} A(k) & 0 \\ 0 & \theta(k) \end{bmatrix} \begin{bmatrix} M_1(k) \\ C(k) \end{bmatrix}^{-1} \begin{bmatrix} z(k) \\ y_1(k) \end{bmatrix} \tag{78}$$

$$+ \begin{bmatrix} B(k) \\ \Gamma(k) \end{bmatrix} u(k) + \begin{bmatrix} 0 \\ \xi(k) \end{bmatrix}.$$

Thus

$$\begin{bmatrix} z(k+1) \\ y_1(k+1) \end{bmatrix} = M(k+1) \begin{bmatrix} A(k) & 0 \\ 0 & \theta(k) \end{bmatrix}$$

$$\times \begin{bmatrix} M_1(k) \\ C(k) \end{bmatrix}^{-1} \begin{bmatrix} z(k) \\ y_1(k) \end{bmatrix} + M(k+1) \begin{bmatrix} B(k) \\ \Gamma(k) \end{bmatrix} u(k) \tag{79}$$

$$+ M(k+1) \begin{bmatrix} 0 \\ \xi(k) \end{bmatrix}.$$

We may rewrite (79) as

$$z(k+1) = A_{11}(k, k+1)z(k) + A_{12}(k, k+1)y_1(k)$$

$$+ B_1(k, k+1)u(k) + \xi_1(k) \tag{80}$$

$$y_1(k + 1) = A_{21}(k, k + 1)z(k) + A_{22}(k, k + 1)y_1(k)$$

$$+ B_2(k, k + 1)u(k) + \xi_2(k),$$

where

$$\begin{bmatrix} A_{11} & A_{12} \\ A_{21} & A_{22} \end{bmatrix} = \begin{bmatrix} M_1(k + 1) \\ C(k + 1) \end{bmatrix} \begin{bmatrix} A(k) & 0 \\ 0 & \theta(k) \end{bmatrix} \begin{bmatrix} M_1(k) \\ C(k) \end{bmatrix}^{-1}$$

$$\begin{bmatrix} B_1(k, k + 1) \\ B_2(k, k + 1) \end{bmatrix} = M(k + 1) \begin{bmatrix} B(k) \\ \Gamma(k) \end{bmatrix}$$

$$\begin{bmatrix} \xi_1(k) \\ \xi_2(k) \end{bmatrix} = M(k + 1) \begin{bmatrix} 0 \\ \xi(k) \end{bmatrix},$$

and where A_{11}, A_{12}, A_{22}, B_1, and B_2 are, respectively, $(n - l) \times (n - l)$, $(n - l) \times l$, $l \times (n - l)$, $l \times l$, $(n - l) \times m$, and $l \times m$ matrices, and ξ_1 and ξ_2 are $(n - l)$- and l-dimensional vectors of Gaussian white noise.

Consider the second equation of (80). We can rewrite it as

$$z_2(k) = y_1(k + 1) - A_{22}(k, k + 1)y_1(k)$$

$$-B_2(k, k + 1)u(k) \qquad (81)$$

$$= A_{21}(k, k + 1)z(k) + \xi_2(k).$$

Let us take the first equation of system (80) as the state equation of a new object with measurements given by (74) and another equation to be developed later. Clearly, $z_2(k)$ can be calculated from the precise measurements $y_1(k + 1)$ and $y_1(k)$.

On rewriting the noise part of (74) in another form

$$y_2(k) = \Omega(k)x(k) + v(k) \qquad (82)$$

$$= \Omega(k)M^{-1}(k)\begin{bmatrix} z(k) \\ y_1(k) \end{bmatrix} + v(k),$$

and representing $\Omega(k)M^{-1}(k)$ by the following:

$$\Omega(k)M^{-1}(k) = [H_1(k):H_2(k)], \tag{83}$$

where H_1 and H_2 are $q \times (n - l)$ and $q \times l$ matrices, respectively, we get, after rearranging terms,

$$z_3(k) = y_2(k) - H_2(k)y_1(k) \tag{84}$$

$$= H_1(k)z(k) + v(k).$$

The left-hand side of (84) can be calculated by the use of available measurements of $y_2(k)$ and $y_1(k)$. That is, we can assume that there is a vector of accessible measurements

$$z_3(k) = H_1(k)z(k) + v(k). \tag{85}$$

Now the new problem is to estimate the vector $z(k)$ given by the first equation of system (80) with measurements given by (81) and (85).

Introduce the following ($l+ q$)-dimensional augmented measurements

$$z_a(k) = \begin{bmatrix} z_2(k) \\ z_3(k) \end{bmatrix} = H_a(k, k + 1)z(k) + \xi_a(k), \tag{86}$$

where

$$H_a(k, k + 1) = \begin{bmatrix} A_{21}(k, k + 1) \\ H_1(k, k + 1) \end{bmatrix}$$

$$\xi_a(k) = \begin{bmatrix} \xi_2(k) \\ v(k) \end{bmatrix}.$$

4.   Equation of the Observer

For the new system given by the equations

$$z(k + 1) = A_{11}(k, k + 1)z(k) + A_{12}(k, k + 1)y_1(k)$$

$$+ B_1(k, k + 1)u(k) + \xi_1(k) \tag{87}$$

$$z_a(k) = H_a(k, k + 1)z(k) + \xi_a(k)$$

we will write the equation of the observer following the procedures in Refs. [145, 146]:

$$\hat{z}(k + 1) = K_1(k)\hat{z}(k) + K_2(k)z_a(k) \tag{88}$$

$$+ K_3(k)[B_1(k, k + 1)u(k) + A_{12}(k, k + 1)y_1(k)],$$

where K_1, K_2, and K_3 are $(n - l) \times (n - l)$-, $(n - l) \times (l + q)$-, and $(n - l) \times (n - l)$-dimensional matrices of unknown observer coefficients, respectively.
We now define the error in estimation by

$$e(k) = z(k) - \hat{z}(k). \tag{89}$$

By direct application of (87) and (88), (89) takes the following form:

$$e(k + 1) = [A_{11}(k, k + 1) - K_1(k) - K_2(k)H_a(k, k + 1)]z(k)$$

$$+ K_1(k)e(k) - K_2(k)\xi_a(k) + [I_{n-l} - K_3(k)][B_1(k, k + 1)u(k)$$

$$+ A_{12}(k, k + 1)y_1(k)] + \xi_1(k), \tag{90}$$

where I_{n-l} represents the $(n - l) \times (n - l)$-dimensional identity matrix.
Considering the fact that we want to develop an unbiased linear estimator, we should guarantee the following:

$$E[e(0)] = 0, \quad E[e(k + 1)] = 0, \quad k = 0, 1, ..., N. \tag{91}$$

Thus

$$E[e(k + 1)] = E[A_{11}(k, k + 1)z(k)] - K_1(k)E[z(k)] - K_2(k)E[H_a(k, k + 1)z(k)]$$

$$+ K_1(k)E[e(k)] - K_2(k)E[\xi_a(k)] + [I_{n-l} - K_3(k)] \tag{92}$$

$$\times \{E[B_1(k, k + 1)]u(k) + E[A_{12}(k, k + 1)]y_1(k)\} + E[\xi_1(k)] = 0.$$

Hence we get from (91)

$$K_3(k) = I_{n-l} \tag{93}$$

$$K_1(k) = E[A_{11}(k, k + 1)] - K_2(k)E[H_a(k, k + 1)]$$

and the observer equation [i.e., (88)] can be written

$$\hat{x}(k + 1) = \{E[A_{11}(k, k + 1)] - K_2(k)E[H_a(k, k + 1)]\}\hat{x}$$

$$+ K_2(k)z_a(k) + B_1(k, k + 1)u(k) + A_{12}(k, k + 1)y_1(k)$$

In a similar procedure, by consideration of the error covariance matrix equation for the estimator, it is possible to find K_2 [133].

According to (77), the optimal mean-square estimate of the state vector will be given by

$$\hat{x}(k) = M^{-1}(k)\begin{bmatrix} \hat{x}(k) \\ y_1(k) \end{bmatrix} \tag{96}$$

In a manner similar to the continuous-time case, the linear feedback control law can be derived based on the Hamiltonian approach using the estimates $x(k)$ with the appropriate gain matrix to be calculated.

D.   IDENTIFICATION AND CONTROL DESIGN
       OF STOCHASTIC SYSTEMS

The analysis, design, and optimization of complex control systems under a high degree of uncertainty involve, as a fundamental requirement, identification, estimation/filtering, and stochastic optimal control. Identification is necessary when knowledge regarding a system's characteristics is incomplete or partial, or change within the system mechanisms is unpredictable or random. In such cases signals or outputs from the system can be measured and be applied to construct an analytical representation of the system. There are, obviously, numerous ways of accomplishing the above, from complicated observation systems specifically designed to generate required information, to simple transient response measurements

[147]. Identification can be divided into system identification and parameter identification. These are carried out in the time or frequency domains. We will first present parameter identification.

1.   Parameter Identification

In order to clarify the concept of parameter identification, let us denote a set of data received at time t by y(t), a vector of several different measurements. In the discrete-time situation (which is normally the case), $y(k) = (y_1(k), \ldots, y_n(k))^T$ and the total record of data until time k is given by

$$y_k(k) = \{y(k), y(k-1), \ldots, y(1)\}. \tag{97}$$

The overall problem of modeling and identification is postulating a class of models for the given data, estimating the unknown parameters of the model from the available data, and assessing the goodness of fit of the model to the given data. In general, a specific model from the class of models is selected according to an optimal criterion based on analysis of the available data [148]. Under certain conditions the model is put in a parametric representation with an unknown parameter vector θ. Thus, the main objective of the identification process then is to identify θ. The mapping that takes the recorded data $y_k(k)$ into an analytical representation of the parameter vector θ in order to study its characteristic properties is usually determined with some algorithm.

In on-line or recursive identification the estimates of $\theta(k)$, $\hat{\theta}(k)$ is required for each k. In off-line or batch identification, $y_N(k)$ (data up to some time N) is recorded and the functional representation of the mapping $\hat{\theta} = \hat{\theta}(N, y_N(k))$ is computed. Clearly, the mapping $\hat{\theta}_N$ should give a good estimate of θ according to some criterion. There are various means and criteria for such an estimate [2]. Such estimates are called unbiased, uniformly minimum mean-square error, minimum variance unbiased, best linear unbiased, maximum likelihood, etc. For a good source of references, see Ref. [149].

Stochastic identification methods deal with the numerical evaluation of a large body of observation data measured on the process or system under consideration. There is an inherent assumption that the knowledge of the parameters sought is imbedded in the measurement data gathered from the experiments performed. However, these measurements are contaminated with noise that satisfies some statistical properties (e.g., some distribution and statistical moments can be attributed to it). The estimates generated must satisfy some common types of statistical convergence criteria and the error dispersion of the estimates can be computed [150]. The robustness issue of course is fundamental in these processes. It concerns the stability of the algorithm used under conditions of changes. Robustness can be expressed with respect to distribution (or any other assumptions) since the probability distribution functions of the parameters are never known correctly and the cost functions are often unstable even for small perturbations. In recent years a great deal of interest is generated in approximate maximum likelihood methods of identification. Under these techniques the algorithms converge under less restrictive conditions and are more robust [151].

A problem of paramount importance in control system design is the analysis of the system under perturbations and random effects. Such a system is termed optimal if it is designed to follow a desired trajectory. When the system deviates from the optimal trajectory, the important question is whether the deviation will increase or will eventually decrease and once again follow the optimal trajectory. When the disturbances affect the state of the system in a direct manner, then this is a stability problem. When only the system parameters are influenced by the disturbances, then structural instability, sensitivity, robustness, etc., come into play.

In stochastic control system design, stochastic stability theory [152] is utilized to produce the required design parameters for the control system. Moreover, stochastic Lyapunov functions and sensitivity analysis in the statistical framework are used, and covariance matrices are computed from stochastic differential equations [153]. Stability is the most fundamental characteristic of a control system as a precautionary measure against uncertainty. In various situations it becomes essential to "estimate" the uncertainties as accurately as possible. Moreover, the stability conditions are also required to be known as precisely as possible. If the stability condition of a control system is very sharp, then this will result in a necessary and sufficient condition for stability of the control system. When the model of the uncertainties "adequately" represents the difference between the real system and the analytical model, then we have a better grasp at the stability requirements. Thus, stochastic optimal control design involves identification of uncertainties (parametric, structural), sensitivity/robustness analysis, modeling and control, and optimization under existing uncertainty.

2.   System Identification

Most analytical models are postulated from physical laws on dynamical properties. Hence, the class of models for a given control system is generally well defined. However, there are situations where an acceptable model is not available and a class of models needs to be postulated according to some given information.

Once the class of models is determined, the problem of system identification, i.e., choosing a specific model from the postulated class, is performed, according to some optimization criterion and based on an analysis of the available data. Various approaches exist for specific model selection or system identification [148]. These can be divided into time domain and frequency domain techniques. In the first approach the parameter estimates are generated by least-squares, maximum likelihood, recursive, or other related techniques. However, in the frequency domain approach, spectral estimates, identification of frequency response characteristics, and decomposition into modal representations via frequency measurements are obtained to identify parameters.

Time domain system identification can be stated in general terms in the following manner [148]:

$$C = \{M(\theta) \mid \theta \in H\}, \tag{98}$$

where C is the class of models, $M(\theta)$ is the specific model based on the unknown parameters θ, and H is an appropriate set. There is a set of available (observed) data given by

$$Z_T = \{Z(t), t \in T\}, \tag{99}$$

where Z_T is the set of data (input and output), t is time, and T is the interval of time (continuous or discrete). The general system identification problem is then that, given Z_T, select $M(\theta)$ from C based on a given optimization criterion related to the error $\varepsilon(t, \theta)$ between the "true" (observed) and predicted data. Then optimal system identification comprises selection of $M(\theta)$ by choosing that value of θ which will minimize a scalar function of the error. In least-squares optimization the functional is the square of the absolute error, $|\varepsilon|^2$. For linear systems a quadratic cost functional is chosen and explicit formulas give the estimates $\hat{\theta}$ of the parameter vector θ. Thus, if

$$\hat{y}(t \mid \theta) = \theta^T \Phi(t), \tag{100}$$

where $y(t)$ is the output and $\hat{y}(t \mid \theta)$ is the predicted estimate, and $\Phi(t)$ is a continuous function of time, then

$$\hat{\theta} = \left(\sum_{i=1}^{N} \Phi(t_i) \Phi^T(t_i) \right)^{-1} \sum_{i=1}^{N} \Phi(t_i) y^T(t_i) \tag{101}$$

for the discrete-time case, and

$$\hat{\theta} = \left(\int_0^T \Phi(t) \Phi^T(t) \, dt \right)^{-1} \int_0^T \Phi(t) y^T(y) \, dt \tag{102}$$

for the continuous-time case.

For more general systems, optimization techniques such as gradient search may be necessary for the optimal estimate of the parameters.

The most important issue in estimation is, of course, convergence of the estimates to their "true" value (convergence with probability, almost sure, etc.). Moreover, when the system model is nonlinear but the class of identification models C are chosen to be linear, then the convergence of the estimates leads only to the closest value in the sense of projection of the true model onto the subspace of linear models.

Verification and validation of analytical models of complex control systems such as aircraft and spacecraft are often a fundamental requirement. In structural dynamic analysis, for instance eigenvalues and eigenvectors, as well as damping parameters of a structure, have to be determined by complex modal testing procedures (both by ground and by flight tests). Two main techniques that exist for such testing are referred to as phase resonance and phase separation. In the first approach, systems are forced to vibrate in one natural mode, and thus a single degree of freedom is isolated for modeling purposes; in the phase-separation procedures, modal quantities are estimated from dynamic response analyses. The first approach is expensive and is based on trial and error. Especially difficult is the determination of closely spaced frequencies. Harmonic excitation procedures to measure dynamic response of the eigensystem (phase-separation techniques) are also utilized via coherence-function analysis for frequency resolution [81]. When random errors of measurements, partial test data, partial knowledge of system parameters, and components are considered, multiple degree-of-freedom analysis and identification are required. Then statistical procedures should be utilized in conjunction with modern estimation techniques such as Kalman filtering or other approaches to estimate the parameters involved.

IV.   CONCLUSIONS

There is an appreciable amount of literature on bilinear control systems that deals mostly with deterministic situations. The stochastic problem of bilinear systems with random disturbances has close connections to the systems presented in this article [154]. Recent developments in the controllability, stability, and other aspects of this problem are also reported [155].

A wide range of problems may be approximated by linear stochastic systems [156]. Diffusion processes, especially in nuclear fission, in heat transfer and in biological systems, may be modeled appropriately by bilinear stochastic systems [157]. An additional term of the form $N(t, U(t))x(t)$ added to (30) on the right-hand-side results in such a system. The characteristics of bilinear stochastic systems are derived in several papers [158, 159]. Most of the studies treat such systems as a first-stage generalization of linear stochastic systems, especially under finite-dimensional suboptimal filters. The problem of identification of bilinear stochastic systems needs further research [159]. State-dependent and control-dependent noise problems can be considered special cases of bilinear stochastic systems, and most of the research is in this area. The analysis and synthesis of bilinear stochastic systems need further development, and to this end many researchers continue to study various aspects of the problem [160, 161].

For the past two decades linear stochastic systems in the infinite-dimensional spaces have been of interest to many researchers [13]. The theory of semigroups in functional analysis, especially that of linear operators developed recently, has proved very valuable and advantageous in solving very general classes of optimal control problems. Some of the disadvantages of semigroup theory, such as its applicability to only time-invariant systems, have created the need for extensions to time-dependent "evolution" equations [162]. However, there seems to be a great deal of work still ahead in this area for this approach to lend itself to practical aspects of the problems in stochastic control theory.

In (30), $A(t)$ would represent an infinitesimal generator of a strongly continuous semigroup $S(t)$ over an appropriate Hilbert space when $A(t) = A$ for all t and $I = t$, $0 < t < T$. Moreover, B, $F_{i,\ Gj}$, and E would all be linear bounded transformations mapping appropriately defined separable Hilbert spaces into the Hilbert space over which $S(t)$ is defined. In a similar manner, the observation equation can be generalized to infinite-dimensional Hilbert spaces. The quadratic cost functional in (31) will also have to be placed in an appropriate infinite-dimensional setting, and then the control problem is to find an admissible controller that will minimize (31). We should note here that the closed-loop optimal stochastic infinite-dimensional problem under partial and noisy measurements (to the author's knowledge) and with multiplicative and additive noise has not been solved to this day.

The infinite-dimensional representation of control systems is only an idealization of reality under the assumption that matter is a continuum and that internal and external forces and moments are distributed. However, under practical circumstances, when real control systems have to be implemented on real structures, only finite-dimensional models and controllers are meaningful (at least until the present). Hence, even though infinite-dimensional models, for instance models composed of partial differential equations, can give deeper understanding and insight into subtle characteristics of a system's behavior, there are no physically implementable distributed controllers (in the practical sense of the word), nor are there infinitely distributed sensors for observation that can be practically useful.

There are various approaches of approximating infinite-dimensional distributed parameter systems by finite-dimensional ordinary differential (difference) equation systems. The widely used techniques, known as Rayleigh–Ritz–Galerkin, finite element, finite difference, etc., are but a few of many others [59]. These numerical methods are translated into computer codes and are widely utilized in generating finite-dimensional ordinary differential equation models for structural systems.

Linear stochastic systems with multiplicative and additive noise can actually be considered nonlinear systems with respect to stochastic variations. The state vector, the control vector, and the multiplicative noise matrices are expressed as products of each other, thus creating a nonlinear setting. It is well known that the optimal filter for such systems is an infinite-dimensional nonlinear filter [3, 112]. Only suboptimal linear filters can be formulated for linear stochastic systems with multiplicative and additive noise, or optimal filters in a class of linear filters [143].

The complexity of linear systems with multiplicative and additive noise speaks for itself. It is obvious that for large-order finite-dimensional systems there could be an unrealistically large amount of statistical information required. For situations of non-Gaussian distributions, the problem gets more complicated, especially when filtering is performed under partial and noisy observation.

The computational aspect of the problem is extremely complex, even if the distributions of the statistical parameters are well known and the order of the system is relatively small [39]. Thus, in order to formulate a control-system model in the stochastic setting presented herein, it is necessary to make certain assumptions, simplifications, and approximations. However, this is the case in any modeling situation, and it is not considered a severe limitation. An important aspect of control systems is that a valid approximation in the form of a mathematical model, whether it be stochastic or deterministic, linear or nonlinear, distributed or lumped, must be as close to the real plant as practically possible according to some criterion.

We have presented a brief review of the state of the art of the algorithms and numerical techniques that are required for the analysis and control design of stochastic linear systems with multiplicative and additive noise. Both the discrete-time and continuous-time cases were exposed in a general setting, and some of the important developments in the field were brought to light. A unified approach to the linear stochastic optimal control and estimation problems with multiplicative and additive noise was presented, and new results that extend the existing theory were developed. It should be noted that it is very difficult to treat many of the significant theoretical achievements in this area and still remain within the limitations of publication guidelines. However, we have tried to include those which we thought should be discussed. The advent of supersonic aircraft with very high performance requirements and the futuristic space structures, such as the space station, seem to promise some realistic ground for modeling and control design with multiplicative and additive noise of complex control systems.

REFERENCES

1.   G. C. GOODWIN and K. S. SIN, "Adaptive Filtering, Prediction and Control." Prentice-Hall, Englewood Cliffs, New Jersey, 1984.
2.   G. C. GOODWIN and R. L. PAYNE, "Dynamic Systems Identification." Academic Press, New York, 1977.
3.   M. AOKI, "Optimization of Stochastic Systems." Academic Press, New York, 1967.
4.   H. KWAKERNAAK and R. SIVAN, "Linear Optimal Control Systems" Wiley, New York, 1972.
5.   J. M. MENDEL and D. G. GIESEKING, Bibliography of the linear quadratic Gaussian problem. *IEEE Trans. Autom. Control* AC-16(6), 847–869 (1971).
6.   R. BELLMAN, "Dynamic Programming" Princeton Univ. Press, Princeton, New Jersey, 1956.

7. N. N. KRASSOVSKII and E. A. LIDSKII, Analytic construction of regulators in the systems with random properties. I–III. *Avtom. Telemekh.* **22**(9–11) (1961).

8. R. F. DRENICK and L. SHAW, Optimal control of linear plants with random parameters. *IEEE Trans. Autom. Control* **AC-9**, 236–244 (1964).

9. T. L. GUNKEL, II and G. F. FRANKLIN, A general solution for linear, sampled-data control. *J. Basic Eng.* **85**, 197–203 (1963).

10. N. N. KRASOVSKII, Stabilization of systems in which noise is dependent on the value of the control signal. *Eng. Cybernet.* **2**, 44–53 (1965).

11. M. AOKI, Optimal control of some class of imperfectly known control systems. *J. Basic Eng.*, pp. 306–310 (1966).

12. A. V. BALAKRISHNAN, "Applied Functional Analysis," 2nd ed. Springer-Verlag, Berlin and New York, 1981.

13. P. S. MAYBECK, "Stochastic models, Estimation, and Control," Vols. 1–3. Academic Press, New York, 1979.

14. M. ATHANS, The role and use of the stochastic linear-quadratic-Gaussian problem in control systems design. *IEEE Trans. Autom. Control* **AC-16**(6), 529–552 (1971).

15. A. A. FELDBAUM, Dual control theory. I–IV. *Autom. Remote Control (Engl. Transl.)* **21**, 1240–1249, 1453–1464 (1960); **22**, 3–16, 129–142 (1961).

16. I. R. PETERSEN, Quadratic stabilization of uncertain linear systems: Existence of a nonlinear stabilizing control does not imply existence of a linear stabilizing control. *IEEE Trans. Autom. Control* **AC-30**(3), 291–293 (1985).

17. B. R. BARMISH and G. LEITMANN, On ultimate boundedness control of uncertain systems in the absence of matching conditions. *IEEE Trans. Autom. Control* **AC-27**, 153–161 (1982).

18. B. R. BARMISH, I. R. PETERSON, and A. FEVER, Linear ultimate boundedness control of uncertain dynamical systems. *Automatica* **19**, 523 (1983).

19. B. R. BARMISH, M. CORLESS, and G. LEITMAN, A new class of stabilizing controllers for uncertain dynamical systems. *SIAM J. Control Optim.* **21**, 246 (1983).

20. B. R. BARMISH, Necessary and sufficient conditions for quadratic stabilizability of an uncertain linear system. *J. Opt. Theory Appl.* **46**, 399 (1985).

21. M. CORLESS and G. GEITMANN, Continuous state feedback guaranteeing uniform ultimate boundedness of uncertain dynamic systems. *IEEE Trans. Autom. Control* **AC-26**, 1139 (1981).

22. I. R. PETERSEN, Structural stabilization of uncertain systems: Necessity of the matching condition. *SIAM J. Control Optim.* **23**, 286–296 (1985).

23. A. LINDQUIST and G. PICCI, Realization theory for multivariate stationary Gaussian processes. *SIAM J. Control Optim.* **23**(6) (1985).

24. G. ADOMIAN, "Stochastic Systems." Academic Press, New York, 1983.

25. M. ATHANS, The role and use of the stochastic linear-quadratic-Gaussian problem on control system design. *IEEE Trans. Autom. Control* **AC-16**(6), 529–552 (1971).

26. L. S. PONTRYAGIN, Some mathematical problems arising in connection with the theory of optimal control systems. *Proc. Conf. Basic Probl. Autom. Control Regul., 1957.*

27. L. S. PONTRYAGIN, V. G. BOLTYANSKII, R. V. GAMKRELIDZE, AND E. F. MISCHENKO, "The Mathematical Theory of Optimal Processes." Wiley (Interscience), New York, 1962.

28. R. E. KALMAN and R. S. BUCY, New results in linear filtering and prediction theory. *J. Basic Eng.* **83**, 95–108 (1961).

29. R. L. KOSUT, H. SALZWEDEL, and A. EMAMI-NAEINI, Robust control of flexible spacecraft. *J. Guidance, Control, Dyn.* **6**(2), 104–111 (1983).

30. P. J. McLANE, Asymptotic stability of linear autonomous systems with state-dependent noise. *IEEE Trans. Autom. Control* **AC-14**, 752–753 (1969).

31. P. J. McLANE, Linear optimal stochastic control using instantaneous output feedback. *Int. J. Control* **13**(2), 383–396 (1971).

32. P. J. McLANE, Optimal stochastic control of linear systems with state-dependent and control-dependent disturbances. *IEEE Trans. Autom. Control* **AC-16**(6), 793–798 (1971).

33.   G. CHOW, "Analysis and Control of Dynamic Economic Systems." Wiley, New York, 1975.

34.   M. AOKI, Control of linear discrete-time stochastic dynamic systems with multiplicative disturbances. *IEEE Trans. Autom. Control* AC-20, 388–392 (1975).

35.   J. L. WILLEMS and J. C. WILLEMS, Feedback stabilizability for stochastic systems with state and control dependent noise. *Automatica* 12, 277–283 (1976).

36.   J. Y. S. LUH and M. MAGUIRAGA, Differential games with state-dependent and control-dependent noises. *IEEE Trans. Autom. Control* AC-15(2), 205–209 (1970).

37.   H. PANOSSIAN, Optimal adaptive stochastic control of linear dynamical systems with multiplicative and additive noise. Ph.D. Dissertation, University of California at Los Angeles (1981).

38.   W. L. DeKONING, Infinite horizon optimal control of linear discrete-time systems with stochastic parameters. *Automatica* 18(4), 443–453 (1982).

39.   A. S. WILLSKY, S. I. MARCUS, and D. N. MARTIN, On the stochastic stability of linear systems containing colored multiplicative noise. *IEEE Trans. Autom. Control* AC-20(5), 711–713(1975).

40.   R. TSE-MIN KU, Adaptive stochastic control of linear systems with random parameters. Ph.D. Dissertation, Massachusetts Institute of Technology, Cambridge (1978).

41.   V. I. IVANENKO, Control in the case of stochastic indeterminacy, *Sov. Autom. Control (Engl. Transl.)* 15(6), 63–71 (1982).

42.   J. J. FLORENTIN, Optimal control of continuous-time, Markov, stochastic systems. *J. Electron. Control* 10, 473–488 (1961).

43.   J. J. FLORENTIN, Partial observability of optimal control, *J. Electron. Control* 13(3), 263–279 (1962).

44.   J. J. FLORENTIN, Optimal probing adaptive control of a simple Bayesian system. *J. Electron. Control* 11, 165 (1962).

45.   J. J. FLORENTIN, Optimal control of systems with generalized Poisson inputs. *J. Basic Eng.* 85, 217–221 (1963).

46.   W. GERSCH and F. KOZIN, Optimal control of multivariable perturbed Markov stochastic systems. *Proc. Allerton Conf. Circuits Syst. Theory, 1963* (1963).

47.   N. N. KRASOVSKII, On optimal control in the presence of random disturbances. *J. Appl. Math. Mech.* 24(1), 82–102 (1960).

48.   W. M. WONHAM, Optimal stationary control of a linear system with state-dependent noise. *SIAM J. Control* 5(3), 486–500 (1967).

49.   D. GORMAN and J. ZABORSKII, Stochastic optimal control of continuous-time systems with unknown gain. *IEEE Trans. Autom. Control* AC-13(6), 630–638 (1968).

50.   D. L. KLEINMAN, Optimal stationary control of linear systems with control-dependent noise. *IEEE Trans. Autom. Control* AC-14(6), 677–677 (1969).

51.   J. T. TOU, System optimization via learning and adaptation. *Int. J. Control* 10, 21–31 (1965).

52.   F. KOZIN, A survey of stability of stochastic systems. *Automatica* 5, 95–112 (1969).

53.   J. J. McKEOWN, Aspects of parallel computation in numerical optimization. *In* "Numerical Techniques for Stochastic Systems" (Archetti and Cubiani, eds.). North-Holland Publ., Amsterdam, 1980.

54.   N. BELLAMO, On a class of stochastic dynamical systems: Mathematical analysis, some optimization problems and applications. *In* "Numerical Techniques for Stochastic Systems" (Archetti and Cugiani, eds.). North-Holland Publ., Amsterdam, 1980.

55.   K. BELLMAN, "Adaptive Control Processes." Princeton Univ. Press, Princeton, New Jersey, 1961.

56.   L. MEIROVITCH, "Analytical Methods in Vibrations." Macmillan, New York, 1967.

57.   D. L. DEAN, "Discrete Field Analysis of Structural Systems." Springer-Verlag, Berlin and New York, 1976.

58.   L. S. WESSTEIN, Introduction and survey on continuum models for repetitive lattice structures. *In* "Proceedings of the Workshop on Applications of Distributed Parame-

ter System Theory to the Control of Large Space Structures" (G. Rodriguez, ed.), pp. 63–70, NASA, JPL, Washington, D.C., 1983.

59.   G. STRANG and G. J. FIX, "An Analysis of the Finite Element Method." Prentice-Hall, Englewood Cliffs, New Jersey, 1973.

60.   L. MEIROVITCH, H. BARUH, and H. OZ, A comparison of control techniques for large flexible systems. *J. Guidance, Control, Dyn.* 6(4), 302–310 (1983).

61.   J. F. GARIBOTTI, R. HERZBERG, K. SOOSAAR, N. K. GUPTA, J. KIEGLER, B. MORAIS, and C. A. NATHAN, "SSTAC Ad Hoc Subcommittee on Controls/Structures Interaction," Final Report. NASA, Washington, D.C., 1983.

62.   G. RODRIGUES, ed., "Proceedings of the Workshop on Applications of Distributed Parameter System Theory to the Control of Large Space Structures," NASA, JPL, Washington, D.C., 1983.

63.   H. V. PANOSSIAN, Uncertainty management in modeling and control of large flexible structures. *Soc. Automat. Eng. {Spec. Pub.]* SP-596, 55–58 (1984).

64.   H. V. PANOSSIAN, Uncertainty management technique in adaptive control. *Control Dyn. Syst.* 25, 1–53 (1987).

65.   D. C. HYLAND, Active control of large flexible spacecraft: A new approach based on minimum information modeling of parameter uncertainties. *VPI ESV/AIAA Symp., 1981* (1981).

66.   D. C. HYLAND, Maximum entropy approach to control design for uncertain structural systems. *IEEE Autom. Control Conf., 1982*, Pap. No. 9475 (1982).

67.   M. J. BALAS, Trends in large space structure control theory: Fondest hopes, wildest dreams. *IEEE Trans. Autom. Control* AC-27(3), 522–535 (1982).

68.   G. S. NURRE, R. S. RYAN, N. H. SCOFIELD, and J. L. SIMS, Dynamics and control of large flexible structures. *J. Guidance, Control, Dyn.* 7(5), 514–526 (1984).

69.   J. B. KELLER, Wave propagation in random media. *Hydrodyn. Instab., Symp. Appl. Math., 13th, 1960*, pp. 222–246 (1962).

70.   W. E. BOYCE and B. E. GOODWIN, Random transverse vibrations of elastic beams. *SIAM J.* 12, 613–629 (1964).

71.   M. HOSHIYA and C. SHAH, Free vibration of stochastic beam-column. *J. Eng. Mech. Div., Am. Soc. Civ. Eng.* 97, 1239–1255 (1971).

72.   J. D. COLLINS and W. T. THOMSON, The eigenvalue problem for structural systems with statistical properties. *AIAA J.* 7(4), 642–648 (1969).

73.   G. C. HART, Eigenvalue uncertainty in stressed structures. *J. Eng. Mech. Div., Am. Soc. Civ. Eng.*, pp. 481–494 (1973).

74.   P. C. CHEN and W. W. SOROKA, Multi-degree dynamic response of a system with statistical properties. *J. Sound Vibr.* 37(4), 547–556 (1974).

75.   F. ELLYIN and P. CHANDRASEKHAS, Probabilistic dynamic response of beams and frames. *J. Eng. Mech. Div., Am. Soc. Civ. Eng.*, pp. 411–421 (1977).

76.   T. K. HASSELMAN and G. C. HART, Modal analysis of random structural systems. *J. Eng. Mech. Div., Am. Soc. Civ. Eng.* (1972).

77.   W.-HU HUANG, Vibration of some structures with periodic random parameters. *AIAA J.* 20(7), 1001–1008 (1982).

78.   T. K. HASSELMAN, Structural uncertainty in dynamic analysis. *Trans. SAE, 1982*, Pap. No. 811049 (1982).

79.   M. Baruch, Correction of stiffness matrix using vibration tests. *AIAA J.* 20(3), 441–443 (1982).

80.   D. S. BERNSTEIN and D. C. HYLAND, The optimal projection/maximum entropy approach to designing low-order robust controllers for flexible structures. *Proc. Conf. Decision Control, 24th, 1985*, pp. 745–752 (1986).

81.   S. R. IBRAHIM, Modal identification techniques assessment and comparison. *Sound Vib.* 19(8), 10–15 (1985).

82.   B. A. BRINKMAN and D. J. MALIOCE, Understanding modal parameters and mode shape scaling. *Sound Vib.* 19(6), 28–30 (1985).

83.   North Atlantic Treaty Organization, Damping effects in aerospace structures. *AGARD Conf. Proc.* AGARD-CP-277 (1979).

84. V. V. KRYLOV, Modeling the internal structure of dynamical systems from input–output relationships (abstract realization theory). *Autom. Remote Control (Engl. Transl.)* No. 3, pp. 5–19 (1984).

85. L. MEIROVITCH, Modeling and control of distributed structures. *In* "Proceedings of the Workshop on Applications of Distributed Parameter System Theory to the Control of Large Space Structures" (G. Rodriguez, ed.), pp. 1–29. NASA, JPL, Washington, D.C., 1983.

86. P. C. HUGHES, Modal identities for elastic bodies, with application to vehicle dynamics and control. *J. Appl. Mech.* **47**(1), 177–184 (1980).

87. M. HAMIDI, G. RODGRIGUEZ, and D. B. SCHAECHTER, Distributed system modeling of a large space antenna. *In* "Proceedings of the Workshop on Applications of Distributed Parameter System Theory to the Control of Large Space Structures" (G. Rodriguez, ed.), pp. 89–102. NASA, JPL, Washington, D.C., 1983.

88. N. C. NIGAM, "Introduction to Random Vibrations." MIT Press, Cambridge, Massachusetts, 1983.

89. J. ZABCZYK, On optimal stochastic control of discrete-time systems in Hilbert space. *SIAM J. Control* **13**(6), 1217–1234 (1975).

90. P. T. KABAMBA, Model reduction by Euclidean methods. *J. Guidance Control* **3**(6), 555–562 (1980).

91. W. H. GREENE, Effects of random member length errors on the accuracy and internal loads of truss antennas. *J. Spacecr. Rockets* **22**(5), 554–559 (1985).

92. H. V. PANOSSIAN, Model order reduction techniques; a survey. To be published.

93. J. S. GIBSON, An analysis of optimal model regulation: Convergence and stability. *SIAM J. Control Optim.* **19**(5), 686–707 (1981).

94. B. C. MOORE, Principal component analysis in linear systems: Controllability, observability, and model reduction. *IEEE Trans. Autom. Control* **AC-26**(1), 17–32 (1981).

95. J. R. SESAK, P. W. LIKINS, and T. CORADETTI, Flexible spacecraft control by model error sensitivity suppression. *J. Astronaut. Sci.* **27**(2), 131–156 (1979).

96. J. N. AUBRUⁿ, J. A. BREAKWELL, N. K. GUPTA, M. G. LYONS, and G. MARGULIES, "ACOSS (Active Control of Space Structures) Three Phase IA," Final Tech. Rep., RADC-TR-80-131. Lockheed Missiles and Space Co., Sunnyvale, California, 1981.

97. N. K. GUPTA, M. G. LYONS, J. N. AUBRUN, and G. MARGULIES, Modeling, control and system identification methods for flexible structures. *In* "Spacecraft Pointing and Position Control" (P. Ph. Vandenbrock and Sz. Szirmay, eds.), NATO AGARDograph No. 260, pp. 12.1–12.41. 1981.

98. R. C. ROGERS and M. BURTON, Dynamic control of large spacecraft – A survey of techniques. *In* "Spacecraft Pointing and Position Control" (P. Ph. Vandenbrock and Sz. Szirmay, eds.), NATO AGARDograph No. 260, pp. 11.1–11.9. 1981.

99. C. COVINGTON, The space station: An overview of the design process." *Int. Aerosp. Fed. Conf. (AIF), 1983.*

100. B. K. WADA, C. P. KUO, and R. J. GLASES, Multiple boundary condition test approach to update mathematical models of large flexible structures. *SAE Aerosp. Technol. Conf. Expos., 1985.*

101. W. H. GREEN, Effects of random member length errors on the accuracy and internal loads of truss antennas. *J. Spacecr. Rockets* **22**(5), 554–559 (1985).

102. S. B. KLEIBANOV, K. B. NORKIN, and V. B. PRIVAL'SKII, Inversion of the Vandermonde matrix. *Autom. Remote Control (Engl. Transl.)* No. 4, pp. 176–177 (1977).

103. V. I. IVANENKO, Control in the case of stochastic indeterminacy. *Sov. Autom. Control (Engl. Transl.)* **15**(6), 63–71 (1982).

104. A. A. FELDBAUM, Theory of dual control. *Autom. Remote Control (Engl. Transl.)* **21**(9), 1240–1249; (11), 1453–1464 (1960); **22**(1), 3–16; (2), 129–142 (1961).

105. S. M. SELTZER, Dynamics and control of large flexible space structures: An overview. *J. Astronaut. Sci.* **27**(2), 95–101 (1979).

106. J. F. YOCUM and L. I. SLAFER, Control system design in the presence of structural dynamic interaction. *J. Guidance Control* **1**(2), 109–116 (1978).

107. M. E. SEZER and D. D. SILJAK, Validation of reduced-order models for control systems design. *J. Guidance, Control, Dyn.* **5**(5), 430–437 (1982).

108. G. N. VANDERPLAATS, Structural optimization – past, present, and future. *AIAA J.* **20**(7), 992–1000 (1982).

109. Y. BAR-SHALOM and E. TSE, Dual effect, certainty equivalence, and separation in stochastic control. *IEEE Trans. Autom. Control* **AC-19**(15), 494–500 (1974).

110. U. G. HAUSSMANN, Optimal stationary control with state and control-dependent noise. *SIAM J. Control* **9**(2) (1971).

111. S. NIWA, M. HAYASE, and I. SUGIURA, Stability of linear time-varying systems with state-dependent noise. *IEEE Trans. Autom. Control* **AC-21** (1976).

112. V. I. TIMOFEEV and S. M. CHERNYAVSKII, Optimal object control with worst random parameter distribution. *Sov. Autom. Control (Engl. Transl.* **9**, 78–83 (1976).

113. J.-M. BISMUT, Linear quadratic optimal stochastic control with random coefficients. *SIAM J. Control Optim.* **14**(3), 419–444 (1976).

114. M. M. CONNORS, Controllability of discrete, linear random dynamical systems. *SIAM J. Control* **5**(2), 183–210 (1967).

115. W. J. MURPHY, Optimal stochastic control of discrete linear systems with unknown gain. *IEEE Trans. Autom. Control* **AC-13**(4), 338–344 (1968).

116. A. J. GRAMMATICOS and B. M. HOROWITZ, The optimal adaptive control law for a linear plant with unknown input gains. *Int. J. Control* **12**(2), 337–346 (1970).

117. R. KU and M. ATHANS, On the adaptive control of linear systems using the open-loo feedback–optimal approach. *IEEE Trans. Autom. Control* **AC-18**, 484–493 (1973).

118. Y. BAR-SHALOM and R. SIVAN, On the optimal control of discrete-time linear systems with random parameters. *IEEE Trans. Autom. Control* **AC-12**(1), 3–8 (1969).

119. V. M. KONSTANTINOV, The stability of stochastic difference systems. *Probl. Inf. Transm. (Engl. Transl.)* **6**, 70–75 (1970).

120. M. K. P. MISHRA and A. K. MAHALANABIS, On the stability of nonlinear feedback systems with control-dependent noise. *Int. J. Syst. Sci.* **6**(10), 945–949 (1975).

121. D. KENRICK, Applications of control theory to macroeconomics. *Ann. Econ. Soc. Meas.* **5**(2), 171–185 (1976).

122. F. R. SHUPP, Uncertainty and optimal policy intensity in fiscal and incomes policies. *Ann. Econ. Soc. Meas.* **5**(2), 225–237 (1976).

123. T. KATAYAMA, On the matrix Riccati equation for linear systems with random gain. *IEEE Trans. Autom. Control* **AC-21**, 770–771 (1976).

124. M. ATHANS, R. KU, and S. B. GERSHWIN, The uncertainty threshold principle: Some fundamental limitations of optimal decision making under dynamic uncertainty. *IEEE Trans. Autom. Control* **AC-22**, 491–495 (1977).

125. R. T. KU and M. ATHANS, Further results on the uncertainty threshold principle. *IEEE Trans. Autom. Control* **AC-22**(5) (1977).

126. B. WITTENMARK, Stochastic adaptive control methods: A survey. *Int. J. Control* **21**(5), 705–730 (1975).

127. S. M. JOSHI, On optimal control of linear systems in the presence of multiplicative noise. *IEEE Trans. Aerosp. Electron. Syst.* **AES-12**, 80–85 (1976).

128. S. E. HARRIS, Stochastic controllability of linear discrete systems with multiplicative noise. *Int. J. Control* **27**(2), 213–227 (1978).

129. P. V. PAKSHIN, State estimation and control synthesis for discrete linear systems with additive and multiplicative noise. *Autom. Remote Control (Engl. Transl.)* No. 4, pp. 75–85 (1978).

130. P. V. PAKSHIN, Optimal control of discrete plants with state- and control-dependent noises. *Autom. Remote Control (Engl. Transl.)* No. 3, pp. 43–54 (1978).

131. P. V. PAKSHIN, Suboptimal control of stochastic linear objects using a nonquadratic quality criterion. *Sov. Autom. Control (Engl. Transl.)* No. 6, pp. 62–70 (1981).

132. J. K. TUGNAIT, Stability of optimum linear estimators of stochastic signals in white multiplicative noise. *IEEE Trans. Autom. Control* **AC-26**(3) (1981).

133. H. V. PANOSSIAN and C. T. LEONDES, Observers for optimal estimation of the state of linear stochastic discrete systems. *Int. J. Control* **37**(3), 645–655 (1983).

134. H. PANOSSIAN and C. T. LEONDES, On discrete-time Riccati-like matrix difference equations with random coefficients. *Int. J. Syst. Sci.* **14**(4), 385–407 (1983).

135. W. L. DeKONING, Detectability of linear discrete-time systems with stochastic parameters. *Int. J. Control* **38**(5), 1035–1046 (1983).

136. W. L. DeKONING, Optimal estimation of linear discrete-time systems with stochastic parameters. *Automatica* **20**(1), 113–115 (1984).

137. I. R. PETERSEN, A Riccati equation approach to the design of stabilizing controllers and observers for a class of uncertain linear systems. *IEEE Trans. Autom. Control* **AC-301**(9), 904–907 (1985).

138. Yu. G. BONDAROS and V. M. KONSTANTINOV, Estimating the state of linear systems with additive and multiplicative noise. *Autom. Remote Control (Engl. Transl.)* No. 5, pp. 34–43 (1976).

139. G. N. MILSHTEIN, Linear optimal controllers of specified structure in systems with incomplete information. *Autom. Remote Control (Engl. Transl.)* No. 8, pp. 48–53 (1976).

140. G. N. MILSHTEIN, Design of stabilizing controller with incomplete state data for linear stochastic systems with multiplicative noise. *Autom. Remote Control (Engl. Transl.)*, No. 5, 98–106 (1982).

141. G. N. MILSHTEIN and L. B. RYASHKO, Estimation in controlled stochastic systems with multiplicative noise. *Autom. Remote Control (Engl. Transl.)*, No. 6, pp. 88–94 (1984).

142. Y. A. PHILLIS, Optimal stabilization of stochastic systems. *J. Math. Anal. Appl.* **94**, 489–50 (1983).

143. Y. A. PHILLIS, Controller design of systems with multiplicative noise. *IEEE Trans. Autom. Control* **AC-30**(10), 1017–1019 (1985).

144. A. V. PANTECEEV and SEMENOV, Optimal control of nonlinear probabilistic systems on the basis of an incomplete state vector," *Autom. Remote Control (Engl. Transl.)* No. 1, pp. 91–100 (1984).

145. M. ATHANS AND E. TSE, A direct derivation of the optimal linear filter using the max principle. *IEEE Trans. Autom. Control* **AC-12**(6), 690–694 (1967).

146. A. I. PETROV and V. V. MININ, Application of observers for optimal control of linear stochastic discrete systems. *Sov. Autom. Control (Engl. Transl.)* **6**, 29–35 (1979).

147. L. LJUNG and T. SODERSTROM, "Theory and Practice of Recursive Identification." MIT Press, Cambridge, Massachusetts, 1983.

148. F. KOZIN and H. G. NATKE, System identification techniques. *Struct. Saf.* **3**, 269–316 (1986).

149. K. J. ÅSTRÖM and P. EYKHOFF, System identification – A survey. *Automatica* **7**, 123–162 (1971).

150. V. STREJC, Trends in identification. *Automatica* **17**(1), 7–21 (1981).

151. Y. Z. TSYPKIN, E. D. AVEDYAN, and O. V. GULINSKII, On convergence of the recursive identification algorithms. *IEEE Trans. Autom. Control* **AC-26**(5), 1009–1017 (1981).

152. H. J. KUSHNER, "Stochastic Stability and Control." Academic Press, New York, 1967.

153. G. JUMARIE, An approach, via entropy, to the stability of random large-scale sampled data systems under structural perturbations. *J. Dyn. Syst., Meas., Control* **104**, 49–57 (1982).

154. R. R. MOHLER and W. J. KOLOD IEJ, An overview of stochastic bilinear control processes. *IEEE Trans. Syst., Man, Cybernet.* **SMC-10**(12), 913–913 (1980).

155. S. G. TZEFESTAS and K. E. ANAGNOSTOU, Stabilization of singularly perturbed strictly bilinear system. *IEEE Trans. Autom. Control* **AC-29**, 943–946 (1984).

156. H. J. SUSSMANN, Semigroup representations, bilinear approximation of input/output maps, and generalized inputs. *In* "Mathematics Systems" (Marchesini and Mitter, eds.). Springer-Verlag, Berlin and New York, 1976.

157. R. R. MOHLER, "Bilinear Control Processes." Academic Press, New York, 1972.
158. R. W. BROCKETT, Stochastic bilinear models. *Proc. J. Autom. Conf., 1979,* pp. 1420–1422 (1979).
159. S.-K. NG, Optimal linear nonanticipative control of partially observable bilinear systems. *IEEE Trans. Autom. Control* AC-29, 271–274 (1984).
160. C. BRUNI, G. DIPILLO, and G. KOCH, Mathematical models and identification of bilinear systems. *In* "Theory and Applications of Variable Structures Systems" (R. R. Mohler and R. Ruberti, eds.), pp. 137–152, Academic Press, New York, 1972.
161. C. S. KUBRUSLY and O. L. COSTA, Mean -square stability conditions for discrete stochastic bilinear systems. *IEEE Trans. Autom. Control* AC-30(11), 1082-1087 (1985).
162. K. YOSIDA, "Functional Analysis," 4th ed., Springer-Verlag, Berlin and New York, 1974.

COMPUTATIONAL TECHNIQUES FOR THE MATRIX PSEUDOINVERSE IN MINIMUM VARIANCE REDUCED-ORDER FILTERING AND CONTROL

THOMAS H. KERR

Massachusetts Institute of Technology
Lincoln Laboratory
Lexington, Massachusetts 02173

There have been two new algorithms of fairly recent origin offered for the calculation of the matrix pseudoinverse. Unfortunately, nonpathological counterexamples can be constructed, as offered herein, that demonstrate the questionable nature of these two algorithms; however, a resolution is offered here to help prevent possible uncritical propagation of the questionable algorithms. As a rigorous alternative, a well-established technique (endorsed by numerical analysts) is reviewed for calculating the correct matrix pseudoinverse using a computer. Additionally, this technique possesses existent independently verified/validated and accessible software code for a convenient implementation. However, historical loose ends in calculating the associated condition number are singled out here as cause for concern and as a topic for future resolution and refinement. Although an optimal control applicatoin of pseudoinverses is also presented here, the primary motivation for considering these pseudoinverse issues is offered in an application example from estimation theory in the implementation and analysis of a minimum variance reduced-order (MVRO) filter, having proper performance that critically hinges on the correct computation of the matrix pseudoinverse. While examples of applying MVRO to navigation applications were provided almost a decade ago, a clear indication of the somewhat restrictive conditions of applicability were wanting, and so are elucidated here, since there appears to be a resurgence of interest in this analytic technique. Another contribution is in providing a tally of the *drawbacks* to be incurred in using MVRO, as well as its previously publicized benefits. This is done in order that a balanced view be offered on what should be considered in a *fair* tradeoff to assess the utility of using MVRO for a particular application.

I.   INTRODUCTION

Although fairly widely utilized in select areas of control and estimation theory (notably in forming bounds and in numerical calculation of the transition matrix and the discrete-time process noise covariance matrix for time-invariant linear systems [19–21]), it is fairly well known that a previous measure thought to be a norm for over twelve years (as evidenced in Refs. [19–21, 39, 110]) has now been demonstrated to be invalid [1–3]. Additional, more severe, analytical misconceptions currently exist in related areas and have been somewhat pervasively propagated (as representatively identified in Refs. [4, 5, 22, 23, 46, 49, 115, 148] for correction). Some counterexamples are presented herein to point out weaknesses in two approaches offered recently for calculating the matrix pseudoinverse. Previously unacknowledged limitations in even the preferred computational technique are offered here as representative of what hurdles are to be encountered in attempting to implement an MVRO filter for navigation applications. These caveats are provided in the same constructive vein as the above-mentioned corrections. A brief theoretical overview is provided in Appendix A of what constitutes a valid pseudoinverse.

Counterexamples are offered in Section II to two recent approaches suggested by researchers, and some textbooks (as identified) for calculating and propagating the matrix pseudoinverse. A technique, currently becoming the standard solution approach, as endorsed by numerical analysts, is reviewed in Section III, along with a brief consideration of implementation details, validation history, and acknowledged although not well-known loose ends in the associated "condition number" estimation (related to the ratio of the largest to smallest eigenvalue encountered in the matrix of concern, being a measure of the degree of ill conditioning encountered). While some varied applications of pseudoinverse calculation are offered in Section IV, Section V concentrates on its impact in minimum variance reduced-order filtering. Section V also provides new insights and explicit restrictions or conditions for valid implementation of an MVRO filter and for the subsequent engineering utility of such an MVRO filter as the main contribution of this article. A brief overall summary is provided in Section VI. Certain augmenting details and illustrative examples are relegated to Appendices A, B, and C.

II.   COUNTEREXAMPLES TO TWO QUESTIONABLE PSEUDOINVERSE ALGORITHMS

Two recent apparently fundamental misconceptions pertaining to the calculation of the matrix pseudoinverse are now identified by means of transparently simple counterexamples.

A.   PSEUDOINVERSE ALGORITHM NUMBER 1

In an application of the generalized likelihood ratio (GLR) to failure detection and other event detections, the telescoping property inherent in the following definition [6, Eq. (46); 7, Eq. (29); 8, Eq. (12)]:

$$C(k; \theta) \overset{\Delta}{=} \sum_{j=N_0}^{k} G^T(j; \theta)V^{-1}(j)G(j; \theta), \tag{1}$$

where θ is a fixed scalar variable representing an unknown event time; j is the time index; k is the current time; $G(j; \theta)$ is an m × n matrix not necessarily of full rank; $V(j)$ is an m × m symmetric positive definite matrix; T as a superscript represents a vector or matrix transpose, and Eq. (1) is used in Refs. [6–8] to establish one means of recursively generating $C(k; \theta)$ as in [6, Eq. (55)]:

$$C(k; \theta) = G^T(k; \theta)V^{-1}(k)G(k; \theta) + Ck - 1; \theta). \tag{2}$$

In Ref. [6, Eq. (56)], the matrix inversion lemma is applied to (2) when each $G(\cdot; \cdot)$ is of full rank, to result in:

$$
\begin{aligned}
C^{-1}(k; \theta) &= \left[G^T(k; \theta)V^{-1}(k)G(k; \theta) + C(k - 1; \theta) \right]^{-1} \\
&= C^{-1}(k - 1; \theta) - C^{-1}(k - 1; \theta)G^T \\
&\quad \times \left[GC^{-1}(k - 1; \theta)G^T + V \right]^{-1}GC^{-1}(k - 1; \theta).
\end{aligned} \tag{3}
$$

However, in Ref. [6, p. 17], it is *asserted* that the matrix inversion lemma can also be used to propagate the pseudoinverse recursively in case all the $G(\cdot; \cdot)$ are *not* of full rank [such that the strict inverse of $C(k - 1; \theta)$ is *not* guaranteed to exist]. However, this assertion was never proved nor referenced in Ref. [6], nor properly qualified as being only a conjecture, and no such matrix-inversion lemma-like property is acknowledged to exist in either of the three recent encyclopedic references [9], [10], or [29], or in other recent specialized discussions ([123, Section 5.2]; [124, Chapter 3]). Indeed, a counterexample to the property asserted in Ref. [6], that the pseudoinverse (denoted herein by a superscript dagger) may be recursively propagated via (3), is offered below.

B.   COUNTEREXAMPLE TO ALGORITHM NUMBER 1

$$C(k - 1; \theta) = \begin{bmatrix} 1 & 2 \\ 2 & 4 \end{bmatrix}; \quad C^{\dagger}(k - 1; \theta) = \frac{1}{25}\begin{bmatrix} 1 & 2 \\ 2 & 4 \end{bmatrix} \tag{4}$$

$$G(k; \theta) = I_2; \quad V(k) = V^{-1}(k) = I_2, \tag{5}$$

where I_2 is the identity matrix, which when used in (2) yields

$$C(k; \theta) = \begin{bmatrix} 2 & 2 \\ 2 & 5 \end{bmatrix} \tag{6}$$

having a valid pseudoinverse (which in this case is the same as the inverse) being

$$C^\dagger(k; \theta) = C^{-1}(k; \theta) = \frac{1}{6}\begin{bmatrix} 5 & -2 \\ -2 & 2 \end{bmatrix}. \tag{7}$$

However, the following *erroneous result*

$$C^\dagger(k; \theta) = \frac{1}{30}\begin{bmatrix} 1 & 2 \\ 2 & 4 \end{bmatrix} \tag{8}$$

is obtained when the matrix inversion lemma of the form of (3) is utilized in an *attempt* to recursively generate the pseudoinverse according to the path advocated in Refs. [6–8]. (The algorithm described above, as offered for pseudoinverse updating in Ref. [6], was encountered in the GLR approach to failure detection and other event detection; however, there are other alternative approaches to failure detection in navigation systems, such as in Refs. [40–46, 55–57, 62], or as surveyed in Refs. [62, 90–92], that do not require any calculation of the pseudoinverse as well as the GLR modification in Ref. [132].) Recent insights that obliquely relate the matrix inversion lemma with calculating pseudoinverses is as provided in Ref. [52, Theorem 5] and Ref. [122, Theorem 3.1]. However, use of the matrix inversion lemma in performing recursive calculations (rather than merely to provide theoretical and structural insight) has been demonstrated to be numerically unstable in general [98, p. 1038]. Valid generalizations of the matrix inversion lemma are in Refs. [130, 131]. Another slightly different, but commonly encountered, theoretical misconception relating to the matrix pseudoinverse in discussed next.

C.   PSEUDOINVERSE ALGORITHM NUMBER 2

In the textbook [11, p. 19], it is *asserted* that the matrix pseudoinverse always takes one or the other of the following two forms:

$$C^\dagger = C^T(CC^T)^{-1} \tag{9}$$

or

$$C^\dagger = (C^TC)^{-1}C^T. \tag{10}$$

It is emphasized here as a *warning of the possible theoretical oversight or definite oversimplification* in the above dichotomy asserted for pseudoinverse calculation in the textbook [11] that the above two forms are appropriate to represent pseudoinverse calculation *only if* either (CC^T) or (C^TC) is nonsingular, respectively.

D.   COUNTEREXAMPLES TO ALGORITHM NUMBER 2

A simple example that illustrates a frequently encountered general case when neither of the above two simple forms is appropriate to represent the pseudoinverse is (Ref. [12, p. 168, Exercise 20], with the solution provided here being original, as derived in Appendix B as an example of the requisite calculations to be performed in determining the pseudoinverse via hand computation for even simple low-dimensional examples):

$$C_1 = \begin{bmatrix} 1 & 2 & 1 \\ 1 & 1 & 0 \\ 1 & 1 & 0 \end{bmatrix} \tag{11}$$

having pseudoinverse

$$C_1^\dagger = \begin{bmatrix} \frac{-1}{3} & \frac{1}{2} & \frac{1}{2} \\ \frac{1}{3} & 0 & 0 \\ \frac{2}{3} & \frac{-1}{2} & \frac{-1}{2} \end{bmatrix} \tag{12}$$

(as can be verified by showing that it satisfies the necessary and sufficient Properties 1–9 of a pseudoinverse [12, p. 165] or as found in Ref. [51, Chapter 4], as previously referenced by Ref. [50]); yet

$$C_1^TC_1 = \begin{bmatrix} 3 & 4 & 1 \\ 4 & 6 & 2 \\ 1 & 2 & 1 \end{bmatrix}; \quad C_1C_1^T = \begin{bmatrix} 6 & 3 & 3 \\ 3 & 2 & 2 \\ 3 & 2 & 2 \end{bmatrix} \tag{13}$$

are both singular (since for $C_1^TC_1$ the sum of the first and third columns equals the second, and for $C_1C_1^T$ the second and third columns are identical). The wording in the dichotomous pseudoinverse definition of Ref. [11] indicates that when C has more columns than rows, then there is no worry that (CC^T) could be singular. The following example demonstrates that this is not the case. Another representative nonsquare matrix that does not fit into either dichotomous alternative offered in Ref. [11, p. 19] of the above Eqs. (9) or (10) is

$$C_2 = \begin{bmatrix} 1 & 3 & 2 & -1 \\ 2 & 5 & 3 & -1 \\ 1 & 0 & -1 & 2 \end{bmatrix} \tag{14}$$

being of rank 2. That both (9) and (10) fall short of adequately handling every case is not just a consequence of the matrix being used for the counterexample being square, since the counterexample of (14) is a rectangular matrix.

This apparently fundamental conceptual error, overlooked in the methodology advocated in Ref. [11] for pseudoinverse calculation, persists in the first through eighth (current 1984) printing.

As indicated in Ref. [100, Sections 7.1 and 7.2], if the general rectangular $m \times n$ matrix C is of rank $r (>0)$, then it admits to a rank factorization of the form

$$C^{(m \times n)} = D^{(m \times r)} E^{(r \times n)} \tag{15}$$

and the corresponding Moore–Penrose generalized inverse (or as simply designated, the pseudoinverse of C) is

$$C^\dagger = E^T (EE^T)^{-1} (D^T D)^{-1} D^T \tag{16}$$

or simply

$$C^\dagger = E^\dagger D^\dagger. \tag{17}$$

The results of (15)–(17) are what is neglected in the textbook of Ref. [11] that would make the story complete. Otherwise, the expressions of (9) and (10) merely represent the right and left inverses of C, respectively, when they exist [124, p. 70]. However, finding the necessary factorization/decomposition indicated in (15) and unequivocally establishing the true rank r are computationally relegated to the use of the SVD, as discussed further in Section III.

While some matrix pseudoinverse examples can be calculated easily because the structure degenerates to a very simple form (as illustrated in the block upper triangular examples of Section V), the calculation of the matrix pseudoinverse in the general case is well known to be quite a formidable problem, as simply discussed in Refs. [51] and [136] for hand calculations. However, for the higher-dimensional matrices to be encountered in most practical applications that are intractable by hand calculation, an accepted computer algorithm is apparently available for pseudoinverse calculation, as now reviewed.

III. PROPER CALCULATION OF MATRIX PSEUDOINVERSE BY VALIDATED SOFTWARE: A STATUS REVIEW

An approach that has been endorsed by numerical analysts [13, pp. 257–258; 14, p. 171; 101] for calculating the matrix pseudoinverse of an arbitrary $n \times m$ matrix C is to utilize the well-known singular value decompositions (SVD), represented as indicated below for the following three (exhaustive) cases (where the asterisk denotes the conjugate transpose of the matrix).

Case 1 (m = n).

$$C = U \begin{bmatrix} \Lambda_r & | & 0 \\ - - | - & - \\ 0 & | & 0_{n-r} \end{bmatrix} V^* \tag{18a}$$

for r such that $1 < r < n$.

Case 2 (n > m).

$$C = U \begin{bmatrix} \Lambda_m \\ -- \\ 0 \end{bmatrix} V^*. \tag{18b}$$

Case 3 (n < m).

$$C = U [\Lambda_n \mid 0] V^*. \tag{18c}$$

In the above, U (the orthogonal eigenvectors of C^*C, denoted as the left singular vectors of C) and V (orthogonal eigenvectors of CC^*, denoted as the right singular vectors of C) are unitary:

$$UU^* = I_n \tag{19}$$

$$VV^* = I_m \tag{20}$$

and Λ_i is a diagonal matrix (not necessarily nonsingular). The pseudoinverse is then available [13, 14] as the corresponding case below.

Case 1' (m = n).

$$C^\dagger = V \begin{bmatrix} \Lambda_r^\dagger & | & 0 \\ - - | - & - \\ 0 & | & 0_{n-r} \end{bmatrix} U^*. \tag{21a}$$

Case 2' (n > m).

$$c^{\dagger} = V \left[\begin{array}{c} \Lambda_m^{\dagger} \\ \hline 0 \end{array} \right] U^*.$$ (21b)

Case 3' (n < m).

$$c^{\dagger} = V [\Lambda_n^{\dagger} \mid 0] U^*.$$ (21c)

where any *i-dimensional diagonal* matrix of the form appearing above,

$$\Lambda_i = \left[\begin{array}{c|c} \text{diag}(\sigma_1, \sigma_2, ..., \sigma_j) & 0 \\ \hline 0 & 0_{i-j} \end{array} \right]$$ (22)

for some fixed j $(1 \leq j \leq i)$ and $\sigma_1 > ... > \sigma_j > 0$, the corresponding pseudoinverse, is *defined* to be

$$\Lambda_i^{\dagger} = \left[\begin{array}{c|c} \text{diag}\left(\dfrac{1}{\sigma_1}, \dfrac{1}{\sigma_2}, ..., \dfrac{1}{\sigma_j} \right) & 0 \\ \hline 0 & 0_{i-j} \end{array} \right].$$ (23)

If r = n in Case 1', then the original square matrix is nonsingular and the pseudoinverse is identical to the standard inverse; consequently, the SVD is not really required where a standard matrix inversion routine will suffice, unless particular caution is being exercised in situations of possible numerical ill conditioning, as can occur in some Kalman filtering applications. {In the calculation of the covariance of estimation error for some Kalman filter applications, the additional expense incurred in utilizing the less severely affected SVD-based procedure is justified to enable added insight into pinpointing any sources of ill conditioning due to pathological circumstances not initially anticipated to be encountered in the application, and to allow the "robustness" of being able to continue the numerical evaluations of covariances unhindered by indicated underflows or by zeros occurring on the principal diagonal that would otherwise halt computations without use of an SVD-based (or UDU^T-based [45]) procedure.} This particular detailed structural specification in terms of the above three separate cases was presented here to avail the reader of the exact form of the correct solution (for ease in actual computational verification) and to avoid any possible slight confusion on where the zeros should occur within the solution matrix, as has arisen in the past in some references (e.g., Ref. [14, Theorem, Section III, p. 166] trying to include the slightly different structural forms encountered in each of these three cases in one apparently overly compact statement). A brief historical summary of the evolution of the correct SVD solution procedures for each of the cases of square/rectangular matrices having real/complex elements is provided in Ref. [14, introduction to Section III]; thus, no further comments on this topic are warranted here.

Decompositions of the form illustrated in Cases 1, 2, and 3, as appropriate, can be computationally accomplished using a commercially available implementation as an EISPACK [15] software routine (as recommended in Ref. [14, p. 167] as being perhaps the best version for SVD currently available). The LINPACK [26] implementation of SVD is similar to that of EISPACK; however, in the years following [14], it became apparent that there may be a slight error in the LINPACK version. The IMSL version of SVD (as LSVDF) is an implementation based on the routine SVDRs, written by Charles Lawson and Richard Hanson [95], and should be similar to that available with EISPACK. Details of the EISPACK validation and, in particular, the validation of the SVD routine by seventeen cooperative but independent universities and government laboratories across the country, are available in Ref. [15] (which additionally serves to compare the efficiencies of different machines for the same test problems). The practical decision as to which of the σ_i's should be effectively considered to be zero in computer calculations (affected by roundoff and truncation errors) is usually accomplished for so-called "equilibrated" matrices C, i.e., scaled such that $\sigma_1 = 1$, by a simple comparison to a tolerance threshold consisting of the larger of the following two quantities: (1) the square root of the particular machine's precision or, (2) a constant reflecting the uncertainty in the data comprising the most uncertain element of the matrix C [14, p. 171]. Alternative suggestions also exist (e.g., Ref. [51, p. 71]) for the proper choice of a decision tolerance threshold to determine an effective zero.

Additionally, a so-designated "backwards error analysis" has been previously performed by Wilkinson and Reinsch for the SVD implementation utilized in EISPACK so that an approximate measure of the "condition number" [13] is ostensibly available (as asserted in Refs. [15, p. 78; 27]) for user monitoring as a gauge of the degree of numerical ill conditioning encountered during the computations that consequently dictate the degree of confidence to be assigned to the final "answer" that is ultimately output. (Less reassuring open research questions pertaining to SVD condition numbers are divulged in Refs. [33, 38], indicating that some aspects of its calculation are still open questions, even though the earlier user manual [15] offers only reassurances of its validity.) An update to the condition number calculation has recently become available [53; cf. Ref. [121, pp. 289–301].

Upon computationally completing the indicated decomposition for the particular case of (18) via an SVD software routine, the reciprocals indicated in (23) should be performed; then the corresponding recombining matrix multiplications of (21) carried to completion to yield a valid matrix pseudoinverse (of minimum norm, denoted as a Moore–Penrose generalized inverse), as the primary goal. While other approaches to matrix pseudoinverse computation are available (e.g., Refs. [19, 109]), only the SVD-based approach has been successfully validated to this author's knowledge. However, other approaches to SVD computation have recently emerged [47, 48] and are undergoing further independent testing/corroboration, including a version that is feasible as a systolic array [71], implementable using VHSIC or other commercially available multiprocessor chips such as the NCR45CG72 geometric arithmetic parallel processor (GAPP).

IV. A SURVEY OF PSEUDOINVERSE APPLICATIONS

As further motivation warranting such detailed consideration of the above SVD computational issues, consider the following reasonable prediction in Ref. [14, p. 166]: "It is likely that within five or ten years SVD will be one of the most important and fundamental working tools for the control/systems community, particularly in the area of linear systems." Evidence substantiating the validity of this prediction is in Ref. [128]. Indeed, the usefulness of the SVD in accomplishing a factorization generally required in order to apply the so-called surely locally unbiased (SLU) decentralized filtering approach [24, 32, p. 17], but apparently not previously recognized, has recently been demonstrated in Ref. [25, Section 2.2.2]. New high-resolution signal detection also exploits use of SVD [99, 104–106, 116]. {However, some complaints by way of counterexamples do exist to the use of the pseudoinverse in lieu of the true inverse in the calculation of array gains in the direction of jammers when using the sampled matrix inversion (SMI) technique for adaptive beamforming and in estimating jammer bearings via the maximum likelihood (ML) method in spectral analysis [106]. Perhaps these counterexamples should be more thoroughly re-examined.} Additionally, SVD variants constitute the preferred method of verifying or establishing positive definiteness or semidefiniteness of matrices encountered in realistically dimensioned computer problem simulations and typical industrial implementations [93]. The SVD has been referred to in Refs. [14, 96] as the only reliable method for determining the rank of a matrix. However, for large symmetric matrices of dimension 200, and even up to 500, Lanczos techniques [97] may be the preferred approach for eigenvalue/eigenvector determination. Practical applications of the Moore–Penrose generalized inverse (which is a continuous operator [29]) already abound in statistics [28], electrical engineering [29, Chapter 5], and linear programming [29, Chapter 11]. Reference [29] also offers multitudinous applications of the extremely useful, alternative Drazin inverse in such areas as Markov chains and linear systems theory [29, Chapters 8 and 9]. Generalized inverses of polynomial matrices of the form of transfer function matrices (normalized by multiplication throughout by the least common denominator), as encountered in linear systems theory in the frequency/transform domain, have also been considered [30]. The topic of generalized inverses has also been considered in the design of Luenberger observers [50, 119] and in image restoration and pattern recognition [129]. The importance of this pseudoinverse topic is illustrated in a particularly lucid application example appearing in Ref. [12, p. 162], where employing the pseudoinverse neatly provides the explicit minimum energy optimum control solution for a linear system with specified initial conditions, final conditions, and final time, as demonstrated in Appendix C. The expert system symbolic manipulation program MACSYMA, developed over approximately ten years at MIT (now available from Symbolics, Inc., and from National Energy Software/Argonne National Laboratory) has recently been successfully used by Charles Stark Draper Laboratory in providing explicit pseudoinverse representations for concatenations of direction cosine matrices representing successive rotations or the referencing of one coordinate frame to another, as occurs with robotic linkages and navigation systems. The matrices encountered in this application routinely involve numerous trigonometric functions that must be manipulated and ultimately simplified, using identities. Estimation theory examples, where the correct computation of the matrix pseudoinverse is *critical* for proper performance, are discussed in Section V.

V. DEPENDENCE OF MINIMUM VARIANCE REDUCED-ORDER FILTERING ON THE PSEUDOINVERSE

The standard linear dynamical system for which Kalman-type filters are designed has a discrete-time representation consisting of an n-dimensional state vector x_k and a p-dimensional measurement vector z_k of the following well-known form:

$$x_{k+1} = \Phi x_k + w_k \qquad (24)$$

$$z_k = H x_k + v_k, \qquad (25)$$

where w_k and v_k are zero-mean, white Gaussian process and measurement noises (independent of the Gaussian initial condition) of covariance level Q and R, respectively. The usual conditions of observability/controllability (or less restrictive detectability/stabilizability conditions [82, p. 82], or even nondetectable [134]) are assumed to be satisfied here by the system of (24) and (25). [Only the standard unadorned form of the linear estimation/filtering problem is addressed here [81]. Straightforward modifications of what is offered here can be routinely accommodated according to existing accepted techniques in order to handle the less standard, but still tractable, variations of linear filtering, such as the cases of having a singular R (i.e., some measurements being uncorrupted by the measurement noise), of a system (24) failing to be process noise controllable/stabilizable and having cross-correlated process and measurement noises, time or serially correlated Gaussian noises, nonindependent initial condition, non-Gaussian initial condition and noises (but distributed according to an "elliptical" family). There can be comprehensive handling of filter replicates for multitarget tracking, the Magill–Laniotis bank-of-filter multimode hypothesis discrimination, use of noises that are centered white Poisson processes rather than Gaussian, and use of mixed combinations of Gaussian and point processes for tracking. These variations are also of significance in seeking something other than LQG feedback control of stochastic systems where filtering is to be performed first to obtain adequate estimates of the current state of the system before corrective control is applied.]

Use of a reduced-order suboptimal filter model of a smaller dimension m (<n) is frequently necessitated to meet constraints on the computational capacity available for the filtering function on board ships or aircraft in aided navigation applications [18, 34, 43, 62, 65, 92]. However, standard *a priori* covariance analysis can still be carried out to account for this expedient reduced-order approximation by establishing the anticipated realistic error of estimation as obtained by *both* (1) acknowledging use of a reduced-order filter model as required as a compromise fit to computer resources available for the particular application, and (2) utilizing any known higher-order real-world model of dimension n (m < n). Standard conventional methodology for accomplishing such an exacting evaluation [11, Chapter 7; 17; 18, pp. 325–341; 63, 88] usually involves working with an augmented state vector of the form

$$x'(t) \triangleq \left[\begin{array}{c} Tx(t) - \hat{x}(t) \\ - - - - - - \\ x(t) \end{array} \right] \tag{26}$$

where, in the above, $T^{(m \times n)}$ (usually consisting of only zeros and ones) is used to circumvent a dimensional incompatibility that would otherwise exist. The second moment of the augmented vector x', being $E[x'(t)x'(t)^T]$, satisfies a so-called time-varying Lyapunov or variance equation that constitutes a computer burden that goes as $(n + m)^3$ following the completion of a first pass of order m^3 needed to specify (and store for use in the final pass) the suboptimal filter gains as calculated by the reduced-order filter (cf. operations counts in [94]).

A self-contained original derivation of the so-called minimum variance reduced-order (MVRO) filter introduced in [16, 35, 36, 111; cf. Ref. 118] is provided below by following the basic steps of Ref. [36], but by further augmenting them here to include subtle crucial intermediate steps and to explicitly feature critical assumptions (left implicit in Refs. [16, 35, 36, 111]), and to further elucidate previously unacknowledged limitations in the MVRO approach as it currently stands.

Suppose that the reduced-order filter to be utilized models a subset of m states of the full n states, x_k, as represented by

$$y_k = T^{(m \times n)} x_k \tag{27}$$

where the transformation T (possibly time varying as treated in Ref. [36, Eq. (5)] and Ref. [16, Eq. (29)] but *not* assumed to be so here for simplicity, and as the prevalent case to be encountered in practice of having fixed constant state selection) effectively serves to delete undesired less important states from consideration in the filter model.

The following three assumptions are implicitly utilized in Refs. [16, 35, 36].

Assumption 1 (state subset selection).

$$TT^\dagger = I_{m \times m} \tag{28}$$

[(28) can usually be met when availed of complete freedom in selecting T. As noted following [16, Eq. (2)], $T^\dagger T$ is an $n \times n$ matrix which is *not* the identity matrix.]

Assumption 2 (extrapolate structure).

$$\hat{y}_{k+1|k} = T\Phi T^\dagger \hat{y}_{k|k}. \tag{29}$$

Assumption 3 (update structure).

$$\hat{y}_{k|k} = \hat{y}_{k|k-1} + K_k [z_k - HT^\dagger \hat{y}_{k|k-1}]. \tag{30}$$

(Assumptions 2 and 3 can also be interpreted as computational constraints being complied with in using an MVRO filter.)

If the residual in (30) were in fact $[z_k - H\hat{x}_{k|k-1}]$, then the filter gain in (30) should be

$$K_k = TK_k^* \tag{31}$$

(where K_k^* is the standard well-known Kalman gain), as could be justified by premultiplying the standard Kalman filtering mechanization equations throughout by T. However, since the residual term in (30) *is* nonstandard, K_k is open for specification, as pursued in the MVRO approach to minimize the variance of estimation error as reflected in the following criterion:

$$\operatorname{tr}\tilde{P}_{k|k} \stackrel{\Delta}{=} \operatorname{tr} E\left[\tilde{e}_{k|k}\tilde{e}_{k|k}^T\right], \tag{32}$$

where

$$\tilde{e}_{k|k} \stackrel{\Delta}{=} \hat{y}_{k|k} - Tx_k. \tag{33}$$

It is frequently more convenient to work instead with

$$e_{k|k} \triangleq T^\dagger \hat{y}_{k|k} - x_k, \tag{34}$$

which may be premultiplied by T throughout to yield

$$Te_{k|k} = T\left(T^\dagger \hat{y}_{k|k} - x_k\right) \tag{35a}$$

$$= TT^\dagger \hat{y}_{k|k} - Tx_k. \tag{35b}$$

By Assumption 1 in (28), (35b) simplifies to yield

$$Te_{k|k} = \hat{y}_{k|k} - Tx_k \triangleq \tilde{e}_{k|k}. \tag{36}$$

Now, utilizing the constrained structural form of (30) to substitute for $\hat{y}_{k|k}$, (34) can be re-expressed as

$$e_{k|k} = T^\dagger\left(\hat{y}_{k|k-1} + K_k[z_k - HT^\dagger \hat{y}_{k|k-1}]\right) - x_k \tag{37a}$$

$$= (I - T^\dagger K_k H)e_{k|k-1} + (I - T^\dagger K_k H)x_k - x_k \tag{37b}$$

$$+ T^\dagger K_k H x_k + T^\dagger K_k v_k$$

$$= (I - T^\dagger K_k H)e_{k|k-1} + T^\dagger K_k v_k, \tag{37c}$$

where a fairly obvious notation consistent with (34) as

$$e_{k|k-1} \triangleq T^\dagger \hat{y}_{k|k-1} - x_k \tag{38}$$

is utilized in (37). It should be noted that a term $T^\dagger K_k H x_k$ was both added and subtracted in order to obtain (37b).

Using (37c) to form $[e_{k|k}e_{k|k}^T]$, and taking the total expectation throughout, yields:

$$P_{k|k} = [I - T^\dagger K_k H]P_{k|k-1}[I - T^\dagger K_k H]^T + T^\dagger K_k R_k K_k^T (T^\dagger)^T \tag{39}$$

with

$$P_{k|k-1} \triangleq E\left[e_{k|k-1} e_{k|k-1}^T\right]. \tag{40}$$

Now combining the criterion of (32) to be minimized with (36), (39), and (40) yields:

$$\text{tr}[\tilde{P}_{k|k}] = \text{tr}\left\{E\left[(\hat{y}_{k|k} - Tx_k)(\hat{y}_{k|k} - Tx_k)^T\right]\right\} \tag{41a}$$

$$= \text{tr}\left[T(I - T^\dagger K_k H)P_{k|k-1}(I - T^\dagger K_k H)^T T^T \right.$$
$$\left. + TT^\dagger K_k R K_k^T (T^\dagger)^T T^T\right]. \tag{41b}$$

By using standard matrix gradient formulas [37], a necessary condition (that is additionally a sufficient condition for the specific nonnegative definite quadratic form within the trace) for achieving the minimization of the criterion of (32) [re-expressed as (41b)] with respect to the filter gain K_k is

$$0 = \frac{\partial}{\partial K_k}\text{tr}[\tilde{P}_{k|k}] = -2(T^\dagger)^T T^T TP_{k|k-1}H^T$$

$$+ 2(T^\dagger)^T T^T T(T^\dagger)K_k\left[HP_{k|k-1}H^T + R\right] \tag{42a}$$

$$= -2TP_{k|k-1}H^T + 2K_k\left[HP_{k|k-1}H^T + R\right], \tag{42b}$$

where the simplification of (42b) is obtained via Assumption 1 as (28). It then comes immediately from (42b) that the MVRO filter gain that minimizes the error in estimation for filters of the form of Assumptions 2 and 3 is

$$K_k = TP_{k|k-1}H^T\left[HP_{k|k-1}H^T + R\right]^{-1}. \tag{43}$$

To complete the MVRO filter specification, a recursive expression for the time evolution of $P_{k|k-1}$ is needed. Returning to (38) and substituting structural Assumption 2 from (29), yields

$$e_{k|k-1} = T^\dagger T\Phi T^\dagger \hat{y}_{k-1|k-1} - x_k \tag{44a}$$

$$= T^\dagger T\Phi T^\dagger \hat{y}_{k-1|k-1} - \Phi x_{k-1} - w_{k-1} \tag{44b}$$

$$= T^\dagger T\Phi T^\dagger \hat{y}_{k-1|k-1} + \Phi T^\dagger \hat{y}_{k-1|k-1} - x_{k-1}$$
$$- \Phi T^\dagger \hat{y}_{k-1|k-1} - w_{k-1} \tag{44c}$$

$$= \Phi e_{k-1|k-1} + (T^\dagger T - I)\Phi T^\dagger \hat{y}_{k-1|k-1} - w_{k-1}. \tag{44d}$$

For systems having the following structural form {identified in Ref. [36, following Eq. (17)], but not explicitly identified in Ref. [16] except for a passing allusion in Ref. [16, Eq. (54)]}:
Assumption 4.

$$(T^\dagger T - I)\Phi T^\dagger \hat{y}_{k-1|k-1} = 0. \tag{45}$$

The middle term of (44d) is zero; so (44) reduces to

$$e_{k|k-1} = \Phi e_{k-1|k-1} - w_{k-1}. \tag{46}$$

from which

$$P_{k|k-1} \triangleq E\left[e_{k|k-1} e^T_{k|k-1}\right] \tag{47a}$$

$$= E\left[\Phi e_{k-1|k-1} e^T_{k-1|k-1} \Phi^T\right] + E\left[w_{k-1} w^T_{k-1}\right] \tag{47b}$$

$$= \Phi P_{k-1|k-1} \Phi^T + Q \tag{47c}$$

since cross terms between $e_{k-1|k-1}$ and w_{k-1} are uncorrelated and have zero mean. Use of (47c) for covariance propagation in conjunction with (39) for updating the covariance to reflect measurement incorporation completes the specification of the MVRO filter of (29), (30), and (43), as summarized in Table 1 in juxtaposition with the standard mechanization equations of Kalman filtering to facilitate a later comparison.

If the condition of Assumption 4 in (45) does not hold, then MVRO filtering can still be done by state augmentation, as offered in Ref. [16, Eqs. (42)–(52)], but the computational burden is then of the order of $(n + m)^3$, and thus of no significant computational benefit over the conventional approaches of Refs. [11, 17, 18]. This is a point that had not previously been adequately emphasized.

There are generally two well-known ways that this rather severe structural constraint of (45) can be satisfied. One way this constraint is satisfied is when

$$(T^\dagger T - I)\Phi T^\dagger = 0, \tag{48}$$

as occurs when the structure of the original system of (24) is block upper-triangular *and* the filter model states constitute a *precise proper subset* of the upper truth model states with a line of demarcation that matches exactly the block partitioning of the original system (as obtained in exhibiting its block upper-triangular structure). The other way the constraint of (45) can be easily satisfied, even if (48) does not hold, is if control compensation is being performed, such as subtracting off the estimates from the system at the end of each filter measurement incorporation cycle (as is frequently done for navigation applications in the resetting of gyro drift rates and in the correcting of platform tilts through torquing, as discussed in Ref. [18, pp. 306–307]), so that

$$\hat{y}_{k-1|k-1} = 0 \tag{49}$$

and the condition of (45) is thus trivially satisfied. However, all of the states of the filter must be reset to result in (49), but not all applications offer this flexibility or capability. A third milder situation that is less well known (and

TABLE 1. Explicit Comparison Between MVRO and Standard Kalman Filter Implementation Equations[a]

	Standard Kalman filter mechanization	MVRO filter mechanization[b,c,d]
Covariance of estimation error		
Propagate step	$P_{k+1}^- = \Phi_{k+1} P_k^+ \Phi_{k+1}^T + Q_k$	$P_{k+1}^- = \Phi_{k+1} P_k^+ \Phi_{k+1}^T + Q_k$
Update step	$P_k^+ = [I - \tilde{K}_k H] P_k^- [I - \tilde{K}_k H]^T + \tilde{K}_k R \tilde{K}_k^T$	$P_k^+ = [I - T^\dagger K_k H] P_k^- [I - T^\dagger K_k H]^T + T^\dagger K_k R K_k^T (T^\dagger)^T$
Filter		
Propagate step	$\hat{x}_{k+1}^- = \Phi_{k+1} \hat{x}_k^+$	$\hat{y}_{k+1}^- = T\Phi_{k+1} T^\dagger \hat{y}_k^+$
Update step	$\hat{x}_k^+ = \hat{x}_k^- + \tilde{K}_k [z_k - \tilde{H}_k^-]$	$\hat{y}_k^+ = \hat{y}_k^- + K_k [z_k - HT^\dagger \hat{y}_k^-]^d$
Filter gain calculation	$\tilde{K}_k = P_k^- H^T [H P_k^- H^T + R]^{-1}$	$K_k = T P_k^- H^T [H P_k^- H^T + R]^{-1}$

[a]Use of plus (+) and minus (−) superscript convention for update and propagate steps, respectively, is the notation popularized in Ref. [11].
[b]Even when the condition of (45) holds, the computational burden of the n-dimensional on-line real-time covariance calculation is seldom acceptable in filtering applications (unless filter gains are precalculated and stored on magnetic tape or disk).
[c]If assumption 4 does not hold, then MVRO mechanization is considerably more complex, as explicitly stated in Ref. [16, Eqs. (42)–(51)].
[d]Please note that $y_k = T^{(m \times n)} x_k$.

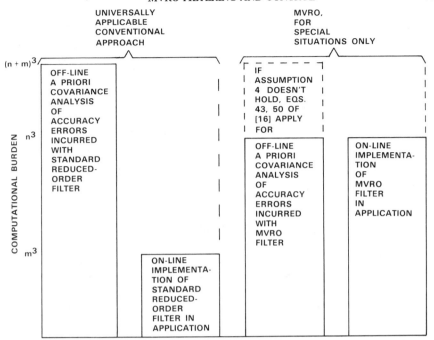

Fig. 1. A comparison of the allocation of computational burden for conventional application filters versus MVRO filters.

seldom occurs, but is indeed a possibility) is for neither (48) nor (49) to be satisfied exactly, but for each to be partially satisfied in such a way that the existing zeros of each exactly cancel the nonzero terms of the other in a complementary fashion in the indicated multiplication of the left-hand side of (48) with the left-hand side of (49) to yield the left-hand side of (45), being appropriately zero to satisfy the condition.

A fundamental comparison of MVRO filtering versus conventional filtering approaches is available from Fig. 1. The penalty associated with an on-line implementation of an MVRO filter is that the covariance calculations are n dimensional (rather than m dimensional for a conventional reduced-order filter). The reduced computational burden of exact *a priori* covariance analysis available with MVRO filters is appropriately consistent only if an MVRO filter is actually used in the physical application. Before an MVRO filter is selected for use in an application, the benefit of the *less* burdensome *a priori* MVRO covariance analysis should be balanced with a consideration of the *greater* burden to be encountered in an on-line MVRO implementation (that could perhaps even preclude satisfying the required constraint of being a real-time mechanization). The point that is being made here for the first time is that the computational burden of MVRO in the on-line implementation is greater than that of a conventional reduced-order filter implementation of the same number of states. This revelation is substantiated by the detailed consideration of the underlying MVRO derivation, as recounted herein with emphasis on previously unstated structural assumptions.

A direct explicit comparison between the mechanization equations of a standard Kalman filter (of dimension n) and an MVRO filter (of dimension m, m < n) is provided in Table 1. Please note that the covariance calculations of both approaches are of dimension n. Also notice that any standard filter mechanization (or any conventional suboptimal filtering analysis mechanization) may be expediently converted to an MVRO mechanization simply by the additional inclusion or insertion of the appropriate transformation matrices T and T†, as indicated in the bottom line of Table 1. Notice the ample opportunity of MVRO results to be adversely affected by any errors in the pseudoinverse calculation since, as clearly portrayed in Table 1, three of the five MVRO mechanization equations rely explicitly upon employing the correct pseudoinverse. While only the case of a time-invariant transformation matrix T was considered here (since most physical applications use a constant subset of truth model states as the filter model states for the duration of a mission), where only *one* pseudoinverse computation of T† suffices for this MVRO mechanization, the presentations in Ref. [36, following Eq. (5)] and Ref. [16, following Eq. (29)] deal with a time-varying transformation T_k that therefore exhibits increased MVRO sensitivity to pseudoinverse calculation. This increased sensitivity occurs because a new $T_k{}^†$ is needed at each time step (see Ref. [49] also). In addition, a further consideration is that pseudoinverse computations are fairly time-consuming calculations, except for extremely simple degenerate cases.

Since structural Assumption 1 was utilized twice in developing the equations describing the MVRO framework, this condition of (28) is now examined to demonstrate that it is sometimes satisfied by coincidence or by objective selection in specific applications. To motivate how the condition of (28) could be invoked so readily, please consider the following example.

A.   A BLOCK UPPER-TRIANGULAR EXAMPLE

Consider the following time-invariant continuous-time block upper-triangular system of the form

$$
\begin{bmatrix} \dot{x}_1(t) \\ \hline \dot{x}_2(t) \\ \hline \dot{x}_3(t) \end{bmatrix} = \begin{bmatrix} F_{11} & F_{12} & F_{13} \\ 0 & F_{22} & F_{23} \\ 0 & 0 & F_{33} \end{bmatrix} \begin{bmatrix} x_1(t) \\ \hline x_2(t) \\ \hline x_3(t) \end{bmatrix} + \begin{bmatrix} w_1(t) \\ \hline w_2(t) \\ \hline w_3(t) \end{bmatrix} \tag{50}
$$

(where the discrete-time formulation has the corresponding block upper-triangular structure) that is to be tracked from its measurements by a filter that estimates the block subset of states

$$
y(k) = \begin{bmatrix} x_1(k) \\ \hline x_2(k) \end{bmatrix} \tag{51}
$$

where x_1, x_2, and x_3 are of dimension n_1, n_2, and n_3, respectively. A straightforward observation is that

$$y(k) = \begin{bmatrix} x_1(k) \\ ---- \\ x_2(k) \end{bmatrix} = \begin{bmatrix} I_{n_1} & 0 & 0 \\ 0 & I_{n_2} & 0 \end{bmatrix} \begin{bmatrix} x_1(k) \\ ---- \\ x_2(k) \\ ---- \\ x_3(k) \end{bmatrix} \tag{52}$$

From (52), the transformation T is therefore implicitly defined to be

$$T = \begin{bmatrix} I_{n_1} & 0 & 0 \\ 0 & I_{n_2} & 0 \end{bmatrix} \tag{53}$$

and, consequently,

$$T^\dagger = T^T(TT^T)^{-1} \tag{54a}$$

$$= \begin{bmatrix} I_{n_1} & 0 \\ 0 & I_{n_2} \\ 0 & 0 \end{bmatrix} \left(\begin{bmatrix} I_{n_1} & 0 & 0 \\ 0 & I_{n_2} & 0 \end{bmatrix} \begin{bmatrix} I_{n_1} & 0 \\ 0 & I_{n_2} \\ 0 & 0 \end{bmatrix} \right)^{-1} \tag{54b}$$

$$= \begin{bmatrix} I_{n_1} & 0 \\ 0 & I_{n_2} \\ 0 & 0 \end{bmatrix} \tag{54c}$$

so structural Assumption 1 is indeed satisfied, since

$$TT^\dagger = \begin{bmatrix} I_{n_1} & 0 & 0 \\ 0 & I_{n_2} & 0 \end{bmatrix} \begin{bmatrix} I_{n_1} & 0 \\ 0 & I_{n_2} \\ 0 & 0 \end{bmatrix} \tag{55a}$$

$$
= \begin{bmatrix} I_{n_1} & 0 \\ 0 & I_{n_2} \end{bmatrix} = I_{n_1 + n_2}. \tag{55b}
$$

Even if the constraint of the application is that no resets can be performed to satisfy (49), a system structure such as (50) and (53) also leads to the condition of (45) holding, since the transition matrix corresponding to the dynamics matrix of (50) is of the form

$$
\Phi = \begin{bmatrix} A_{11} & A_{12} & A_{13} \\ 0 & A_{22} & A_{23} \\ 0 & 0 & A_{33} \end{bmatrix} \tag{56}
$$

which simply yields the following calculation:

$$
(T^{\dagger}T - I)\Phi T^{\dagger} = \begin{bmatrix} 0 & 0 & 0 \\ 0 & 0 & 0 \\ 0 & 0 & -I_{n_3} \end{bmatrix} \begin{bmatrix} A_{11} & A_{12} & A_{13} \\ 0 & A_{22} & A_{23} \\ 0 & 0 & A_{33} \end{bmatrix} \begin{bmatrix} I_{n_1} & 0 \\ 0 & I_{n_2} \\ 0 & 0 \end{bmatrix} \tag{57a}
$$

$$
= 0. \tag{57b}
$$

B.   AN EXAMPLE THAT IS NOT BLOCK UPPER-TRIANGULAR

A different selection for a filter model that is also a proper subset of the block upper-triangular truth model is

$$
y(k) = \begin{bmatrix} x_2(k) \\ \hdashline x_3(k) \end{bmatrix} \tag{58}
$$

as represented by the transformation

$$
T = \begin{bmatrix} 0 & I_{n_2} & 0 \\ 0 & 0 & I_{n_3} \end{bmatrix}. \tag{59}
$$

For this example, the critical Assumption 1 [as (28)] holds, and the pseudoinverse again degenerates to $T^\dagger = T^T$, but Assumption 4 is violated in general [since (48) does *not* hold] unless it is possible (and practically desirable from the standpoint of convenience and economic feasibility) to implement control compensation in the particular application, such that (48) holds. Thus, two cases, one conveniently tractable and one less tractable, have been presented to illustrate realistic MVRO implementation considerations for a time-invariant block upper-triangular system truth model, such as is frequently encountered in realistic navigation and guidance (and even passive bearings-only sonobuoy target tracking) filter applications (e.g., [34, 43, 55–62, 72–80, 146, 147]). A block-diagonal example and one- and two-state filter subsets of an inherent third-order system are treated in Ref. [16, pp. 790–791] with all details visible, while the more realistic navigation examples involving 18-state, 15-state, and 11-state MVRO implementations treated in Ref. [16] unfortunately do *not* expose any of the detailed considerations needed to establish that the Assumptions 1–4 hold, as has been demonstrated here to be of fundamental importance.

Several useful surveys of Kalman filter procedures, experiences, and successes have been offered over the years [54, 64, 65], the most recent being in Ref. [54]. In Ref. [54, p. 503], it is stated that "systematic implementation and analysis of reduced-order models were unavailable" prior to the introduction of MVRO (in 1972 [35] to 1973 [36]). The use of MVRO is advocated in Ref. [54] as a systematic way to handle reduced-order filtering applications and is asserted to be much preferred to current covariance and Monte Carlo simulation techniques, which are referred to in Ref. [54] as being "expensive in both time and computer cost" and essentially "*ad hoc.*" On the face of it, MVRO offers a type of analytic beauty that appears to continually entice unwary onlookers (in 1973 [35], in 1979 [44], in 1981 [63], and in 1986 [111]). The other worrisome aspect is encountering these exhortations to use MVRO without corresponding explanations, such as that provided here, of what lies beneath the surface (or what likely disappointments each new enthusiast should expect to encounter after devoting time and effort toward implementing this apparent panacea). It is acknowledged in a somewhat astonished tone in Ref. [54] that conventional approaches to reduced-order filtering continue to be routinely used in practice rather than MVRO. This section explains why, in general, the conventional reduced-order filtering practices are apparently the prudent approach to follow, and should be continued until MVRO is refined beyond its current state, such that the open questions raised herein are adequately answered and resolved. Much stronger objections to the use of MVRO (along other lines) appear in [142] than (charitably) are raised here; these are endorsed here as valid criticisms. The scrutiny of [142] was evidently spawned by my earlier critique of [112].

Other objections to standard reduced-order filtering practice (also embracing the MVRO approach) have been raised in the past [31] on the grounds that explicit consideration of the bias introduced in utilizing a reduced-order filter had not yet been explicitly evaluated. However, current practice is to perform a representative off-line bias evaluation tailored to the intended mission scenario to enable rigorous verification of a satisfactorily low bias magnitude such that the bias does *not* interfere with the goal of filtering: "to tractably provide reasonably close estimates on-line in real time of the true states of interest."

A UDU^T-type square-root factorization of the type associated with Bierman [45] has more recently been performed for the MVRO [44] under somewhat restrictive conditions. These conditions are [44, p. 578] that:

1) The block-partitioned state vector is arranged so that

$$y = [I \mid 0] \begin{bmatrix} x_1 \\ \text{---} \\ x_2 \end{bmatrix}; \tag{60}$$

2) The filter error estimate is instantaneously reset to zero through impulsive control;

3) The measurement covariance matrix R is diagonal.

It is further suggested in Ref. [44, p. 578] that the condition of 1) is *not* restrictive since such ordering of the state vector can be either performed[1] by the analyst in setting up the problem or be automatically performed via pointer arrays in the resulting computer code, 2) will depend on the structure and flexibility of the particular application, and 3) can be attained, if not already present, by using well-known "whitening" procedures. It is agreed here that 3) can be attained using data "whitening" procedures since

$$y' = R^{-1/2}y = R^{-1/2}Hx + R^{-1/2}v \tag{61a}$$

$$= H'x + v' \tag{61b}$$

$$E\left[v'_k v'^T_k \right] = I. \tag{62}$$

However, we note here that these whitening procedures are cumbersome if R is time varying. Moreover, it is noted here that such a whitening would violate any state rearrangement that resulted in the condition of 1) as (60) being satisfied. Thus, in general, it appears that requiring an arbitrary system to satisfy both 1) *and* 3) is contradictory, while either 1) *or* 3) is routinely achievable.

Besides the use of MVRO and safer conventional approaches to reduced-order filtering discussed at the beginning of Section IV, many other novel approaches to reduced-order filtering exist [82–85, 102, 103, 107, 108, 117, 118], but the utility of these other results to navigation applications is yet to be demonstrated. Indeed, kneejerk response commentaries/caveats for some of these other approaches are that:

1) Reference [82] requires that a full two-point boundary-value problem (TPBVP) be solved for reduced-order filtering. (While solving backward and for-

---

[1] However, an explicit algorithm for achieving this prescribed reordering was not provided in Ref. [44], nor referenced as being easily available.

ward in time for Kalman smoothing as a Bryson–Frazier two-filter smoother is standard practice [87], having this comparable computational burden for just filtering is somewhat unexpected, i.e., defying prior physical intuition, and would tend to preclude a convenient real-time implementation.)

2) Reference [83] is less computationally burdensome than Ref. [82], but requires that the state size of the reduced-order filter be the same as the dimension of the measurements in (25) [while the identities of the original underlying states x in (24) are lost]. While the approach of Ref. [83] appears to be mathematically correct, it is of almost no interest for most navigation applications where the dimension of the underlying states can be fairly large: 15–100 states, while the dimension of the measurements is usually fairly small (on the order of 2 or 3). If the method of Ref. [83] were applied to these navigation applications, the dimension of the resulting reduced-order filter would correspondingly be only 2 or 3, respectively, depending on the actual measurement dimension. This is a severely confining restriction on the dimension of the tolerable reduced-order filter that is to capture the essence of the system's underlying dynamics.

3) While Ref. [84] offers a wonderful historical survey and insightful revelations into the various alternative approaches developed to handle filtering situations with some noise-free measurements present, the technique that is developed and advocated in Ref. [84] invokes a similarity transformation where, in general, underlying physical state identities are lost. Practical navigation applications routinely utilize reasonableness tests based on anticipated behavior of the physically enumerated states. In order to employ reasonableness tests (e.g., Ref. [89, p. 288]) for the reduced-order filter of Ref. [84], such tests would have to also be converted to the newly established coordinate system and later backed out for problem isolation (thus constituting a nontrivial computational burden). The advanced algebraic techniques of Ref. [84] are applicable only for time-invariant systems, while many navigation applications are inherently time varying due to the way specific forces and/or gravity anomalies/vertical deflections are handles [114].

4) Reference [85] is in the same vein as Ref. [83], but remedies many of the above-mentioned concerns. However, Ref. [85] is applicable only to time-invariant systems (see caveats above for Ref. [84]) and (as acknowledged in Ref. [85]) does not offer a numerical method for solving the simultaneous matrix equations that arise, nor does it offer a way of avoiding spurious solutions associated with likely multiple local minima that would satisfy the same optimal projection equations. More significant is that the problem formulation is only concerned with asymptotically good estimation and tracking as time gets large rather than being concerned with good tracking for finite horizon mission epochs of usual concern in navigation.

Perhaps newly emerging approaches to reduced-order modeling, such as in Refs. [102, 103, 107, 108, 138, 139, 141–144], will be more fruitful. References [102, 103] require further optimization operations and by so doing depart from a standard Kalman filter formulation, with an additional computational burden incurred. Reasonable complaints have already been raised in Ref. [120] concerning the approach of Refs. [102, 103]. The author also has strong reservations regarding the practical applicability of Refs. [117, 118], but constraints on space prevent further elaboration here. References [108], [139], and [141] appear to be particularly promising for future filtering applications.

VI.   SUMMARY

        Simple nonpathological counterexamples have been provided to demonstrate that two recently proposed algorithms for matrix pseudoinverse calculation are unsatisfactory by not giving the correct answer in the general case. The elements of a widely endorsed computational approach for calculating the matrix pseudoinverse of Penrose, based upon an SVD algorithm, as available in either an EISPACK or IMSL software package, were reviewed as a correct approach to solving this problem. The reader was also availed with insights into related issues and less-well-known open questions and the corresponding followups pertaining to currently used approximate estimates of "condition numbers" employed as a gauge of numerical ill conditioning actually encountered in pseudoinverse calculation of specific matrices. Pointers were supplied to constructive impacts of pseudoinverse calculation across a fairly broad spectrum of application areas as the reason the applications-oriented engineer should be concerned about the proper calculation of the pseudoinverse.
        Focusing attention on a likely beneficial impact of pseudoinverse calculation in estimation theory for navigation applications, the so-called minimum variance reduced-order design methodology for selecting reduced-order filters was explored in detail here. The outputs of this investigation are:
        1) Analytical statements of inherent assumptions and conditions being offered here as clarifications of requirements that must be met in order to validly use MVRO (but were not previously made explicit).
        2) A revelation of the heavy reliance on a *correct* matrix pseudoinverse computation within the MVRO filtering mechanization equations, thus evidence exists of:
                a) Sensitivity of MVRO to computation time expended in forming the pseudoinverse;
                b) Sensitivity of MVRO performance to accuracy of pseudoinverse calculations as a required intermediate computation.
        3) A balanced treatment of *both* benefits and drawbacks that should be considered in pursuing an MVRO implementation for a particular application.
        Throughout this investigation, constructive remedies were offered whenever possible: 1) to strengthen observed weakness in previously recommended approaches for pseudoinverse calculations and, 2) to bolster the MVRO design methodology.
        By alerting Kalman filter practitioners to these weaknesses associated with MVRO, the previous pitfalls can be circumvented. It is hoped that the cautions extended here are viewed constructively along with the following other warnings in the Kalman filter analysis and application area:

1) On limitations of a structural reformation for solving an algebraic Riccati equation [68] associated with filtering;

2) On some pitfalls in seeking to use age-weighted filters [66];

3) On problems in particular formulations of extended Kalman filtering [69] (with additional remedies offered in Ref. [86]);

4) On problems in the early analytic proofs of the stability of the Kalman filter [67; 70, Appendix C] and even in later proofs (see Ref. [25, Section 4.2 and Appendix A.1] for additional occurrences and ramifications);

5) On tradeoffs existing between degree of accuracy achievable versus computational time delay incurred (as gauged in terms of operations counts) for several popular alternative square-root filter formulations [18, Chapter 7].

6) Some problems relating to the lack of numerical stability when using the widely hailed "Schur Approach" for calculating Matrix Riccati equation solution [135];

7) Some problems associated with certain approaches to Matrix Spectral Factorization (as discussed in [137]) in putting a problem involving serially time-correlated additive noise into standard Kalman filter form (which expects only uncorrelated white additive noises) via "state augmentation" [11, pp. 133–135].

VII. APPENDIX A: THEORETICAL BASIS FOR THE PSEUDOINVERSE OF A CONTINUOUS LINEAR TRANSFORMATION

The significance of working with Hilbert spaces as done here is simply explained in Ref. [12, Chapter 3] as being motivated by the capability to carry over geometric intuition and experience honed in two- and three-dimensional Euclidean space to other situations [133], such as in achieving a better understanding of the underlying geometric structure of spaces of functions given that the *domain space* G is a *Hilbert space* (i.e., it is a linear vector space that has an *inner product* and is "complete" in the sense that all Cauchy sequences converge to a point within the space without "gaps").

H, the *range space*, is a Hilbert space.

θ_x and θ_y are the *null elements* or *additive identities* in the linear vector spaces G and H, respectively.

B(G, H) is notation for the class of *bounded (continuous) linear functions* from domain G *into* range H (notation: f:G $\rightarrow$ H or the function f *maps* G into H and f is continuous on G).

f is a function from B(G, H).

The main idea associated with the above preliminary definitions is portrayed geometrically in Fig. 2.

In Fig. 2, $\mathscr{R}(f)$ is the notation for the *range of f*. The fact that f is merely

into H means that there may exist y in H such that there is no $\overset{\circ}{x}$ in G with

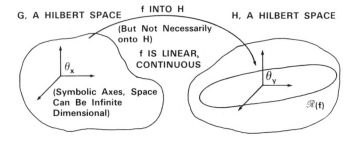

Fig. 2. Function f maps the domain space G into the range space H.

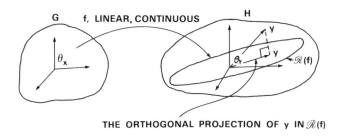

Fig. 3. Projecting y into $\mathscr{R}(f)$ by the Hilbert space projection theorem.

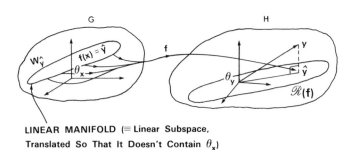

Fig. 4. Obtaining the manifold of x values such that $f(x) = \hat{y}$.

$$f(\overset{o}{x}) = \overset{o}{y}.$$

(63)

If f were *onto* H, then for every y in H, there would exist an $\overset{o}{x}$ in G such that (63)

holds. If, in addition, f were *one-to-one* (notation: 1–1) then, for every $\overset{o}{y}$ in H there would exist only *one* x in G, such that (63) holds (i.e., two or more points in G could not map into the same y value in H). If f were 1–1 *and* onto, then an ordinary inverse function would exist and there would be no need to consider a pseudoinverse since it would reduce to this *unique* ordinary inverse. The situations of interest for potential use of the pseudoinverse occur when f is *not* 1–1 and onto. (For finite-dimensional matrices, these cases of interest correspond to either the situation of a square matrix being singular or the situation of having a nonsquare matrix where the finite-dimensional Euclidean domain space has a dimension different from that of the Euclidean range space.)

The range of f, $\mathscr{R}(f)$ is a *linear subspace* (in analogy to a plane through the origin in Euclidean 3-space, E^3). If G or H is finite dimensional (or if it can be otherwise shown), then $\mathscr{R}(f)$ is *closed* [125]. Consequently, $\mathscr{R}(f)$ is a *closed linear subspace*. This is just what is needed in the hypothesis to apply the Hilbert space projection theorem [126, p. 76, Theorem 4.11] in specifying what rigorously constitutes a pseudoinverse of the transformation f.

A.   CONSTRUCTION OF THE GENERAL PSEUDOINVERSE

Given a particular arbitrary y in H (notation: $y \in H$), consider all the x_1 in G (notation: $x_1 \in G$) such that

$$\|f(x_1) - y\| = \min_{x \in G} \|f(x) - y\|.$$

(64)

The norm $\|\cdot\|$ here is defined naturally in terms of the existing inner product associated with the Hilbert space as $\|\cdot\| = \sqrt{(\cdot \mid \cdot)}$.

Approximation of y in H. As seen in Fig. 3,

$$\min_{x \in G} \|f(x) - y\|$$

exists since, by the Hilbert space projection theorem, any arbitrary y in H may be approximated in the closed linear subspace $\mathscr{R}(f)$ by its orthogonal projection, $\hat{y}$. Since $\mathscr{R}(f)$ is the range space of f, there exists an x_1 in G [not necessarily unique, as shown in Fig. 4 (since there may be more than one x_1 value in G)], such that

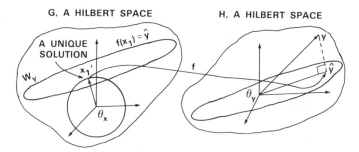

Fig. 5. x_0' is the unique point of $W_{\hat{y}}$ which has minimum norm.

$$f(x_1) = \hat{y} \tag{65}$$

[this occurs since f is onto $\mathscr{R}(f)$].
      Therefore, the following equalities hold:

$$\|f(x_1) - y\| = \min_{x \in G} \|f(x) - y\| = \min_{p \in \mathscr{R}(f)} \|p - y\| = \|\hat{y} - y\|. \tag{66}$$

The following device is used to obtain a unique x_1 that satisfies (65).
      Uniqueness by Minimizing Norm in G. Represent the linear *manifold* of Fig. 4 by

$$W_{\hat{y}} = \{x_1 \text{ such that } f(x_1) = \hat{y}\}. \tag{67}$$

That (67) describes a linear manifold (also known as a linear *variety* or linear *flat*) can be demonstrated by showing that $W_{\hat{y}}$ satisfies the requirements to be classified as a linear manifold as presented in Ref. [12, Chapter 3]. Now

$$W_{\theta_y} = \{x_1 \text{ such that } f(x_1) = \theta_y\} \overset{\Delta}{=} \text{null space of } f = \eta(f) \tag{68}$$

so $W_{\hat{y}}$ is just a translation of the null space of (68). While $W_{\hat{y}}$ is not a subspace, since it does not contain θ_x, it is a complete convex subset of Hilbert space; hence, by Ref. [126, p. 78, Theorem 4.10], there is a unique point x_1' which is closest to the origin (the null element) θ_x of G. Figure 5 amply portrarys this situation.

The point of tangency of the smallest ball, centered at the origin of θ_x which intereseets $W_{\hat{y}}$, is x_1'. The point x_1', defined in this way, is now unique. The above-described mechanism of *associating a unique x_1' with an arbitrary fixed y such that x_1' satisfies (66)* defines a function from H *into* G which is the pseudoinverse, $f^\dagger$. A nice analytic proof of the minimum norm property of the pseudoinverse is in Ref. [124, pp. 89–90, Theorem 3.7].

By an alternative approach, since $\mathscr{R}$ (f) is a closed linear subspace in a Hilbert space H, and $\eta(f)$ is a closed linear subspace in a Hilbert space G, invocation of the Hilbert space decomposition theorem [126, p. 79, Theorem 4.11] yields that

$$G = \eta(f) \oplus [\eta(f)]^\perp \tag{69}$$

$$H = \mathscr{R}(f) \oplus [\mathscr{R}(f)]^\perp \tag{70}$$

where (69) and (70) have the following interpretation: for arbitrary fixed x in G, there exists a *unique* $\bar{x}$ and $\tilde{x}$ with

$$\bar{x} \text{ in } \eta(f) \tag{71}$$

$$\tilde{x} \text{ in } [\eta(f)]^\perp \tag{72}$$

{i.e., each element of $[n(f)]^\perp$ results in zero when an inner product is formed with it and every element of $\eta(f)$}, such that

$$x = \bar{x} + \tilde{x} \tag{73}$$

(i.e., this is an *orthogonal decomposition*, with one element in the linear subspace and the other element orthogonal to it!). Similarly, for arbitrary fixed y in H, there exists a *unique* $\hat{y}$ and $\tilde{y}$ with

$$\hat{y} \text{ in } R(f) \tag{74}$$

and

$$\tilde{y} \text{ in } [R(f)]^\perp \tag{75}$$

i.e., each element of $[R(f)]^\perp$ results in zero when an inner product is formed with it and every element of R(f), such that

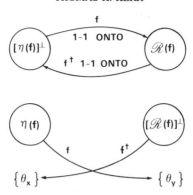

Fig. 6. The pseudoinverse as an extension of the ordinary inverse function associated with an original function that is 1–1 and onto [12, p. 164; 113, p. 578, Fig. C.17.1].

$$y = \hat{y} + \tilde{y} \tag{76}$$

As discussed in Ref. [12, Chapter 3], the continuous function, when restricted to have only domain $[\eta(f)]^{\perp}$, can be regarded as a function from the Hilbert space $[\eta(f)]^{\perp}$ onto the Hilbert space $\mathscr{R}(f)$. This closed linear subset of a Hilbert space is itself again a Hilbert space [125].

Between $[\eta(f)]^{\perp}$ and $\mathscr{R}(f)$, f is *one-to-one* and *onto*, and it has an inverse that is continuous and linear. The inverse of f defines $f^{\dagger}$ on $\mathscr{R}(f)$. Its domain is extended to all of H by defining the function's extension as

$$f^{\dagger}(y) = \theta_x \text{ for all } y \text{ in } [R(f)]^{\perp}. \tag{77}$$

This alternate but equivalent interpretation of the pseudoinverse afforded by (69)–(77) is summarized in Fig. 6.

B.   PROPERTIES OF THE GENERAL PSEUDOINVERSE

For a continuous linear function f, having its range R(f) closed and pseudoinverse being $f^{\dagger}$, then [12, p. 165]:

(a) $f^{\dagger}$ is linear;

(b) $f^{\dagger}$ is continuous;

(c) $(f^{\dagger})^{\dagger} = f$;

(d) $(f*)^{\dagger} = (f^{\dagger})*$;

(e) $f^\dagger \circ f \circ f^\dagger = f^\dagger$;

(f) $f \circ f^\dagger \circ f = f$;

(g) $(f^\dagger \circ f)^* = f^\dagger \circ f$;

(h) $f^\dagger = (f^* \circ f)^\dagger \circ f^*$;

(i) $f^\dagger = f^* \circ (f \circ f^*)^\dagger$;   (78)

where, in the above, $f \circ g \overset{\Delta}{=} f[g(\cdot)]$ is the composite function, and $*$ is the adjoint operator, and represents the adjoint of f, which is defined using the following definitions of *inner product* on the domain $(\cdot \mid \cdot)_G$ and on the range $(\cdot \mid \cdot)_H$. The adjoint operator f^* is defined so that $(x \mid f^*(y))_G = (f(x) \mid y)_H$ for each fixed y in H and all x in G. Therefore, f^* is unique, linear, continuous, and identical in norm to f as $\|f\| = \|f^*\|$.

In *certain limiting cases* it is possible to give a *simple explicit formula for $f^\dagger$* as follows: If $f \circ f^*$ is invertible, then

$$f^\dagger = [f^* \circ f]^{-1} \circ f^*.$$ (79)

If $f \circ f^*$ is invertible, then

$$f^\dagger = f^* \circ [f \circ f^*]^{-1}.$$ (80)

In general, however, a simple explicit closed-form formula for $f^\dagger$ does not exist [12, Chapter 3].

C.   MANIPULATING IDENTITIES

As an example of how the identities of Section VII,B can be manipulated to analytically establish certain desired relationships, consider the following exercise of seeking to establish that

$$(I + f)^{-1} \overset{?}{=} (I - f^\dagger \circ f) + (I + f^\dagger)^{-1} \circ f^\dagger,$$ (81)

where I is the identity transformation.

To establish the above identity as the goal, proceed by performing a sequence of completely reversible operations that eventually reduce to an identity that is obvious; then by retracing the steps in reverse order, the desired identity is obtained. To this end, first perform a composite "postmultiplication" by $(I + f)$ to yield

$$I = (I - f^\dagger \circ f) \circ (I + f) + (I + f^\dagger)^{-1} \circ f^\dagger \circ (I + f) \tag{82a}$$

$$= I - f^\dagger \circ f + [f - f^\dagger \circ f \circ f] + (I + f^\dagger)^{-1} \circ f^\dagger + (I + f^\dagger)^{-1} \circ f^\dagger \circ f \tag{82b}$$

$$= I - f^\dagger \circ f + [f - f \circ f^\dagger \circ f] + (I + f^\dagger)^{-1} \circ f^\dagger + (I + f^\dagger)^{-1} \circ f \circ f^\dagger \tag{82c}$$

$$= I + (I + f^\dagger)^{-1} \circ [-(I + f^\dagger) \circ f \circ f^\dagger + f^\dagger + f \circ f^\dagger] \tag{82d}$$

$$= I + (I + f^\dagger)^{-1} \circ [-f \circ f^\dagger + [-f^\dagger \circ f \circ f^\dagger + f^\dagger] + f \circ f^\dagger] \tag{82e}$$

$$= I + (I + f^\dagger)^{-1} \circ [-f \circ f^\dagger + f \circ f^\dagger] \tag{82f}$$

$$= I, \tag{82g}$$

where in going from (82a) to (82b) the indicated expansions were performed. In going from (82b) to (82c), the expressions within brackets in both are equivalent. In going from (82c) to (82d), the expression within brackets is zero via the identity of (78f). In going from (82d) to (82e), the expression $(I + f^\dagger)$ within the brackets is expanded out with its composite "postmultipliers." In going from (82e) to (82f), the expression within the brackets is zero via the identity of (78e). In going from (82f) to (82g), the expression within the brackets is the zero transformation which, when composed with $(I + f^\dagger)$, is also zero. Thus, retracing steps in reverse order, and finally using a composite function "postmultiplication" by $(I + f)^{-1}$, yields the desired identity of (81). Thus, this exercise demonstrates standard manipulations that can be performed with pseudoinverse transformations in accordance with the established "rules" or identities of (78). The exercise of Eq. (82), as used to verify Eq. (81), was actually solicited from the author within an application by James Taylor in seeking a more general result as an extension of those in [145], as evident from his acknowledgment of me.

VIII. APPENDIX B: LONGHAND CALCULATION OF A MATRIX PSEUDOINVERSE

A. MATRIX PSEUDOINVERSE AS A SPECIAL CASE OF THE GENERAL PSEUDOINVERSE OF PENROSE

Please consider the diagram of Fig. 5 with the Hilbert domain space $G \equiv E^n$ and the range space $H \equiv E^m$, where E represents Euclidean space (i.e., E^1 is the real line). All linear continuous functions f from E^n to E^m can be represented as

$$y^{(m \times 1)} = f(\underline{x}) = C^{(m \times n)} \underline{x}^{(n \times 1)} \tag{83}$$

where C is an $(m \times n)$ matrix.

For matrices, properties of (78d)–(78g) completely specify a unique $C^\dagger$ and are sometimes used as the definition of $C^\dagger$. Alternatively,

$$C^\dagger C \underline{y} = \underline{y} \text{ for all } \underline{y} \text{ in } \mathscr{R}(C^T) \tag{84}$$

$$C^\dagger \underline{z} = 0 \text{ for all } \underline{z} \text{ in } \eta(C^T) \tag{85}$$

$$C^\dagger(\underline{y} + \underline{z}) = C^\dagger \underline{y} + C^\dagger \underline{z} \text{ for all } \underline{y} \text{ in } \mathscr{R}(C) \text{ and all } \underline{z} \text{ in } \eta(C^T) \tag{86}$$

and (84)–(86) may be used as definitions of $C^\dagger$, where in the above the adjoint of C is merely the matrix transpose.

By Ref. [51, Theorem 4.22], if any solution to

$$C\underline{x} = \underline{y} \tag{87}$$

exists, it can be expressed as

$$\underline{x} = C^\dagger \underline{y} + (I - C^\dagger C)\underline{z}, \tag{88}$$

where $\underline{z}$ is any arbitrary conformable vector.

{As an aside, the expression within parentheses in the second term in (88) is idempotent in that it is its own square [123, p. 41]. Hence, the pseudoinverse can be routinely used to create examples of idempotent matrices.}

B. EXPLICIT PROCEDURE FOR CALCULATING THE PSEUDOINVERSE

The following procedure is from Ref. [51].
Situation 1. Given a diagonal matrix

$$\Lambda = \text{diag}(\lambda_1, \lambda_2, ..., \lambda_n) \tag{89}$$

where some λ_i may be zero, then the corresponding pseudoinverse is

$$\Lambda^\dagger \triangleq \text{diag}(\lambda_1^{-1}, \lambda_2^{-1}, ..., \lambda_n^{-1}), \tag{90}$$

where

$$\lambda_i^{-1} = \begin{cases} \dfrac{1}{\lambda_i}, & \text{if } \lambda_i \neq 0 \\ 0, & \text{if } \lambda_i = 0 \end{cases} \tag{91}$$

[cf. (22), (23)].

Situation 2. Given a Hermitian matrix, i.e.,

$$H = \overline{H}^T, \tag{92}$$

where the vinculum represents the complex conjugate, let

$$H = U\Lambda\overline{U}^T, \tag{93}$$

where U is a unitary matrix

$$\overline{U}^T = U^{-1}. \tag{94}$$

(U is simply the normalized eigenvector matrix associated with H, and the eigenvectors of an Hermitian matrix are always distinct and H can always be diagonalized [127, Sections 7.12 and 7.13].) The corresponding pseudoinverse is

$$H^\dagger = U\Lambda^\dagger \overline{U}^T, \tag{95}$$

where $\Lambda^\dagger$ can be found from the procedure of Situation 1 above. Naturally,

$$\overline{U}^T = U^T \tag{96}$$

for H and U real.

Situation 3. Given an arbitrary m × n matrix C, let

$$H \triangleq C^T C; \tag{97}$$

then

$$C^\dagger \triangleq H^\dagger C^T, \tag{98}$$

where $H^\dagger$ can be computed by the procedure of Situations 1 and 2 above.

The above procedure can be put in perspective by considering the following direct quote from Ref. [19, p. 136]: "Several proposals for computing $C^\dagger$ have been made in the literature. These algorithms are often very inefficient from the point of view of numerical computation (although they may be useful for getting exact answers in simple cases)." For instance, in establishing the existence of the Penrose inverse for a symmetric matrix Λ, we used the existence of a diagonalizing transformation, but this involved finding all the eigenvalues of C, which is a more difficult mathematical problem than the computation of $\Lambda^\dagger$. Moreover, other algorithms proposed thus far do not simplify when the actual inverse C exists, since then it should be that

$$C^\dagger = C^{-1}. \tag{99}$$

C.   A NUMERICAL EXAMPLE OF PSEUDOINVERSE CALCULATION

The following direct quote from Ref. [19, p. 145] shows what order of difficulty to anticipate by way of computational burden incurred in this calculation: "The exact computation of the generalized inverse involves a very large amount of work." This may be an understatement. In seeking to find the pseudoinverse of the matrix C_1 in (11) of Section II,D, first form

$$H \triangleq C_1^* C_1 = C_1^T C_1 \tag{100}$$

as

$$H = \begin{bmatrix} 1 & 1 & 1 \\ 2 & 1 & 1 \\ 1 & 0 & 0 \end{bmatrix} \begin{bmatrix} 1 & 2 & 1 \\ 1 & 1 & 0 \\ 1 & 1 & 0 \end{bmatrix} = \begin{bmatrix} 3 & 4 & 1 \\ 4 & 6 & 2 \\ 1 & 2 & 1 \end{bmatrix}. \tag{101}$$

As observed in Section II,D, both $C_1^T C_1$ and $C_1 C_1^T$ are singular; so there can be no recourse to the simple expressions of (9) or (10) [cf. (80) and (79), respectively, for specifying the pseudoinverse]. The pseudoinverse must instead be determined from the general expression of (98); therefore, as an intermediate step $H^\dagger$ must be determined via the procedure of Situation 2 of Section VIII,B.

Finding the Eigenvalues of H.

$$0 = \det[H - \lambda I_3] = \det \begin{bmatrix} 3 - \lambda & 4 & 1 \\ 4 & 6 - \lambda & 2 \\ 1 & 2 & 1 - \lambda \end{bmatrix}$$

$$= \lambda(-6 + 10\lambda - \lambda^2). \tag{102}$$

Therefore, the eigenvalues of H correspond to the solutions of

$$\lambda = 0 \tag{103}$$
$$\lambda^2 - 10\lambda + 6 = 0, \tag{104}$$

where further use of the quadratic formula for (104) yields the following three eigenvalues of H:

$$\lambda = 0, 5 \pm \sqrt{19}. \tag{105}$$

The corresponding eigenvectors are now calculated. For $\lambda = 0$:

$$H - (0)I_3 = \begin{bmatrix} 3 & 4 & 1 \\ 4 & 6 & 2 \\ 1 & 2 & 1 \end{bmatrix}. \tag{106}$$

It may be verified that an unnormalized eigenvector of H may be obtained by finding the cofactors associated with the first row of (106) as

$$\underline{e}_1^T = [2, -2, 2]^T. \tag{107}$$

Normalizing (107) so that

$$e_{1j}^2 + e_{2j}^2 + e_{3j}^2 = 1, \text{ for } j = 1 \tag{108}$$

yields:

$$\hat{\underline{e}}_1^T = \left[\frac{1}{\sqrt{3}}, \frac{-1}{\sqrt{3}}, \frac{1}{\sqrt{3}}\right]^T. \tag{109}$$

For $\lambda = 5 + \sqrt{19}$:

$$H - (5 + \sqrt{19})I_3 = \begin{bmatrix} -2 - \sqrt{19} & 4 & 1 \\ 4 & 1 - \sqrt{19} & 2 \\ 1 & 2 & -4 - \sqrt{19} \end{bmatrix}. \tag{110}$$

Similarly, an unnormalized eigenvector may be obtained by finding the cofactors associated with the first row of (110) as

$$\underline{e}_2^T = \left[11 + 3\sqrt{19}, \, 18 + 4\sqrt{19}, \, 7 + \sqrt{19}\right]^T. \tag{111}$$

Normalizing (111) so that (108) holds with $j = 2$ yields

$$\hat{\underline{e}}_2^T = \left[\frac{11 + 3\sqrt{19}}{\left(988 + 224\sqrt{19}\right)^{1/2}}, \, \frac{18 + 4\sqrt{19}}{\left(988 + 224\sqrt{19}\right)^{1/2}}, \, \frac{7 + \sqrt{19}}{\left(988 + 244\sqrt{19}\right)^{1/2}}\right]. \tag{112}$$

Similarly, for $\lambda = 5 - \sqrt{19}$:

$$H - (5 - \sqrt{19})I_3 = \begin{bmatrix} -2 - \sqrt{19} & 4 & 1 \\ 4 & 1 + \sqrt{19} & 2 \\ 1 & 2 & -4 + \sqrt{19} \end{bmatrix}. \tag{113}$$

An unnormalized eigenvector may be obtained by finding the cofactors associated with the first row of (110) as

$$\underline{e}_3^T = \left[11 - 3\sqrt{19}, \, 18 - 4\sqrt{19}, \, 7 - \sqrt{19}\right]^T. \tag{114}$$

Similarly, normalizing (114) so that (108) holds with $j = 3$, yields

$$\hat{\underline{e}}_3^T = \left[\frac{11 - 3\sqrt{19}}{\left(988 - 244\sqrt{19}\right)^{1/2}}, \frac{18 - 4\sqrt{19}}{\left(988 - 224\sqrt{19}\right)^{1/2}}, \frac{7 - \sqrt{19}}{\left(988 - 244\sqrt{19}\right)^{1/2}} \right]. \qquad (115)$$

A check on these calculations occurs in noting that: $\hat{\underline{e}}_1, \hat{\underline{e}}_2, \hat{\underline{e}}_3$ are mutually orthogonal, as theoretically predicted and, consequently, for the normalized eigenvector matrix

$$U \triangleq \left[\hat{\underline{e}}_1 \mid \hat{\underline{e}}_2 \mid \hat{\underline{e}}_3 \right] \qquad (116)$$

it checks that

$$UU^T = I_{(3 \times 3)}. \qquad (117)$$

Now the normalized eigenvector matrix U so obtained diagonalizes the symmetric matrix H as

$$U^T H U = \text{diag}\left\{ 0, \; 5 + \sqrt{19}, \; 5 - \sqrt{19} \right\}. \qquad (118)$$

As discussed in Situation 1 of Section VIII,B, the pseudoinverse of the diagonal matrix is:

$$\Lambda^\dagger \triangleq \text{diag}\left\{ 0, \; 1/(5 + \sqrt{19}), \; 1/(5 - \sqrt{19}) \right\} \qquad (119)$$

$$= \text{diag}\left\{ 0, \; 0.1069, \; 1.560 \right\}. \qquad (120)$$

By (95) of Situation 2 of Section VIII,B, the pseudoinverse of the symmetrix matrix is:

$$H^\dagger \triangleq \begin{bmatrix} 0.5774 & 0.5432 & -0.6096 \\ -0.5774 & 0.7995 & 0.1657 \\ 0.5774 & 0.2563 & 0.7752 \end{bmatrix} \begin{bmatrix} 0 & 0 & 0 \\ 0 & 0.1069 & 0 \\ 0 & 0 & 1.560 \end{bmatrix} U^T$$

$$= \begin{bmatrix} 0 & 0.0580 & -0.9508 \\ 0 & 0.0854 & 0.2584 \\ 0 & 0.0274 & 1.209 \end{bmatrix} \begin{bmatrix} 0.5774 & -0.5774 & 0.5774 \\ 0.5432 & 0.7995 & 0.2563 \\ -0.6096 & 0.1657 & 0.7752 \end{bmatrix}$$

$$= \begin{bmatrix} 0.61\overline{1} & -0.11\overline{1} & -0.72\overline{2} \\ -0.11\overline{1} & 0.11\overline{1} & 0.22\overline{2} \\ -0.72\overline{2} & 0.22\overline{2} & 0.94\overline{4} \end{bmatrix} \tag{121}$$

By (96) of Situation 3 of Section VIII,B, the pseudoinverse is:

$$C^{\dagger} \triangleq \begin{bmatrix} 0.61\overline{1} & -0.11\overline{1} & -0.72\overline{2} \\ -0.11\overline{1} & 0.11\overline{1} & 0.22\overline{2} \\ -0.72\overline{2} & 0.22\overline{2} & 0.94\overline{4} \end{bmatrix} \begin{bmatrix} 1 & 1 & 1 \\ 2 & 1 & 1 \\ 1 & 0 & 0 \end{bmatrix} \tag{122}$$

$$= \begin{bmatrix} -0.33\overline{3} & 0.5 & 0.5 \\ 0.33\overline{3} & 0.0 & 0.0 \\ 0.66\overline{6} & -0.5 & -0.5 \end{bmatrix} = \begin{bmatrix} \dfrac{-1}{3} & \dfrac{1}{2} & \dfrac{1}{2} \\ \dfrac{1}{3} & 0 & 0 \\ \dfrac{2}{3} & \dfrac{-1}{3} & \dfrac{-1}{2} \end{bmatrix},$$

which corresponds to (12) in Section II,D.

IX. APPENDIX C: AN APPLICATION OF THE PSEUDOINVERSE IN MINIMUM ENERGY OPTIMAL CONTROL

Given a linear dynamic system described by a set of differential equations of the form

$$\dot{\underline{x}}(t) = F\underline{x}(t) + \underline{b}u(t), \tag{123}$$

where $\underline{x}$ is an n vector, F is an $n \times n$ matrix, $\underline{b}$ is an n vector, and u is a scalar control function. Assume that initial condition $x(0) = \theta_y$ (the null element of the range space) and that the goal is to transfer the system to the final state $\underline{x}(T) = \underline{x}_1$ by application of suitable control u(t). Of the class of controls which accomplish the desired state transfer, our objective is to determine the one that minimizes the energy:

$$\int_0^T u^2(t) \, dt. \tag{124}$$

The explicit solution to the differential equation of state (123) is

$$x(T) = \int_0^T e^{F(T - t)} \underline{b} u(t) \, dt.$$

Thus, defining the function f mapping $L_2[0, T]$ into Euclidean n space E^n by

$$f(u) = \int_0^T e^{F(T - t)} \underline{b} u(t) \, dt \tag{125}$$

yields the following associations in terms of the notation of Appendix A:

$$G = L^2[0, T]; \quad H = E^n,$$

and the corresponding appropriate inner products are

$$(x_1 \mid x_2)_G = (x_1 \mid x_2)_{L^2} \overset{\Delta}{=} \int_0^T x_1(t) \cdot x_2(t) \, dt \tag{126}$$

and

$$(y_1 \mid y_2)_H = (\underline{y}_1 \mid \underline{y}_2)_{E^n} \overset{\Delta}{=} \underline{y}_1^T \cdot \underline{y}_2, \tag{127}$$

and the corresponding norm for the control (in terms of the specified inner product) is

$$\|u\|_{L^2} \overset{\Delta}{=} \sqrt{(u \mid u_2)_L} = \left(\int_0^T u^2(t) \, dt \right)^{1/2}. \tag{128}$$

The problem of minimizing (124) is equivalent to that of determining the *u of minimum norm* in (128) satisfying

$$f(u) = \underline{x}'_1. \tag{129}$$

Since the range of f, $\mathscr{R}$ (f), is finite dimensional, it is therefore closed. Thus, the results of the following theorem apply.

Theorem 1 [12, p. 161]. Let G and H be Hilbert spaces and let arbitrary $f \in B(G, H)$ with range closed in H. The vector x of minimum norm satisfying

$$f(x) = \underline{y} \tag{130}$$

is given by

$$x = f^*(z), \tag{131}$$

where z is any solution of the composite function

$$f \circ f^*(\underline{z}) = \underline{y}. \tag{132}$$

By virtue of the above Theorem 1, the optimal solution of (129) is

$$u = f^*(\underline{z}), \tag{133}$$

where

$$f \circ f^*(z) = \underline{x}'_1. \tag{134}$$

It remains to compute the above functions f* and f ∘ f* for this specific application. For any $u \in L_2, \underline{y} \in E^n$

$$(\underline{y} \ll f(u))_{E^n} = \underline{y}^T \int_0^T e^{F(T - t)} \underline{b} u(t) \, dt = \int_0^T \left[\underline{y}^T e^{F(T - t)} \underline{b} \right] u(t) \, dt$$

$$= (f^*(y) \mid u)_{L^2}; \tag{135}$$

hence, by the property of adjoint transformations

$$f^*(y) \underline{b}^T e^{F^T(T-t)} \underline{y}. \tag{136}$$

It turns out that f o f* is the following n × n matrix

$$f \circ f^* = \int_0^T e^{F(T-t)} \underline{bb}^T e^{F^T(T-t)} \, dt. \tag{137}$$

If the matrix [f o f* is invertible [i.e., if (F, b) is a controllable pair], then the optimal control u(t) can be found directly to be of the form

$$u(t) = f^* \circ [f \circ f^*]^{-1} \underline{x}_1', \tag{138}$$

or, more explicitly, as

$$u(t) = \underline{b}^T e^{F^T(T-t)} \left(\int_0^T e^{F(T-s)} \underline{bb}^T e^{F^T(T-s)} \, ds \right)^{-1} \underline{x}_1'. \tag{139}$$

Another unrelated pseudoinverse application in control and estimation theory relates to computationally determining a basis for the null space of an arbitrary matrix [109].

ACKNOWLEDGMENTS

The author wishes to thank Joseph D'Appolito for comments pertaining to implementation of MVRO, which motivated this further investigation into MVRO algorithms.

This investigation was partially funded by NADC contracts Nos. N62269-79-D-0301 and N62269-81-C-0086 as items encountered in conjunction with performing contractual tasks at Intermetrics, Inc., the author's previous affiliation. Publication of this article does not constitute approval by the U.S. Navy of the findings or conclusions contained herein. It is disseminated only for the exchange and stimulation of ideas. This article is an outgrowth of an earlier paper [112] that appeared in IEEE Transactions on Aerospace and Electronic Systems.

REFERENCES

1.   T. H. KERR, An invalid norm appearing in control and estimation. *IEEE Trans. Autom. Control*, Vol. AC-23, pp. 73, 74 (1978).
2.   T. H. KERR, Correction to 'An invalid norm appearing in control and estimation.' *IEEE Trans. Autom. Control (Tech. Notes Corresp.)*, Vol. AC-23, pp. 1117, 1118 (1978).

3. C.-H. J. HSU, Comments on 'An invalid norm appearing in control and estimation.' *IEEE Trans. Autom. Control (Tech. Notes Corresp.)* **AC-25**(5), 1012 (1980).

4. T. H. KERR, Three important matrix inequalities currently impacting control and estimation applications. *IEEE Trans. Autom. Control*, Vol. AC-23, pp. 1110, 1111 (1978).

5. T. H. KERR, Rectifying several pervasive errors appearing in estimation and control theory. (internal memo available from author upon request).

6. A. S. WILLSKY and H. L. JONES, "A Generalized Likelihood Ratio Approach to State Estimation in Linear Systems Subject to Abrupt Changes," Rep. No. ESL-P-538. Electron. Syst. Lab., Massachusetts Institute of Technology, Cambridge, 1974.

7. A. S. WILLSKY and H. L. JONES, A generalized likelihood ratio approach to state estimation in linear systems subject to abrupt changes. *Proc. Conf. Decision Control*, pp. 846–853 Phoenix, AZ (1974).

8. A. S. WILLSKY and H. L. JONES, A generalized likelihood ratoi approach to detection and estimation of jumps in linear systems. *IEEE Trans. Autom. Control* AC-21(1), 108–112 (1976).

9. A. BEN-ISRAEL and T. N. E. GREVILLE, "Generalized Inverses: Theory and Applications." Wiley, New York, 1974.

10. C. R. RAO and S. K. MITR , "Generalized Inverses of Matrices and Its Applications." Wiley, New York, 1971.

11. A. GELB, ed., "Applied Optimal Estimation." MIT Press, Cambridge, Massachusetts, 1974.

12. D. G. LUENBERGER, "Optimization by Vector Space Methods." Wiley, New York, 1969.

13. E. K. BLUM, "Numerical Analysis and Computation Theory and Practice." Addison-Wesley, Reading, Massachusetts, 1972.

14. V. C. KLEMA and A. J. LAUB, The singular value decomposition: It's computation and some applications. *IEEE Trans. Autom. Control* AC-25(2), 164–176 (1980).

15. B. S. GARBOW J. M. BOYLE, J. J. DONGARRA, and C. B. MOLER, Matrix eigensystem routines EISPACK guide extension. *Lect. Notes Comput. Sci.* **51** (1977).

16. C. E. HUTCHINSON, J. A. D'APOLITO, and K. J. ROY, Applications of minimum variance reduced-state estimators. *IEEE Trans. Aerosp. Electron. Syst.* AES-11(5), pp. 785–794 (1975).

17. E. M. DUIVEN, Suboptimal linear filtering. *J. Spacecr. Rockets* **11**(3), 196–198 (1974).

18. P. S. MAYBECK, "Stochastic Models, Estimation, and Control," Vol. 1. Academic Press, New York, 1979.

19. R. E. KALMAN and T. S. ENGLAR, A user's manual for the automatic synthesis program (Program C). *NASA [Contract. Rep.]*, CR NASA **CR-475** (1966).

20. G. J. BIERMAN, Power series evaluation of transition and covariance matrices. *IEEE Trans. Autom. Control* AC-17(2), 228–232 (1972).

21. P. R. BELANGER and T. P. McGILLIVRAY, Computational experience with the solution of the matrix Lyapunov equations. *IEEE Trans. Autom. Control (Tech. Notes Corresp.)* AC-21(5), 799–800 (1976).

22. E. FOGEL, A comment on the use of spectral radius of a matrix. *IEEE Trans. Autom. Control* AC-26(3), 798–799 (1981).

23. T. H. KERR, A conservative view on the GLR failure and event detection approach, March, 1982 (internal memo available from author on request).

24. C. W. SANDERS, E. C. TACKER, T. D. LINTON, and R.Y.-S. LING, Specific structures for large-scale state estimation algorithms having information exchange. *IEEE Trans. Autom. Control* AC-23(2), pp. 255–261 (1978).

25. T. H. KERR and L. CHIN, The theory and techniques of discrete-time decentralized filters. *In* "Advances in the Theory and Technology of Nonlinear Filters and Kalman Filters" (C. T. Leondes, ed.). NATO Advis. Group Aerosp. Res. Dev., AGARDograph Noordhoff International Publishing, Leiden, 1981.

26. J. J. DONGARRA C. B. MOLER, J. R. BUNCH, and G. W. STEWART, "LINPACK User's Guide." SIAM, Philadelphia, Pennsylvania, 1979.

27. A. K. CLINE, C. B. MOLER, G. W. STEWART, and J. H. WILKINSON, An estimate for the condition number of a matrix. *SIAM J. Numer. Anal.* **16**(2), 368–375 (1979).

28. S. MAXUMDAR, C. C. LI, and G. R. BRYCE, Correspondence between a linear restriction and a generalized inverse in linear model analysis.. *Am. Stat.* **34**(2), 103–105 (1980).

29. S. L. CAMPBELL and C. D. MEYER, "Generalized Inverse of Linear Transformations." Pitman, San Francisco, California, 1979.

30. E. D. SONTAG, On generalized inverses of polynmomial and other matrices. *IEEE Trans. Autom. Control* **AC-25**(3), 514–517 (1980).

31. R. B. ASHER, K. D. HERRING, and J. C. RYLES, Bias, variance, and estimation error in reduced-order filters. *Automatica* **12**, 589–600 (1976).

32. C. W. SANDERS, E. C. TACKER, and T. D. LINTON, "Decentralized Estimation Via Constrained Filters," Tech. Rep. ECE-73-1. University of Wisconsin, Madison, 1973.

33. C. B. MOLER, Three research problems in numerical linear algebra. *Numer. Anal. Proc. Symp. Appl. Math.* **22** (1978).

34. T. H. KERR, Modeling and evaluating and empirical INS difference monitoring procedure used to sequence SSBN navaid fixes. *Navigation, J. Inst. Navig.* **28**(4), pp. 263–285 (1981).

35. C. E. HUTCHINSON and J. A. D'APPOLITO, Minimum variance reduced state filters. *Proc. Conf. Decision Control, 1972*, pp. 670–671 (1973).

36. J. A. D'APPOLITO and K. J. ROY, Reduced order filtering with applications in hybrid navigation. *Proc. Electron. Aerosp. Syst. Conv. (EASCON), 1973*, pp. 1–7 (1973).

37. M. ATHANS and F. C. SCHWEPPE, "Gradient Matrices and Matrix Calculations," TN 1965-63. Lincoln Lab., Massachusetts Institute of Technology, Lexington, 1965.

38. G. W. STEWART, On the perturbation of pseudo-inverses, projections, and least squares problems. *SIAM Rev.* **19**, 634–662 (1977).

39. R. K. MEHRA, Digital simulation of multidimensional Gauss–Markov random processes. *IEEE Trans. Autom. Control* **AC-14**(2), 112–113 (1969).

40. T. H. KERR, Real-time failure detection: A static nonlinear optimization problem that yields a two-ellipsoid overlap test. *J. Optim. Theory Appl.* **22**, pp. 509–536 (1977).

41. T. H. KERR, Statistical analysis of a two-ellipsoid overlap test for real-time failure detection. *IEEE Trans. Autom. Control* **AC-25**(4), 762–772 (1980).

42. T. H. KERR, False alarm and correct detection probabilities over a time interval for restricted classes of failure detection algorithms. *IEEE Trans. Inf. Theory* **IT-28**(4), pp. 619–631 (1982).

43. P. SINHA, "Covariance Analysis Program: User's Guide," GPS IV&V Memo No. 21-80. Intermetrics, 1980 (program under configuration control No. B13704A-00.00A).

44. J. VAGNERS and J.. WITTE, Design of numerically stable flight filters from minimum variance reduced-order estimators. *Proc. Nat. Aerosp. Electron. Conf. (NAECON), 1979* (1979).

45. G. J. BIERMAN, "Factorization Methods for Discrete Sequential Estimation." Academic Press, New York, 1977.

46. T. H. KERR, Examining the controversy over the acceptability of SPRT and GLR techniques in some applications. *Proc. Am. Control Conf.* **3**, 966–977 (1983).

47. T. F. CHAN, Algorithm 581: An improved algorithm for computing the singular value decomposition F1. *ACM Trans. Math. Software* **5**(1), 84–88 (1982).

48. T. F. CHAN, An improved algorithm for computing the singular value decomposition. *ACM Trans. Math. Software* **8**(1), 72–83 (1982).

49. B. SHEFAI, R. L. CARROLL *et al.*, Comments on "On the application of matrix generalized inverses to the design of observers for time-varying and time-invariant linear systems." *IEEE Trans. Autom. Control* **AC-29**(12), 1125–1126 (1984).

50. D. G. LUENBERGER, An introduction to observers. *IEEE Trans. Autom. Control* AC-16(6), pp. 596–602 (1971).

51. D. M. WIBERG, "Schaum's Outline Series: State Space and Linear Systems." McGraw-Hill, New York, 1971.

52. D. E. CATLIN and R. L. GEDDES, State estimation and divergence analysis. *IEEE Trans. Aerosp. Electron.* AES-20(5), 594–602 (1984).

53. R. BYERS, A LINPACK-style condition estimator for the equation $AX - XB^T = C$. *IEEE Trans. Autom. Control* AC-29(10), 926–928 (1984).

54. C. E. HUTCHINSON, The Kalman filter applied to aerospace and electronic systems. *IEEE Trans. Aerosp. Electron. Syst.* AES-20(4), 500–504 (1984).

55. T. H. KERR, "Poseidon Improvement Studies: Real-Time Failure Detection in the SINS/ESGM," TASC Rep. TR-418-20, Reading, MA, 1974 (confidential).

56. T. H. KERR, "Failure Detection in the SINS/ESGM System," TASC Rep. TR-528-3-1, Reading, MA, 1975 (confidential).

57. T. H. KERR, "Improving ESGM Failure Detection in the SINS/ESGM System (U)," TASC Rep. TR-678-3-1, Reading, MA, 1976 (confidential).

58. T. H. KERR, Preliminary Quantitative Evaluation of Accuracy/Observables Trade-off in Selecting Loran/NAVSAT Fix Strategies," TASC Tech. Inf. Memo. TIM-889-3-1, Reading, MA, 1977 (confidential).

59. T. H. KERR, "Improving C-3 SSBN Navaid Utilization," TASC Tech. Inf. Memo. TIM-1390-3-1, Reading, MA, 1979 (secret).

60. T. H. KERR, "Stability Conditions for the RelNav Community as a De-Centralized Estimator – Final Report," Rep. No. IR-480, Intermetrics, Cambridge, MA, 1980.

61. J. E. SACKS, N. A. CARLSON, and T. H. KERR, "Integrated Navigation Concept Study," Rep. IR-MA-321, Intermetrics, 1984.

62. T. H. KERR, Decentralized filtering and redundancy management/failure detection for multisensor integrated navigation systems. *Proc. Inst. Navig. Nat. Tech. Meet., Avion. Sess., pp. 191–208, 1985* (1985).

63. P. S. MAYBECK, Reduced-order Kalman filter design and performance analysis. *In* "Advances in the Theory and Technology of Applications of Nonlinear Filters and Kalman Filters (C. T. Leondes, ed.). NATO Advis. Group Aerosp. Res. Deve., AGARDograph Noordhoff International Publishing, Leiden, Chapter 10, 1981.

64. C. T. LEONDES, ed., "Practical Aspects of Kalman Filtering Implementation, AGARD Lec. Ser. No. 82. NATO Advis. Group Aerosp. Res. Dev., AGARDograph Noordhoff International Publishing, Leiden, 1976.

65. S. F. SCHMIDT, The Kalman filter: Its recognition and development for aerospace applications. *J. Guidance Control* 4(1), 4–7 (1981).

66. G. W. GAWRYS and V. D. VANDELINDE, On the steady-state error of the fading memory filter. *IEEE Trans. Autom. Control* AC-21(4), 624–625 (1976).

67. K. L. HITZ, T. E. FORMANN, and B. D. O. ANDERSON, A note on bounds on solutions of Riccati equations. *IEEE Trans. Autom. Control* AC-20(1), 178 (1972).

68. G. J. BIERMAN, Commens on an analytic solution for an algebraic matrix Riccati equation. *IEEE Trans. Autom. Control* AC-20(2), 300–301 (1975).

69. H. E. EMARA-SHABAIK and C. T. LEONDES, A note on the extended Kalman filter. *Automatica* 17(2), 411–412 (1981).

70. T. P. McGARTY, "Stochastic Systems and State Estimation." Wiley (Interscience), New York, 1974.

71. I. C. F. IPSEN, "Singular Value Decomposition with Systolic Arrays," NASA Tech. Rep. NASA-CR-172396. Langley Research Center, Hampton, Virginia, 1984.

72. T. H. KERR, Failure detection aids for human operator decisions in a precision inertial navigation system complex. *Proc. Symp. Appl. Decision Theory Probl. Diagn. Repair.* Sponsored by the American Statistical Association, Fairborn, Ohio, 1976.

73. T. H. KERR and L. CHIN, A stable decentralized filtering implementation for JTIDS RelNav. *Proc. IEEE Positin, Location, Navig. Symp. (PLANS), pp. 318–329, 1980* (1981).

74. T. H. KERR, "Phase III GPS Integration," Vol. 1, Rep. No. IR-MA-177. Intermetrics, Cambridge, MA, 1983.

75.   T. H. KERR, "Navy GPS/SSN Phase II User Equipment DT&E: Magnavox Modification Center (Mod Center) Test Report," Rep. No. IR-MA-391 (NADC Rep. No. GPS-85-19432-032). Intermetrics, Cambridge, MA, 1984.
76.   T. H. KERR, "Navy GPS/SSN Phase II User Equipment DT&E: Rockwell–Collins Developmental Test & Evaluation (Operational Readiness) [DT&E(OR)] Test Report)," Rep. No. IR-MA-484 (NADC No. GPS-85-19600-061). Intermetrics, Cambridge, MA, 1985.
77.   T. H. KERR, "Functional and Mathematical Structural Analysis of the Passive Tracking Algorithm (PTA)," Rep. IR-MA-208 for Naval Air Development Center. Intermetrics (1983).
78.   T. H. KERR, "Assessment of the Status of the Current Post-Coherent Localization Algorithm," Rep. IR-MA-319 for NADC. Intermetrics, Cambridge, MA (1984).
79.   C. S. HWANG and R. R. MOHLER, "Nonlinear Observability and Mixed-Coordinate Bearings-Only Signal Processing," Rep. No. OSU-OWR TR 84-4 for ONR. Naval Postgraduate School, Monterey, CA, 1984.
80.   S. E. HAMMEL and V. J. AIDALA, Observability requirements for three-dimensional tracking via angle measurements. *IEEE Trans. Aerosp. Electron. Syst.* **AES-21**(2) (1985).
81.   B. D. O. ANDERSON and J. B. MOORE, "Optimal Filtering." Prentice-Hall, Englewood Cliffs, New Jersey, 1979.
82.   C. S. SIMS and R. B. ASHER, Optimal and suboptimal results in full- and reduced-order linear filtering. *IEEE Trans. Autom. Control* **AC-23**(3) (1978).
83.   C. S. SIMS, Reduced-order modeling and filtering. *Control Dyn. Syst.* **18** (1982).
84.   V. B. HAAS, Reduced-order state estimation for linear systems with exact measurements. *Automatica* **21**(2) (1984).
85.   D. S. BERSTEIN and D. C. HYLAND, The optimal projection equations for reduced-order state estimation. *IEEE Trans. Autom. Control* **AC-30**(6) , pp. 1201–1211 (1985).
86.   G. B. DiMASI, An approximation for the nonlinear filtering problem, with error bound. *Stochastics* **14**, 247–271 (1985).
87.   J. E. WALL, A. S. WILLSKY, and N. R. SANDELL, On the fixed-interval smoothing problem. *Stochastics* **5**, 1–41 (1981).
88.   M. AOKI and J. R. HUDDLE, Estimation of the state vector of a linear stochastic system with a constrained estimator. *IEEE Trans. Autom. Control* **AC-12**(4) (1967).
89.   D. F. LIANG, J. C. McMILLAN *et al.*, Low cost integrated marine navigation system. *Navigation, J. Inst. Navig.* **30**(4) , pp. 281–300, (1983–1984).
90.   R. ISERMAN, Process fault detection based on modeling and estimation methods – A survey. *Automatica* **20**(4), 387–404 (1984).
91.   B. WALKER, Recent developments in fault diagnosis and accommodation. Presented at *AIAA Guidance Control Conf.*, but too late for inclusion in proceedings (available from author), August, 1983.
92.   T. H. KERR, Decentralized filtering and redundancy management for multisensor navigation. *IEEE Trans. Aerosp. Electron. Syst.* **AES-23**(2) (1987).
93.   T. H. KERR, Testing matrices for positive definiteness and semidefiniteness and application examples that spawn the need. *AIAA J. Guidance, Control, Dyn.* **10**(5) (1987).
94.   M. VERHAEGEN and P. VAN DOOREN, Numerical aspects of different Kalman filter implementations. *IEEE Trans. Autom. Control* **AC-31**(10), 907–917 (1986).
95.   C. L. LAWSON and R. J. HANSON, "Solving Least-Squares Problems (Appendix C)," Prentice-Hall, Englewood Cliffs, New Jersey, 1974.
96.   G. H. GOLUB and C. F. VAN LOAN, "Matrix Computations." Johns Hopkins Univ. Press, Baltimore, Maryland, 1983.
97.   J. K. CULLUM and R. A. WILLOUGHBY, "Lanczos Algorithms for Large Symmetric Eigenvalue Computations," Vols. 1 and 2, Birkhaeuser, Boston, Massachusetts, 1985.
98.   R. SCHREIBER, Implementation of adaptive array algorithms. *IEEE Trans. Acoust., Speech, Signal Process.* **ASSP-34**(5), 1038–1045 (1986).

99.   D. W. TUFTS and C. D. MELLISSINOS, Simple, effective computation of principal eigenvalues and their eigenvectors and application to high resolution estimation of frequencies. *IEEE Trans. Acoust., Speech, Signal Process.* **ASSP-34**(5), 1046–1053 (1986).

100.   R. DEUTSCH, "Estimation Theory." Prentice-Hall, Englewood Cliffs, New Jersey, 1965.

101.   G. GOLUB and W. KAHAN, Calculating the singular values and pseudo-inverse of a matrix. *SIAM J. Numer. Anal. Ser. B* **2**, 205–224 (1965).

102.   F. W. FAIRMAN, Reduced-order state estimation for discrete time stochastic systems. *IEEE Trans. Autom. Control* **AC-22** , pp. 874–876 (1977).

103.   E. FOGEL and Y. F. HUANG, Reduced-order optimal state estimator for linear systems with partially noise-corrupted measurement. *IEEE Trans. Autom. Control* **AC-25**(5), 994–996 (1980).

104.   D. W. TUFTS and C. D. MELISSINOS, Effective computation of principal eigenvectors and their eigenvalues and application to high-resolution estimation of frequencies. *IEEE Trans. Acoust., Speech, Signal Process.* **ASSP-34**(5), 1046–1053 (1986).

105.   R. O. SCHMIDT, Multiple emitter location and signal parameter estimation. *Proc. RADC Spectrum Estim. Workshop, 1979*, pp. 243–258 (1979).

106.   E. K. L. HUNG, R. M. TURNER, and R. W. HERRING, A pitfall in using the pseudoinverse of a singular covariance matrix in adaptive signal processing. *Proc. ASSP Spectrum Estim. Workshop, 2nd, 1983*, pp. 253–258 (1984).

107.   P. G. COXSON, Structured model reduction. *Proc. Conf. Decision Control, 23rd, 1984*, pp. 139–142 (1985).

108.   U. B. DESAI, Reduced-order modeling of stochastic processes with applications in estimation. *In* "Modeling and Application of Stochastic Processes" (U. B. Desai, ed.), pp. 43–74. Kluwer Academic Publ., Boston, Massachusetts, 1986.

109.   J. D. APLEVICH, A simple method for finding a basis for the null-space of a matrix. *IEEE Trans. Autom. Control* **AC-21**(3), 402 (1976).

110.   M. L. LION, Author's reply to 'On the evaluation of e^{At} by power series.' *IEEE Proc.* **55**, 413 (1967).

111.   J. A. D'APPOLITO, Kalman filter theory and application – A short course. A tutorial presented at NAECON 86 and included in *Tutorial Proc. NAECON , 1986* (1986).

112.   T. H. KERR, The proper computation of the matrix pseudoinverse and its impact in MVRO filtering. *IEEE Trans. Aerosp. Electron. Syst.* **AES-21**(5), 711–724 (1985).

113.   L. A. ZADEH and C. A. DESOER, "Linear System Theory: The State Space Approach." McGraw-Hill, New York, 1963.

114.   W. H. FINCKE and A. J. KLEINMAN, Maneuver-dependent component error models and synchronized reset filters for inertial navigation systems. *Proc. Position, Location, Navig. Symp. (PLANS), 1980*, pp. 107–114 (1981).

115.   T. H. KERR, Cautions concerning occasional misuse of shaping filters for marginally stable systems. *IEEE Trans. Aerosp. and Electron. Syst* (to be published).

116.   A. PAULRAJ, R. ROY, and T. KAILATH, A subspace approach to signal parameter estimation. *Proc. IEEE* **74**(7), 1044–1045 (1986).

117.   K. YONEZAWA, Reduced--order Kalman filtering with incomplete observability. *AIAA J. Guidance Control* **3**(3), 280–282 (1980).

118.   A. K. MAHALANABIS, On minimizing the divergence in discrete filters. *IEEE Trans. Autom. Control* **AC-17**(2), 239–240 (1972).

119.   W. P. M. P. DAYAWANSA, Comments on 'On the application of matrix generalized inverses to the design of observers for time-varying and time-invariant linear systems.' *IEEE Trans. Autom. Control* **AC-27**(5), 1137–1138 (1982).

120.   J. O'REILLY, Reply to author's reply to 'Commens on two recent papers on reduced-order optimal state estimation for linear systems with partially noise-corrupted measurement.' *IEEE Trans. Autom. Control* **AC-27**(6), 1266–1267 (1982).

121.   G. W. STEWART, "Introduction to Matrix Computations." Academic Press, New York, 1973.

122.   T. S. LEE, Numerical aspects of the inverse function theory. *Proc. Conf. Decision Control, 22nd, 1983* , pp. 424–429 (1984).

123.   M. J. R. HEALY, "Matrices for Statistics." Oxford Univ. Press (Clarendon), London and New York, 1986.

124.   R. A. USMANI, "Applied Linear Algebra." Dekker, New York, 1987.

125.   S. K. BERBERIAN, "Introduction to Hilbert Spaces." Oxford Univ. Press, London and New York, 1961.

126.   W. RUDIN, "Real and Complex Analysis." McGraw-Hill, New York, 1966.

127.   E. KREYSZIG, "Advanced Engineering Mathematics." Wiley, New York, 1963.

128.   *Proceedings of the International Workshop on SVD and Signal Processing.* Sponsored by European Association for Signal Processing (EURASIP), Les Houches, Grenoble, France, 1987.

129.   C. L. PATTERSON, G. BUECHLER, and H. C. ANDREWS, Pseudoinversion in digital image restoration. *Proc. Conf. Decision Control, 1974*, pp. 449–452 (1975).

130.   E. VERRIEST, B. FRIEDLANDER, and M. MORF, Distributed processing in estimation and detection. *Proc. Conf. Decision Control, 18th, 1979*, pp. 153–158 (1980).

131.   D. J. TYLAVSKY and G. R. L. SOHIE, Generalization of the matrix inversion lemma. *Proc. IEEE* **74**(7), 1050–1052 (1986).

132.   C. B. CHANG and K. P. DUNN, On the GLR detection and estimation of unexpected inputs in linear discrete systems. *IEEE Trans. Autom. Control* **AC-24**(3), 499–500 (1979).

133.   G. R. L. SOHIE and L. H. SIBUL, Application of Hilbert space theory to optimal and adaptive space–time processing. *Proc. Conf. Inf. Sci. Syst.*, pp. 17–22 (1982).

134.   P. BURRIDGE and A. HALL, Convergence of the Kalman filter gain for a class of nondetectable signal extraction problems, *IEEE Trans. Autom. Control*, AC-32(11), 1036–1039 (1987).

135.   P. H. PETKOV, N. D. CHRISTOV, and M. M. KONSTANTINOV, On the numerical properties of the Schur approach for solving the matrix Riccati equation, *Sys. Control Lett.* **9**(3), 197–201 (1987).

136.   C. BRUNI, A. ISIDORI, and A. RUBERTI, "On the calculation of pseudo-inverses," *IEEE Trans. Autom. Control*, AC-11(2), 204–205 (1966).

137.   T. H. KERR, "Multichannel Shaping Filter Formulations for BRVAD Using Matrix Spectral Factorization," Report No. PA-500. MIT Lincoln Laboratory, Lexington (1987).

138.   A. L. DORAN, Coordinate Selection Issues in the Order Reduction of Linear Systems. In "Control and Dynamic Systems: Advances in Theory and Applications," Vol. 25: System Identification and Adaptive Control, Part 1 of 3 (C. T. Leondes, ed.). Academic Press, NY (1987).

139.   Y. BARAM and G. KALIT, Order reduction in linear state estimation under performance constraints, *IEEE Trans. Autom. Control* AC-32(11), 983–989 (1987).

140.   R. SETTERLUND, New insights into minimum variance reduced order filters, *AIAA J. Guidance Control, Dyn.* (1988).

141.   U. M. AL-SAGGAF and G. F. FRANKLIN, An error bound for a discrete reduced order model of a linear multivariable system, *IEEE Trans. Autom. Control* AC-32 (9), 815–819 (1987).

142.   H.-F. CHEN and L. GUO, Consistent estimation of the order of stochastic control systems, *IEEE Trans. Autom. Control* AC-32 (6), 531–535 (1987).

143.   E. A. JONCKHEEVE, On stochastic model reduction, *IEEE Trans. Autom. Control* AC-32 (6), 530–531 (1987).

144.   H. D. MITTELMANN and J. A. CADZOW, Continuity of closest rank-p approximations to matrices, *IEEE Trans. Acoustics, Speech, and Sig. Proc.* ASSP-35(8), 1211–1212 (1987).

145.   J. H. TAYLOR, Cramer–Rao estimation error lower bound analysis for nonlinear systems with unknown deterministic variables, *IEEE Trans. Autom. Control* AC-24 (2), 343–344 (1979).

146.   T. H. KERR, An almost completely analytic closed-form implementation example of a Schweppe likelihood ratio detector, submitted.

147.   T. H. KERR, Kalman filter tracking in the multitarget case and an associated practical sonobuoy selection procedure, submitted.
148.   T. H. KERR, Overview status of Cramer–Rao-like bounds for nonlinear filtering, submitted.

DECOMPOSITION TECHNIQUE IN MULTIOBJECTIVE DISCRETE-TIME DYNAMIC PROBLEMS: THE ENVELOPE APPROACH

DUAN LI and YACOV Y. HAIMES

Department of Systems Engineering
University of Virginia
Charlottesville, Virginia 22901

I. INTRODUCTION

The fundamental characteristic of large-scale systems is their inescapably multifarious nature: for instance, the structure of such systems may be multilevel or hierarchical, they may have multiple objectives which are usually noncommensurable, and the evolution of such systems may be multistage or dynamical. This necessitates the development of a comprehensive framework for a theory of how to handle decision making in large-scale multiobjective systems.

The past decade has seen an increasing concern about the integration of two well-known approaches – hierarchical systems theory and the multiobjective optimization technique – into a unified framework that is appropriate for large-scale systems. Theoretical and methodological results of hierarchical multiobjective analysis for large-scale systems have been developed in recent years [1–16]. A survey paper on hierarchical multiobjective analysis for large-scale systems is presented by Haimes and Li [17].

The multiobjective optimization problem for large-scale dynamic systems that this study considers is the problem of finding the set of all noninferior solutions. An envelope approach that finds the set of noninferior solutions of large-scale multiobjective systems problems by decomposition and coordination is developed. The main contribution of the work described in this article is the presentation of a new, unified approach to the decomposition-coordination problem of large-scale multiobjective systems. In addition, the solution procedure gives a great deal of insight into large-scale multiobjective optimization problems.

In Section II, the definition of an envelope is given and the formulas for envelopes with parametric form are derived. One basic theorem that explores the relationship between the envelope approach and multiobjective optimization is proved. Computational simplification of the envelope approach for convex problems is also obtained. Section III deals with the multiobjective dynamic programming problem, and shows how adoption of the envelope approach leads to a new version of multiobjective dynamic programming. The principles of hierarchical generating methods for finding the set of noninferior solutions of a large-scale multiobjective system by using a two-level decomposition-coordination scheme are established in Section IV, where two versions of hierarchical generating methods are also developed. The concluding section offers suggestions for future research.

II.   BASIC THEOREM OF THE ENVELOPE APPROACH

A.   ENVELOPES

The subject of envelopes is generally studied in the areas of differential equations and differential geometry (see, e.g., Refs. [18–22]). However, few papers in the literature deal with envelopes that have a parametric form. For the purpose of this study, this section will give a derivation for formulas for envelopes that have a parametric form.

1.   Parametrized Curves, Surfaces, and Hypersurfaces

A parametrized curve in the real Euclidean space R^2 is a map

$$F_1\colon \Theta_1 \to R^2, \tag{1}$$

where Θ_1 is an interval in R and

$$F_1(\theta) = [f_1(\theta), f_2(\theta)]^T, \quad \theta \in \Theta_1. \tag{2}$$

We assume here that functions f_1 and f_2 both have derivatives for all $\theta \in \text{int } \Theta_1$. The variable θ is called a parameter. The curve F_1 is called regular provided there

$$\text{does not exist } \theta \in \text{int } \Theta_1 \text{ with } \left[\frac{\partial f_1(\theta)}{\partial \theta}, \frac{\partial f_2(\theta)}{\partial \theta}\right]^T = 0.$$

A parametrized surface in the real Euclidean space R^3 is a map

$$F_2\colon \Theta_2 \to R^3, \tag{3}$$

where Θ_2 is a set in R^2 and

$$F_2(\theta) = [f_1(\theta), f_2(\theta), f_3(\theta)]^T, \quad \theta = [\theta_1, \theta_2]^T \in \Theta_2. \tag{4}$$

We assume here that all three functions – f_1, f_2, and f_3 – have partial derivatives with respect to θ_1 and θ_2 for all $\theta \in \text{int } \Theta_2$. The variable θ is called a parameter vector. The surface F_2 is called regular if for all $\theta \in \text{int } \Theta_2$,

$$\text{rank} \left[\frac{\partial f_1(\theta)}{\partial \theta}, \frac{\partial f_2(\theta)}{\partial \theta}, \frac{\partial f_3(\theta)}{\partial \theta} \right] = 2. \tag{5}$$

A parametrized hypersurface in the real Euclidean space R^n, $n > 3$, is a map

$$F_n : \Theta_{n-1} \rightarrow R^n, \tag{6}$$

where Θ_{n-1} is a set in R^{n-1} and

$$F_n(\theta) = [f_1(\theta), f_2(\theta), ..., f_n(\theta)]^T, \tag{7}$$

$$\theta = [\theta_1, \theta_2, ..., \theta_{n-1}]^T \in \Theta_{n-1}.$$

We assume here that all n functions f_1, f_2, ..., f_n have partial derivatives with respect to θ_1, θ_2, ..., θ_{n-1}. The variable θ is called a parameter vector. The hypersurface F_n is called regular if for all $\theta \in \text{int } \Theta_{n-1}$,

$$\text{rank} \left[\frac{\partial f_1(\theta)}{\partial \theta}, \frac{\partial f_2(\theta)}{\partial \theta}, ..., \frac{\partial f_{n-1}(\theta)}{\partial \theta} \right] = n - 1. \tag{8}$$

In the following study, we assume that all parametrized curves, surfaces, and hypersurfaces are regular.

2.   Families and Envelopes

A family of curves may be given by the following parametrized form:

$$f_1 = f_1(\theta; \alpha) \tag{9a}$$

$$f_2 = f_2(\theta; \alpha), \tag{9b}$$

where $\theta \in \Theta_1 \subseteq R$ is the parameter of curves and $\alpha \in A \subseteq R$ is the parameter of the family. By giving α a specific numerical value, we obtain the equations of one curve of the family, while if we let α run through all possible values, we obtain the entire family of curves. We assume here that functions f_1 and f_2 both have continuous derivatives up to the second order with respect to θ and α, for all $\theta \in$ int Θ_1 and $\alpha \in$ int A.

Definition 1. Given a family of curves, then a curve that is only tangent at each of its points to some curve of the family is called the envelope curve of the given family of curves.

Note. Not all families of curves have envelopes. For example, a family of concentric circles and a family of parallel straight lines have no envelopes.

Lemma 1. If a family of regular curves that is expressed in the parametric form given in (9) has an envelope curve, then the points of the envelope curve satisfy the following equations:

$$f_1 = f_1(\theta; \alpha) \tag{10a}$$

$$f_2 = f_2(\theta; \alpha) \tag{10b}$$

$$\frac{\partial f_2}{\partial \theta} \frac{\partial f_1}{\partial \alpha} - \frac{\partial f_1}{\partial \theta} \frac{\partial f_2}{\partial \alpha} = 0. \tag{10c}$$

Remark. If the conditions of the implicit function theorem are satisfied for (10c), then we can solve α as a function of θ in (10c). Thus, we can get the parametric form for the envelope curve by substituting α in (10a) and (10b).

Proof. Since each point on the envelope curve is also on one curve with the corresponding α of the family, and since both the envelope curve and the curve of the family have the same tangents at that point, we have

$$\frac{\partial f_2}{\partial \alpha} \bigg/ \frac{\partial f_1}{\partial \alpha} = \frac{\partial f_2}{\partial \theta} \bigg/ \frac{\partial f_1}{\partial \theta} \tag{11}$$

which gives us (10). Q.E.D.

Remark. (1) If it is difficult to get the analytic expression for α as a function of θ on the envelope, α will be solved for some fixed values of θ. Then, a curve-fitting technique, such as least squares, can be used to determine $\alpha(\theta)$.

(2) Since we assume each curve of the family is regular, all points satisfying (10) are thus on the envelope curve.

(3) If α is of dimension $n > 1$, we can still use (10) to determine the envelope. The proof is similar.

A family of surfaces may be given by the following parametrized form:

$$f_1 = f_1(\theta; \alpha) \tag{12a}$$

$$f_2 = f_2(\theta; \alpha) \tag{12b}$$

$$f_3 = f_3(\theta; \alpha), \tag{12c}$$

where $\theta \in \Theta_2 \subseteq R^2$ is the parameter vector of surfaces and $\alpha \in A \subseteq R^m$, $m \geq 1$, is the parameter vector of the family. By giving α a specific numerical value, we get the equations of one surface of the family, while if we let α run through all possible values, we obtain the entire family of surfaces. We assume that all three functions – f_1, f_2, and f_3 – have continuous derivatives up to the second order with respect to θ and α, for all $\theta \in$ int Θ_2 and $\alpha \in$ int A.

Definition 2. Given a family of surfaces, then a surface that is only tangent at each of its points to some surface of the family is called the envelope surface of the given family of surfaces.

Lemma 2. If a family of regular surfaces that is expressed in the parametric form given in (12) has an envelope surface, then the points of the envelope surface satisfy the following equations:

$$f_1 = f_1(\theta; \alpha) \tag{13a}$$

$$f_2 = f_2(\theta; \alpha) \tag{13b}$$

$$f_3 = f_3(\theta; \alpha) \tag{13c}$$

$$\frac{\partial(f_2, f_3)}{\partial(\theta_1, \theta_2)} \frac{\partial f_1}{\partial \alpha} + \frac{\partial(f_3, f_1)}{\partial(\theta_1, \theta_2)} \frac{\partial f_2}{\partial \alpha} + \frac{\partial(f_1, f_2)}{\partial(\theta_1, \theta_2)} \frac{\partial f_3}{\partial \alpha} = 0. \tag{13d}$$

Remark. If the conditions of the implicit function theorem are satisfied for (13d), then we can solve α as a function of θ in (13d). Thus, we can get the parametric form for the envelope surface by substituting α in (13a)–(13c).

Proof. For the family of surfaces expressed in a parametric form, we know the normal vector of each surface in the family is given by

$$\left[\frac{\partial(f_2, f_3)}{\partial(\theta_1, \theta_2)}, \frac{\partial(f_3, f_1)}{\partial(\theta_1, \theta_2)}, \frac{\partial(f_1, f_2)}{\partial(\theta_1, \theta_2)}\right]^T.$$

From the requirement that the tangents of the envelope surface at $[f_1(\theta; \alpha), f_2(\theta; \alpha), f_3(\theta; \alpha)]^T$ be orthogonal to the normal vector of the corresponding surface, we have the results given in (13). Q.E.D.

Remark. (1) If it is difficult to get the analytic expression for α as a function of θ on the envelope, α will be solved for some fixed values of θ. Then, a curve-fitting technique, such as least squares, can be used to determine $\alpha(\theta)$.

(2) Since we assume that each surface of the family is regular, all points satisfying (13) are thus on the envelope surface.

A family of hypersurfaces may be given by the following parametrized form:

$$f_1 = f_1(\theta; \alpha) \tag{14a}$$

$$f_2 = f_2(\theta; \alpha) \tag{14b}$$
$$\vdots$$
$$f_n = f_n(\theta; \alpha), \tag{14c}$$

where $n > 3$; $\theta \in \Theta_{n-1} \subseteq R^{n-1}$ is the parameter vector of hypersurfaces, and $\alpha \in A \subseteq R^m$, $m \geq 1$, is the parameter vector of the family. By giving α a specific numerical value, we get the equations of one hypersurface of the family, while if we let α run through all possible values, we obtain the entire family of hypersurfaces. We assume that all n functions – $f_1, f_2, \ldots, f_n$ – have continuous derivatives up to the second order with respect to θ and α, for all $\theta \in$ int Θ_{n-1}, and $\alpha \in$ int A.

Definition 3. Given a family of hypersurfaces, then a hypersurface that is only tangent at each of its points to some hypersurface of the family is called the envelope hypersurface of the given family of hypersurfaces.

Lemma 3. If a family of regular hypersurfaces that is expressed in the parametric form given in (14) has an envelope hypersurface, then the points of the envelope hypersurface satisfy the following equations:

$$f_1 = f_1(\theta; \alpha) \tag{15a}$$

$$f_2 = f_2(\theta; \alpha) \tag{15b}$$

$$\vdots$$

$$f_n = f_n(\theta; \alpha) \tag{15c}$$

$$\frac{\partial(f_2, f_3, \ldots, f_n)}{\partial(\theta_1, \theta_2, \ldots, \theta_{n-1})} \frac{\partial f_1}{\partial \alpha} - \frac{\partial(f_1, f_3, \ldots, f_n)}{\partial(\theta_1, \theta_2, \ldots, \theta_{n-1})} \frac{\partial f_2}{\partial \alpha} \tag{15d}$$

$$+ \ldots + (-1)^{n-1} \frac{\partial(f_1, f_2, \ldots, f_{n-1})}{\partial(\theta_1, \theta_2, \ldots, \theta_{n-1})} \frac{\partial f_n}{\partial \alpha} = 0.$$

Remark. If the conditions of the implicit function theorem are satisfied for (15d), then we can solve α as a function of θ in (15d). Thus, we can get the parametric form for the envelope hypersurface by substituting α in the first n equations of expression (15).

Proof. For the family of hypersurfaces in the parametric form, we know that the normal vector of each hypersurface in the family is given by

$$\left[\frac{\partial(f_2, f_3, \ldots, f_n)}{\partial(\theta_1, \theta_2, \ldots, \theta_{n-1})}, -\frac{\partial(f_1, f_3, \ldots, f_n)}{\partial(\theta_1, \theta_2, \ldots, \theta_{n-1})}, \ldots, (-1)^{n-1} \frac{\partial(f_1, f_2, \ldots, f_{n-1})}{\partial(\theta_1, \theta_2, \ldots, \theta_{n-1})} \right]^T$$

From the requirement that the tangents of the envelope hypersurface at $[f_1(\theta; \alpha),$ $f_2(\theta; \alpha), \ldots, f_n(\theta; \alpha)]^T$ be orthogonal to the normal vector of the corresponding hypersurface, we have the results given in (15). Q.E.D.

Remark. (1) If it is difficult to get the analytic expression for α as a function of θ on the envelope, α will be solved for some fixed values of θ. Then a curve-fitting technique, such as least squares, can be used to determine $\alpha(\theta)$.

(2) Since we assume that each hypersurface of the family is regular, all points satisfying (15) are thus on the envelope hypersurface.

B.   RELATIONSHIP BETWEEN ENVELOPES
        AND MULTIOBJECTIVE OPTIMIZATION

Several basic concepts of multiobjective optimization were developed in economics. The notion of utility was introduced in the eighteenth century. Indifference curves as contour lines of a utility function were introduced by Pareto [23]. More than a half-century later, theoretical mathematical results of multiobjective optimization were developed by Kuhn and Tucker [24] and Koopmans [25]. In 1963, Zadeh [26] first presented the question of system design with respect to several performance indices. Since then, both theory and methodology for multiobjective optimization has rapidly spread from the areas of static optimization problems to dynamical systems, and currently it has become an important part of control theory.

Methodological results about multiobjective optimization are found and reviewed (e.g., Refs. [27–32]). The book by Chankong and Haimes [33] is concerned with a unified treatment of both theory and methodology. The text by Salukvadze [34] is devoted to vector-valued optimization problems in control theory.

Consider the following multiobjective problem:

$$\min f(x) = \begin{bmatrix} f_1(x) \\ f_2(x) \\ \vdots \\ f_k(x) \end{bmatrix} \tag{16a}$$

$$\text{s.t. } g(x) \le 0 \tag{16b}$$

$$h(x) = 0 \tag{16c}$$

$$x \in S \tag{16d}$$

where x is an n-dimensional vector of decision variables; $f_i(x)$, $i = 1, 2, \ldots, k$, is a real-valued function that represents the i-th objective; $g(x)$ and $h(x)$ are m_1- and m_2-dimensional real-valued vector functions that represent the system constraints; the set $S \subseteq R^n$ denotes other forms of constraints which cannot be expressed as functions g and h; and f, g, and h are all continuously differentiable over their domain.

Definition 4. The decision space of the problem given in (16) is characterized by the set

$$X = \{x \mid g(x) \le 0, h(x) = 0, \text{ and } x \in S\}, \tag{17}$$

and the objective space or the functional space is defined as

$$F = \{f(x) \mid x \in X\}. \tag{18}$$

The problem outlined in (16) includes one purely mathematical stage: determining noninferior solutions. Conceptually, a noninferior solution is one which is not dominated by any other feasible solution. Precisely, we have the following definition.

Definition 5 [33]. x^* is said to be a noninferior solution of problem (16) if there exists no other feasible x such that $f_j(x) \leq f_j(x^*)$ for all $j = 1, ..., k$, with strict inequality for at least one j.

Remark. The set of noninferior solutions in functional space of the problem posed in (16) can be denoted by $\text{Ext}[F \mid R_+^k]$, which is based on the concept of the cone extreme point introduced by Yu [35].

In various approaches proposed to handle multiobjective optimization problems, the interactions between the decision maker and the analyst take several forms. The so-called generating methods [36] represent an extremely reduced form, where the entire noninferior set or a representative subset is identified for the decision maker, who in turn selects his or her preferred solution from among this set.

The most common strategy in generating methods is to characterize noninferior solutions in terms of optimal solutions of appropriate scalar optimization problems. Among the many suggested ways of obtaining a scalar problem from a vector optimization problem, the weighting problem [26, 37] and the l-th objective ε-constraint method [38] are the most common.

Lemma 4. The dimension of the solution set, $\text{Ext}[F \mid R_+^k]$, of problem (16) satisfies

$$d\left(\text{Ext}[F \mid R_+^k]\right) \leq \min(n, k - 1). \tag{19}$$

Proof. See Chu [39].
Definition 6. If

$$d\left(\text{Ext}[F \mid R_+^k]\right) = k - 1 \tag{20}$$

is satisfied for problem (16), the problem is called regular. Otherwise the problem is degenerate.

If the problem is regular, the efficient frontier in functional space is a curve when $k = 2$, or it is a surface when $k = 3$, or it is a hypersurface when $k > 3$. If the problem is degenerate, we may divide the solution set into several regions. In each region, there exist two or more objective functions that do not conflict with each other. Thus, we may reduce the number of objective functions of degenerate multiobjective problems without violating the primary problem considerations.

In the work that follows, we will consider only regular problems of multiobjective systems.

Let

$$f_1 = f_1(\theta; \alpha) \tag{21a}$$

$$f_2 = f_2(\theta; \alpha) \tag{21b}$$

$$\vdots$$

$$f_k = f_k(\theta; \alpha) \tag{21c}$$

represent a family of curves (if $k = 2$) or of surfaces (if $k = 3$) or of hypersurfaces (if $k > 3$) in a k-dimensional space, where $\theta \in \Theta \subseteq R^{k-1}$ is the parameter vector of the curve (if $k = 2$), the surface (if $k = 3$), or the hypersurface (if $k > 3$), and $\alpha \in A \subseteq R^m$ is the parameter vector of the family. Then we have the following theorem relating envelopes to multiobjective optimization. This theorem plays an essential role in the development of the envelope approach.

Theorem 1. If all members in the family given in (21) are regular, then all noninferior solutions, $(\hat{\theta}, \hat{\alpha})$, with $\hat{\theta} \in$ int Θ, $\hat{\alpha} \in$ int A, of the following problem:

$$\min_{\theta, \alpha} \begin{bmatrix} f_1 = f_1(\theta; \alpha) \\ f_2 = f_2(\theta; \alpha) \\ \vdots \\ f_k = f_k(\theta; \alpha) \end{bmatrix} \tag{22}$$

lie on the envelope of the family. Here we assume that all f_i's, $i = 1, ..., k$, have partial derivatives with respect to θ and α.

Proof. From the paper given by Chu [39], we know that for $(\hat{\theta}^T, \hat{\alpha}^T)^T$ to be a noninferior solution, there must exist a k-dimensional nonzero vector $\mu \geq 0$ such that

$$\left[\frac{\partial f_1}{\partial \theta}, \frac{\partial f_2}{\partial \theta}, ..., \frac{\partial f_k}{\partial \theta} \right] \mu = 0 \tag{23}$$

and

$$\left[\frac{\partial f_1}{\partial \alpha}, \frac{\partial f_2}{\partial \alpha}, ..., \frac{\partial f_k}{\partial \alpha}\right]\mu = 0. \tag{24}$$

According to the assumption, we have

$$\text{rank}\left[\frac{\partial f_1}{\partial \theta}, \frac{\partial f_2}{\partial \theta}, ..., \frac{\partial f_k}{\partial \theta}\right] = k - 1. \tag{25}$$

Thus, from (23), we know that μ belongs to the orthogonal complementary space

of $\left[\frac{\partial f_1}{\partial \theta}, \frac{\partial f_2}{\partial \theta}, ..., \frac{\partial f_k}{\partial \theta}\right]^T$. Then we have

$$\frac{\partial f_2}{\partial \theta}\frac{\partial f_1}{\partial \alpha} - \frac{\partial f_1}{\partial \theta}\frac{\partial f_2}{\partial \alpha} = 0, \quad \text{if } k = 2 \tag{26a}$$

or

$$\frac{\partial(f_2, f_3)}{\partial(\theta_1, \theta_2)}\frac{\partial f_1}{\partial \alpha} + \frac{\partial(f_3, f_1)}{\partial(\theta_1, \theta_2)}\frac{\partial f_2}{\partial \alpha} + \frac{\partial(f_1, f_2)}{\partial(\theta_1, \theta_2)}\frac{\partial f_3}{\partial \alpha} = 0, \quad \text{if } k = 3 \tag{26b}$$

or

$$\frac{\partial(f_2, f_3, ..., f_k)}{\partial(\theta_1, \theta_2, ..., \theta_{k-1})}\frac{\partial f_1}{\partial \alpha} - \frac{\partial(f_1, f_3, ..., f_k)}{\partial(\theta_1, \theta_2, ..., \theta_{k-1})}\frac{\partial f_2}{\partial \alpha}$$

$$+ ... + (-1)^{k-1}\frac{\partial(f_1, f_2, ..., f_{k-1})}{\partial(\theta_1, \theta_2, ..., \theta_{k-1})}\frac{\partial f_k}{\partial \alpha} = 0, \quad \text{if } k > 3. \tag{26c}$$

That is, $(\hat{\theta}^T, \hat{\alpha}^T)^T$ is on the envelope of the family.   Q.E.D.

   Remark. (1) θ may be any kind of parameter vector; it is not necessarily the weighting coefficient vector or the ε vector used in the ε-constraint method.

   (2) If the problem in (22) is neither convex nor concave, the set of noninferior solutions will not necessarily be entirely identified if we adopt the weighting method. Using either the weighting method or the ε-constraint method to solve (22) is more complicated than the envelope approach, since more vari-

ables (i.e., the weighting coefficient vector or the ε vector) will be introduced in those methods.

(3) If there exist some constraints in the problem given in (22), Theorem 1 is still valid for noninferior solutions, $(\hat{\theta}, \hat{\alpha})$, provided that all constraints are inactive at point $(\hat{\theta}, \hat{\alpha})$.

(4) In the following study for multiobjective optimization problems, we assume the existence of the envelope; i.e., we exclude the cases where no noninferior solution or only a finite number of noninferior solutions belong to int $X(\theta, \alpha)$, where $X(\theta, \alpha)$ is the feasible region for θ and α.

C.   COMPUTATIONAL SIMPLIFICATION OF THE ENVELOPE APPROACH FOR CONVEX PROBLEMS

In this subsection, the computational simplification of envelope approaches for convex problems will be investigated. If the weighting method is used to solve the corresponding weighting problem given in (16), the noninferior solutions can be expressed by functions of the weighting coefficient vector θ; i.e.,

$$x^* = x^*(\theta_1, \theta_2, ..., \theta_{k-1}) \tag{27a}$$

$$f_i^* = f_i^*(\theta_1, \theta_2, ..., \theta_{k-1}), \quad i = 1, 2, ..., k \tag{27b}$$

$$f^* = f^*(\theta) = \sum_{i=1}^{k} \theta_i f_i^*(\theta_1, \theta_2, ..., \theta_{k-1}), \tag{27c}$$

where $(\theta_1, \theta_2, ..., \theta_{k-1}, 1 - \Sigma_{j=1}^{k-1}\theta_j) \in \Theta$, and

$$\Theta = \left\{ \theta \mid \theta \in R^k, \theta_j \geq 0, \text{ and } \sum_{j=1}^{k} \theta_j = 1 \right\}. \tag{27d}$$

Here, $f^*(\theta)$ is considered to be class C^2; i.e., $f^*(\theta)$ has continuous derivatives up to the second order with respect to θ. The justification for considering $f^*(\theta)$ as a class-C^2 function is based on the differentiability of the system of equations (Kuhn–Tucker conditions) as the optimality conditions for the minimization of f. If the conditions of the implicit function theorem are satisfied, x and the Lagrangian multipliers are differentiable with respect to the weighting coefficient vector θ. The elements of $f^*(\theta)$, which are themselves differentiable functions of x, are then differentiable with respect to θ by the chain rule of differentiation.

Lemma 5. If $f_i^*(\theta_1, \theta_2, \ldots, \theta_{k-1})$, $i = 1, 2, \ldots, k$, is a noninferior solution of the problem given in (16), generated by the weighting method, then we have

$$\sum_{i=1}^{k} \hat{\theta}_i \frac{\partial f_i^*(\hat{\theta}_1, \hat{\theta}_2, \ldots, \hat{\theta}_{k-1})}{\partial \theta_j} = 0, \; j = 1, 2, \ldots, k-1, \tag{28}$$

where $\hat{\theta} \in \theta$ and $\hat{\theta}_i > 0$, $i = 1, 2, \ldots, k$.

Proof. The proof is similar to the one given by Reid and Vemuri [40]. Since $f^*(\hat{\theta}) = \Sigma_{i=1}^{k} \hat{\theta}_i f_i(\hat{\theta}_1, \hat{\theta}_2, \ldots, \hat{\theta}_{k-1})$ is the minimum point of the weighting problem, $\min \Sigma_{i=1}^{k} \hat{\theta}_i f_i$, any admissible variation df about the point $f^*(\hat{\theta})$ must satisfy

$$\sum_{i=1}^{k} \hat{\theta}_i \, df_i^*(\hat{\theta}_1, \hat{\theta}_2, \ldots, \hat{\theta}_{k-1}) \geq 0, \tag{29}$$

where

$$df_i^*(\hat{\theta}) \approx \sum_{j=1}^{k-1} \frac{\partial f_i^*(\hat{\theta}_1, \hat{\theta}_2, \ldots, \hat{\theta}_{k-1})}{\partial \theta_j} \Delta \theta_j \tag{30}$$

$$+ \frac{1}{2} \sum_{j=1}^{k-1} \sum_{l=1}^{k-1} \frac{\partial^2 f_i^*(\hat{\theta}_1, \hat{\theta}_2, \ldots, \hat{\theta}_{k-1})}{\partial \theta_j \partial \theta_l} \Delta \theta_j \Delta \theta_l.$$

Since $\Delta \theta_j$, $j = 1, 2, \ldots, k-1$, can be of any sign, we must have (28) to guarantee that the inequality expressed in (28) is satisfied. Q.E.D.

Theorem 2 (orthogonality theorem). If $f_i^*(\theta_1, \theta_2, \ldots, \theta_{k-1}; \alpha)$, $i = 1, 2, \ldots, k$, is a noninferior solution of a regular multiobjective problem in a family with parameter α, generated by the weighting method, then on the envelope of this family of noninferior frontiers with parameter α, we have

$$\sum_{i=1}^{k} \hat{\theta}_i \frac{\partial f_i^*(\hat{\theta}_1, \hat{\theta}_2, \ldots, \hat{\theta}_{k-1}; \alpha)}{\partial \alpha} = 0, \tag{31}$$

where $\hat{\theta} \in \Theta$, and $\hat{\theta}_i > 0$, $i = 1, 2, ..., k$.

Proof. Since we assume the problem is regular, the space T spanned by

$$
\begin{bmatrix} \dfrac{\partial f_1}{\partial \theta_1} \\ \vdots \\ \dfrac{\partial f_k}{\partial \theta_1} \end{bmatrix}
\begin{bmatrix} \dfrac{\partial f_1}{\partial \theta_2} \\ \vdots \\ \dfrac{\partial f_k}{\partial \theta_2} \end{bmatrix}
\cdots
\begin{bmatrix} \dfrac{\partial f_1}{\partial \theta_{k-1}} \\ \vdots \\ \dfrac{\partial f_k}{\partial \theta_{k-1}} \end{bmatrix}
$$

is a $k - 1$-dimensional hyperplane. From Lemma 5, we know $[\hat{\theta}_1, \hat{\theta}_2, ..., \hat{\theta}_{k-1}, 1 - \Sigma_{j=1}^{k-1}\hat{\theta}_j]^T$ is in the one-dimensional space T*, which is the orthogonal complementary space of T. We also know that

$$
\left[\frac{\partial(f_2, f_3, ..., f_k)}{\partial(\theta_1, \theta_2, ..., \theta_{k-1})}, -\frac{\partial(f_1, f_3, ..., f_k)}{\partial(\theta_1, \theta_2, ..., \theta_{k-1})}, ..., (-1)^{k-1} \frac{\partial(f_1, f_2, ..., f_{k-1})}{\partial(\theta_1, \theta_2, ..., \theta_{k-1})} \right]^T
$$

constitutes the basis of T*. Thus, on the noninferior frontier, we have

$$
\left[\frac{\partial(f_2, f_3, ..., f_k)}{\partial(\theta_1, \theta_2, ..., \theta_{k-1})}, ..., (-1)^{k-1} \frac{\partial(f_1, f_2, ..., f_{k-1})}{\partial(\theta_1, \theta_2, ..., \theta_{k-1})} \right]^T
$$

(32)

$$
= c \left[\theta_1, ..., \theta_{k-1}, 1 - \sum_{j=1}^{k-1} \theta_j \right]^T,
$$

where c is a constant. A proof of Theorem 2 is then based on Lemma 3, which says $\left[\dfrac{\partial f_1}{\partial \alpha}, \dfrac{\partial f_2}{\partial \alpha}, ..., \dfrac{\partial f_k}{\partial \alpha} \right]^T$ is orthogonal to T*. Q.E.D.

III.   MULTIOBJECTIVE DYNAMIC PROGRAMMING METHOD USING THE ENVELOPE APPROACH

In many practical problems decisions have to be made sequentially at different points of time. Multiobjective optimization problems in which decisions are to be made sequentially are called sequential multiobjective decision problems. They are also referred to as multiobjective multistage decision problems. Multiobjective dynamic programming is a mathematical methodology well suited to multiobjective multistage decision problems.

Multiobjective dynamic programming methods, when applicable, decompose a multistage multiobjective problem into a sequence of single-stage multiobjective problems. In most cases, this sequence of subproblems is easier to solve than the original problem.

At present, multiobjective dynamic programming still remains one of the most provocative topics in the area of multiobjective optimization [41–50]. On the one hand, a large number of multiobjective sequential decision-making problems necessarily lead to the multiobjective dynamic programming formulation and, on the other hand, available methodologies for handling multiobjective dynamic programming still require further improvement to be more effective.

The aim of most existing generating methods of multiobjective dynamic programming schemes is to convert the original multiobjective multistage decision problem into a series of single-objective multistage decision problems, either by the weighting method or by the ε-constraint method, and then to apply single-objective dynamic programming to these single-objective multistage decision problems. However, these schemes have some limitations.

For multiobjective dynamic programming schemes that use the weighting method, unless each overall objective function f_i is of additive form with respect to the i-th objective function of each stage, the weighting sum $\Sigma_i \theta_i f_i$ will make separability invalid.

For multiobjective dynamic programming schemes that use the ε-constraint method, one limitation is that in most cases the ε constraints may not be separable with respect to each stage. If some new state variables corresponding to ε constraints are introduced, the scheme will run into a dimensionality problem as the number of state variables increases with the number of objective functions.

In this section we will investigate the use of the envelope approach in multiobjective dynamic programming. Using the envelope approach, we can handle a general class of multiobjective dynamic problems, and at each stage we can identify the vector cost-to-go without doing any optimization operations in the process.

A.   THE PRINCIPLE OF OPTIMALITY IN MULTIOBJECTIVE DYNAMIC PROGRAMMING

Consider a class of discrete-time dynamic systems described by difference equations of the form

$$x(t + 1) = H_t(x(t), u(t), t), \quad t = 0, 1, ..., T - 1, \tag{33}$$

$x(0)$ given, and where $x(t) \in R^n$ denotes the state, $u(t) \in R^p$ denotes the control, and

$$H_t(\cdot, \cdot, \cdot): R^n \times R^p \times R \rightarrow R^n, \quad t = 0, 1, ..., T - 1.$$

Assume further that the state vector and the control vector are constrained by the following equations:

$$g_t(x(t), u(t)) \leq 0, \quad t = 0, 1, ..., T - 1 \tag{34a}$$

$$g_T(x(T)) \leq 0. \tag{34b}$$

The stage's objectives are assumed to be as follows:

$$f_j^t = f_j^t(x(t), u(t)), \quad t = 0, 1, ..., T - 1; \quad j = 1, 2, ..., k \tag{35a}$$

$$f_j^T = f_j^T(x(T)), \quad j = 1, 2, ..., k \tag{35b}$$

and the overall objective $f_j, j = 1, 2, ..., k$, is a function of $f_j^t, t = 0, 1, ..., T - 1, T$; i.e.,

$$f_j = f_j\left(f_j^0, f_j^1, ..., f_j^{T-1}, f_j^T\right), \quad j = 1, 2, ..., k. \tag{36}$$

The multiobjective optimization problem of this class of dynamic systems can be posed as follows:

$$\min_{x, u} f = \begin{bmatrix} f_1(f_1^0, f_1^1, ..., f_1^{T-1}, f_1^T) \\ f_2(f_2^0, f_2^1, ..., f_2^{T-1}, f_2^T) \\ \vdots \\ f_k(f_k^0, f_k^1, ..., f_k^{T-1}, f_k^T) \end{bmatrix} \tag{37}$$

s.t. (33) and (34).

In the following study, we assume that all functions, H_t, $t = 0, 1, ..., T - 1$; g_t, $t = 0, 1, ..., T - 1$; g_T; f_j^t, $t = 0, 1, ..., T - 1$, $j = 1, ..., k$; f_j^T, $j = 1, ..., k$; and f_j, $j = 1, ... k$, are differentiable on their domains.

In order to apply multiobjective dynamic programming to the systems given by (37), the system has to satisfy the conditions of forward (backward) separability and forward (backward) monotonicity. These can be viewed as an extension of the work of Yu and Seiford [44].

Definition 7. Forward separability and backward separability: The vector $f = [f_1, f_2, ..., f_k]^T$ in (37) is forward separable (backward separable) if there exist functions φ_i^t ($t = 1, 2, ..., T$, $i = 1, 2, ..., k$, each φ_i^t: $R \times R \rightarrow R$) such that

$$f_i = \varphi_i^T \left(f_i^T, \varphi_i^{T-1}(f_i^{T-1}, \varphi_i^{T-2}(..., \varphi_i^2(f_i^2, \varphi_i^1(f_i^1, f_i^0))...))) \right), \quad i = 1, 2, ..., k \tag{38}$$

$$\left(f_i = \varphi_i^1(f_i^0, \varphi_i^2(f_i^1, \varphi_i^3(..., \varphi_i^{T-1}(f_i^{T-2}, \varphi_i^T(f_i^{T-1}, f_i^T))...))) \right), \quad i = 1, 2, ..., k. \tag{39}$$

Remark. (38) and (39) can be expressed, respectively, in more distinct forms: forward separability:

$$f = f^0 \vec{o} f^1 \vec{o} f^2 \vec{o} ... \vec{o} f^{T-1} \vec{o} f^T; \tag{40}$$

backward separability:

$$f = f^0 \overleftarrow{o} f^1 \overleftarrow{o} f^2 \overleftarrow{o} ... \overleftarrow{o} f^{T-1} \overleftarrow{o} f^T, \tag{41}$$

where

$$f^i = [f_1^i, f_2^i, ..., f_k^i]^T, \quad i = 0, 1, ..., T. \tag{42}$$

Note that each $\vec{o}$ (or $\overleftarrow{o}$) represents a forward (or backward) operator that may denote different operations in its components and may vary from stage to stage.

Example 1. These two objective functions,

$$f_1 = f_1^0 + f_1^1 f_1^2$$

$$f_2 = f_2^0 \exp(f_2^1 / f_2^2)$$

are backward separable, but not forward separable. And these two,

$$f_1 = f_1^0 f_1^1 f_1^2$$

$$f_2 = f_2^0 + f_2^1 + f_2^2$$

are both forward separable and backward separable.

Definition 8. Forward monotonicity and backward monotonicity: A forward separable (backward separable) multiobjective function $f = f^0 \vec{o} f^1 \vec{o} \dots \vec{o} f^T$ ($f = f^0 \overleftarrow{o} f^1 \overleftarrow{o} \dots \overleftarrow{o} f^T$) is forward (backward) monotonic iff

$$\hat{f}^0 \vec{o} \hat{f}^1 \vec{o} \dots \vec{o} \hat{f}^t > \tilde{f}^0 \vec{o} \tilde{f}^1 \vec{o} \dots \vec{o} \tilde{f}^t \tag{43a}$$

implies

$$\hat{f}^0 \vec{o} \hat{f}^1 \vec{o} \dots \vec{o} \hat{f}^t \vec{o} f^{t+1} > \tilde{f}^0 \vec{o} \tilde{f}^1 \vec{o} \dots \vec{o} \tilde{f}^t \vec{o} f^{t+1} \tag{43b}$$

$$(\hat{f}^{t+1} \overleftarrow{o} \hat{f}^{t+2} \overleftarrow{o} \dots \overleftarrow{o} \hat{f}^T > \tilde{f}^{t+1} \overleftarrow{o} \tilde{f}^{t+2} \overleftarrow{o} \dots \overleftarrow{o} \tilde{f}^T \tag{44a}$$

implies

$$f^t \overleftarrow{o} \hat{f}^{t+1} \overleftarrow{o} \hat{f}^{t+2} \overleftarrow{o} \dots \overleftarrow{o} \hat{f}^T > f^t \overleftarrow{o} \tilde{f}^{t+1} \overleftarrow{o} \tilde{f}^{t+2} \overleftarrow{o} \dots \overleftarrow{o} \tilde{f}^T) \tag{44b}$$

where $0 \le t \le T - 1$.

Example 2. A backward separable multiobjective function

$$f_1 = f_1^0 + f_1^1 f_1^2$$

$$f_2 = f_2^0 \exp(f_2^1/f_2^2)$$

is not backward monotonic.

For multiobjective multistage systems that satisfy forward separability and forward monotonicity, we may develop a forward version of multiobjective dynamic programming. This forward version can be used for the purpose of impact analysis. However, its computation requires that the system described in (33) be convertible. Traditionally, most multiobjective dynamic programming schemes adopt the backward version.

In the following we will give a new version of the principle of optimality for multiobjective dynamic programming, which is similar to the one adopted in single-objective control theory. The derivation is based on the assumption that the system given in (37) satisfies the conditions for backward separability and backward monotonicity. For other systems that satisfy forward separability and forward monotonicity, the results will be similar [6].

Theorem 3 (the principle of optimality). If the problem given in (37) satisfies the conditions of backward separability and backward monotonicity, then the principle of optimality holds when we adopt the multiobjective dynamic programming method; i.e., each noninferior control sequence has the property that whatever the initial state is, the existing control subsequence must constitute a noninferior policy with respect to this initial state.

Proof. Assume that $\{\tilde{u}(0), \tilde{u}(1), ..., \tilde{u}(T-1)\}$ is a control sequence and $\{\tilde{x}(0) = x(0), \tilde{x}(1), \tilde{x}(2), ..., \tilde{x}(T)\}$ is its corresponding state trajectory. If, at $\tilde{x}(t)$, $0 \le t \le T - 1$, the point $\left[f_1^t(\tilde{x}(t), \tilde{u}(t)) \,^\sigma\, f_1^{t+1}(\tilde{x}(t+1), \tilde{u}(t+1)) \,^\sigma ... \,^\sigma\, f_1^T(\tilde{x}(T)), \right.$
$\left. ..., f_k^t(\tilde{x}(t), \tilde{u}(t)) \,^\sigma\, f_k^{t+1}(\tilde{x}(t+1), \tilde{u}(t+1)) \,^\sigma\, ... \,^\sigma\, f_k^T(\tilde{x}(T)) \right]^T$ is not on the efficient frontier with respect to $\tilde{x}(t)$ as the initial point, then there exist a control subsequence $\{\hat{u}(t), \hat{u}(t+1), ..., \hat{u}(T-1)\}$ and a corresponding state subsequence $\{\hat{x}(t) = \tilde{x}(t), \hat{x}(t+1), ..., \hat{x}(T)\}$ such that

$$f_i^t(\hat{x}(t), \hat{u}(t)) \,^\sigma\, f_i^{t+1}(\hat{x}(t+1), \hat{u}(t+1)) \,^\sigma\, ... \,^\sigma\, f_i^T(\hat{x}(T))$$

$$\le f_i^t(\tilde{x}(t), \tilde{u}(t)) \,^\sigma\, f_i^{t+1}(\tilde{x}(t+1), \tilde{u}(t+1)) \,^\sigma\, ... \,^\sigma\, f_i^T(\tilde{x}(T)) \tag{45}$$

$$i = 1, 2, ..., k$$

and at least one strict inequality holds. Therefore, if we select the control sequence $\{\tilde{u}(0), \tilde{u}(1), ..., \tilde{u}(t-1), \hat{u}(t), \hat{u}(t+1), ..., \hat{u}(T-1)\}$, its corresponding state sequence is $\{x(0), \tilde{x}(1), \tilde{x}(2), ..., \tilde{x}(t), \hat{x}(t+1), \hat{x}(t+2), ..., \hat{x}(T)\}$. According to the backward monotonicity assumption, we have

$$f_i^0(x(0), \tilde{u}(0)) \,^\sigma\, f_i^1(\tilde{x}(1), \tilde{u}(1)) \,^\sigma ... \,^\sigma\, f_i^{t-1}(\tilde{x}(t-1), \tilde{u}(t-1))$$

$$\sigma \ f_i^t(\tilde{x}(t),\ \hat{u}(t))\ \sigma \ f_i^{t+1}(\hat{x}(t+1),\ \hat{u}(t+1))\ \sigma \ ...\ \sigma \ f_i^T(\hat{x}(T))$$

$$\leq f_i^0(x(0),\ \tilde{u}(0))\ \sigma \ f_i^1(\tilde{x}(1),\ \tilde{u}(1))\ \sigma \ ...\ \sigma \ f_i^T(\tilde{x}(T)),$$

$$i = 1, 2, ..., k, \tag{46}$$

and at least one strict inequality holds. Therefore, the control sequence $\{\tilde{u}(0),\ \tilde{u}(1),$ ..., $\tilde{u}(T-1)\}$ generates an inferior point. Q.E.D.

Theorem 3 can be seen as an extension of the work of Brown and Strauch [41], in which the same associative operation is used to combine the returns from successive stages. Such limitation is removed in our study. In our version of the principle of optimality, the operators do not have to be associative and they may vary from stage to stage.

B.   A RECURSIVE RELATIONSHIP IN
MULTIOBJECTIVE DYNAMIC PROGRAMMING

The principle of optimality stated in the above subsection gives us the basis for a new multiobjective dynamic programming method that uses the envelope approach. Recognizing the following fact is essential to understanding the applicability of the envelope approach to the multiobjective dynamic programming problem. At stage t, $0 \leq t \leq T - 2$, for given $x(t)$, adopting a different control $u(t)$ leads to a different state $x(t + 1)$ at stage $t + 1$. If the noninferior frontiers available at various $x(t + 1)$ are mapped back to the functional space at given $x(t)$, a family of objective curves (or surfaces or hypersurfaces) is formed. If the family is regular, then, based on Theorem 1, the envelope of this family represents the noninferior frontier at $x(t)$. The above claim may be stated more formally as follows. Let

$$E_i^t = f_i^t\ \sigma \ f_i^{t+1}\ \sigma ...\ \sigma \ f_i^T,\ \ i = 1, 2, ..., k \tag{47}$$

be the i-th accumulative objective function from $x(t)$, and assume that the noninferior frontier at various points $x(t + 1)$ is expressed by

$$E_1^{t+1*} = E_1^{t+1*}(x(t+1), \theta) \tag{48a}$$

$$E_2^{t+1^*} = E_2^{t+1^*}(x(t+1), \theta) \tag{48b}$$

$$\vdots$$

$$E_k^{t+1^*} = E_k^{t+1^*}(x(t+1), \theta), \tag{48c}$$

where θ is the parameter vector. Then, for a given $x(t)$, the family of objective curves (or surfaces, or hypersurfaces) is

$$E_1^t = f_1^t(x(t), u(t)) \, \overset{\sigma}{} \, E_1^{t+1^*}(H_t(x(t), u(t), t), \theta) \tag{49a}$$

$$E_2^t = f_2^t(x(t), u(t)) \, \overset{\sigma}{} \, E_2^{t+1^*}(H_t(x(t), u(t), t), \theta) \tag{49b}$$

$$\vdots$$

$$E_k^t = f_k^t(x(t), u(t)) \, \overset{\sigma}{} \, E_k^{t+1^*}(H_t(x(t), u(t), t), \theta). \tag{49c}$$

Here $u(t)$ is dealt with as a parameter vector of the family. If the family is regular, then, based on Theorem 1, finding the set of noninferior solutions for the given $x(t)$ is equivalent to finding the envelope of this family. And the envelope can be identified by solving the following equations:

$$\frac{\partial(E_2^t, E_3^t, ..., E_k^t)}{\partial(\theta_1, \theta_2, ..., \theta_{k-1})} \frac{\partial E_1^t}{\partial u(t)} - \frac{\partial(E_1^t, E_3^t, ..., E_k^t)}{\partial(\theta_1, \theta_2, ..., \theta_{k-1})} \frac{\partial E_2^t}{\partial u(t)} + ...$$

$$+ (-1)^{k-1} \frac{\partial(E_1^t, E_2^t, ..., E_{k-1}^t)}{\partial(\theta_1, \theta_2, ..., \theta_{k-1})} \frac{\partial E_k^t}{\partial u(t)} = 0. \tag{50}$$

If the conditions of the implicit function theorem are satisfied, we may express $u(t)$ as a function of θ and $x(t)$. Otherwise, or if it is too difficult to get an analytic solution, we will solve $u(t)$ for some fixed values of θ and $x(t)$. Then, a curve-fitting technique such as least squares can be used to determine $u^*(t)$ as a function of θ and $x(t)$. Substituting $u^*(t)$ back into (49) gives us the vector of cost-to-go at $x(t)$,

$$E_1^{t^*} = E_1^{t^*}(x(t), \theta) \tag{51a}$$

$$E_2^{t*} = E_2^{t*}(x(t), \theta) \tag{51b}$$

$$\vdots$$

$$E_k^{t*} = E_k^{t*}(x(t), \theta). \tag{51c}$$

This approach leads to a recurrence relation for solving the problem given in (37).

Algorithm 1. Multiobjective dynamic programming using the envelope approach. At stage T: For every given point $x(T)$, calculate the values of objective functions,

$$f_i^T = f_i^T(x(T)), \quad i = 1, 2, ..., k. \tag{52}$$

At stage $T - 1$: For every given point $x(T - 1)$, identify the noninferior frontier of the following problem either by the weighting method or the ε-constraint method:

$$\min_{u(T-1)} \begin{bmatrix} f_1^{T-1}(x(T-1), u(T-1)) & \circ & f_1^T(H_{T-1}(x(T-1), u(T-1), T-1)) \\ \vdots & & \\ f_k^{T-1}(x(T-1), u(T-1)) & \circ & f_k^T(H_{T-1}(x(T-1), u(T-1), T-1)) \end{bmatrix} \tag{53a}$$

$$\text{s.t. } g_{T-1}(x(T-1), u(T-1)) \le 0 \tag{53b}$$

and express the noninferior frontier in a parametric form

$$E_1^{T-1*} = E_1^{T-1*}(x(T-1), \theta) \tag{54a}$$

$$E_2^{T-1*} = E_2^{T-1*}(x(T-1), \theta) \tag{54b}$$

$$\vdots$$

$$E_k^{T-1*} = E_k^{T-1*}(x(T-1), \theta). \tag{54c}$$

Here θ may be either the weighting coefficient vector or the ε vector.

At stage t, $0 \le t \le T - 2$: For every given point $x(t)$, use (50) to identify the envelope of the family given in (49). Record only the noninferior part of the envelope.

The noninferior frontier at $x(0)$ corresponds to the set of noninferior solutions of the problem given in (37).

Example 3.

$$\min \left[\begin{array}{l} f_1 = x^2(0) + x^2(1) + \exp[x^2(1)][2x^2(2) + x^2(3)] \\ f_2 = u^2(0) + \exp[u^2(0)][u^2(1) + u^2(2)] \end{array} \right]$$

s.t. $x(3) = x(2) + u(2)$
      $x(2) = [1 + u(1)]x(1)$

      $x(1) = x(0)^{u(0)}$
      $x(0) = 15.$

Stage 3. For given $x(3)$

$E_1^3 = x^2(3)$

$E_2^3 = 0.$

Stage 2. For given $x(2)$, we have

$E_1^2 = 2x^2(2) + [x(2) + u(2)]^2$

$E_2^2 = u^2(2).$

Use the weighting method and form the Lagrangian

$L_2 = \theta\{2x^2(2) + [x(2) + u(2)]^2\} + (1 - \theta)u^2(2).$

We then get the solutions by solving $\partial L_2/\partial u(2) = 0$,

$u*(2) = -\theta x(2)$

$$E_1^{2*} = (3 - 2\theta + \theta^2)x^2(2)$$

$$E_2^{2*} = \theta^2 x^2(2).$$

Stage 1. For given $x(1)$, the family of noninferior frontiers is

$$E_1^1 = x^2(1) + \exp[x^2(1)](3 - 2\theta + \theta^2)[1 + u(1)]^2 x^2(1)$$

$$E_2^1 = u^2(1) + \theta^2[1 + u(1)]^2 x^2(1).$$

The envelope of this family can be identified by solving

$$\frac{\partial E_1^1}{\partial \theta} \frac{\partial E_2^1}{\partial u(1)} - \frac{\partial E_2^1}{\partial \theta} \frac{\partial E_1^1}{\partial u(1)} = 0.$$

In other words,

$$(-2 + 2\theta)\{2u(1) + 2\theta^2[1 + u(1)]x^2(1)\} - 4\theta(3 - 2\theta + \theta^2)[1 + u(1)]x^2(1) = 0.$$

Therefore, on the envelope, we have

$$u*(1) = \frac{-(3\theta - \theta^2)x^2(1)}{1 - \theta + (3\theta - \theta^2)x^2(1)}$$

$$E_1^{1*} = x^2(1) + (3 - 2\theta + \theta^2)\left(\frac{1 - \theta}{1 - \theta + (3\theta - \theta^2)x^2(1)}\right)^2 x^2(1)\exp[x^2(1)]$$

$$E_2^{1*} = \left(\frac{(3\theta - \theta^2)x^2(1)}{1 - \theta + (3\theta - \theta^2)x^2(1)}\right)^2 + \theta^2\left(\frac{1 - \theta}{1 - \theta + (3\theta - \theta^2)x^2(1)}\right)^2 x^2(1).$$

Stage 0. For given $x(0) = 15$, the family of noninferior frontiers is

$$E_1^0 = 225 + 225^{u(0)} + (3 - 2\theta + \theta^2)\left(\frac{1 - \theta}{1 - \theta + (3\theta - \theta^2)225^{u(0)}}\right)^2 225^{u(0)}$$

$$\times \exp(225^{u(0)})$$

$$E_2^0 = u^2(0) + \exp[u^2(0)]\left[\left(\frac{(3\theta - \theta^2)225^{u(0)}}{1 - \theta + (3\theta - \theta^2)225^{u(0)}}\right)^2\right.$$

$$\left. + \theta^2\left(\frac{1 - \theta}{1 - \theta + (3\theta - \theta^2)225^{u(0)}}\right)^2 225^{u(0)}\right]$$

The envelope of this family can be identified by solving

$$\frac{\partial E_2^0}{\partial \theta}\frac{\partial E_1^0}{\partial u(0)} - \frac{\partial E_1^0}{\partial \theta}\frac{\partial E_2^0}{\partial u(0)} = 0.$$

After some simplification, we have

$$\frac{2(1 - \theta)u(0)}{\exp[u^2(0)]} + \frac{\theta \ln 225 \cdot 225^{u(0)}}{\exp(225^{u(0)})}$$

$$+ \theta(1 - \theta)225^{u(0)}\{(\theta - 1)\ln 225[\theta - 3 - (\theta^2 - 2\theta + 3)225^{u(0)}]$$

$$+ 2u(0)\theta[(1 - \theta)^2 + (3 - \theta)^2 225^{u(0)}]\}/[1 - \theta + (3\theta - \theta^2)225^{u(0)}]^2 = 0.$$

For given θ, the value of $u(0)$ can be evaluated by GINO on the IBM-PC. Table I gives some noninferior solutions of the overall system.

TABLE I. A SAMPLE OF NONINFERIOR SOLUTIONS FOR EXAMPLE 3[a]

	1	2	3	4	5
θ	0	0.2	0.4	0.6	0.8
$u(0)$	0	-0.366942	-0.490894	-0.608804	-0.776224
$x(1)$	1	0.3702054	0.2646451	0.1923052	0.1222052
$u(1)$	0	-0.087538	-0.108256	-0.117491	-0.116155
$x(2)$	1	0.3377982	0.2359958	0.1697111	0.1080104
$u(2)$	0	-0.067560	-0.094398	-0.101827	-0.086408
$x(3)$	1	0.2702386	0.1415975	0.0678844	0.021602
f_1	234.15485	225.48255	225.21101	225.10154	225.03909
f_2	0	0.148636	0.2672288	0.4056605	0.6408089

[a]At stage 1 and stage 0, θ is no longer the weighting coefficient.

C.   COMPUTATIONAL PROCEDURE FOR MULTIOBJECTIVE DYNAMIC PROGRAMMING USING THE ENVELOPE APPROACH

As we already know, the recurrence relation of multiobjective dynamic programming can be obtained by finding the envelope of the family of objective curves (or surfaces, or hypersurfaces) which result from the efficient frontiers at the next stage and from the controls adopted at the present stage.

In most cases, it is difficult or impossible to get the analytic solutions for envelopes at each stage. Thus it is necessary to investigate the computational procedure for multiobjective dynamic programming using the envelope approach.

To make the computational procedure feasible, it is necessary to quantize the admissible state and control values into a finite number of levels. At each grid of state values, quantized controls are to be tried. Efficient solutions are identified by checking if the resulting point of the vector objective lies on the envelope. Interpolation will be required to get the values of the vector cost-to-go, $[E_1{}^t(x(t), \theta), \ldots, E_k{}^t(x(t), \theta)]^T$, if $x(t)$ does not fall exactly on a grid value.

In the following, Example 3 will be solved numerically, which shows the mechanism of the computational procedure.

Consider the problem

$$\min \begin{bmatrix} f_1 = x^2(0) + x^2(1) + \exp[x^2(1)][2x^2(2) + x^2(3)] \\ f_2 = u^2(0) + \exp[u^2(0)][u^2(1) + u^2(2)] \end{bmatrix}$$

s.t. $x(3) = x(2) + u(2)$
$\quad\quad x(2) = [1 + u(1)]x(1)$
$\quad\quad\quad\quad\quad u(0)$
$\quad\quad x(1) = x(0)$
$\quad\quad x(0) = 15.$

At stage 2, 21 noninferior solutions are calculated by the weighting method for each of 20 grid points of state $x(2)$.

At each grid point of $x(1)$, $\tilde{x}(1)$, for each value of grid points of $\theta, \tilde{\theta}$, the corresponding noninferior control $\tilde{u}(1)$ is searched as follows.

Step 1. The corresponding $\tilde{x}(2)$ is generated by the equation

$$\tilde{x}(2) = [1 + \tilde{u}(1)]\tilde{x}(1).$$

The two state grid points that are next to $\tilde{x}(2)$ are identified.

Step 2. Three points on the vector cost-to-go from $\tilde{x}(2)$ are obtained by the quadratic interpolation:

$$E_i^2(\tilde{x}(2), \theta) = E_i^2(\underline{x}(2), \theta)\frac{[\tilde{x}(2) - \hat{x}(2)][\tilde{x}(2) - \overline{x}(2)]}{[\underline{x}(2) - \hat{x}(2)][\underline{x}(2) - \overline{x}(2)]}$$

$$+ E_i^2(\hat{x}(2), \theta)\frac{[\tilde{x}(2) - \underline{x}(2)][\tilde{x}(2) - \overline{x}(2)]}{[\hat{x}(2) - \underline{x}(2)][\hat{x}(2) - \overline{x}(2)]}$$

$$+ E_i^2(\overline{x}(2), \theta)\frac{[\tilde{x}(2) - \underline{x}(2)][\tilde{x}(2) - \hat{x}(2)]}{[\overline{x}(2) - \underline{x}(2)][\overline{x}(2) - \hat{x}(2)]}$$

where $i = 1, 2$; $\theta = \underline{\theta}, \overline{\theta}, \overline{\theta}$ (here $\underline{\theta}$ and $\overline{\theta}$ are grid points, which are next to $\tilde{\theta}$); $\underline{x}(2)$, $\hat{x}(2)$, $\overline{x}(2)$ are three consecutive grid points; and either $\tilde{x}(2)\epsilon[\underline{x}(2), \hat{x}(2)]$ or $\tilde{x}(2)\epsilon$ $[\hat{x}(2), \overline{x}(2)]$.

Step 3. The partial derivatives, $\dfrac{\partial E_i^2(\tilde{x}(2), \tilde{\theta})}{\partial \theta}$, $i = 1, 2$, and

$\dfrac{\partial E_i^2(\tilde{x}(2), \tilde{\theta})}{\partial x(2)}$, $i = 1, 2$, are estimated by the following formulas. Recall:

$$\frac{d}{dx}\sum_{j=1}^{3}\prod_{\substack{i=1\\i\neq j}}^{3}\left(\frac{x-x_i}{x_j-x_i}\right)y_j = \sum_{j=1}^{3}\frac{2x-\displaystyle\sum_{i=1,i\neq j}^{3}x_i}{\displaystyle\prod_{\substack{i=1\\i\neq j}}^{3}(x_j-x_i)}y_j.$$

Thus, we have

$$\frac{\partial E_i^2(\tilde{x}(2),\tilde{\theta})}{\partial\theta} = E_i^2(\tilde{x}(2),\underline{\theta})\frac{\tilde{\theta}-\bar{\theta}}{(\underline{\theta}-\tilde{\theta})(\underline{\theta}-\bar{\theta})} + E_i^2(\tilde{x}(2),\tilde{\theta})\frac{2\tilde{\theta}-\underline{\theta}-\bar{\theta}}{(\tilde{\theta}-\underline{\theta})(\tilde{\theta}-\bar{\theta})}$$

$$+ E_i^2(\tilde{x}(2),\bar{\theta})\frac{\tilde{\theta}-\underline{\theta}}{(\bar{\theta}-\underline{\theta})(\bar{\theta}-\tilde{\theta})}, \quad i=1,2$$

$$\frac{\partial E_i^2(\tilde{x}(2),\tilde{\theta})}{\partial x(2)} = E_i^2(\underline{x}(2),\tilde{\theta})\frac{2\tilde{x}(2)-\hat{x}(2)-\bar{x}(2)}{[\underline{x}(2)-\hat{x}(2)][\underline{x}(2)-\bar{x}(2)]}$$

$$+ E_i^2(\hat{x}(2),\tilde{\theta})\frac{2\tilde{x}(2)-\underline{x}(2)-\bar{x}(2)}{[\hat{x}(2)-\underline{x}(2)][\hat{x}(2)-\bar{x}(2)]}$$

$$+ E_i^2(\bar{x}(2),\tilde{\theta})\frac{2\tilde{x}(2)-\underline{x}(2)-\hat{x}(2)}{[\bar{x}(2)-\underline{x}(2)][\bar{x}(2)-\hat{x}(2)]}, \quad i=1,2.$$

Step 4. The partial derivatives

$$\frac{\partial E_i^1(\tilde{x}(1),\tilde{\theta},u(1))}{\partial\theta} \text{ and } \frac{\partial E_i^1(\tilde{x}(1),\tilde{\theta},u(1))}{\partial u(1)}, \quad i=1,2,$$

are obtained as follows:

$$\frac{\partial E_1^1}{\partial \theta} = \exp [x^2(1)]\frac{\partial E_1^2}{\partial \theta}$$

$$\frac{\partial E_2^1}{\partial \theta} = \frac{\partial E_2^2}{\partial \theta}$$

$$\frac{\partial E_1^1}{\partial u(1)} = \exp [x^2(1)]\frac{\partial E_1^2}{\partial x(2)}x(1)$$

$$\frac{\partial E_2^1}{\partial u(1)} = 2u(1) + \frac{\partial E_2^2}{\partial x(2)}x(1).$$

Step 5. Calculate the value of

$$R = \frac{\partial E_2^1}{\partial \theta}\frac{\partial E_1^1}{\partial u(1)} - \frac{\partial E_1^1}{\partial \theta}\frac{\partial E_2^1}{\partial u(1)}.$$

If $R \neq 0$, try the next grid of $u(1)$ (and go back to Step 1). In most cases, the noninferior control $u(1)$, which satisfies $R = 0$, will be calculated by the linear interpolation of two adjacent grid points of $u(1)$.

At $x(0) = 15$, for each value of grid points of θ, $\tilde{\theta}$, the corresponding noninferior control $\tilde{u}(0)$ is searched as follows.

Step 1. The corresponding $\tilde{x}(1)$ is generated by the equation

$$\tilde{x}(1) = x(0)^{\tilde{u}(0)}.$$

The two state grid points that are next to $\tilde{x}(1)$ are identified.

Step 2. Three points on the vector cost-to-go from $\tilde{x}(1)$ are obtained in the same manner as in Stage 1.

Step 3. The partial derivatives,

$$\frac{\partial E_i^1(\tilde{x}(1), \tilde{\theta})}{\partial \theta}, i = 1, 2, \text{ and } \frac{\partial E_i^1(\tilde{x}(1), \tilde{\theta})}{\partial x(1)}, i = 1, 2,$$

are estimated in the same manner as in Stage 1.

Step 4. The partial derivatives,

$$\frac{\partial E_i^0(x(0), \tilde{\theta}, u(0))}{\partial \theta} \quad \text{and} \quad \frac{\partial E_i^0(x(0), \tilde{\theta}, u(0))}{\partial u(0)}, \quad i = 1, 2,$$

are obtained as follows:

$$\frac{\partial E_1^0}{\partial \theta} = \frac{\partial E_1^1}{\partial \theta}$$

$$\frac{\partial E_2^0}{\partial \theta} = \exp[u^2(0)]\frac{\partial E_2^1}{\partial \theta}$$

$$\frac{\partial E_1^0}{\partial u(0)} = \frac{\partial E_1^1}{\partial x(1)}x(0)^{u(0)} \ln x(0)$$

$$\frac{\partial E_2^0}{\partial u(0)} = 2u(0) + 2u(0)\exp[u^2(0)]E_2^1(\tilde{x}(1), \tilde{\theta})$$

$$+ \exp[u^2(0)]\frac{\partial E_2^1}{\partial x(1)}x(0)^{u(0)} \ln x(0).$$

Step 5. The value of

$$R = \frac{\partial E_2^0}{\partial \theta}\frac{\partial E_1^0}{\partial u(0)} - \frac{\partial E_1^0}{\partial \theta}\frac{\partial E_2^0}{\partial u(0)}$$

is calculated. The noninferior control $u(0)$, which satisfies $R = 0$, is reached in the same manner as in Stage 1.

Table II gives four noninferior solutions on the envelope at $x(0) = 15$. For detailed computational results, see Ref. [5]. Compared with the analytical results in Example 3, we can conclude that this numerical approach gives a very good approximation.

TABLE II. A SAMPLE OF NONINFERIOR SOLUTIONS FOR EXAMPLE 3
BY THE NUMERICAL METHOD

	1	2	3	4
θ	0.2	0.4	0.6	0.8
u(0)	-0.367450	-0.492279	-0.609770	-0.790158
f_1	225.4814	225.2097	225.1012	225.0368
f_2	0.1489596	0.2683672	0.4066228	0.6593875

D.   ANALYTICAL RESULTS OF MULTIOBJECTIVE
      DYNAMIC PROGRAMMING FOR
      LINEAR-QUADRATIC PROBLEMS

In this section we consider the discrete system described by the state
equation

$$x(t + 1) = A(t)x(t) + B(t)u(t), \tag{55}$$

where $x \in R^n$ is the state vector, $u \in R^p$ is the control vector, and the states and
controls are not constrained by any boundaries. The problem is to find the set of
noninferior control policies $u^*(x(t), t; \theta)$ that minimizes the vector quadratic performance measure

$$F = \begin{bmatrix} f_1 = \frac{1}{2}x^T(N)H_1^N x(N) + \sum_{t=0}^{N-1} H_1^t(x(t), u(t)) \\ \vdots \\ f_k = \frac{1}{2}x^T(N)H_k^N x(N) + \sum_{t=0}^{N-1} H_k^t(x(t), u(t)) \end{bmatrix} \tag{56}$$

where

$$H_i^t(x(t), u(t)) = \frac{1}{2}x^T(t)Q_i^t x(t) + \frac{1}{2}u^T(t)R_i^t u(t),$$

$$i = 1, 2, \ldots, k; \, t = 0, 1, \ldots, N - 1. \tag{57}$$

H_i^N ($i = 1, 2, ..., k$) and Q_i^t ($i = 1, 2, ..., k$; $t = 0, 1, ..., N - 1$) are real symmetric positive semidefinite $n \times n$ matrices. R_i^t ($i = 1, 2, ..., k$; $t = 0, 1, ..., N - 1$) is a real symmetric positive definite $p \times p$ matrix.

The approach we will derive is to solve the recursive envelope equation (50) analytically. We begin by defining

$$E_1^N = \frac{1}{2} x^T(N) H_1^N x(N) \tag{58a}$$

$$\vdots$$

$$E_k^N = \frac{1}{2} x^T(N) H_k^N x(N). \tag{58b}$$

The cost over the final interval is given by

$$E_1^{N-1} = H_1^{N-1}(x(N-1), u(N-1)) + \frac{1}{2}[A(N-1)x(N-1)$$

$$+ B(N-1)u(N-1)]^T H_1^N [A(N-1)x(N-1) + B(N-1)u(N-1)] \tag{59a}$$

$$\vdots$$

$$E_k^{N-1} = H_k^{N-1}(x(N-1), u(N-1)) + \frac{1}{2}[A(N-1)x(N-1)$$

$$+ B(N-1)u(N-1)]^T H_k^N [A(N-1)x(N-1) + B(N-1)u(N-1)]. \tag{59b}$$

To minimize this vector cost function, we adopt the weighting method and minimize the following weighting objective function:

$$L_{N-1} = \sum_{i=1}^{k} \theta_i \Big\{ H_i^{N-1}(x(N-1), u(N-1)) + \frac{1}{2}[A(N-1)x(N-1)$$

$$+ B(N-1)u(N-1)]^T H_i^N [A(N-1)x(N-1) + B(N-1)u(N-1)] \Big\}. \tag{60}$$

Taking the partial derivative with respect to $u(N-1)$, we get the optimal control $u^*(N-1; \theta)$ for given θ,

$$\sum_{i=1}^{k} \theta_i \Big\{ R_i^{N-1} u(N-1) + B^T(N-1)H_i^N[A(N-1)x(N-1)$$

$$+ B(N-1)u(N-1)] \Big\} = 0. \tag{61}$$

In other words,

$$u^*(N-1; \theta) = -\left[\sum_{i=1}^{k} \theta_i R_i^{N-1} + B^T(N-1)\left(\sum_{i=1}^{k} \theta_i H_i^N \right) B(N-1) \right]^{-1}$$

$$\times B^T(N-1)\left(\sum_{i=1}^{k} \theta_i H_i^N \right) A(N-1)x(N-1)$$

$$= -K_{N-1}(\theta)x(N-1), \tag{62}$$

where

$$K_{N-1}(\theta) = \left[\sum_{i=1}^{k} \theta_i R_i^{N-1} + B^T(N-1)\left(\sum_{i=1}^{k} \theta_i H_i^N \right) B(N-1) \right]^{-1}$$

$$\times B^T(N-1)\left(\sum_{i=1}^{k} \theta_i H_i^N \right) A(N-1). \tag{63}$$

Substituting the expression for $u^*(N-1; \theta)$ into E_i^{N-1}, $i = 1, 2, \ldots, k$, gives us the vector of cost-to-go at $x(N-1)$,

$$E_1^{N-1*} = \frac{1}{2}x^T(N-1)P_1^{N-1}(\theta)x(N-1) \tag{64a}$$

$$\vdots$$

$$E_k^{N-1*} = \frac{1}{2}x^T(N-1)P_k^{N-1}(\theta)x(N-1), \tag{64b}$$

where

$$P_i^{N-1}(\theta) = Q_i^{N-1} + K_{N-1}^T(\theta)R_i^{N-1}K_{N-1}(\theta)$$

$$+ [A(N-1) - B(N-1)K_{N-1}(\theta)]^T H_i^N [A(N-1) - B(N-1)K_{N-1}(\theta)],$$

$$i = 1, 2, ..., k. \tag{65}$$

Assume that at stage t, $t = 1, 2, ..., N - 1$, the vector of cost-to-go at $x(t)$ is

$$E_1^{t*} = \frac{1}{2}x^T(t)P_1^t(\theta)x(t) \tag{66a}$$

$$\vdots$$

$$E_k^{t*} = \frac{1}{2}x^T(t)P_k^t(\theta)x(t). \tag{66b}$$

Then, at $x(t-1)$, the family of noninferior frontiers is expressed as

$$E_1^{t-1} = H_1^{t-1}(x(t-1), u(t-1)) + \frac{1}{2}[A(t-1)x(t-1)$$

$$+ B(t-1)u(t-1)]^T P_1^t(\theta)[A(t-1)x(t-1) + B(t-1)u(t-1)] \tag{67a}$$

$$\vdots$$

$$E_k^{t-1} = H_k^{t-1}(x(t-1), u(t-1)) + \frac{1}{2}[A(t-1)x(t-1)$$

$$+ B(t-1)u(t-1)]^T P_k^t(\theta)[A(t-1)x(t-1) + B(t-1)u(t-1)]. \tag{67b}$$

According to Theorem 2, the envelope of this family can be identified by solving

$$\theta_1 \frac{\partial E_1^{t-1}}{\partial u(t-1)} + \theta_2 \frac{\partial E_2^{t-1}}{\partial u(t-1)} + \ldots + \theta_k \frac{\partial E_k^{t-1}}{\partial u(t-1)} = 0, \tag{68}$$

i.e.,

$$\sum_{i=1}^{k} \theta_i \left\{ R_i^{t-1} u(t-1) + B^T(t-1) P_i^t(\theta) [A(t-1)x(t-1) \right.$$

$$\left. + B(t-1)u(t-1)] \right\} = 0. \tag{69}$$

Thus, the optimal control $u^*(t-1; \theta)$ for given θ is

$$u^*(t-1; \theta) = -\left[\sum_{i=1}^{k} \theta_i R_i^{t-1} + B^T(t-1) \left(\sum_{i=1}^{k} \theta_i P_i^t(\theta) \right) B(t-1) \right]^{-1}$$

$$\times B^T(t-1) \left(\sum_{i=1}^{k} \theta_i P_i^t(\theta) \right) A(t-1)x(t-1)$$

$$= -K_{t-1}(\theta)x(t-1), \tag{70}$$

where

$$K_{t-1}(\theta) = \left[\sum_{i=1}^{k} \theta_i R_i^{t-1} + B^T(t-1) \left(\sum_{i=1}^{k} \theta_i P_i^t(\theta) \right) B(t-1) \right]^{-1}$$

$$\times B^T(t-1) \left(\sum_{i=1}^{k} \theta_i P_i^t(\theta) \right) A(t-1). \tag{71}$$

Substituting the expression for $u^*(t-1; \theta)$ into E_i^{t-1}, $i = 1, 2, \ldots, k$, gives us the vector of cost-to-go at $x(t-1)$,

$$E_1^{t-1*} = \frac{1}{2}x^T(t-1)P_1^{t-1}(\theta)x(t-1) \tag{72a}$$

$$\vdots$$

$$E_k^{t-1*} = \frac{1}{2}x^T(t-1)P_k^{t-1}(\theta)x(t-1), \tag{72b}$$

where

$$P_i^{t-1}(\theta) = Q_i^{t-1} + K_{t-1}^T(\theta)R_i^{t-1}K_{t-1}(\theta)$$

$$+ [A(t-1) - B(t-1)K_{t-1}(\theta)]^T P_i^t(\theta)[A(t-1) - B(t-1)K_{t-1}(\theta)]$$

$$i = 1, 2, ..., k. \tag{73}$$

By solving an N-stage process recursively, we can get the vector cost-to-go with initial state x(0) as follows:

$$E_1^{0*} = \frac{1}{2}x^T(0)P_1^0(\theta)x(0) \tag{74a}$$

$$\vdots$$

$$E_k^{0*} = \frac{1}{2}x^T(0)P_k^0(\theta)x(0). \tag{74b}$$

IV.   HIERARCHICAL GENERATING METHODS

A.   GENERAL PRINCIPLES FOR
HIERARCHICAL GENERATING METHODS

One basic task in dealing with optimization problems for large-scale multiobjective systems is generating the set of noninferior solutions. Hierarchical generating methods are defined here to be methods that find the set of noninferior solutions of a large-scale multiobjective system by using decomposition and coordination.

The idea of decomposition was first treated theoretically in mathematical programming by Dantzig and Wolfe [51], who dealt with large linear programming problems possessing special structures. Motivated by the salient hierarchical structure of organizations and certain areas of control of complex industrial systems, Mesarovic, Lefkowitz, and their colleagues at the Systems Research Center of Case Western Reserve University, starting about 1961, conducted theoretical investigations in axiomatizing the decoupled approach that is termed the multilevel or hierarchical approach. A detailed exposition of these first and fundamental developments is found in the classic book by Mesarovic *et al.* [52], which presents a discussion of coordination principles such as the interaction prediction principle, the interaction balance principle, and the interaction estimation principle. Three basic decomposition-coordination schemes – the feasible method, the nonfeasible method, and the contraction mapping method – have been reported by Brosilow *et al.* [53], Lasdon and Schoeffler [54], and Takahara [55], respectively. During the past two decades the development of hierarchical systems theory has grown by leaps and bounds. Detailed survey papers in this area are presented by Mahmoud [56], Singh [57], and Nachane [58]. The hierarchical multilevel approach has been successful primarily in social systems [59] and water resources systems [60].

The purpose of this section is to extend hierarchical single-objective optimization methods to hierarchical generating methods for the multiobjective case. Some general principles for hierarchical generating methods will first be postulated. These principles will provide guidance in synthesizing structures for two versions of hierarchical generating methods, which will then be developed.

1. General Problem Formulation

Suppose an overall system and N interacting subsystems are given for a two-level system. The overall system is described as follows:

overall process: $P: U \rightarrow X$ (75)

vector overall objective: $G: U \times X \rightarrow F,$ (76)

where U is the set of control vectors, X the set of output vectors, and F the set of k-dimensional vector objective functions. The sets U, X, and F are abstract sets with F having the semiorder of their components in functional space. Let g be defined on U by the equation

$g(u) = G[u, P(u)].$ (77)

The overall control problem D is to find the subset of U which generates the set $\text{Ext} [F|R_+^k]$.

Let $U = U_1 \times U_2 \times ... \times U_N$ and $X = X_1 \times X_2 \times ... \times X_N$. For each i = 1, 2, ..., N, let there be given the subsystem which is described as follows:

subprocess: $P_i: U_i \times Z_i \rightarrow X_i$ (78)

vector subobjective: $G_i: U_i \times Z_i \times X_i \rightarrow F,$ (79)

where Z_i is the set of interaction vector inputs which are generated by the following mapping:

interaction input: $H_i: X \rightarrow Z_i.$ (80)

Let g_i be defined on $U_i \times Z_i$ by the equation

$$g_i(u_i, z_i) = G_i[u_i, z_i, P_i(u_i, z_i)].$$ (81)

2.   General Principles for Hierarchical Generating Methods

Hierarchical generating methods involve solving a global problem, D, by solving a number of subproblems $D_i(\alpha)$ which are parametrized with respect to coordination variable α. The first step in hierarchical generating methods is to define the subproblems, $D_i(\alpha)$. The following two types of a decomposition-coordination scheme appear in parallel with those used in the scalar objective case [52].

Type I. Model coordination. Let $\alpha = (\alpha_1, \alpha_2, ..., \alpha_n)$ be given in $X = X_1 \times X_2 \times ... \times X_n$ as the prediction of the subsystems' outputs. Then a parametrized overall problem $D(\alpha)$ may decompose into N separate subproblems, $D_i(\alpha)$, $i = 1, 2, ..., N$. For each α in X, the infimal control problem $D_i(\alpha)$ is to find the subset of U_i which generates the set Ext $[F_i(\alpha)|R_+^k]$, where

$$F_i(\alpha) = \left\{ G_i[u_i, z_i, \alpha_i] \mid (u_i, z_i) \in S_i(\alpha) \right\}$$ (82)

$$S_i(\alpha) = \left\{ (u_i, z_i) \mid z_i = H_i(\alpha); P_i(u_i, z_i) = \alpha_i \right\}.$$ (83)

Type II. Goal coordination. Let B be a given set such that each β in B specifies a parametrized overall problem $D(\beta)$ which may decompose into N separate subproblems, $D_i(\beta)$, $i = 1, 2, ..., N$. For each β in B, a modified performance function $G_{i\beta}: U_i \times Z_i \times X_i \rightarrow F$ can be specified. Thus, the infimal control problem $D_i(\beta)$ is to find the subset of $U_i \times Z_i \times X_i$ which generates the set Ext $[F_i(\beta)|R_+^k]$, where

$$F_i(\beta) = \left\{ G_{i\beta}[u_i, z_i, x_i] \mid (u_i, z_i, x_i) \in S_i \right\} \tag{84}$$

$$S_i = \left\{ (u_i, z_i, x_i) \mid P_i(u_i, z_i) = x_i \right\}. \tag{85}$$

Vector optimization is over both sets U_i and Z_i. The interaction inputs, z_i, $i = 1$, $2, ..., N$, are treated as free variables.

Having generated the solution sets for each infimal problem, $D_i(\alpha)$ [or $D_i(\beta)$], $i = 1, 2, ..., N$, the second step that immediately arises in hierarchical generating methods is to map the local solutions sets to an overall parametrized problem solution set, i.e., to construct a map T such that

$$T: \text{Ext}\,[F_1(\gamma) \mid R_+^k] \times \text{Ext}\,[F_2(\gamma) \mid R_+^k] \times ... \times \text{Ext}\,[F_N(\gamma) \mid R_+^k]$$

$$\rightarrow \text{Ext}\,[F(\gamma) \mid R_+^k], \tag{86}$$

where $\gamma = \alpha, \beta$, and Ext $[F(\gamma)|R_+^k]$ is the solution set of problem $D(\gamma)$, $\gamma = \alpha, \beta$.

Remark. The domain of T is a proper subset of Ext $[F_1(\gamma)|R_+^k] \times ... \times$ Ext $[F_N(\gamma)|R_+^k]$. In other words, not every combination of local solutions constitutes a noninferior solution of the corresponding overall parametrized problem.

For different values of the parameter γ, $\gamma = \alpha, \beta$, we may get a family of Ext $[F(\gamma)|R_+^k]$'s which are solution sets for parametrized overall problems. The third step in hierarchical generating methods is to attain the solution set, Ext $[F|R_+^k]$, of the overall problem D from the parametrized solution family of Ext $[F(\gamma)|R_+^k]$'s, i.e., to identify Ext $[F|R_+^k]$ among the elements of $\cup$ Ext $[F(\gamma)|R_+^k]$. Based on Theorem 1, the envelope approach is suitable for dealing with this task.

B.   A FEASIBLE VERSION OF
     HIERARCHICAL GENERATING METHODS

1.   Problem Statement

Let us consider a system consisting of N intercoupled subsystems. In each subsystem, $i = 1, 2, ..., N$, let x_i be the output vector of subsystem i, $x_i \in$

R^{n_i}; let u_i be the control vector of subsystem i, $u_i \in R^{p_i}$; and let z_i be the interaction input vector of subsystem i, $z_i \in R^{m_i}$.

The subsystem is completely described by giving its outputs as functions of its control and interaction input:

$$x_i = H_i(u_i, z_i), \quad i = 1, 2, ..., N, \tag{87}$$

where the function H_i, $i = 1, 2, ..., N$, is differentiable with respect to u_i and z_i.

A model for the overall system is obtained by adding to (87) a set of relations describing how the subsystems are interconnected:

$$z_i = C_i(x_1, x_2, ..., x_N), \quad i = 1, 2, ..., N, \tag{88}$$

where the function C_i, $i = 1, 2, ..., N$, is differentiable with respect to x_j, $j = 1, 2, ..., N$.

This nonlinear model (87) with a nonlinear coupling, (88), among the subsystems covers a general class of systems. In addition, the assumption of nonlinear coupling gives us the flexibility to define the subsystem and enables us to do a coordinate transformation on the input-output relationship for some subsystems in order to simplify the treatment of the problem.

The system's multiobjective function, which is what we want to minimize, is assumed to be of the additively separable form:

$$f = \begin{bmatrix} f_1 = \displaystyle\sum_{i=1}^{N} f_1^i(x_i, u_i, z_i) \\ f_2 = \displaystyle\sum_{i=1}^{N} f_2^i(x_i, u_i, z_i) \\ \vdots \\ f_k = \displaystyle\sum_{i=1}^{N} f_k^i(x_i, u_i, z_i) \end{bmatrix} \tag{89}$$

The following assumption is made in this multiobjective optimization model: for each subsystem p_i, the dimension of control u_i is greater than or equal to n_i, the dimension of x_i.

2. A Feasible Decomposition Theorem

In a case where the system is large, it may be difficult to tackle directly, in a global way, the nonlinear multiobjective optimization problem given by (87)–(89). A way to avoid such difficulties may be found among the hierarchical generating methods that solve the problem of optimization for large-scale multiobjective systems by decomposition and coordination.

If we temporarily fix the values of x_i, $i = 1, 2, \ldots, N$, we can decompose the large-scale multiobjective optimization problem given in (87)–(89) into the following N multiobjective subproblems:

$$\min \begin{bmatrix} f_1^i(x_i, u_i, z_i) \\ f_2^i(x_i, u_i, z_i) \\ \vdots \\ f_k^i(x_i, u_i, z_i) \end{bmatrix} \tag{90a}$$

$$\text{s.t. } x_i = H_i(u_i, z_i) \tag{90b}$$

$$z_i = C_i(x_1, x_2, \ldots, x_N). \tag{90c}$$

In this feasible decomposition scheme, at each subsystem the criteria are not changed; however, the output vector x_i is fixed, as is the interaction input z_i, through (88). We call x_i, $i = 1, 2, \ldots, N$, the coordination variables.

For different coordination variables, we get a family of noninferior frontiers with parameters x in the functional space. We will prove in the following that the envelope of this family gives us all the noninferior solutions of the primal problem outlined in (87)–(89).

Theorem 4. The feasible decomposition theorem

$$\text{Ex}\left[F(S) | \mathbb{R}_+^k \right] = \text{Ext}\left[\left\{ \bigcup_{x \in X} \text{Ext}[f(S(x)) | \mathbb{R}_+^k] \right\} | \mathbb{R}_+^k \right], \tag{91}$$

where

$$x = \left[x_1^T, x_2^T, \ldots, x_N^T \right]^T, \; u = \left[u_1^T, u_2^T, \ldots, u_N^T \right]^T, \; z = \left[z_1^T, z_2^T, \ldots, z_N^T \right]^T;$$

$$S = \left\{ (x, u, z) \mid x_i = H_i, z_i = C_i, i = 1, 2, ..., N \right\};$$

$$F(S) = \left\{ f(x, u, z) \mid (x, u, z) \in S \right\};$$

$$X = \left\{ x \mid \text{there exists } u \text{ such that } (x, u, z) \in S \right\};$$

$$S(x) = \left\{ (x, u, z) \mid (x, u, z) \in S, x \text{ is fixed and } x \in X \right\}; \text{ and}$$

$$f(S(x)) = \left\{ f(x, u, z) \mid (x, u, z) \in S(x) \right\}.$$

Proof. Necessity: Assume $f(\hat{x}, \hat{u}, \hat{z}) \in \text{Ext}[F(S) \mid R_+^k]$. We know $\hat{x} \in X$ and $f(\hat{x}, \hat{u}, \hat{z}) \in \text{Ext}[f(S(\hat{x})) \mid R_+^k]$. Furthermore, $f(\hat{x}, \hat{u}, \hat{z})$ must belong to $\text{Ext}[\{ \cup \text{Ext}[f(S(x)) \mid R_+^k]\} \mid R_+^k]$; otherwise, it will lead to a contradiction of the assumption.

Proof. Sufficiency: Assume $f(\hat{x}, \hat{u}, \hat{z}) \in \text{Ext}\left[\left\{ \cup \text{Ext}[f(S(x)) \mid R_+^k]\right\} \mid R_+^k \right]$. If $f(\hat{x}, \hat{u}, \hat{z}) \notin \text{Ext}[F(S) \mid R_+^k]$, then there exists $(\tilde{x}, \tilde{u}, \tilde{x}) \in S$ such that $f(\hat{x}, \hat{u}, \hat{z}) \in f(\tilde{x}, \tilde{u}, \tilde{z}) + R_+^k$. If $f(\tilde{x}, \tilde{u}, \tilde{z}) \in \text{Ext}[f(S(\tilde{x})) \mid R_+^k]$, this leads to a contradiction of the assumption. If $f(\tilde{x}, \tilde{u}, \tilde{z}) \notin \text{Ext}[f(S(\tilde{x})) \mid R_+^k]$, then there exists $(\bar{x}, \bar{u}, \bar{z}) \in S(\tilde{x})$ such that $f(\bar{x}, \bar{u}, \bar{z}) \in \text{Ext}[f(S(\tilde{x})) \mid R_+^k]$ and $f(\bar{x}, \bar{u}, \bar{z}) \in f(\tilde{x}, \tilde{u}, \tilde{z}) + R_+^k$. Thus we have $f(\hat{x}, \hat{u}, \hat{z}) \in f(\bar{x}, \bar{u}, \bar{z}) + R_+^k$, which is a contradiction. Q.E.D.

It is clear to conclude from Theorem 4 that large-scale nonlinear multiobjective optimization problems may be solved by multilevel methods. At the lower level, the inner multiobjective optimization of (91), $\text{Ext}[f(S(x)) \mid R_+^k]$, is dealt with, that is, each subsystem solves the problem given in (90) for a fixed value of x. At the upper level, if the family is regular, then, based on Theorem 1, the coordination may be accomplished by the envelope approach, which gives us the set of noninferior solutions of the primal overall system, that is, $\text{Ext}[F(S) \mid R_+^k]$.

3.   Feasible Decomposition and Envelope Coordination

We do not make an assumption of the convexity for the problem given in (87)–(89), and the weighting approach is not appropriate for some nonconvex cases, due to the duality gap [33]. Because of these considerations, we adopt the ε-constraint approach [38] to deal with those multiobjective optimization problems that may be nonconvex.

The l-th-objective ε-constraint formulation for the problem in (87)–(89) with a fixed value $\overline{x}$ is defined for some $\varepsilon = [\varepsilon_1, ..., \varepsilon_{l-1}, \varepsilon_{l+1}, ..., \varepsilon_k]^T$:

$$P_l(\varepsilon; \overline{x}): \quad \min f_l = \sum_{i=1}^{N} f_l^i(\overline{x}_i, u_i, z_i) \tag{92a}$$

$$\text{s.t.} \quad f_j = \sum_{i=1}^{N} f_j^i(\overline{x}_i, u_i, z_i) \le \varepsilon_j, \ j = 1, ..., k, \ j \ne l \tag{92b}$$

$$\overline{x}_i = H_i(u_i, z_i), \ i = 1, 2, ..., N \tag{92c}$$

$$z_i = C_i(\overline{x}_1, \overline{x}_2, ..., \overline{x}_N), \ i = 1, 2, ..., N. \tag{92d}$$

For a given point $[\overline{x}^T, u^{*T}, z^T]^T$, we use the symbol $P_l(\varepsilon^*; \overline{x})$ to represent the problem $P_l(\varepsilon; \overline{x})$, where $\varepsilon_j = \varepsilon_j^* = f_j(\overline{x}, u^*, z^*), j = 1, ..., k, j \ne l$. It follows from Theorem 4.2 in Ref. [33] that if $[\overline{x}^T, u^{*T}, z^{*T}]^T$ is the unique solution of $P_l(\varepsilon^*; \overline{x})$, then $[\overline{x}^T, u^{*T}, z^{*T}]^T$ is a noninferior solution of the problem in (87)–(89) with a fixed value $\overline{x}$.

Similarly, the l-th-objective ε-constraint formulation for subsystem i, (90), with a fixed $\overline{x}$ is defined for some $\varepsilon^i = [\varepsilon_1^i, ..., \varepsilon_{l-1}^i, \varepsilon_{l+1}^i, ..., \varepsilon_k^i]^T$,

$$P_l^i(\varepsilon^i, \overline{x}): \quad \min f_l^i(\overline{x}_i, u_i, z_i) \tag{93a}$$

$$\text{s.t.} \quad f_j^i(\overline{x}_i, u_i, z_i) \le \varepsilon_j^i, \ j = 1, ..., k, \ j \ne l \tag{93b}$$

$$\overline{x}_i = H_i(u_i, z_i) \tag{93c}$$

$$z_i = C_i(\overline{x}_1, \overline{x}_2, ..., \overline{x}_N).$$ (93d)

For a given point $[\overline{x}_i^T, u_i^{*T}, z_i^{*T}]^T$, we use the symbol $P_l^i(\varepsilon^{i*}; \overline{x})$ to represent the problem $P_l^i(\varepsilon^i; \overline{x})$, where $\varepsilon_j^i = \varepsilon_j^{i*} = f_j^i(\overline{x}_i, u_i^*, z_i^*)$, $j = 1, ..., k, j \neq l$. And we know that if $[\overline{x}_i^T, u_i^{*T}, z_i^{*T}]^T$ is the unique solution of $P_l^i(\varepsilon^{i*}; \overline{x})$, then $[\overline{x}_i^T, u_i^{*T}, z_i^{*T}]^T$ is a noninferior solution of the problem in (90) with a fixed value $\overline{x}$.

In the following, we are going to investigate the relationship between the noninferior solutions of the problem given in (87)–(89) with a fixed value $\overline{x}$ and the noninferior solutions of N subsystems, which are expressed by the problem in (90) with the fixed value $\overline{x}$.

Theorem 5. Assume $[\overline{x}_i^T, u_i^{*T}, z_i^{*T}]^T$ is the unique solution of $P_l^i(\varepsilon^i; \overline{x})$ and is a regular point, $i = 1, 2, ..., N$. If $[\overline{x}_1^T, u_1^{*T}, z_1^{*T}; \overline{x}_2^T, u_2^{*T}, z_2^{*T}; ...; \overline{x}_N^T, u_N^{*T}, z_N^{*T}]^T$ solves problem $P_l(\varepsilon^*; \overline{x})$, where $\varepsilon^* = \Sigma_{i=1}^N \varepsilon^{i*}$, then we have

$$\lambda_{lj}^1(\varepsilon^{1*}) = \lambda_{lj}^2(\varepsilon^{2*}) = ... = \lambda_{lj}^N(\varepsilon^{N*}), \quad j = 1, ..., k, j \neq l,$$ (94)

where λ_{lj}^i is the optimal Kuhn–Tucker multiplier of problem $P_l^i(\varepsilon^{i*}; \overline{x})$ with respect to the j-th ε constraint.

Remark. 1) The assumption of regularity guarantees the existence of the Kuhn–Tucker multipliers.

2) The assumption of uniqueness guarantees that the l-th-objective ε-constraint formulation for each subsystem generates a noninferior solution of the problem given in (90).

3) To assure that $[\overline{x}_i^T, u_i^{*T}, z_i^{*T}]^T$ is a regular point of $P_l^i(\varepsilon^{i*}; \overline{x})$, the condition $p_i \geq n_i + (k - 1)$ must be satisfied.

Proof. Introduce variables ε_j^i, $i = 1, ..., N$; $j = 1, ..., k, j \neq l$, and rewrite $P_l(\varepsilon^*; \overline{x})$ in (92) as follows:

$$\min f_l = \sum_{i=1}^N f_l^i(\overline{x}_i, u_i, z_i)$$ (95a)

$$\text{s.t. } f_j^i(\overline{x}_i, u_i, z_i) \leq \varepsilon_j^i, \quad j = 1, ..., k, j \neq l; i = 1, 2, ..., N$$ (95b)

$$\sum_{i=1}^N \varepsilon_j^i = \sum_{i=1}^N \varepsilon_j^{i*} = \varepsilon_j^*, \quad j = 1, ..., k, j \neq l$$ (95c)

$$\bar{x}_i = H_i(u_i, z_i), \quad i = 1, 2, ..., N \tag{95d}$$

$$z_i = C_i(\bar{x}_1, \bar{x}_2, ..., \bar{x}_N), \quad i = 1, 2, ..., N. \tag{95e}$$

Form the Lagrangian of the problem in (95):

$$L = \sum_{i=1}^{N} f_l^i(\bar{x}_i, u_i, z_i) + \sum_{i=1}^{N} \sum_{\substack{j=1 \\ j \neq l}}^{k} \lambda_{lj}^i \left[f_j^i(\bar{x}_i, u_i, z_i) - \varepsilon_j^i \right]$$

$$+ \sum_{\substack{j=1 \\ j \neq l}}^{k} \lambda_j \left(\sum_{i=1}^{N} \varepsilon_j^i - \varepsilon_j^* \right) + \sum_{i=1}^{N} \mu_i^T \left[\bar{x}_i - H_i(u_i, z_i) \right]$$

$$+ \sum_{i=1}^{N} \sigma_i^T \left[z_i - C_i(\bar{x}_1, \bar{x}_2, ..., \bar{x}_N) \right], \tag{96}$$

where λ_{lj}^i, $i = 1, ..., N$, $j = 1, ..., k$, $j \neq l$, are Kuhn–Tucker multipliers; and λ_j ($j = 1, ..., k$, $j \neq l$), μ_i ($i = 1, ..., N$), and σ_i ($i = 1, ..., N$) are Lagrangian multipliers. We may get the first-order necessary conditions for the optimal solutions of problem (95) as follows:

$$\frac{\partial L}{\partial \lambda_j} = \sum_{i=1}^{N} \varepsilon_j^i - \varepsilon_j^* = 0, \quad j = 1, ..., k, \ j \neq l \tag{97}$$

$$\frac{\partial L}{\partial \varepsilon_j^i} = -\lambda_{lj}^i + \lambda_j = 0, \quad i = 1, 2, ..., N; \ j = 1, ..., k, \ j \neq l \tag{98}$$

$$\frac{\partial L}{\partial u_i} = \frac{\partial f_l^i(\bar{x}_i, u_i, z_i)}{\partial u_i} + \sum_{\substack{j=1 \\ j \neq l}}^{k} \lambda_{lj}^i \frac{\partial f_j^i(\bar{x}_i, u_i, z_i)}{\partial u_i}$$

$$-\frac{\partial H_i^T(u_i, z_i)}{\partial u_i}\mu_i = 0, \quad i = 1, ..., N \tag{99}$$

$$\frac{\partial L}{\partial z_i} = \frac{\partial f_l^i(\bar{x}_i, u_i, z_i)}{\partial z_i} + \sum_{\substack{j=1 \\ j \neq l}}^{k} \lambda_{lj}^i \frac{\partial f_j^i(\bar{x}_i, u_i, z_i)}{\partial z_i} - \frac{\partial H_i^T(u_i, z_i)}{\partial z_i}\mu_i + \sigma_i = 0,$$

$$i = 1, ..., N \tag{100}$$

$$\frac{\partial L}{\partial \lambda_{lj}^i} = f_j^i(\bar{x}_i, u_i, z_i) - \varepsilon_j^i \leq 0, \quad \lambda_{lj}^i \geq 0, \quad \lambda_{lj}^i \frac{\partial L}{\partial \lambda_{lj}^i} = 0,$$

$$i = 1, ..., N; j = 1, ..., k, j \neq l \tag{101}$$

$$\frac{\partial L}{\partial \mu_i} = \bar{x}_i - H_i(u_i, z_i) = 0, \quad i = 1, ..., N \tag{102}$$

$$\frac{\partial L}{\partial \sigma_i} = z_i - C_i(\bar{x}_1, \bar{x}_2, ..., \bar{x}_N) = 0, \quad i = 1, ..., N \tag{103}$$

If we choose ε_j^i equal to ε_j^{i*}, $i = 1, ..., N$, $j = 1, ..., k$, $j \neq l$, (97) is satisfied. Equations (99)–(103) are the first-order necessary conditions for $[\bar{x}_i^T, u_i^{*T}, z_i^{*T}]^T$ to be the optimal solution of $P_i^l(\varepsilon^{i*}; \bar{x})$. The necessary condition (94) in Theorem 5 follows directly from (98). Q.E.D.

In the following, we consider the case where the noninferior frontier for each subsystem (90) with a fixed x, $i = 1, 2, ..., N$, is of $k - 1$ dimension, and the optimal Kuhn–Tucker multiplier λ_{lj}^i, $i = 1, ..., N$, $j = 1, ..., k$, $j \neq l$, is a strictly monotonic function of ε_j^i, $j = 1, ..., k$, $j \neq l$. The scheme to map the noninferior frontiers of N subsystems into the noninferior frontier of the overall system is established by using the tradeoff information in the subsystems in accordance with Theorem 5.

Each subsystem i solves (90) with the fixed $\bar{x}$ independently by using the ε-constraint approach. The parametric form of the set of noninferior solutions of subsystem i can be expressed with the corresponding tradeoff values in the following way:

$$f_l^i = \varepsilon_l^i \cdots \lambda_{l1}^i = \lambda_{l1}^i(\varepsilon_1^i, ..., \varepsilon_{l-1}^i, \varepsilon_{l+1}^i, ..., \varepsilon_k^i; \bar{x}) \tag{104a}$$

$$\vdots$$

$$f^i_{l-1} = \varepsilon^i_{l-1} \ \cdots \ \lambda^i_{l,l-1} = \lambda^i_{l,l-1}(\varepsilon^i_1, \ \ldots, \ \varepsilon^i_{l-1}, \varepsilon^i_{l+1}, \ \ldots, \ \varepsilon^i_k; \ \overline{x}) \qquad (104b)$$

$$f^i_l = f_l(\varepsilon^i_1, \ \ldots, \ \varepsilon^i_{l-1}, \varepsilon^i_{l+1}, \ \ldots, \ \varepsilon^i_k; \ \overline{x}) \qquad (104c)$$

$$f^i_{l+1} = \varepsilon^i_{l+1} \ \cdots \ \lambda^i_{l,l+1} = \lambda^i_{l,l+1}(\varepsilon^i_1, \ \ldots, \ \varepsilon^i_{l-1}, \varepsilon^i_{l+1}, \ \ldots, \ \varepsilon^i_k; \ \overline{x}) \qquad (104d)$$

$$\vdots$$

$$f^i_k = \varepsilon^i_k \ \cdots \ \lambda^i_{lk} = \lambda^i_{lk}(\varepsilon^i_1, \ \ldots, \ \varepsilon^i_{l-1}, \varepsilon^i_{l+1}, \ \ldots, \ \varepsilon^i_k; \ \overline{x}). \qquad (104e)$$

The set of noninferior solutions of the problem in (87)–(89) with this fixed $\overline{x}$ can be obtained by summing the objectives of the corresponding points in efficient frontiers of each subsystem that are satisfied by the necessary condition, (94). Since there are N $(k-1)$ unknowns in the $(N-1)$ $(k-1)$ tradeoff equations of (94), it is possible to express ε^i_j, $i = 1, \ldots, N$, $i \neq s$, $j = 1, \ldots, k$, $j \neq l$, as the function of $\varepsilon^s_1, \varepsilon^s_2, \ldots, \varepsilon^s_{l-1}, \varepsilon^s_{l+1}, \ldots, \varepsilon^s_k$, where $1 \leq s \leq N$. Thus, the parametric form of the set of noninferior solutions of the problem in (87)–(89) with fixed $\overline{x}$ can be expressed as

$$f_1 = f_1(\varepsilon^s_1, \ \ldots, \ \varepsilon^s_{l-1}, \varepsilon^s_{l+1}, \ \ldots, \ \varepsilon^s_k; \ \overline{x}) \qquad (105a)$$

$$f_2 = f_2(\varepsilon^s_1, \ \ldots, \ \varepsilon^s_{l-1}, \varepsilon^s_{l+1}, \ \ldots, \ \varepsilon^s_k; \ \overline{x}) \qquad (105b)$$

$$\vdots$$

$$f_k = f_k(\varepsilon^s_1, \ \ldots, \ \varepsilon^s_{l-1}, \varepsilon^s_{l+1}, \ \ldots, \ \varepsilon^s_k; \ \overline{x}). \qquad (105c)$$

For different values of the coordination variable x, we get a family of noninferior frontiers as expressed in (105). If the family is regular, then, based on Theorem 4, the coordination algorithm is designed to identify the set of noninferior solutions of the primal problem given in (87)–(89) by using the envelope approach. In fact, the union of $\text{Ext}[f(S(x)) \mid R_+^k]$ composes a family and the multiobjective optimization problem, $\text{Ext}[\{\cup \text{Ext}[f(S(x)) \mid R_+^k]\} \mid R_+^k]$, may be solved by identifying the envelope of this family based on Theorem 1.

The envelope of the family defined by (105), which has parameters x, can be obtained by the following formulas.

For $k = 2$ (without loss of generality, take $l = 1$),

$$f_1 = f_1(\varepsilon_2^s; x) \tag{106a}$$

$$f_2 = f_2(\varepsilon_2^s; x) \tag{106b}$$

$$\frac{\partial f_2}{\partial \varepsilon_2^s} \frac{\partial f_1}{\partial x} - \frac{\partial f_1}{\partial \varepsilon_2^s} \frac{\partial f_2}{\partial x} = 0. \tag{106c}$$

For $k \geq 3$ (without loss of generality, take $l = 1$),

$$f_1 = f_1(\varepsilon_2^s, \ldots, \varepsilon_k^s; x) \tag{107a}$$

$$f_2 = f_2(\varepsilon_2^s, \ldots, \varepsilon_k^s; x) \tag{107b}$$

$$\vdots$$

$$f_k = f_k(\varepsilon_2^s, \ldots, \varepsilon_k^s; x) \tag{107c}$$

$$\frac{\partial(f_2, f_3, \ldots, f_k)}{\partial(\varepsilon_2^s, \varepsilon_3^s, \ldots, \varepsilon_k^s)} \frac{\partial f_1}{\partial x} - \frac{\partial(f_1, f_3, \ldots, f_k)}{\partial(\varepsilon_2^s, \varepsilon_3^s, \ldots, \varepsilon_k^s)} \frac{\partial f_2}{\partial x} + \ldots$$

$$+ (-1)^{k-1} \frac{\partial(f_1, f_2, \ldots, f_{k-1})}{\partial(\varepsilon_2^s, \varepsilon_3^s, \ldots, \varepsilon_k^s)} \frac{\partial f_k}{\partial x} = 0, \tag{107d}$$

where

$$\frac{\partial(f_1, f_2, \ldots, f_{k-1})}{\partial(\varepsilon_2^s, \varepsilon_3^s, \ldots, \varepsilon_k^s)} = \begin{vmatrix} \dfrac{\partial f_1}{\partial \varepsilon_2^s} & \cdots & \dfrac{\partial f_1}{\partial \varepsilon_k^s} \\ \vdots & & \\ \dfrac{\partial f_{k-1}}{\partial \varepsilon_2^s} & \cdots & \dfrac{\partial f_{k-1}}{\partial \varepsilon_k^s} \end{vmatrix}$$

4. Application to Multiobjective Discrete Dynamic Systems

Consider the following multiobjective discrete dynamic system:

$$
\min \begin{bmatrix} f_1 = \displaystyle\sum_{t=0}^{T-1} f_1^t(x(t), u(t), t) \\ f_2 = \displaystyle\sum_{t=0}^{T-1} f_2^t(x(t), u(t), t) \\ \vdots \\ f_k = \displaystyle\sum_{t=0}^{T-1} f_k^t(x(t), u(t), t) \end{bmatrix} \tag{108a}
$$

s.t. $x(t + 1) = h(x(t), u(t))$

$$
x(0) = x_0, \, x(T) = x_T. \tag{108b}
$$

The coordination variable $z(t)$ is defined as

$$
z(t - 1) = x(t). \tag{109}
$$

Thus, the subproblem t, $t = 1, \ldots, T - 2$, could be written directly as

$$
\min \begin{bmatrix} f_1^t(x(t), u(t), t) \\ f_2^t(x(t), u(t), t) \\ \vdots \\ f_k^t(x(t), u(t), t) \end{bmatrix} \tag{110a}
$$

s.t. $z(t) = h(x(t), u(t))$ \hfill (110b)

$x(t) = z(t - 1)$ for given $z(t - 1)$ and $z(t)$. \hfill (110c)

To take the initial state into account, the first subproblem becomes:

$$
\min
\begin{bmatrix}
f_1^0(x_0, u(0), 0) \\
f_2^0(x_0, u(0), 0) \\
\vdots \\
f_k^0(x_0, u(0), 0)
\end{bmatrix}
\tag{111a}
$$

s.t. $z(0) = h(x_0, u(0))$ for given $z(0)$.   (111b)

The condition on the final state requires that subproblem $T - 1$ be:

$$
\min
\begin{bmatrix}
f_1^{T-1}(x(T-1), u(T-1), T-1) \\
f_2^{T-1}(x(T-1), u(T-1), T-1) \\
\vdots \\
f_k^{T-1}(x(T-1), u(T-1), T-1)
\end{bmatrix}
\tag{112a}
$$

s.t. $x_T = h\big(x(T-1), u(T-1)\big)$ (112b)

$x(T-1) = z(T-2)$ for given $z(T-2)$.   (112c)

As we stated earlier, the hierarchical generating method with feasible decomposition is only applicable if the dimension of $u \geq$ the dimension of $x + (k - 1)$.

C.   A NONFEASIBLE VERSION OF HIERARCHICAL GENERATING METHODS

1.   The Vector Lagrangian Problem

Consider the following multiobjective optimization problem:

$$
\min_x f(x) = \min_x [f_1(x), f_2(x), \ldots, f_k(x)]^T
\tag{113a}
$$

s.t. $h(x) = 0$ (113b)

$$g(x) \leq 0 \tag{113c}$$

$$x \in S, \tag{113d}$$

where $x \in R^n$ is the decision vector, h and g are m_1-dimensional and m_2-dimensional vector-valued functions, respectively, and $S \subseteq R^n$. Equation (113) is called here the primal problem.

We assume in this section that the decision space

$$X = \{x \mid h(x) = 0, g(x) \leq 0, x \in S\}$$

is convex and the vector objective function $f(x)$ is an R_+^k-convex function (see Yu [35]). Since the problem given in (113) is a convex multiobjective optimization problem, it is appropriate to adopt the weighting method to generate noninferior solutions. The weighting problem is defined as follows:

$$\min_x \sum_{i=1}^{k} \theta_i f_i(x) \tag{114a}$$

$$\text{s.t. } h(x) = 0 \tag{114b}$$

$$g(x) \leq 0 \tag{114c}$$

$$x \in S, \tag{114d}$$

where the weighting coefficients θ_i's satisfy

$$\theta_i \geq 0, \quad i = 1, 2, \ldots, k \tag{115a}$$

$$\sum_{i=1}^{k} \theta_i = 1. \tag{115b}$$

Given the problem in (114), we form a Lagrangian function,

$$L = \sum_{i=1}^{k} \theta_i f_i(x) + \lambda_1^T h(x) + \lambda_2^T g(x), \tag{116}$$

where $\lambda_1 \in R^{m_1}$ and $\lambda_2 \in R_+^{m_2}$ are Lagrangian multipliers. Since

$$\lambda_1^T h(x) + \lambda_2^T g(x) = \sum_{i=1}^{k} \left\{ \theta_i [\lambda_1^T h(x) + \lambda_2^T g(x)] \right\}, \tag{117}$$

we can view the Lagrangian L in (116) as being associated with the following multiobjective problem:

$$\min \begin{bmatrix} f_1(x) + \lambda_1^T h(x) + \lambda_2^T g(x) \\ f_2(x) + \lambda_1^T h(x) + \lambda_2^T g(x) \\ \vdots \\ f_k(x) + \lambda_1^T h(x) + \lambda_2^T g(x) \end{bmatrix} \tag{118}$$

s.t. $x \in S$.

The problem given in (118) is defined as the vector Lagrangian problem of the problem given in (113), and

$$L(x; \lambda_1, \lambda_2) = \begin{bmatrix} f_1(x) + \lambda_1^T h(x) + \lambda_2^T g(x) \\ f_2(x) + \lambda_1^T h(x) + \lambda_2^T g(x) \\ \vdots \\ f_k(x) + \lambda_1^T h(x) + \lambda_2^T g(x) \end{bmatrix} \tag{119}$$

is called the vector Lagrangian function.

2.   Separable Problems

By forming the vector-valued Lagrangian function, a constrained vector optimization problem has been converted into an unconstrained one (except for the restriction $x \in S$). This formulation is especially useful when the problem is separable, that is, when x, f, h, and g can be partitioned as

$$x = (x_1^T, x_2^T, ..., x_p^T)^T, \ p \leq n \tag{120a}$$

$$f_i(x) = \sum_{j=1}^{p} f_i^j(x_j), \ \ i = 1, 2, ..., k \tag{120b}$$

$$h(x) = \sum_{j=1}^{p} h^j(x_j) \tag{120c}$$

$$g(x) = \sum_{j=1}^{p} g^j(x_j) \tag{120d}$$

$$S = S_1 \times S_2 \times ... \times S_p, \tag{120e}$$

where $x_i \in S_i$, $i = 1, 2, ..., p$. Then the vector Lagrangian problem, (118), is separable with respect to x_i and can be minimized by solving, independently, the following subproblems with fixed values of λ_1 and λ_2:

$$\min_{x_j} \begin{bmatrix} f_1^j(x_j) + \lambda_1^T h^j(x_j) + \lambda_2^T g^j(x_j) \\ f_2^j(x_j) + \lambda_1^T h^j(x_j) + \lambda_2^T g^j(x_j) \\ \vdots \\ f_k^j(x_j) + \lambda_1^T h^j(x_j) + \lambda_2^T g^j(x_j) \end{bmatrix} \tag{121a}$$

$$\text{s.t.} \ \ x_j \in S_j, \tag{121b}$$

$$j = 1, 2, ..., p.$$

For large-scale multiobjective optimization problems, there may be no satisfactory methods for solving the primal problem, but the subproblems, if they involve only a few variables, may be handled easily.

3.   Duality Theorem

Definition 9. A dual map φ is a point-to-set map from $R^{m_1} \times R_+^{m_2}$ to R^k, which is defined as

$$\varphi(\hat{\lambda}_1, \hat{\lambda}_2) = \text{Ext}\left[\left\{ L(x; \hat{\lambda}_1, \hat{\lambda}_2) \mid x \in S \right\} \mid R_+^k \right]. \tag{122}$$

More specifically, the parametric form of $\varphi(\hat{\lambda}_1, \hat{\lambda}_2)$ is given as follows:

$$\bar{f}_1 = \bar{f}_1(\theta; \hat{\lambda}_1, \hat{\lambda}_2) \tag{123a}$$

$$\bar{f}_2 = \bar{f}_2(\theta; \hat{\lambda}_1, \hat{\lambda}_2) \tag{123b}$$
$$\vdots$$

$$\bar{f}_k = \bar{f}_k(\theta; \hat{\lambda}_1, \hat{\lambda}_2), \tag{123c}$$

where we assume the weighting method is used to identify $\varphi(\hat{\lambda}_1, \hat{\lambda}_2)$, θ is the weighting coefficient vector satisfying the conditions in (115), and $\bar{f}_i$ is the i-th element of the vector-valued Lagrangian function L.

Lemma 6. $\varphi(\lambda_1, \lambda_2)$ is an R_+^k-concave point-to-set map. Namely, for any $\hat{\lambda}_1, \tilde{\lambda}_1 \in R^{m_1}$; $\hat{\lambda}_2, \tilde{\lambda}_2 \in R_+^{m_2}$; and any $\alpha, 0 \le \alpha \le 1$,

$$\varphi\left(\alpha\hat{\lambda}_1 + (1-\alpha)\tilde{\lambda}_1, \alpha\hat{\lambda}_2 + (1-\alpha)\tilde{\lambda}_2\right) \subseteq \alpha\varphi(\hat{\lambda}_1, \hat{\lambda}_2)$$

$$+ (1-\alpha)\varphi(\tilde{\lambda}_1, \tilde{\lambda}_2) + R_+^k. \tag{124}$$

Proof. See Tanino and Sawaragi [61]. Q.E.D.

Theorem 6. Duality theorem. If $\hat{x}$ is a noninferior solution of the problem given in (113) and Slater's constraint qualification is satisfied (i.e., there exists $x' \in X$), then

$$f(\hat{x}) \in \text{Ext}\left[\bigcup_{\lambda_1 \in R^{m_1}, \lambda_2 \in R_+^{m_2}} \varphi(\lambda_1, \lambda_2) \mid R_-^k\right],$$ (125)

Proof. The proof is similar to the one given in Tanino and Sawaragi [61]. If $\hat{x}$ is a noninferior solution of the problem in (113) and Slater's constraint qualification is satisfied, we know that there exist $\hat{\lambda}_1$ and $\hat{\lambda}_2$ such that $f(\hat{x}) \in \varphi(\hat{\lambda}_1, \hat{\lambda}_2)$. [Since $h(\hat{x}) = 0$, $\lambda_2^T g(\hat{x}) = 0$, this leads to $f(\hat{x}) = L(\hat{x}; \hat{\lambda}_1, \hat{\lambda}_2)$.] If

$$f(\hat{x}) \notin \text{Ext}\left[\bigcup_{\lambda_1 \in R^{m_1}, \lambda_2 \in R_+^{m_2}} \varphi(\lambda_1, \lambda_2) \mid R_-^k\right],$$ (126)

then there exist $\tilde{\lambda}_1 \in R^{m_1}$, $\tilde{\lambda}_2 \in R_+^{m_2}$, and $L(\tilde{x}; \tilde{\lambda}_1, \tilde{\lambda}_2) \in \varphi(\tilde{\lambda}_1, \tilde{\lambda}_2)$ such that

$$f(\hat{x}) = L(\tilde{x}; \tilde{\lambda}_1, \tilde{\lambda}_2) - \gamma,$$ (127)

where $\gamma \in R_+^k$ and $\gamma \neq 0$. Therefore, we have

$$L(\hat{x}; \tilde{\lambda}_1, \tilde{\lambda}_2) = f(\hat{x}) + \begin{bmatrix} \tilde{\lambda}_1^T h(\hat{x}) + \tilde{\lambda}_2^T g(\hat{x}) \\ \vdots \\ \tilde{\lambda}_1^T h(\hat{x}) + \tilde{\lambda}_2^T g(\hat{x}) \end{bmatrix}$$

$$= L(\tilde{x}; \tilde{\lambda}_1, \tilde{\lambda}_2) - \gamma + \begin{bmatrix} \tilde{\lambda}_1^T h(\hat{x}) + \tilde{\lambda}_2^T g(\hat{x}) \\ \vdots \\ \tilde{\lambda}_1^T h(\hat{x}) + \tilde{\lambda}_2^T g(\hat{x}) \end{bmatrix}$$

$$= L(\tilde{x}; \tilde{\lambda}_1, \tilde{\lambda}_2) - \gamma',$$ (128)

where $\gamma' \in R_+^k$ and $\gamma' \neq 0$. In the last equality, we have used the facts of $h(\hat{x}) = 0$, $\tilde{\lambda}_2 \in R_+^{m_2}$, and $g(\hat{x}) \leq 0$. This leads to a contradiction of $L(\tilde{x}; \tilde{\lambda}_1, \tilde{\lambda}_2) \in \varphi(\tilde{\lambda}_1, \tilde{\lambda}_2)$. Q.E.D.

If all f_i's, $i = 1, 2, ..., k$, in (123) are differentiable with respect to θ, λ_1, and λ_2 and the family $\bigcup_{\lambda_1 \in R^{m_1}, \lambda_2 \in R_+^{m_2}} \varphi(\lambda_1, \lambda_2)$ is regular, then, based on

Theorems 1 and 6, all noninferior solutions of the problem given in (113) lie on the envelope of the family of noninferior frontiers expressed by (123).

4.   Hierarchical Generating Method with Nonfeasible Decomposition for Multiobjective Discrete Dynamic Systems

In this subsection, we will consider a class of discrete dynamic systems described by difference equations of the form

$$x(t + 1) = Ax(t) + Bu(t), \quad t = 0, 1, ..., T - 1, \tag{129}$$

$x(0)$ given, and where $x(t) \in R^n$ denotes the state, $u(t) \in R^p$ denotes the control, A is an $n \times n$ matrix, and B is an $n \times p$ matrix.

We assume further that the state vector and the control vector are constrained by the following equations:

$$g_t(x(t), u(t)) \leq 0, \quad t = 0, 1, ..., T - 1 \tag{130a}$$

$$g_T(x(T)) \leq 0, \tag{130b}$$

where g_t, $t = 0, 1, ..., T - 1$, and g_T are R_+^m-convex functions.

The stage's objectives are assumed to be functions of the stage variables,

$$f_j^t = f_j^t(x(t), u(t), t), \quad j = 1, 2, ..., k; t = 0, 1, ..., T - 1 \tag{131a}$$

$$f_j^T = f_j^T(x(T)), \quad j = 1, 2, ..., k, \tag{131b}$$

and the overall objectives are of an additive form of stage objectives. Thus, the overall problem can be stated as follows:

$$
\min
\begin{bmatrix}
f_1 = \displaystyle\sum_{t=0}^{T-1} f_1^t(x(t),\, u(t),\, t) + f_1^T(x(T)) \\[2mm]
f_2 = \displaystyle\sum_{t=0}^{T-1} f_2^t(x(t),\, u(t),\, t) + f_2^T(x(T)) \\[2mm]
\vdots \\[2mm]
f_k = \displaystyle\sum_{t=0}^{T-1} f_k^t(x(t),\, u(t),\, t) + f_k^T(x(T))
\end{bmatrix}
\tag{132}
$$

s.t. (129) and (130),
where $f = [f_1, f_2, \ldots, f_k]^T$ is an R_+^k-convex vector objective function. We assume here that all functions f_j, $j = 1, 2, \ldots, k$ and g_t, $t = 0, 1, \ldots, T$, are differentiable with respect to $x(t)$ and $u(t)$.

In the following, we will consider decomposing the original problem in (132) by the discrete time index t, thereby reducing a "functional" multiobjective optimization problem to a series of "parameteric" multiobjective optimization problems at the first level of a two-level structure. This decomposition can be considered a temporal decomposition, in contrast with the spatial one developed in Li and Haimes [7].

We first form the vector-valued Lagrangian by introducing the n-dimensional costate vector p,

$L(x, u; p) =$

$$
\begin{bmatrix}
\bar{f}_1 = \displaystyle\sum_{t=0}^{T-1} f_1^t(x(t),\, u(t),\, t) + f_1^T(x(T)) + \displaystyle\sum_{t=0}^{T-1} p^T(t)[Ax(t) + Bu(t) - x(t+1)] \\[2mm]
\bar{f}_2 = \displaystyle\sum_{t=0}^{T-1} f_2^t(x(t),\, u(t),\, t) + f_2^T(x(T)) + \displaystyle\sum_{t=0}^{T-1} p^T(t)[Ax(t) + Bu(t) - x(t+1)] \\[2mm]
\vdots \\[2mm]
\bar{f}_k = \displaystyle\sum_{t=0}^{T-1} f_k^t(x(t),\, u(t),\, t) + f_k^T(x(T)) + \displaystyle\sum_{t=0}^{T-1} p^T(t)[Ax(t) + Bu(t) - x(t+1)]
\end{bmatrix}
\tag{133}
$$

Define

$$
H_i^t(x(t),\, u(t),\, t) = f_i^t(x(t),\, u(t),\, t) + p^T(t)[Ax(t) + Bu(t)],
$$

$$
i = 1, 2, \ldots, k;\ t = 0, 1, \ldots, T - 1. \tag{134}
$$

We can set the target for the first level as follows:

$$\min \begin{bmatrix} \displaystyle\sum_{t=0}^{T-1} \left[H_1^t(x(t), u(t), t) - p^T(t-1)x(t) \right] + f_1^T(x(T)) - p^T(T-1)x(T) \\[2mm] \displaystyle\sum_{t=0}^{T-1} \left[H_2^t(x(t), u(t), t) - p^T(t-1)x(t) \right] + f_2^T(x(T)) - p^T(T-1)x(T) \\[2mm] \vdots \\[2mm] \displaystyle\sum_{t=0}^{T-1} \left[H_k^t(x(t), u(t), t) - p^T(t-1)x(t) \right] + f_k^T(x(T)) - p^T(T-1)x(T) \end{bmatrix} \qquad (135a)$$

s.t. $g_t(x(t), u(t)) \le 0, \quad t = 0, 1, \ldots, T-1$ (135b)

$\qquad g_T(x(T)) \le 0,$ (135c)

where $x(0)$ is given and $p(-1)$ is defined to be zero.

Since the problem given in (135) is separable in the time index for fixed $p(t)$, $t = 0, 1, \ldots, T-1$, the multiobjective subproblems at the first level then become, for $t = 0$:

$$\min_{u(0)} \begin{bmatrix} H_1^0(x(0), u(0), 0) \\ H_2^0(x(0), u(0), 0) \\ \vdots \\ H_k^0(x(0), u(0), 0) \end{bmatrix} \qquad (136a)$$

s.t. $g_0(x(0), u(0)) \le 0,$ (136b)

where $x(0)$ is given. For $t = 1, 2, \ldots, T-1$:

$$\min_{x(t),u(t)} \begin{bmatrix} H_1^t(x(t), u(t), t) - p^T(t-1)x(t) \\ H_2^t(x(t), u(t), t) - p^T(t-1)x(t) \\ \vdots \\ H_k^t(x(t), u(t), t) - p^T(t-1)x(t) \end{bmatrix} \qquad (137a)$$

s.t. $g_t(x(t), u(t)) \le 0.$ (137b)

For $t = T$:

$$
\min_{x(T)} \begin{bmatrix} f_1^T(x(T)) - p^T(T-1)x(T) \\ f_2^T(x(T)) - p^T(T-1)x(T) \\ \vdots \\ f_k^T(x(T)) - p^T(T-1)x(T) \end{bmatrix} \tag{138a}
$$

$$
\text{s.t. } g_T(x(T)) \le 0. \tag{138b}
$$

Theorem 7. Assume that, for a fixed-parameter p and a weighting co-efficient vector θ, $u^*(0)$ solves the weighting form of the problem given in (136); $(x^*(t), u^*(t))$, $t = 1, 2, \ldots, T - 1$, solves the weighting form of the problem given in (137); and $x^*(T)$ solves the weighting form of the problem given in (138). Then $(u^*(0), x^*(1), u^*(1), \ldots, x^*(T-1), u^*(T-1), x^*(T))$ solves the weighting form of the problem given in (135) with the fixed-parameter vector p and the weighting coefficient vector θ.

Proof. The problem given in (135) is separable in the time index for fixed p. The weighting form of the objective functions of the overall problem given in (135) is

$$
L = \sum_{j=1}^{k} \left[\theta_j \left(\sum_{t=0}^{T-1} f_j^t(x(t), u(t), t) + f_j^T(x(T)) \right) \right]
$$
$$
+ \sum_{t=0}^{T-1} p^T(t)[Ax(t) + Bu(t) - x(t+1)] = \sum_{t=0}^{T} L_t, \tag{139}
$$

where

$$
L_0 = \sum_{j=1}^{k} \theta_j H_j^0(x(0), u(0), 0) \tag{140a}
$$

$$
L_t = \sum_{j=1}^{k} \left[\theta_j H_j^t(x(t), u(t), t) \right] - p^T(t-1)x(t), \tag{140b}
$$

$$
t = 1, 2, \ldots, T-1
$$

$$
L_T = \sum_{j=1}^{k} \left[\theta_j f_j^T(x(T)) \right] - p^T(T-1)x(T), \tag{140c}
$$

which are exactly the weighting forms of the objective functions of the subproblems given in (136)–(138). Q.E.D.

Theorem 8. All noninferior solutions of the problem given in (132) lie on the envelope of the following family of noninferior frontiers of the problem given in (135) with parameter p:

$$\bar{T}_1 = \bar{T}_1(\theta; p) \tag{141a}$$

$$\bar{T}_2 = \bar{T}_2(\theta; p) \tag{141b}$$

$$\vdots$$

$$\bar{T}_k = \bar{T}_k(\theta; p) \tag{141c}$$

where $\bar{T}_i$, $i = 1, 2, ..., k$, is the i-th element of the vector-valued Lagrangian given in (133), and the parametric form of the noninferior frontier given in (141) is obtained at the first level.

Remark. We assume here that the family in (141) is regular.

Proof. Note that Theorem 1 is a first-order necessary condition, which is also applicable to vector maximization problems. Then, following Theorem 6 and Theorem 1 will give us the proof. Q.E.D.

The above temporal-decomposition envelope-coordination scheme can be summarized in the following algorithm

Algorithm 2. Temporal decomposition and envelope coordination of multiobjective dynamic systems.

Step 1. The second level sends down a set of coordination variables $p(t)$ to the first level.

Step 2. For given p, each subsystem t solves its corresponding problem in (136)–(138) and obtains the parametric form of the set of noninferior solutions,

$$\bar{f}_1^t = \bar{f}_1^{t*}(\theta; p) \tag{142a}$$

$$\bar{f}_2^t = \bar{f}_2^{t*}(\theta; p) \tag{142b}$$

$$\vdots$$

$$\bar{f}_k^t = \bar{f}_k^{t*}(\theta; p), \tag{142c}$$

where $\bar{f}_j^t$ is the j-th objective of subsystem t in (136)–(138).

Step 3. Set

$$\bar{f}_j(\theta; p) = \sum_{t=0}^{T} \bar{f}_j^{t*}(\theta; p), \quad j = 1, 2, ..., k. \tag{143}$$

Step 4. Identify the envelope of the family given in (143) with parameter p. All efficient solutions of the problem given in (132) lie on the envelope.

5. A Three-Level Structure for the Hierarchical Generating Method for Large-Scale Discrete-Time Dynamic Systems

A minimization is to be performed on a dynamic system that comprises N interconnected subsystems,

$$x_i(t + 1) = A_i x_i(t) + B_i u_i(t) + C_i z_i(t),$$

$$t = 0, 1, ..., T - 1, \quad x_i(0) \text{ given,}$$

$$i = 1, 2, ..., N, \tag{144}$$

where $x_i(t)$ is the state vector of subsystem i, $x_i \in R^{n_i}$; $u_i(t)$ is the control vector of subsystem i, $u_i \in R^{p_i}$; and $z_i(t)$ is the interaction input of subsystem i, $z_i \in R^{n_i}$, which satisfies

$$z_i(t) = \sum_{j=1}^{N} D_j^i x_j(t), \quad t = 0, 1, ..., T - 1; \, i = 1, 2, ..., N. \tag{145}$$

A_i is an $n_i \times n_i$ matrix; B_i is an $n_i \times p_i$ matrix; C_i is an $n_i \times n_i$ matrix; and D_j^i is an $n_i \times n_j$ matrix.

The problem is to minimize the following multiobjective problem:

$$\min \begin{bmatrix} f_1 = \sum_{i=1}^{N} \left(\sum_{t=0}^{T-1} f_1^{it}(x_i(t), u_i(t), z_i(t), t) + f_1^{iT}(x_i(T)) \right) \\ f_2 = \sum_{i=1}^{N} \left(\sum_{t=0}^{T-1} f_2^{it}(x_i(t), u_i(t), z_i(t), t) + f_2^{iT}(x_i(T)) \right) \\ \vdots \\ f_k = \sum_{i=1}^{N} \left(\sum_{t=0}^{T-1} f_k^{it}(x_i(t), u_i(t), z_i(t), t) + f_k^{iT}(x_i(T)) \right) \end{bmatrix} \tag{146}$$

s.t. (144) and (145),

where $f = [f_1, f_2, ..., f_k]^T$ is an R_+^k-convex objective function and is differentiable on its domain.

By using the results of the spatial decomposition approach and the temporal decomposition as a base, we can develop a three-level coordination scheme to find the set of noninferior solutions for this hierarchical large-scale dynamical system.

Introducing the Lagrangian multipliers $\lambda_i(t)$, $t = 0, 1, ..., T - 1$, $i = 1, 2, ..., N$, we can transform the problem given in (146) into the following vector Lagrangian problem:

$$
\min \begin{bmatrix}
\sum_{i=1}^{N} \left\{ f_1^{iT}(x_i(T)) + \sum_{t=0}^{T-1} \left[f_1^{it}(x_i(t), u_i(t), z_i(t), t) \right. \right. \\
\left. \left. + \lambda_i^T(t)\left(z_i(t) - \sum_{j=1}^{N} D_j^i x_j(t) \right) \right] \right\} \\[4pt]
\sum_{i=1}^{N} \left\{ f_2^{iT}(x_i(T)) + \sum_{t=0}^{T-1} \left[f_2^{it}(x_i(t), u_i(t), z_i(t), t) \right. \right. \\
\left. \left. + \lambda_i^T(t)\left(z_i(t) - \sum_{j=1}^{N} D_j^i x_j(t) \right) \right] \right\} \\[4pt]
\vdots \\[4pt]
\sum_{i=1}^{N} \left\{ f_k^{iT}(x_i(T)) + \sum_{t=0}^{T-1} \left[f_k^{it}(x_i(t), u_i(t), z_i(t), t) \right. \right. \\
\left. \left. + \lambda_i^T(t)\left(z_i(t) - \sum_{j=1}^{N} D_j^i x_j(t) \right) \right] \right\}
\end{bmatrix} \tag{147a}
$$

s.t. $x_i(t + 1) = A_i x_i(t) + B_i u_i(t) + C_i z_i(t),$ \hfill (147b)

$$t = 0, 1, ..., T - 1; \ i = 1, 2, ..., N.$$

Thus, as in the hierarchical generating method for large-scale static systems [7], it is possible to separate the overall system into N independent subsystems for given $\lambda(t)$ sequences supplied by the upper level.

The multiobjective problem of the i-th subsystem can be expressed as follows:

$$
\min
\begin{bmatrix}
f_1^{iT}(x_i(T)) + \sum_{t=0}^{T-1}\left[f_1^{it}(x_i(t), u_i(t), z_i(t), t) \right. \\[2mm]
\left. + \lambda_i^T(t)z_i(t) - \left(\sum_{j=1}^{N} \lambda_j^T(t)D_i^j \right) x_i(t) \right] \\[4mm]
f_2^{iT}(x_i(T)) + \sum_{t=0}^{T-1}\left[f_2^{it}(x_i(t), u_i(t), z_i(t), t) \right. \\[2mm]
\left. + \lambda_i^T(t)z_i(t) - \left(\sum_{j=1}^{N} \lambda_j^T(t)D_i^j \right) x_i(t) \right] \\[3mm]
\vdots \\[4mm]
f_k^{iT}(x_i(T)) + \sum_{t=0}^{T-1}\left[f_k^{it}(x_i(t), u_i(t), z_i(t), t) \right. \\[2mm]
\left. + \lambda_i^T(t)z_i(t) - \left(\sum_{j=1}^{N} \lambda_j^T(t)D_i^j \right) x_i(t) \right]
\end{bmatrix}
\tag{148a}
$$

s.t. $x_i(t + 1) = A_i x_i(t) + B_i u_i(t) + C_i z_i(t),$ (148b)

$t = 0, 1, ..., T - 1$, $x_i(0)$, $z_i(0)$ given.

Instead of solving the problem in (148) – the multiobjective problem of the i-th dynamic subsystem, $i = 1, 2, ..., N$ – directly, we will further decompose the i-th dynamic subsystem, $i = 1, 2, ..., N$, by the discrete-time index t, thereby reducing a "functional" optimization problem at the first level of a two-level structure to one of a "parametric" optimization at the first level of a three-level structure.

In order to determine the optimal strategy of this three-level structure, let us introduce the costate vector $p_i(t)$, $t = 0, 1, ..., T - 1$, $i = 1, 2, ..., N$, and form the vector-valued Lagrangian problem of (148):

$$\min \begin{bmatrix} f_1^{iT}(x_i(T)) + \sum_{t=0}^{T-1} \left[f_1^{it}(x_i(t), u_i(t), z_i(t), t) \right. \\ \left. + \lambda_i^T(t)z_i(t) - \left(\sum_{j=1}^{N} \lambda_j^T(t)D_i^j \right) x_i(t) \right. \\ \left. + p_i^T(t)\left[A_i x_i(t) + B_i u_i(t) + C_i z_i(t) - x_i(t+1) \right] \right] \\ \vdots \\ f_k^{iT}(x_i(T)) + \sum_{t=0}^{T-1} \left[f_k^{it}(x_i(t), u_i(t), z_i(t), t) \right. \\ \left. + \lambda_i^T(t)z_i(t) - \left(\sum_{j=1}^{N} \lambda_j^T(t)D_i^j \right) x_i(t) \right. \\ \left. + p_i^T(t)\left[A_i x_i(t) + B_i u_i(t) + C_i z_i(t) - x_i(t+1) \right] \right] \end{bmatrix} \quad (149)$$

$i = 1, 2, ..., N.$

Define

$$R_j^{it}(x_i(t), u_i(t), z_i(t), t) = f_j^{it}(x_i(t), u_i(t), z_i(t), t)$$

$$+ \lambda_i^T(t)z_i(t) - \left(\sum_{j=1}^{N} \lambda_j^T(t)D_i^j \right) x_i(t)$$

$$+ p_i^T(t)\left[A_i x_i(t) + B_i u_i(t) + C_i z_i(t) \right],$$

$$j = 1, 2, ..., k; t = 0, 1, ..., T - 1. \tag{150}$$

Then the computation of the problem given in (149) for fixed λ and p can be performed by minimizing the multiobjective subproblems for each time index as follows: For $t = 0$:

$$\min_{u_i(0)} \begin{bmatrix} R_1^{i0}(x_i(0), u_i(0), z_i(0), 0) \\ \vdots \\ R_k^{i0}(x_i(0), u_i(0), z_i(0), 0) \end{bmatrix} \tag{151a}$$

s.t. $x_i(0)$, $z_i(0)$ given.

For $t = 1, 2, ..., T - 1$:

$$\min_{x_i(t), u_i(t), z_i(t)} \begin{bmatrix} R_1^{it}(x_i(t), u_i(t), z_i(t), t) - p_i^T(t-1)x_i(t) \\ \vdots \\ R_k^{it}(x_i(t), u_i(t), z_i(t), t) - p_i^T(t-1)x_i(t) \end{bmatrix} \tag{151b}$$

For $t = T$:

$$\min_{x_i(T)} \begin{bmatrix} f_1^{iT}(x_i(T)) - p_i^T(T-1)x_i(T) \\ \vdots \\ f_k^{iT}(x_i(T)) - p_i^T(T-1)x_i(T) \end{bmatrix} \tag{151c}$$

All noninferior solutions of the problem given in (148) for a fixed λ lie on the envelope of the family (with parameter p and the fixed λ) of noninferior frontiers which are obtained by solving (151). Furthermore, all noninferior solutions of the primal problem given in (146) lie on the envelope of the family of noninferior frontiers with parameter λ, which are obtained by solving (148).

Therefore, by virtue of this three-level hierarchical structure and the envelope approach, the large-scale multiobjective optimal control problem defined by (146) can be solved by the following algorithm.

Algorithm 3. Three-level-structure hierarchical generating method.

Step 1. The third level sends down a set of $\lambda(t)$'s to the second level.

Step 2. The second level sends down sets of $\lambda(t)$'s and $p(t)$'s, each of which contains one $\lambda(t)$ sequence and one corresponding set of $p_i(t)$'s, to the first level.

Step 3. At the first level, for given Lagrangian multiplier $\lambda(t)$ and costate vector $p(t)$, each subsystem (i, t) solves the problem given in (151) and gets the parametric form of the set of noninferior solutions,

$$\bar{f}_1{}^{it} = \bar{f}_1{}^{it*}(\theta; p_i, \lambda) \tag{152a}$$

$$\bar{f}_2{}^{it} = \bar{f}_2{}^{it*}(\theta; p_i, \lambda) \tag{152b}$$

$$\vdots$$

$$\bar{f}_k{}^{it} = \bar{f}_k{}^{it*}(\theta; p_i, \lambda) \tag{152c}$$

$$i = 1, 2, ..., N; \ t = 0, 1, ..., T - 1, T,$$

where $\bar{f}_j^t$, $j = 1, 2, ..., k$, is the j-th objective function of subsystem (i, t) given in (151).

Step 4. Set

$$\bar{f}_j^i(\theta; p_i, \lambda) = \sum_{t=0}^{T} \bar{f}_j^{it*}(\theta; p_i, \lambda), \ j = 1, 2, ..., k. \tag{153}$$

Step 5. At the second level, identify the envelope of the following family with parameter $p_i(t)$ and fixed $\lambda(t)$:

$$\bar{f}_1{}^i = \bar{f}_1{}^i(\theta; p_i, \lambda) \tag{154a}$$

$$\bar{f}_2{}^i = \bar{f}_2{}^i(\theta; p_i, \lambda) \tag{154b}$$

$$\vdots$$

$$\bar{f}_k{}^i = \bar{f}_k{}^i(\theta; p_i, \lambda) \tag{154c}$$

for each subsystem i in the problem given in (148), i = 1, 2,..., N.
Assume that the parametric form of the envelopes is

$$\bar{T}_1{}^i = \bar{T}_1{}^{i*}(\theta; \lambda) \tag{155a}$$

$$\bar{T}_2{}^i = \bar{T}_2{}^{i*}(\theta; \lambda) \tag{155b}$$

$$\vdots$$

$$\bar{T}_k{}^i = \bar{T}_k{}^{i*}(\theta; \lambda) \tag{155c}$$

where $\bar{f}_j^i$, j = 1, 2, ..., k, is the j-th objective of subsystem i in (148).

Step 6. S e t

$$\bar{f}_j(\theta; \lambda) = \sum_{i=1}^{N} \bar{f}_j^{i*}(\theta; \lambda), \;\; j = 1, 2, ..., k. \tag{156}$$

Step 7. At the third level, identify the envelope of the following family with parameter $\lambda(t)$:

$$\bar{T}_1 = \bar{T}_1(\theta; \lambda) \tag{157a}$$

$$\bar{T}_2 = \bar{T}_2(\theta; \lambda) \tag{157b}$$

$$\vdots$$

$$\bar{T}_k = \bar{T}_k(\theta; \lambda) \tag{157c}$$

All noninferior solutions of the problem given in (146) lie on this envelope.

V. CONCLUSIONS

In this study, a new method, termed here the envelope approach, has been proposed to solve some classes of large-scale multiobjective optimization problems. Investigation of the use of the envelope approach in multiobjective dynamic programming and in the hierarchical generating methods shows that this approach is suitable for the decomposition-coordination of large-scale multiobjective systems.

A.   MULTIOBJECTIVE DYNAMIC PROGRAMMING
      USING THE ENVELOPE APPROACH

The multiobjective dynamic programming method using the envelope approach derived in this study is applicable to general multiobjective multistage problems. Assumptions (such as that each overall objective function is of additive form with respect to the corresponding objective function at each stage required by the weighting method, or that associative operations are the same for all stages) are not needed in multiobjective dynamic programming using the envelope approach.

Under the assumptions of separability and monotonicity, the theorem of the principle of optimality for multiobjective dynamic systems is proved. The principle of optimality and the relationship between the envelope approach and multiobjective optimization give a theoretical basis for the multiobjective dynamic programming using the envelope approach. Using the envelope approach, we can find the set of noninferior solutions without requiring the performance of a large number of auxiliary scalar dynamic programming problems (not to mention the fact that auxiliary scalar dynamic programming methods fail in some cases). Moreover, this approach gives a clearer insight into multiobjective multistage optimization problems than do conventional methods that invoke scalar dynamic programming.

There is only one severe limitation to this approach – the curse of dimensionality in dynamic programming. This drawback is more serious than it is in scalar dynamic programming, since instead of recording the scalar cost-to-go and its associated optimal control, the vector cost-to-go and its associated set of noninferior solutions have to be recorded for each grid of the state at each stage.

One possibility for future research is to integrate some of the computational procedures used in scalar dynamic programming (for example, the differential dynamic programming) with the envelope approach as used in multiobjective cases.

B.   HIERARCHICAL GENERATING METHODS

The principle of hierarchical generating methods has been proposed in this study, in which two versions of hierarchical generating methods have been developed. By means of this study, a theoretical basis and methodological grounding for decomposition and coordination in a unified hierarchical multiobjective framework have been established. On the one hand, the advantages of the hierarchical generating methods accrue to the analyst: the approach helps him to deal with only the lower-dimensioned multiobjective subsystems and to coordinate the subproblems efficiently. On the other hand, for the decision maker, the benefits of hierarchical generating methods lie in the facts that 1) no interaction is necessary during the generating process for the set of noninferior solutions and, 2) the decision maker will acquire a fuller knowledge and better understanding of the system.

1.   Comparison of Two Versions of Hierarchical Generating Methods

Hierarchical generating methods can be divided into two types, according to whether their decomposition is feasible or nonfeasible. Assumption of the existence of saddle points is essential to the hierarchical generating method with nonfeasible decomposition. Unlike the hierarchical generating method with nonfeasible decomposition, the hierarchical generating method with feasible decomposition can be applied to hierarchical multiobjective systems with nonconvex objectives, nonlinear subsystems, and nonseparable interactions among subsystems. Also, local multiobjective optimization problems at the lower level seem to be simpler than in the nonfeasible version, since the vector objective function for each subsystem is not modified, and all the subsystem's outputs (and thus all interaction inputs) are specified at the upper level. However, the feasible version has a severe applicability condition: the dimension of u_i must be equal to or larger than the dimension of $x_i + (k - 1)$, $i = 1, 2, ..., N$, in order to guarantee a necessary condition for regular points. In addition, in the feasible version it is much more complex to get the corresponding efficient frontier of the overall system from the efficient frontiers of the subsystems than it is in the nonfeasible version.

2.   Comparison of Hierarchical Generating Methods and Straightforward Hierarchical Multiobjective Schemes

Straightforward hierarchical multiobjective schemes usually involve two steps. In the first step, some of the multiobjective optimization approaches, such as the weighting method and the ε-constraint method, are used to convert the original multiobjective problem into a series of single-objective problems. Then, in the second step, the ordinary hierarchical methods (see Mesarovic *et al.* [52]) can be directly applied to each single-objective problem in the series.

The straightforward methods are effective in many cases. In some aspects, however, the framework of the hierarchical generating methods presented in this study is more general. For example, when the original multiobjective large-scale system is nonconvex, the straightforward hierarchical multiobjective scheme adopts the ε-constraint method to convert it to a series of single-objective problems. In this case, the ordinary feasible decomposition method usually fails, since the ε-constraints are not separable with respect to subsystems in the feasible decomposition.

As viewed from the aspect of coordination, the straightforward hierarchical multiobjective methods and the hierarchical generating methods differ in the following. In straightforward hierarchical multiobjective schemes, the weighting coefficients or the values of the ε-constraints are preselected for each formed single-objective problem. Then a noninferior solution is identified as the ordinary hierarchical methods proceed to get the corresponding value of the coordination variable. On the other hand, in the hierarchical generating methods, the value of the coordination variable is assigned for each parametrized multiobjective problem, and a set of noninferior solutions of this parametrized problem is generated. Then, a noninferior solution of the overall system is identified among this set if the envelope properties are satisfied.

Moreover, the hierarchical generating methods deal with the decomposition and coordination in a multiobjective manner. This gives a clearer insight into multiobjective large-scale systems than can be obtained using straightforward hierarchical multiobjective methods that invoke single-objective multilevel methods.

As a final comment on the envelope approach, this approach is applicable to large-scale multiobjective optimization where there exists an envelope as a noninferior frontier in the coordination stage. The conditions for the existence of an envelope as a noninferior frontier for various multiobjective optimization problems need to be derived in future research.

ACKNOWLEDGMENTS

This research was supported in part by the National Science Foundation, Grant No. CEE-8211606, under the project title "The integration of the hierarchical and multiobjective approaches: Phase II," and Grant No. ECE85-13445, under the project title "Hierarchical-mul-tiobjective-dynamic analysis for the maintenance of water and wastewater treatment plants."
The editorial work of Virginia Benade is very much appreciated.

REFERENCES

1.   J. ESTER, C. RIEDEL, and M. PESCHEL, Polioptimal approach to the control of hierarchical multilevel systems. *Proc. World Congr. IFAC, 6th,* pp.19.2.1–6 *(1975).*
2.   A. M. GEOFFRION and W. W. HOGAN, *in* "Techniques of Optimization" (A. V. Balakrishnan, ed.). Academic Press, New York, pp. 455–466, 1972.

3.   Y. Y. HAIMES, in "Large-Scale Systems" (Y. Y. Haimes, ed). North-Holland Publ., Amsterdam, pp. 1–17, 1982.

4.   Y. Y. HAIMES, in "Progress in Ecological Engineering and Management by Mathematical Modeling" (D. Dubois, ed.). Editions Cebedoc, Paris, pp. 11–22, 1981.

5.   D. LI, Optimization of large-scale hierarchical multiobjective systems: The envelope approach. Ph.D. Dissertation, Case Western Reserve University, Cleveland, Ohio, 1987.

6.   D. LI and Y. Y. HAIMES, Proc. IEEE Int. Conf. Syst., Man Cybernet., 1985 , pp. 1039–1046 (1985).

7.   D. LI and Y. Y. HAIMES, J. Optim. Theory Appl. 54, 303 (1987).

8.   D. LI and Y. Y. HAIMES, A hierarchical generating method with feasible decomposition. Proc. World Congr. IFAC, 10th, 1987.

9.   P. NIJKAMP and P. RIETVELD, Eur. Econ. Rev. 15, 63 (1981).

10.   M. PESCHEL and C. RIEDEL, in "Conflict Objectives in Decisions" (D. E. Bell, R. L. Keeney, and H. Raiffa, eds.). Wiley, New York, pp. 97–122, 1977.

11.   K. SHIMIZU and E. AIYOSHI, J. Optim. Theory and Appl. 35, 517 (1981).

12.   K. STRASZAK, Polioptimization of large-scale systems with multilevel control structures. Proc. World Congr. IFAC, 5th, 1972 , pp. 27.4.1–8 (1972).

13.   N. TAKAMA and D. P. Loucks, Water Resour. Bull. 17, 448 (1981).

14.   K. TARVAINEN, On the generating of Pareto optimal alternatives in large-scale systems. IFAC/IFORS Symp. Large Scale Syst., 4th, 1986.

15.   K. TARVAINEN and Y. Y. HAIME , IEEE Trans. Syst., Man, Cybernet. SMC-12, 751 (1982).

16.   K. TARVAINEN, Y. Y. HAIMES, and I. LEFKOWITZ, Automatica 19, 15 (1983).

17.   Y. Y. HAIMES and D. LI, Automatica 24(1), 53 (1988). (The original version was presented in the 4th IFAC/IFOR Symposium on Large Scale Systems, Zurich, 1986).

18.   F. JIN and X. LI, "Ordinary Differential Equations" (in Chinese). Shanghai Scientific and Technological Press, Shanghai, 1962.

19.   V. C. BOLTYANSKII, "Envelopes." Macmillan, New York, 1964.

20.   J. W. BRUCE and P. J. GIBLIN, "Curves and Singularities." Cambridge Univ. Press, London and New York, 1984.

21.   J. J. STOKER, "Differential Geometry." Wiley (Interscience), New York, 1969.

22.   A. GOETZ, "Introduction to Differential Geometry." Addison-Wesley, Reading, Massachusetts, 1970.

23.   V. PARETO, "Cours d'Economie Politique." Rouge, Lausanne, Switzerland, 1896.

24.   H. W. KUHN and A. W. TUCKER, Nonlinear programming. Proc. Berkeley Symp. Math. Stat. Probabil., 2nd, 1951 pp. 481–492.

25.   T. C. KOOPMANS, ed., "Activity Analysis of Production," Cowles Comm. Monogr. No. 13. Wiley, New York, 1951.

26.   L. A. ZADEH, IEEE Trans. Autom. Control AC-8, 59 (1963).

27.   K. R. MacCRIMMON, in "Multiple Criteria Decision Making" (J. L. Cochrane and M. Zeleny, eds.). Univ. of South Carolina Press, Columbia, pp. 18–44, 1973.

28.   J. L. COHON and D. H. MARKS, Water Resour. Res. 11, 208 (1975).

29.   M. ZELENY, "Multiple Criteria Decision Making, Kyoto, 1975." Springer-Verlag, Berlin and New York, 1979.

30.   C. L. HWANG and A. S. M. MASUD, "Multiple Objective Decision Making – Methods and Applications: A State-of-the-Art Survey." Springer-Verlag, Berlin and New York, 1979.

31.   V. CHANKONG and Y. Y. HAIMES, Large Scale Syst. 5, 1 (1983).

32.   L. A. RASTRIGIN and YA. YU. EIDUK, Autom. Remote Control (Engl. Transl.) 46, 1 (1985).

33.   V. CHANKONG and Y. Y. HAIMES, "Multiobjective Decision Making: Theory and Methodology." Elsevier North Holland, New York, 1983.

34.   M. E. SALUKVADZE, "Vector-Valued Optimization Problems in Control Theory." Academic Press, New York, 1979.

35.   P. L. YU, J. Optim. Appl. 14, 319 (1974).

36.   J. L. COHON, "Multiobjective Programming and Planning." Academic Press, New York, 1978.
37.   S. GASS and T. SAATY, *Nav. Res. Logistic Q.* **2**, 39 (1955).
38.   Y. Y. HAIMES, L. LASDON, and D. WISMER, *IEEE Trans. Syst., Man, Cybernet.* **SMC-1**, 296 (1971).
39.   K. CHU, *IEEE Trans. Autom. Control* **AC-15**, 591 (1970).
40.   R. W. REID and V. VEMURI, *J. Franklin Inst.* **291**, 241 (1971).
41.   T. A. BROWN and R. E. STRAUCH, *J. Math. Anal. Appl.* **12**, 364 (1965).
42.   L. G. MITTEN, *Manage. Sci.* **21**, 43 (1974).
43.   M. J. SOBEL, *Manage. Sci.* **21**, 967 (1975).
44.   P. L. YU and L. SEIFORD, *in* "Multiple Criteria Analysis" (P. Nijkamp and J. Sprink, eds.). Gower Press, London, pp. 235–244 (1981).
45.   B. VILLARREAL and M. H. KARWAN, *J. Optim. Theory Appl.* **38**, 43 (1982).
46.   M. I. HENIG, *SIAM J. Control Optim.* **23**, 490 (1983).
47.   M. I. HENIG, *Math. Oper. Res.* **10**, 462 (1985).
48.   G. W. TAUXE, R. R. INMAN, and D. M. MADES, *Water Resour. Res.* **15**, 1398 (1979).
49.   V. CHANKONG, Y. Y. HAIMES, and D. M. GEMPERLINE, *IEEE Autom. Control* **AC-26**, 1195 (1981).
50.   R. R. LEVARY, *Int. J. Syst. Sci.* **15**, 309 (1984).
51.   G. DANTZIG and P. WOLFE, *Oper. Res.* **8**, 101 (1960).
52.   M. D. MESAROVIC, D. MACKO, and Y. TAKAHARA, "Theory of Hierarchical, Multilevel Systems." Academic Press, New York, 1970.
53.   C. BROSILOW, L. S. LASDON, and J. D. PEARSON, Feasible optimization methods for interconnected systems. *Proc. Jt. Autom. Control Conf., 1965* pp. 79–84 (1965).
54.   L. S. LASDON and J. D. SCHOEFFLER, A multilevel technique for optimization. *Proc. Jt. Autom. Control Conf., 1965*, pp. 85–92 (1965).
55.   Y. TAKAHARA, Multilevel approach to dynamic optimization. M.S. Thesis, Case Institute of Technology, Cleveland, Ohio, 1965.
56.   M. S. MAHMOUD, *IEEE Trans. Syst., Man, Cybernet.* **SMC-7**, 125 (1977).
57.   M. G. SINGH, A survey of recent developments in hierarchical optimizations and control. *Proc. Trienn. World Congr. IFAC, 8th, pp. 1271–1278, 1981.*
58.   D. M. NACHANE, *Eur. J. Oper. Res.* **21**, 25 (1984).
59.   D. Q. MAYNE, *in* "Directions in Large Scale Systems" (Y. C. Ho and S. K. Mitter, eds.), pp. 17–23. Plenum, New York, 1976.
60.   Y. Y. HAIMES, "Hierarchical Analyses of Water Resources Systems: Modeling and Optimization of Large-Scale Systems." McGraw-Hill, New York, 1977.
61.   T. TANINO and Y. SAWARAGI, *J. Optim. Theory Appl.* **27**, 509 (1979).

ALGORITHMS AND COMPUTATIONAL TECHNIQUES IN ROBOTIC SYSTEMS

SHIUH-JER HUANG

Department of Mechanical Engineering and Technology
National Taiwan Institute of Technology
Taipei, Taiwan, People's Republic of China

I.   INTRODUCTION

In the past decade, a large number of robots has been used in a number of industrial manufacturing processes to perform routine and repetitive tasks or to work in environments hostile to human appendages. The main advantage of manipulators is that once they are programmed they can perform these tasks at a rapid pace without becoming tired or bored. For applications in nuclear reactor plants, high-speed assemblies, remote manipulator systems of the space shuttle, or submarines, the digital control manipulator is a most useful tool. The computer generates commands for the manipulator control system that will cause a desired motion.

The dynamic analysis of manipulators tends to be rather complicated because of large configuration changes during spatial motion. Due to the changing geometry and Coriolis effect, the equations of motion of an N-degree-of-freedom open kinematic chain are highly nonlinearly coupled, which makes them not amenable to direct analytical solution. This creates a difficult control problem if the manipulator is to operate at a high speed. But it is very desirable to have high-speed motion and good performance to improve productivity and satisfy accuracy requirements.

Traditionally the design of the manipulator's control system is such that it is normally equipped with relatively simple control systems by treating each joint of the robot arm independently as a simple linear servomechanism. However, we know that the dynamics models of industrial robots are characterized by highly nonlinear equations with nonlinear coupling between the variables of motion. The simple linear decoupled model neglects the motion interaction and configuration effects of the whole arm mechanism, which makes it inadequate to obtain good system performance. With increased demand on manipulator performance will come the need for improved manipulator-control techniques. The use of conventional linear control techniques limits the basic dynamic performance of manipulators in a number of ways, two of which are very significant. In the first one, the dynamic characteristics of general spatial manipulators are a highly nonlinear function of the positions and velocities of the manipulator elements. In the other, the dynamic performance characteristics of manipulators will be degraded by the inertial properties of the objects being manipulated. Hence, in general, it is not possible to design a linear control system which will yield uniformly high system performance over a wide range of manipulator tasks. In some cases, the changing of parameters of the controlled system and the interaction between variables is significant enough to render the conventional linear feedback control strategies ineffective. The result will reduce servo response speed and damping, which limit the precision and speed of the end effector.

During the past two decades, various control concepts have been developed to an advanced level (Whitney [26, 27]; Paul [28]; Walker and Luh [13]). These algorithms range from linearized models to nonlinear models, from classical PID control to model reference adaptive control and self-tuning control. Although some reports employing optimal control theory have presented complicated nonlinear control strategies [15, 16], for the most part simpler linear strategies have been suggested [8, 13]. Some of the related algorithms are briefly discussed below. More details are in tutorial papers [8, 9] and reference texts [10, 11].

The disadvantages of these methods are that the detailed mathematical model of the system must be known and the control law cannot be used in a large working space.

The growth of computer technology makes robust adaptive control possible and more attractive in real-time operating time-varying nonlinear control problems. Among the many different approaches that have been proposed for adaptive control, two schemes in particular are of great interest. In the first, which is called model reference adaptive control, the basic idea is to cause the system to behave like a given reference model. A key question in model reference adaptive control, which concerned the stability of the resulting system, was finally resolved in the late 1970s by the combined efforts of many investigators [17].

The second scheme is the self-tuning regulator, which consists of two major stages: an on-line parameter identification scheme and feedback control law design. The recursive parameter estimator gathers available input and output data to estimate the unknown parameters of the system subject to a specified error criterion. Many estimation algorithms are available; however, the recursive least-squares estimation is currently the most popular due to its simplicity and effectiveness. The feedback control design algorithm uses these estimated system parameters to produce a new set of control coefficients for the feedback controller to generate the new control actions. This scheme, which was inherent in the early work of Kalman [29] and Young [30], was further developed by Chang and Rissanen [31]. They proposed the use of a least-squares parameter estimator together with a minimum variance controller, and they showed that this technique was one-step-ahead optimal. Later, a very exciting step forward was made by Astrom and Wittenmark [32] in parameter identification. They showed that if the parameter estimates converged to some value (not necessarily the true value), then a self-tuning minimum variance regulator would be optimal for a general ARMAX model even though the noise parameters were not explicitly estimated. A key observation of Astrom and Wittenmark was that, under certain conditions, it is not necessary to identify the parameters of the process, but instead it is sufficient to directly adjust the control law.

Recently various adaptive control algorithms have been proposed in manipulator control applications. Dubowsky [18] proposed a model reference adaptive control which uses a linear second-order time-invariant differential equation as the reference model for each degree of freedom of the robot arm. The manipulator is controlled by adjusting the position and velocity feedback gains to follow the model. A steepest-descent method is used to update the feedback gains. The coupling terms between the joints are neglected, which considerably simplifies the dynamic model of the manipulator. However, this method does not work for manipulators with gravity terms or stochastic disturbances, and there are some questions concerning the validity of their stability analysis.

Koivo [19] proposed an adaptive self-tuning controller using an autoregressive model to fit the input–output data from the manipulator. This work is an extension of the minimum variance control model of Clarke and Gawthrop [7], who modified the minimum variance algorithm by taking into account the control input constraints and command tracking capability. This algorithm does not require the system to be minimum phase, but the system must be open-loop stable. Thus this restriction makes the scheme inappropriate for the control of flexible manipulators or low-mass (inertia) manipulators which may exhibit open-loop unstable characteristics.

Lee [4] proposed an adaptive control that differs from the above by considering the nonlinear interactions as feedback components to minimize the nonlinear effects of the control system. Chung [20] and Walkers[21] proposed the pole placement assignment algorithm, which used a second-order independent difference model. The poles of the model can be chosen by the designer to reflect the desired specifications.

Elliott [22] showed that while adaptive control using the linear modeling approach can work for certain geometries and loadings, it performs poorly for other cases. Then he introduced a nonlinear model of adaptive control algorithms. He considered all terms in the dynamic model individually and identified the time-invariant parameters for each term. This means that when the system becomes complicated, or it possesses a high degree of freedom, the parameters needed to be identified will increase very quickly; for instance, a 3-degree-of-freedom (DOF)

robot has at least 28 parameters. Nevertheless, it is well documented in the literature that the convergence rate of the parameters of the sequential least-squares estimators deteriorates as the number of parameters to be estimated increases. Furthermore, computation time grows polynomially with an increase in the number
of parameters. This will affect the real-time implementation of practical applications. Therefore, Elliott's algorithm has disadvantages when used for cases with
high degrees of freedom.

The purpose of the present work is to design a simple controller without
many parameters to be estimated. Thus a nonlinear time-varying parameter adaptive control system is developed by considering the estimated angle accelerations,
velocity squared, and the value of the sine of the angle as outputs to estimate the
system parameters. We combine all parameters which have the same physical
significance in order to reduce the number of parameters.

This nonlinear time-varying adaptive control has four advantages. One is
directly using the nonlinear dynamic model in control law design, which can compensate all nonlinear effects, e.g., gravity and Coriolis forces. The second is that
the identification algorithm for the time-varying parameters can adjust the system
parameters from time to time. This is especially useful in systems where the
payload changes during the working task. The third is that this algorithm uses a
simple control law when no detailed mathematical model and system physical dimension is needed. The fourth is that the control law parameters are the same as
the parameter values estimated from identification schemes of system parameters.
Since less computing time is required for this scheme, the real-time implementation would be more practical. Also, if we can prove that the input and output are
bounded sequences, then the system global stability problem can be proved.

II.   MANIPULATOR DYNAMICS
           AND CONTROL METHODS

A.   MODELING OF MANIPULATOR DYNAMICS

The equations of motion for a manipulator with rigid arms are derived by
applying the Lagrange equations:

$$\frac{d}{dt}\left(\frac{\partial T}{\partial \dot{q}}\right) - \frac{\partial T}{\partial q} + \frac{\partial V}{\partial q} + F = Q, \tag{1}$$

where T and V are the kinetic and potential energies of the system, q and $\dot{q}$ are the
joint angles and angular velocities, and Q is the generalized external force corre-

sponding to q. To provide a reasonably accurate yet simplified model of the manipulator gross motion, it is necessary to impose certain assumptions on the analysis. Effects such as link flexibility and motor backlash are neglected. Generally, industrial robots need 6 DOFs, of which the first three control the end-effector position and the other three are for end-effector orientation control. Here we concentrate on system position control. The payload and end-effector mass are idealized as nonextended rigid bodies which have mass but no appreciable inertia. As a result, the effect of wrist and payload motion with respect to link 2 would be negligible. The mass of the wrist was lumped together with the payload mass at the end of link 2, and the links were idealized as rigid bodies, modeled as lumped masses and inertias.

The manipulator system's kinetic energy includes two parts. One is the kinetic energy of concentrated lumped mass moving with the velocity of each link's center of mass. Another is the rotational kinetic energy of each link with respect to center of mass:

$$T = \frac{1}{2}\sum_i M_i \dot{R}_i^2 + \frac{1}{2}\sum_i I_i \omega_i^2. \tag{2}$$

The potential energy of the system is due to gravitational force field,

$$V = \sum_i M_i g R_i \cos(Y_i). \tag{3}$$

After substituting T and V into (1) and taking the derivative with respect to generalized coordinates, the equation of motion of the system can be derived. The manipulator dynamics are described by nonlinear, time-varying, inhomogeneous differential equations and are highly coupled with all degrees of freedom.

The equations of motion of a 3-DOF robot system (Fig. 1) are as follows:

$$[M] \cdot \{A\} + [C] \cdot \{V_i V_j\} + [F] \cdot \{V\} + [G] \cdot \{\sin(Y)\} = \{U\}, \tag{4}$$

where M, C, F, and G matrices have components as follows:

$$M_{11} = J' + \left(\frac{1}{3}m_1 + \frac{1}{4}m_2 + m\right)L_1^2 S_2^2 + \frac{1}{3}m_2 L_2^2 \left(\frac{3L_1}{2L_2}S_2 + S_3\right)^2$$

$$+ m_3 L_2^2 \left(\frac{L_1}{L_2} S_2 + S_3 \right)^2 + m_3 L_2 \left(\frac{L_1}{L_2} S_2 + S_3 \right)^2 \tag{5}$$

$$M_{22} = \left(\frac{1}{3} m_1 - m_2 + m_3 + m \right) L_1^2 + \left(\frac{1}{2} m_2 + m_3 \right) L_1 L_2 C_{23}$$

$$M_{23} = \left(\frac{1}{3} m_2 + m_3 \right) L_2^2 + \left(\frac{1}{2} m_2 + m_3 \right) L_1 L_2 C_{23}$$

$$M_{32} = \left(\frac{1}{2} m_2 + m_3 \right) L_1 L_2 C_{23}$$

$$M_{33} = \left(\frac{1}{3} m_2 + m_3 \right) L_2^2$$

$$C_{11} = \left[\frac{2}{3} m_1 + 2 \left(m_2 + m + m_3 \right) \right] L_1^2 C_2 S_2 + \left(m_2 + 2 m_3 \right) L_1 L_2 C_2 S_3 \tag{6}$$

$$C_{12} = \left(m_2 + 2 m_3 \right) L_1 L_2 S_2 C_3 + \left(\frac{2}{3} m_2 + 2 m_3 \right) L_2^2 C_3 S_3$$

$$C_{23} = - \left(m_2 + m + \frac{1}{3} m_1 + m_3 \right) L_1^2 C_2 S_2 - \left(\frac{1}{2} m_2 + m_3 \right) L_1 L_2 S_{2+3}$$

$$- \left(\frac{1}{3} m_2 + m_3 \right) L_2^2 S_3 C_3$$

$$C_{23} = - \left(\frac{1}{2} m_2 + m_3 \right) L_1 L_2 S_{23}$$

$$C_{25} = \left(\frac{1}{2} m_2 + m_3 \right) L_1 L_2 S_{23}$$

$$C_{33} = - \left(\frac{1}{3} m_2 + m_3 \right) L_2^2 S_3 C_3 - \left(\frac{1}{2} m_2 + m_3 \right) L_1 L_2 S_2 C_3$$

$$C_{34} = - \left(\frac{1}{2} m_2 + m_3 \right) L_1 L_2 S_{23}$$

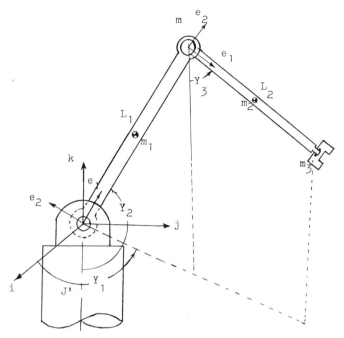

Fig. 1. Rigid arm spatial manipulator system with three-degrees-of-freedom.

$$F_{11} = f_1$$

$$F_{22} = f_2$$

$$F_{23} = -F_{33} = -f_3$$

$$G_{22} = \left(\frac{1}{2}m_1 + m_2 + m + m_3\right)L_1g$$

$$G_{23} = \left(\frac{1}{2}m_2 + m_3\right)L_2g$$

$$G_{33} = \left(\frac{1}{2}m_2 + m_3\right)L_2g$$

$$C_{ij} = \cos\left(Y_i - Y_j\right)$$

$$S_{ij} = \sin\left(Y_i - Y_j\right)$$

$$S_{i+j} = \sin\left(Y_i + Y_j\right),$$

where g is the gravitational field and m_i and L_i are the mass and the length of link i (where i identifies links 1 and 2). The mass of actuators at joints 1 and 2 are m and m_3. J' is the moment of inertia of the rotational base.

B.   TRACKING CONTROL PROBLEM

In the position tracking control, we consider the end effector moving with a prespecified velocity along the trajectory, so that we can program the pathline as a function of time in each joint angle coordinate. This tracking control problem is to design a controller U(t) which causes Y(t) to follow a desired trajectory Y*(t). Here we assume that the actuator can supply the desired torque simultaneously under the command signal of the control law; therefore, no motor dynamics are considered. In order to use a digital computer for calculation of the control law, we use classical sample data methodologies. The controller is designed based on a discrete-time system which will be used to control the continuous system. The first step is to derive a discrete approximation for (4). The simplest approach is to approximate

$$V(k) = \frac{Y(k) - Y(k-1)}{T} \tag{7}$$

$$A(k) = \frac{Y(k+1) - 2Y(k) + Y(k-1)}{T^2} \tag{8}$$

as the discrete-type estimation of velocity and acceleration, where T is the sampling period. If we have the velocity measurements, then the velocity approach is not needed. In this discrete-type tracking control problem we need to find the control input U(k) which satisfies the discrete-type equation of motion (4) step by step in order to produce a system response to Y(k + 1), where

$$Y(k+1) = Y^*(k+1) = Y^*\left((k+1)T\right). \tag{9}$$

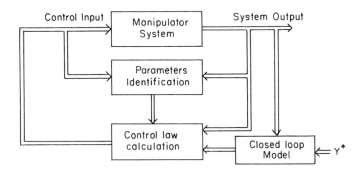

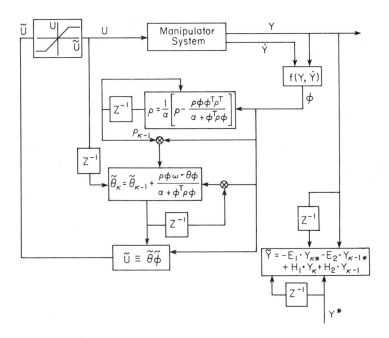

Fig. 2. Adaptive control system block diagram with a modified model.

For practical applications, the desired trajectory is in Cartesian coordinates; we must solve the geometric mechanism's Jacobian transformation to get the trajectory in the joints' coordinate system.

Here we want to take advantage of the reference model in smoothing the deadbeat one-step-ahead response; so a closed-loop control model which was set between reference trajectory input and desired output (see Fig. 2) was designed. This model makes the control effort smoother and the output response approach the desired trajectory asymptotically. Then it uses this desired output value as one part of the control command in calculating control inputs. Assume the closed-loop model can be characterized by the equation

$$\tilde{Y}(k+1) + E_1 \cdot Y(k) + E_2 \cdot Y(k-1) = H_1 \cdot Y^*(k) + H_2 \cdot H^*(k-1), \qquad (10)$$

where $Y^*(k)$ is a vector of the reference trajectory, and E_1, E_2, H_1, and H_2 are constant matrices. These matrices are chosen by the designer, but they need to satisfy two conditions. The first is that the determinant of $(Z^2 + E_1 \cdot Z + E_2)$ must have all its zeros inside the unit circle to ensure the stability of the system. The second is that this control model needs to satisfy the condition of zero steady-state error in order to guarantee the trajectory convergence. That means

$$\tilde{Y} = \frac{H_1 \cdot Z^{-1} + H_2 \cdot Z^{-2}}{1 + E_1 \cdot Z^{-1} + E_2 \cdot Z^{-2}} Y^*(k) \qquad (11)$$

$$\lim_{k \to \infty} Y^*(k) - \tilde{Y}(k) = \lim_{z \to 1}(Z-1) \cdot \frac{1 + \left(E_1 - H_1\right)z^{-1} + \left(E_2 - H_2\right)z^{-2}}{1 + E_1 \cdot Z^{-1} + E_2 \cdot Z^{-2}} \cdot Y^*(k)$$

$$= 0. \qquad (12)$$

For example, the velocity of the end effector on the tracking trajectory is considered to be constant. Thus the desired output $Y^*(t)$ is a ramp input.

$$Y^*(z) = \frac{Tz}{(z-1)^2} \cdot \kappa, \qquad (13)$$

where κ is a constant. Then we can rewrite (12) as

$$e(\infty) = \lim_{z \to 1} Y^*(z) - \tilde{Y}(z) \qquad (14)$$

$$= \lim_{z \to 1}(z-1) \cdot \frac{z^2 + \left(E_1 - H_1\right)z + \left(E_2 - H_2\right)}{z^2 + E_1 \cdot z + E_2} \cdot \frac{Tz}{(z-1)^2}\kappa$$

$$= \lim_{z \to 1} \frac{z^2 + \left(E_1 - H_1\right)z + \left(E_2 - H_2\right)}{z^2 + E_1 \cdot z + E_2} \cdot \frac{Tz}{(z-1)}\kappa$$

$$\equiv 0, \tag{15}$$

where $(z^2 + E_1 \cdot z + E_2)$ has not root at $z = 1$ (first condition). So, in order to get $e(\infty) = 0$, $z^2 + (E_1 - H_1)z + (E_2 - H_2) = 0$ should have repeated roots at $z = 1$. That means $E_1 - H_1 = 2.0$ and $E_2 - H_2 = 1.0$. Another consideration in design of the closed-loop model is to choose higher damping.

Using this idea, two different control algorithms are designed in the present work. One of these control algorithms is based on a classical computed torque control method which is called fixed digital control strategy, and the other is called adaptive control strategy. In the following section we will describe these algorithms and then compare their performance, advantages, and disadvantages by numerical computer simulation.

C.   ADAPTIVE CONTROL STRATEGY

The concept of an adaptive system has been defined by Landau: "An adaptive system measures a certain index of performance (IP) using the inputs, the states and the output of the adjustable system. From the comparison of the measured index of performance values and a set of given ones, the adaptation mechanism modifies the parameters of the adjustable system or generates an auxiliary input in order to maintain the index of performance values close to the set of given ones."

From the manipulator dynamics system we have the equation

$$[M] \cdot \{A\} + [C] \cdot \{V_i V_j\} + [F] \cdot \{V\} + [G] \cdot \{\sin(Y)\} = \{U\}. \tag{16}$$

This control law was defined as

$$U(k) = \tilde{\theta}_{k-1} \cdot \tilde{\varphi}_k, \tag{17}$$

where

$$\tilde{\varphi}_k^T = \left[\tilde{A}(k), \ V_i(k)V_j(k), \ V(k), \ \sin[Y(k)] \right] \tag{18}$$

are estimated or measurement value products, and

$$\tilde{\theta}_{k-1} = \left[\tilde{M}_{k-1}, \ \tilde{C}_{k-1}, \ \tilde{F}_{k-1}, \ \tilde{G}_{k-1} \right] \tag{19}$$

are estimated parameter vectors. The true values of M, C, F, and G are defined in Section A.

In designing the adaptive control strategy, we chose the cost function as

$$J_0(\theta) = \left(\theta - \tilde{\theta}_0 \right) P_0^{-1} \left(\theta - \tilde{\theta}_0 \right)^T \tag{20}$$

$$J_n(\theta) = \alpha J_{n-1}(\theta) + \left(U_n - \theta\varphi_n \right)^2 . \tag{21}$$

The error of the initial parameters guess was accounted for in $J(\theta)$. The "forgetting factor" α was chosen in order to get an exponential forgetting profile in the accumulated criterion J of the system output error signal. Unlike the conventional method, the type of $(Y - \tilde{Y})^2$ needs extra computing time to calculate the control law parameters. Here we choose $[U(k) - \theta\varphi]^2$ instead of $[Y(k) - \theta'\varphi']^2$ in the cost function for the tracking control problem. The advantage is that the cost function still contains the output error squared message, and this choice can reduce the computation time in calculating the control law. When minimizing J with respect to U, we get the optimal control law $U = \theta\varphi$; minimizing J with respect to θ, we can get the equations of the parameter identification scheme. This combination is a simple effectiveness adaptive control law. In this adaptive control we need a good parameter identification algorithm to estimate the θ vector, especially when time-varying system parameters are to be estimated. Note that although the velocity product and trigonometric terms of the control system are highly nonlinear, its parameters have a linear form with respect to the nonlinear terms, so that the standard sequential linear parameter estimation procedures can be applied. It should also be pointed out that technical aspects of stability analysis require that $\tilde{M}$, the first entry in $\tilde{\theta}$, be restricted from converging to zero. According to

Goodwin and Sin [17], some parameter estimator schemes can be used in nonlinear time-varying systems, and the best choice depends on the system's characteristics. Here the least-squares method with exponential weighting [17] is used in simulation, and the results are found to be very good.

D.   LEAST-SQUARES METHOD WITH EXPONENTIAL DATA WEIGHTING

In order to derive the system parameters identification scheme by the method of least squares with exponential data weighting, the most recent data are assumed to be more informative than the past data. We then exponentially discard old data, which leads to the following exponentially weighted cost function:

$$J_0(\theta) = \left(\theta - \tilde{\theta}_0\right)P_0^{-1}\left(\theta - \tilde{\theta}_0\right)^T \tag{22}$$

$$J_n(\theta) = \alpha J_{n-1}(\theta) + \left(U_n - \theta\varphi_n\right)^2, \tag{23}$$

where $0 < \alpha < 1.0$. Note that $\alpha = 1$ gives the standard least-squares cost function. It can be shown that minimization of the cost function $J_n(\theta)$ leads to the following sequential algorithm (Appendix A of Ref. [14]):

$$\tilde{\theta}^T(k) = \tilde{\theta}^T(k-1) + \frac{P(k-1)\varphi(k)\left[U(k) - \tilde{\theta}(k-1)\varphi(k)\right]}{\alpha + \varphi^T(k)P(k-1)\varphi(k)} \tag{24}$$

$$P(k) = \frac{1}{\alpha}\left(P(k-1) - \frac{P(k-1)\varphi(k)\varphi^T(k)P(k-1)}{\alpha + \varphi^T(k)P(k-1)\varphi(k)}\right). \tag{25}$$

E.   ADAPTIVE CONTROL PROCEDURE

The adaptive control procedure operates according to the following steps:
1) We have known values (estimated or measured) of $V(k)$ and $Y(k)$ at k steps and from the closed-loop model

$$\tilde{Y}(k+1) = -E_1 \cdot \tilde{Y}(k) - E_2 \cdot \tilde{Y}(k-1) + H_1 \cdot Y^*(k) + H_2 \cdot Y^*(k-1) \tag{26}$$

or

$$\tilde{Y}(k+1) = -E_1 \cdot Y(k) - E_2 \cdot Y(k-1) + H_1 \cdot Y^*(k) + H_2 \cdot Y^*(k-1). \tag{27}$$

The second equation uses real output $Y(k)$, $Y(k-1)$ to calculate the desired output of the next step. This algorithm obviously gives a system performance change after the payload changes.

2) We can next use the central difference approach to estimate the desired acceleration at each k step:

$$\tilde{A}(k) = \frac{\tilde{Y}(k+1) - 2Y(k) + Y(k-1)}{T^2}. \tag{28}$$

After that these values will be obtained:

$$\tilde{\varphi}_k^T = \left[\tilde{A}(k), \, V_i(k)V_j(k), \, V(k), \, \sin[Y(k)] \right]. \tag{29}$$

3) Calculate the control law

$$U(k) = \tilde{\theta}_{k-1} \cdot \tilde{\varphi}_k. \tag{30}$$

4) Use the values calculated from the control law as the system input and measure the system output response $Y(k+1)$.

5) Compute the system k step actual acceleration by using these output values:

$$A(k) = \frac{Y(k+1) - 2Y(k) + Y(k-1)}{T^2}. \tag{31}$$

6) Use these data:

$$\varphi_k^T = \left[A(k), V_i(k)V_j(k), V(k), \sin[Y(k)] \right],$$ (32)

$\tilde{\theta}_{k-1}$, and $U(k)$ to represent the output error. Substitute this information in the system identification scheme to estimate and update the system parameter's value.

From the new parameter value and the next step reference trajectory position we can carry out another step iteration. The system block diagrams are presented in Fig. 2.

III. STABILITY ANALYSIS AND SIMULATION

A. BOUNDED INPUT–BOUNDED OUTPUT

In order to prove the stability property of this nonlinear adaptive control scheme, we need to prove that the control system input and output are bounded. From the control law equation (4) we get

$$U(k) = \tilde{M}(k-1) \cdot \tilde{A}(k) + \tilde{C}(k-1) \cdot V_i V_j(k)$$

$$+ \tilde{F}(k-1) \cdot V(k) + \tilde{G}(k-1) \cdot \sin[Y(k)].$$ (33)

Let us define the control input error as

$$\delta(k) = U(k) - \tilde{M}(k-1) \cdot A(k) - \tilde{C}(k-1) \cdot V_i V_j(k)$$

$$- \tilde{F}(k-1) \cdot V(k) - \tilde{G}(k-1) \cdot \sin[Y(k)]$$

$$= \tilde{M}(k-1) \cdot \left[\tilde{A}(k) - A(k) \right]$$

$$= \frac{\tilde{M}(k-1)}{T^2} \left[\tilde{Y}(k+1) - Y(k+1) \right]$$

$$= \frac{\tilde{M}(k-1)}{T^2} \left[-E_1 \cdot Y(k) - E_2 \cdot Y(k-1) \right.$$ (34)

$$+ H_1 \cdot Y^*(k) + H_2 \cdot Y^*(k - 1) - Y(k + 1) \Big] \tag{35}$$

or

$$Y(k + 1) + E_1 \cdot Y(k) + E_2 \cdot Y(k - 1)$$

$$= H_1 \cdot Y^*(k) + H_2 \cdot Y^*(k - 1) - T^2 \cdot \tilde{M}^{-1}(k - 1) \cdot \delta(k) \tag{36}$$

since the roots of the $\det(Z^2 + E_1 \cdot Z + E_2)$ have been chosen to lie strictly inside the unit circle and the reference input sequence $Y^*(k)$ is assumed bounded. As a result, the output sequence $Y(k)$ is guaranteed to be bounded provided $\det \tilde{M}(k) > \varepsilon > 0$ for all k, where ε is a small constant:

$$Y(k) \le C_1 + C_2 \cdot \max\big[\delta(k)\big]. \tag{37}$$

Next, from the control law equation, we have

$$U(k) = \tilde{M}(k - 1) \cdot \tilde{A}(k) + \tilde{C}(k - 1) \cdot V_i V_j(k)$$

$$+ \tilde{F}(k - 1) \cdot V(k) + \tilde{G}(k - 1) \cdot \sin\big[Y(k)\big], \tag{38}$$

where

$$\tilde{A}(k) = \frac{\tilde{Y}(k + 1) - 2Y(k) + Y(k - 1)}{T^2} \tag{39}$$

$$V(k) = \frac{Y(k) - Y(k - 1)}{T}. \tag{40}$$

Therefore, $\tilde{A}(k)$, $V(k)$, $V_i(k) \cdot V_j(k)$, and $\sin[Y(k)]$ are also a bounded sequence, which means that the control input signal is also bounded:

$$U(k) \le C_3 + C_4 \cdot \max\big[\delta(k)\big], \tag{41}$$

where C_1, C_2, C_3, and C_4 are some finite constants.

In practical applications, the control torque output of any actuator has physical limitations; therefore the control input U(k) is automatically bounded. Now that the input and output sequences are all bounded, the results of Goodwin and Sin have shown that the system global stability is obtained when a sequential least-squares algorithm is employed.

B.   EXISTENCE OF THE DISCRETE NONLINEAR ADAPTIVE CONTROL

The control law U(k) is given by

$$U(k) = \tilde{M}(k-1) \cdot \tilde{A}(k) + \tilde{C}(k-1) \cdot V_i V_j(k)$$

$$+ \tilde{F}(k-1) \cdot V(k) + \tilde{G}(k-1) \cdot \sin[Y(k)]. \tag{42}$$

Substituting these control inputs into the dynamic equation (4), we can calculate the system output Y(k + 1) for the next step.

$$Y(k+1) = 2 \cdot Y(k) - Y(k-1) + T^2 \cdot M^{-1} \Big\{ U(k)$$

$$- C \cdot V_i V_j(k) - F \cdot V(k) - G \cdot \sin[Y(k)] \Big\}. \tag{43}$$

Let us define

$$E(k+1) = \tilde{Y}(k+1) - Y(k+1); \tag{44}$$

then

$$E(k+1) = \tilde{Y}(k+1) - 2 \cdot Y(k) + Y(k-1) - T^2 \cdot M^{-1}$$

$$\times \Big\{ U(k) - C \cdot V_i V_j(k) - F \cdot V(k) - G \cdot \sin[Y(k)] \Big\}$$

$$= T^2 \Big(\tilde{A}(k) - M^{-1} \Big\{ U(k) - C \cdot V_i V_j(k) - F \cdot V(k) - G \cdot \sin[Y(k)] \Big\} \Big)$$

$$= T^2 \cdot M^{-1} \left\{ M \cdot \tilde{A}(k) - U(k) + C \cdot V_i V_j(k) + F \cdot V(k) + G \cdot \sin[Y(k)] \right\}$$

$$= T^2 \cdot M^{-1} \left\{ (M - \tilde{M}) \cdot \tilde{A}(k) + (C - \tilde{C}) \cdot V_i V_j(k) \right.$$

$$\left. + (F - \tilde{F}) \cdot V(k) + (G - \tilde{G}) \cdot \sin[Y(k)] \right\}$$

$$= T^2 \cdot M^{-1} [M - \tilde{M}, \, C - \tilde{C}, \, F - \tilde{F}, \, G - \tilde{G}] \cdot \begin{bmatrix} \tilde{A}(k) \\ V_i V_j(k) \\ V(k) \\ \sin[Y(k)] \end{bmatrix}$$

$$\equiv T^2 \cdot M^{-1} \cdot \bar{\theta}_{k-1} \tilde{\varphi}_k \tag{45}$$

$$= T^2 \cdot M^{-1} \cdot \bar{\theta}_{k-1} \varphi_k + T^2 \cdot M^{-1} (M - \tilde{M}) \cdot [\tilde{A}(k) - A(k)] \tag{46}$$

$$= T^2 \cdot M^{-1} \cdot \bar{\theta}_{k-1} \varphi_k + M^{-1} \cdot (M - \tilde{M}) \cdot [\tilde{Y}(k+1) - Y(k+1)] \tag{47}$$

$$= T^2 \cdot M^{-1} \cdot \bar{\theta}_{k-1} \varphi_k + E(k+1) - M^{-1} \cdot \tilde{M} \cdot E(k+1). \tag{48}$$

With some rearrangement of the above equation, we obtain

$$\tilde{M} \cdot E(k+1) = T^2 \cdot \bar{\theta}_{k-1} \varphi_k \tag{49}$$

$$E(k+1) = T^2 \tilde{M}^{-1} \bar{\theta}_{k-1} \varphi_k. \tag{50}$$

The control objective point is to determine U(k) such that

$$\lim_{k \to \infty} E(k+1) = \lim_{k \to \infty} \left\{ \tilde{Y}(k+1) - Y(k+1) \mid \mathscr{L}(k) \right\} = 0, \tag{51}$$

where $\mathscr{L}(k)$ is the information set which contains the outputs, output products, and input until time k. In the last section we have proved that $\varphi(k) = [A(k), V_i(k)\cdot V_j(k), \sin[Y(k)]]$ is a bounded sequence. Thus there are two possible ways to satisfy the asymptotic convergence criterion of the output.

1) Since

$$E(k + 1) = T^2 \tilde{M}^{-1} \cdot \bar{\theta}_{k-1} \varphi_k$$

and $\varphi(k)$ is bounded for all time k, if

$$\lim_{k \to \infty} \bar{\theta}(k) = 0 \tag{52}$$

then

$$\lim_{k \to \infty} \bar{\theta}(k - 1)\varphi(k) = 0. \tag{53}$$

$\bar{\theta}(k) = 0$ means that the parameters of the system converge to their true values. In order to obtain the solution, the control input signal should have sufficiently rich frequencies or they must be persistently exciting.

2) Another possibility is not to insist on $\bar{\theta}(k) \to 0$, but simply find any vector $\tilde{\theta}$ such that $\bar{\theta}_\varphi \to 0$, where $\tilde{\theta}$ is linearly related to $\varphi(k)$. It can be readily shown that such a vector $\tilde{\theta}$ exists, because any $\tilde{\theta}(k)$ which makes $\varphi(k)$ orthogonal to $\bar{\theta}(k - 1)$ will satisfy the requirement. From (45) we define

$$\bar{\theta} = \left[M - \tilde{M}, C - \tilde{C}, F - \tilde{F}, G - \tilde{G} \right]. \tag{54}$$

There will be an affine subspace of $(R^n, R^n \times R^n)$ of such vectors with this choice of $\varphi(k)$ such that

$$E(k + 1) = T^2 \tilde{M}^{-1} \bar{\theta}(k - 1)\varphi(k) = 0. \tag{55}$$

Hence, there exists a control law of the form

$$U(k) = \tilde{\theta}(k-1)\tilde{\varphi}(k), \tag{56}$$

where $\varphi(k) \in (R^n, R^n \times R^n)$ space, but the space spanned by $\varphi(k)$ is $H(R^n, R^n \times R^n)$. Therefore, we can find a vector $\bar{\theta}(k-1)$ such that

$$\bar{\theta}(k-1) \neq 0, \quad \varphi \in H(R^n, R^n \times R^n), \tag{57}$$

$$\bar{\theta} \in H^\perp.$$

Thus,

$$E(k+1) = T^2 \tilde{M}^{-1} \bar{\theta}(k-1)\varphi(k) = 0, \tag{58}$$

where the $\theta(k-1)$ are time-varying system parameter vectors. Under the assumption that the system parameters are changing slowly, the convergence of these estimated parameters can be proved [14].

C.   SIMULATION OF A 3-DOF ROBOT SYSTEM

The physical and geometrical characteristics of this spatial manipulator are as follows: $L_1 = 1.0$ m, $L_2 = 0.60$ m, $m_1 = 5.0$ kg, $m_2 = 3.0$ kg, the mass of actuator at joint 2 and end effector are $m = 2.0$ kg, $m_3 = 1.5$ kg, and the moment of inertia of the rotation base is $J' = 3.0$ kg m. The viscous friction dampings are 0.5, 0.35, and 0.35 kg m/sec, corresponding to joints 1, 2, and 3.

Here only the time-varying adaptive control system algorithm was used for simulation, because Elliott's time-invariant method needs to estimate at least 28 parameters instead of 18 for a time-varying system, which is not efficient in adaptive control implementation.

1.   Path Tracking Control

The reference trajectory of the end effector is a circle on the inertial coordinate X–Y plane

$$X^2 + (Y - 0.80)^2 = 0.09 \text{ m}^2$$

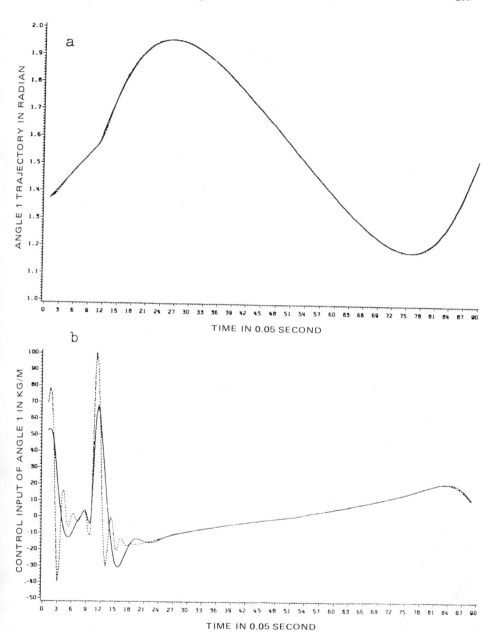

Fig. 3. Angle 1 input and output response trajectories of a spatial manipulator of fixed and adaptive control with $U_{1\,max} = 100$ kg m. (a) Angle trajectory: (–), reference; (---), fixed control; (---), adaptive control. (b) Control input of the angle: (–), fixed control; (- - -) adaptive control.

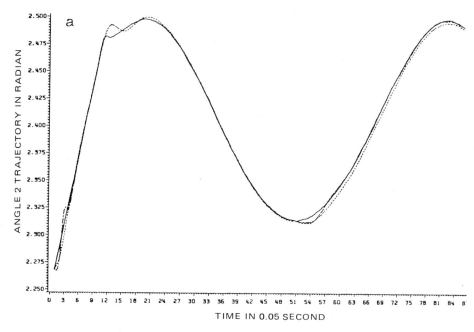

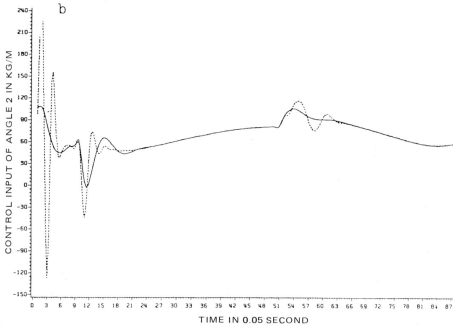

Fig. 4. Angle 2 input and output response trajectories of a spatial manipulator of fixed and adaptive control with $U_{2\ max} = 250$ kg m. Legend as in Fig. 3.

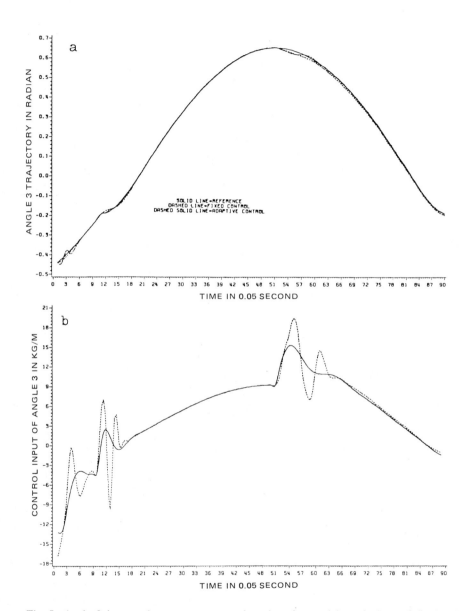

Fig. 5. Angle 3 input and output response trajectories of a spatial manipulator of fixed and adaptive control with $U_{3\ max} = 25$ kg m. Legend as in Fig. 3.

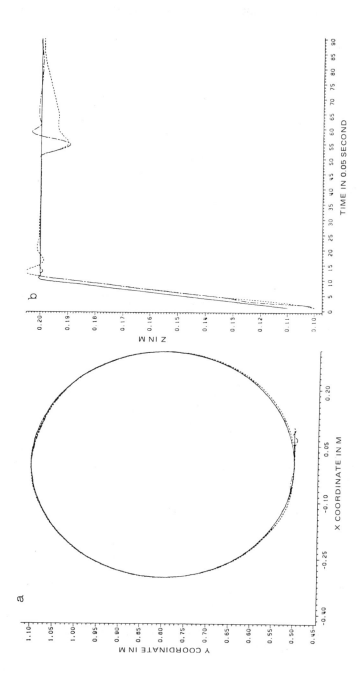

Fig. 6. The end-effector Cartesian coordinate position trajectories. (–), reference; (---), fixed control; (---), adaptive control. (a) End-effector position in the xy plane; (b) in the z coordinate.

204

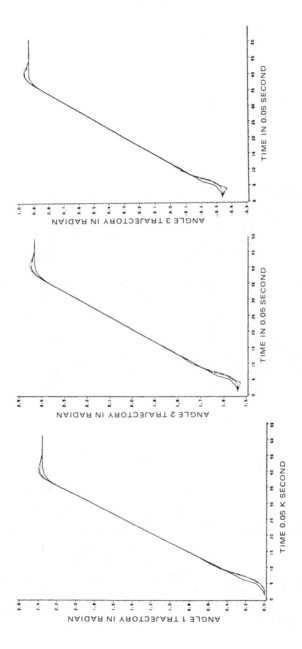

Fig. 7. Angle output response trajectories of a spatial manipulator moving between two positions. Legend as in Fig. 6. (a) Angle 1; (b) angle 2; (c) angle 3.

205

$$X(k) = -0.30 \sin\left(\frac{\pi(k-1)}{40}\right) m$$

$$Y(k) = 0.80 - 0.30 \cos\left(\frac{\pi(k-1)}{40}\right) m$$

$$Z(k) = 0.20 \text{ m}.$$

The sampling time T is 0.05 sec. The model to be matched between Y^* and $\tilde{Y}$ is $H_1 = -E_1 = 1.0$, $H_2 = 0.71$, and $E_2 = 0.29$. The initial parameter guess used for the parameter identification scheme of the adaptive control is chosen within 25–30% of the true initial values. At time t = 2.0 sec the end effector at the end of the second link picks up a payload of 1.5 kg and the robot system continues to move another half-circle.

Figures 3a, 4a, and 5a present the three angle trajectories of reference, fixed control, and adaptive control. The control input differences between these two methods are shown in Figs. 3b, 4b, and 5b. Figure 6a,b illustrates the robot end-effector output trajectories in Cartesian coordinates X, Y, and Z. From these simulation results, we observe that the adaptive control in the first few steps has obvious deviations due to the initial error of the parameter guess. This phenomenon only happens in the first run, and the later runs do not have this undesirable deviation. The small deviation error at the peak of the sinusoidal-type angle trajectory is due to the fact that the linear closed-loop model cannot match the properties of the nonlinear angle trajectory.

2.   Two-Endpoints Response Control

Consider the situation when the end effector of a robot needs to move from (0.8, 0.0, –0.6)m to (–0.8, 0.8, 0.4)m in Cartesian coordinates. The velocity law of the trajectory planning is chosen first as an acceleration from the starting point, followed by a constant velocity motion, and then a deceleration to the endpoint. Figure 7 plots the angle trajectories of reference, fixed control, and adaptive control methods. The observed overshoots are smaller than the step input response case, which was shown in Ref. [14] for a 2-DOF system. Figures 8–10 illustrate more complicated angle trajectories generated when using the block diagram of Fig. 2. The end effector stops at certain specified points for 1 sec, and then it moves to another point midway, where it picks up a payload and moves back.

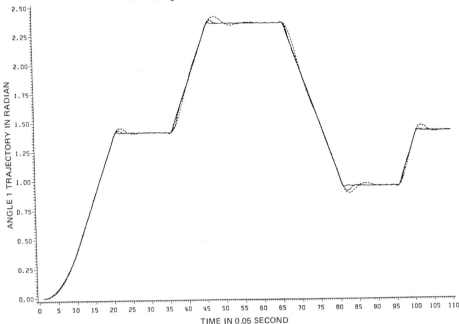

Fig. 8. Angle 1 output response trajectories of a 3-DOF robot in working condition with the closed-loop model. Legend as in Fig. 6.

IV. PHYSICAL MODELING OF FLEXIBLE MANIPULATORS

A. BACKGROUND

To date most manipulators have been designed and built almost rigidly. Dynamically this system could be treated as a rigid one as long as it is designed as a short and rigid element, as well as having speeds which are relatively slow. But this is not an available solution in two notable applications: remote-controlled robot manipulators for space applications and high-speed automatic machinery. Furthermore, an important consideration in connection with the usefulness of robots on a production line is the speed with which they can transfer objects from one point to another. So there has been increasing interest in the effect of link flexibility in computer-controlled manipulators and robots. This interest is spurred by the desire for designing greater-speed lightweight robot systems capable of moving larger payloads without increasing the mass of the linkage and improving the accuracy of the robotic manipulator.

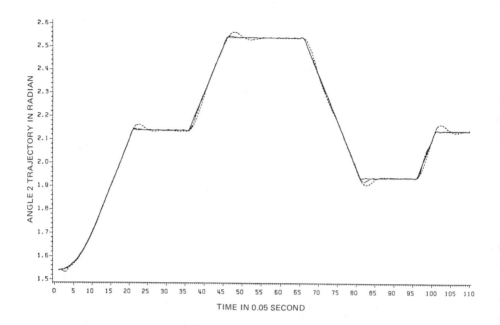

Fig. 9. Angle 2 output response trajectories of a 3-DOF robot in working condition with the closed-loop model. Legend as in Fig. 6.

Research on elastic manipulators has been concerned so far mostly with the difficult dynamic modeling problem [1–3, 5]. Control schemes for flexible manipulators are still in their first stages of development [6, 12, 23–25].

All the above methods that have been proposed for flexible manipulator systems are based on certain assumptions and can only be used in special cases. Those controllers are designed based on linearized systems with respect to some special equilibrium points, and the control system's dynamic response due to system perturbations is investigated. They can be used within a small working range, but we have to accept the obvious error tolerance. Some schemes are not even practically available yet, because generally the elastic vibration states are unknown and are very difficult to measure or estimate. That means we cannot consider these states as avilable information in design control law. Therefore, much effort is still needed to develop a good controller for general flexible manipulator systems. In this study a new approach was developed by combining the system's noise estimation scheme and the rigid arm's system nonlinear adaptive control algorithm. Here a truncated mode shapes method is used in flexible-beam system dynamic modeling. A nonlinear dynamic model is used in control law design di-

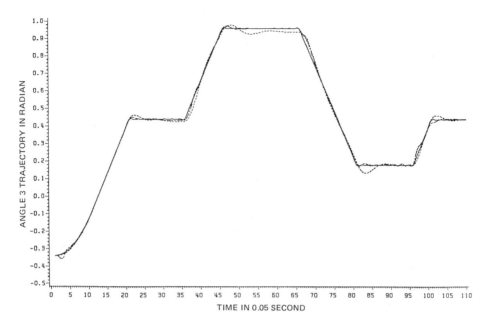

Fig. 10. Angle 3 output response trajectories of a 3-DOF robot in working condition with the closed-loop model. Legend as in Fig. 6.

rectly. The adaptive controller includes a biased term to identify the deflection effect of the manipulator system. This means that we try to modify the nonlinear adaptive control algorithm in Section I for stochastic system applications. Finally, two-dimensional robots were chosen for computer simulation and checking of system performance.

The schematic of the manipulator in Fig. 11 consists of two flexible links and a rigid end-effector/payload combination. Only planar motion is allowed, with the driving force provided by ideal torque sources located at the joints. The two flexible links are modeled as Euler–Bernoulli beams. These links have length l_i, constant elastic modulus E_i, constant section bending moment of inertia I_i, and constant mass per unit length (where i identifies links 1 and 2). The moment of inertia of the rotational base is J', which is associated at joint angle 1.

Assuming that the flexible links are rigidly attached to the joints, the links can be modeled as cantilevered-free beams with a moving base. Each joint is associated with an actuator which provides the control torque; the actuator masses are m and m_3, concentrated at the ends of links 1 and 2, respectively. The end effector and payload are considered as a concentrated mass located at the end of the second flexible link without any moment of inertia.

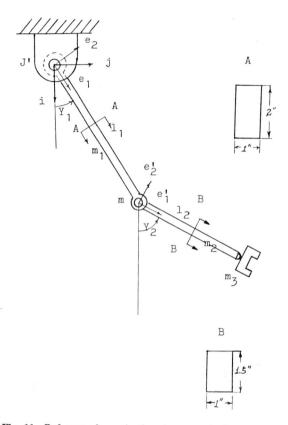

Fig. 11. Reference frame in the planar manipulator system.

B.   PLANAR MECHANISM
       KINEMATIC DESCRIPTION

To describe the motion of the system, three reference frames are defined, as shown in Fig. 11. These frames are: [O, i, j], the inertial reference frame; [O, e_1, e_2], the link 1 reference frame; and [O', e_1', e_2'], the link 2 reference frame. The j and e_1 axes are chosen perpendicular to the respective i and e_2 axes. The rotation of both links relative to the inertial reference frame are specified by the two angles Y_i, where Y_1 is the angle between i and e_1; and Y_2 is the angle between i and e_1'. All angles are positive counterclockwise.

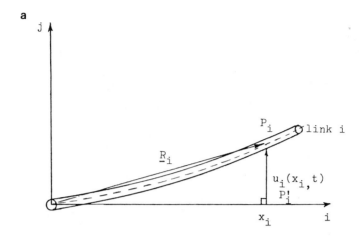

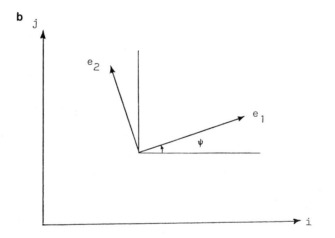

Fig. 12. Beam deflection local position vector and coordinate systems.

An arbitrary point P_i' in an undeformed link is specified by the linear distance from the local origin. As the link bends P_i' will deflect to the new position P_i, as shown in Fig. 12a. The flexible motion in the local coordinate system was defined as $u_i(x, t)$. Assuming the deflection to be small, u_i can be taken perpendicular to the x axis. The local position vector R to O is then given as

$$\mathbf{R}_i = x_i \mathbf{e}_1 + u_i \mathbf{e}_2, \tag{59}$$

where u_i is the magnitude of $u_i(x, t)$.

Figure 12b shows two coordinate systems R_i in Eq. (59) is the vector expression of R in the $[O, e_1, e_2]$ reference frame. Knowing the angle ψ between the i and e_1 axes, the coordinate transformation matrix [B] can be formed:

$$B = \begin{bmatrix} \cos \psi & -\sin \psi \\ \sin \psi & \cos \psi \end{bmatrix}. \tag{60}$$

Premultiplication of R by [B] results in R^0, the vector expression with the components of R_i in the i, j directions as components

$$R_i^0 = [B] \cdot R_i. \tag{61}$$

Coordinate transformation matrices can now be defined for the two moving local coordinate systems of the manipulator. Premultiplying the local position vector R by the appropriate coordinate transformation matrix selected, resulting in the components of R_i in the inertial frame or any reference frame.

The flexible motion of the link i relative to local coordinate systems is described by $u_i(x, t)$. An assumed mode shapes method will be used to describe $u_i(x, t)$. The displacement of a point x units from the local origin is written as:

$$u_i(x, t) = \sum_j^n \Phi_{ij}(x) \cdot q_{ij}(t), \tag{62}$$

where $\Phi(x)$ is the $1 \times n$ vector of link mode shapes and $q(t)$ is the time-dependent $n \times 1$ vector of model amplitudes. Appendix B in Ref. [14] contains the details of the cantilevered-free beam mode shapes used:

$$\Phi_{ij}(x) = \left[\cosh \lambda_{ij} x - \cos \lambda_{ij} x - \sigma_{ij} \left(\sinh \lambda_{ij} x - \sin \lambda_{ij} x \right) \right].$$

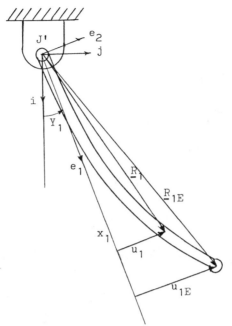

Fig. 13. Link 1 position vector.

C.   LINK-1 KINEMATICS

The relative position vector of P_1 to the first frame R_1 is described as

$$R_1 = xe_1 + u_1 e_2. \tag{63}$$

The local and inertial position vectors of the end of link 1 are also shown in Fig. 13. Denoting the deflection at the end of link 1 by u_{1E}, the local position vector of the end of link 1 is

$$R_{1E} = l_1 e_1 + u_{1E} e_2. \tag{64}$$

The inertial velocity of P_1 is given as

$$v_1 = -\frac{dR_1}{dt} + \dot{Y}_1 e_3 \times R_1$$

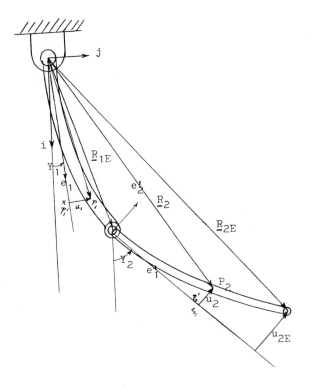

Fig. 14. Link 2 position vector.

$$= -u_1 \dot{Y}_1 e_1 + \left(x \dot{Y}_1 + \dot{u}_1 \right) e_2. \tag{65}$$

Clearly, $\dot{R}_1$ is the velocity of P_1 relative to the local coordinate system expressed in the reference frame $[O, e_1, e_2]$; other terms are the velocity due to local frame rotation with respect to the inertial frame $[O, i, j]$. The inertial velocity of the end of link 1 is

$$v_{1E} = -u_{1E} \dot{Y}_1 e_1 + \left(l_1 \dot{Y}_1 + \dot{u}_{1E} \right) e_2. \tag{66}$$

D.   LINK-2 KINEMATICS

Figure 14 shows the position vectors of an arbitrary point P_2 on link 2 and the inertial position vectors of the ends of links 1 and 2. R_2 is the local position vector of P_2. Using vector addition, the inertial position of P_2 is:

$$R_2 = l_1 e_1 + u_{1E} e_2 + \xi e_1' + u_2 e_2'$$

$$= \left(l_1 + \xi C_{21} - u_2 S_{21} \right) e_1 + \left(u_{1E} + \xi S_{21} + u_2 C_{21} \right) e_2, \tag{67}$$

where $C_{21} = \cos(Y_2 - Y_1)$ and $S_{21} = \sin(Y_2 - Y_1)$. The inertial velocity of an element of mass on link 2 involves the translation of the local coordinate system $[O, e_1, e_2]$, the velocity of the element relative to the local frame, and the velocity cue to the rotation of the local frame relative to the inertial frame $[O, i, j]$:

$$v_2 = -\frac{dR_2}{dt} + \dot{Y}_1 e_3 \times R_2$$

$$= -\left[u_{1E} \dot{Y}_1 + \dot{u}_2 S_{21} + (\xi S_{21} + u_2 C_{21}) \dot{Y}_2 \right] e_1$$

$$+ \left[l_1 \dot{Y}_1 + \dot{u}_{1E} + (\xi C_{21} - u_2 S_{21}) \dot{Y}_2 + \dot{u}_2 C_{21} \right] e_2. \tag{68}$$

Following the same reasoning used for $\dot{R}_{2E}$, the inertial velocity at the end of link 2 is given by:

$$v_{2E} = v_2(l_2, t)$$

$$= -\left[u_{1E} \dot{Y}_1 + \dot{u}_{2E} S_{21} + (l_2 S_{21} + u_{2E} C_{21}) \dot{Y}_2 \right] e_1$$

$$+ \left[l_1 \dot{Y}_1 + \dot{u}_{1E} + (l_2 C_{21} - u_{2E} S_{21}) \dot{Y}_2 + \dot{u}_{2E} C_{21} \right] e_2. \tag{69}$$

E.   KINETIC ENERGY

The kinetic energy of a continuous system is

$$T = \frac{1}{2} \int_0^1 \rho(\dot{R} \cdot \dot{R}) \, dx, \tag{70}$$

where the integration is performed over all bodies in the system and R is the inertial position vector of an element of mass $\rho \, dx$.

Since R_i specifies the inertial position of a section on beam i, the kinetic energy for these two flexible beams is:

$$T_b = \frac{1}{2} \int_0^{l_1} m_1 \dot{R}_1 \cdot \dot{R}_1 \, dx + \frac{1}{2} \int_0^{l_2} m_2 \dot{R}_2 \cdot \dot{R}_2 \, d\xi, \tag{71}$$

where m_1 and m_2 are the link mass densities and l_1 and l_2 are the lengths of links 1 and 2, respectively.

The concentrated mass m, m_3 represents the joints and actuators at the ends of links 1 and 2, and contribute T_c to the system's kinetic energy:

$$T_c = \frac{1}{2} J' \dot{Y}_1^2 + \frac{1}{2} m (\dot{R}_{1E} \cdot \dot{R}_{1E}) + \frac{1}{2} m_3 (\dot{R}_{2E} \cdot \dot{R}_{2E}). \tag{72}$$

The total system kinetic energy is then the sum of the component kinetic energies given in (71) and (72):

$$T = T_b + T_c. \tag{73}$$

Here the assumed mode shapes method is used to describe the flexible motion of links 1 and 2. Link deflections are described as the product of mode shapes $\Phi_{ij}(x)$ and time-dependent modal amplitue $q_{ij}(t)$:

$$u_i(x, t) = \sum_j^n \Phi_{ij}(x) \cdot q_{ij}(t). \tag{74}$$

To use the Lagrange method, the kinetic energy is expressed in terms of the system generalized coordinates. The generalized coordinates consist of: the angles $Y_i(t)$ shown in Fig. 11, and the mode's amplitude vector $q_{ij}(t)$.

The detailed expression of T in terms of the quadratic expression of the generalized coordinates is included in Appendix C for the 2-DOF flexible dynamic system of [14].

F.   POTENTIAL ENERGY

The system potential energy is described by the sum of the energy due to the position of system mass elements in a uniform gravitational field and the strain energy associated with link flexure. For an arbitrary point P on link 1 or 2, the position vector R_i is shown in Fig. 11 and given by (63) and (67):

$$\mathbf{R}_1 = x\mathbf{e}_1 + u_1\mathbf{e}_2$$

$$= (x \cdot \cos Y_1 - u_1 \sin Y_1)\mathbf{i} + (x \cdot \sin Y_1 + u_1 \cos Y_1)\mathbf{j} \tag{75}$$

$$\mathbf{R}_2 = l_1\mathbf{e}_1 + u_{1E}\mathbf{e}_2 + \xi\mathbf{e}_1' + u_2\mathbf{e}_2'$$

$$= (l_1 \cos Y_1 - u_{1E} \sin Y_1 + \xi \cos Y_2 - u_2 \sin Y_2)\mathbf{i}$$

$$+ (l_1 \sin Y_1 + u_{1E} \cos Y_1 + \xi \sin Y_2 + u_2 \cos Y_2)\mathbf{j}. \tag{76}$$

In the reference configuration, $Y_i = 0$ and $u_i = 0$. So

$$\mathbf{R}_i = x_i\mathbf{e}_1 + 0\mathbf{e}_2. \tag{77}$$

Since the gravitational field is parallel to the inertial i direction, the potential energy for P in an arbitrary system configuration is:

$$V_p(dx) = -\rho\, dx\, g(x \cdot \cos Y - u \cdot \sin Y). \tag{78}$$

The gravitation potential for the entire system is then the integral over all mass elements of the two flexible beams plus the potential energy V_c due to the concentrated mass m and m_3:

$$V_p = -\int_0^{l_1} m_1 g(x \cos Y_1 - u_1 \sin Y_1)\, dx + V_c$$

$$-\int_0^{l_2} m_2 g(l_1 \cos Y_1 - u_{1E} \sin Y_1 + \xi \cos Y_2 - u_2 \sin Y_2) \, d\xi. \tag{79}$$

The strain energy associated with link flexure is

$$V_2 = \frac{1}{2}\int_0^{l_1} EI_1 \left(-\frac{\partial^2 u_1}{\partial x^2}\right)^2 dx + \frac{1}{2}\int_0^{l_2} HI_2\left(-\frac{\partial^2 u_2}{\partial \xi^2}\right)^2 d\xi$$

$$+\frac{1}{2}\int_0^{l_1} FT_1\left(-\frac{\partial u_1}{\partial x}\right)^2 dx + \frac{1}{2}\int_0^{l_2} FT_2\left(-\frac{\partial u_2}{\partial \xi}\right)^2 d\xi \tag{80}$$

where E_i is the link elastic modulus, I_i is the bending moment of inertia, and u_i is the beam deflection. The first two terms are the bending strain energy; the last two terms are the strain energy due to axial shortening deflection. In general, robot rotation motion speed is $0 < \omega < 10$ rad/sec, which means $FT_i \sim O(10^2 \sim 10^3)$, and $(\partial^2 u/\partial x^2)$, $(\partial u/\partial x)$ are of about the same order; $EI \sim O(10^7)$. So we can neglect the second half of the strain energy due to the axial shortening effect, since the axial deformation is also very small. But this assumption cannot be used in dealing with high-speed rotation systems, for example $\omega > 10^2$.

Since the assumed mode method is used to describe link flexure, the total system potential energy can be written as:

$$V_s = \frac{1}{2}\int_0^{l_1} EI_1 \sum_i \sum_j q_i \Phi_i'' \Phi_j'' q_j \, dx + \frac{1}{2}\int_0^{l_2} EI_2 \sum_i \sum_j q_i \Phi_i'' \Phi_j'' q_j \, d\xi, \tag{81}$$

where $\Phi_{ij}''(x)$ is the second derivative of the link i mode shape vector with respect to the local coordinate x_i. The system total potential energy is thus strain plus gravitational potential energy:

$$V_t = V_p + V_s. \tag{82}$$

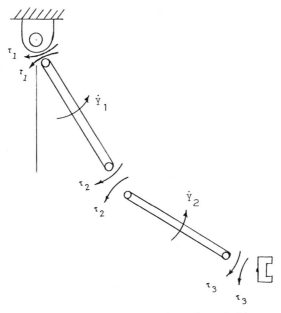

Fig. 15. Positive sense of torque and angular velocities.

G.   GENERALIZED FORCE Q

The system being studied has control torques τ_i applied at each joint. The positive sense of joint torques and angular velocities is shown in Fig. 15. In addition to rigid body movement of the links, the torque excites elastic body dynamics in the manipulator. A generalized force Q_i can be considered as the virtual work done by all the forces acting on the system per unit displacement δq_i. Assuming the other δq's are zero, δq_i is the virtual displacement of generalized coordinate q_i. Using the principle of virtual work, we can obtain

$$\delta W = \tau_1\, \delta Y_1 + \tau_2\,(\delta Y_2 - \delta Y_1 - \delta Y_{1E})$$

$$= (\tau_1 - \tau_2)\, \delta Y_1 + \tau_2\, \delta Y_2 - \tau_2\, \delta Y_{1E}, \tag{83}$$

where $\tau_i\, \delta Y_i$ is the virtual work done by τ_i in a rigid body virtual displacement δY_i. The virtual work done by a torque τ_i in bending a link is represented by the terms $\tau_i\, \delta T_{1E}$ and $\tau_i\, \delta Y_{2E}$, where the δY_{iE} are the virtual slopes at the ends of links

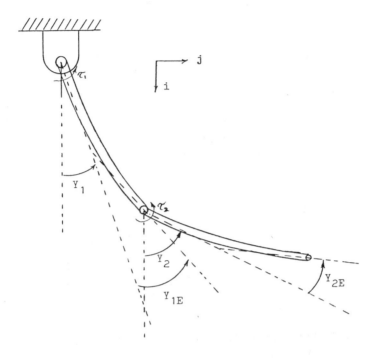

Fig. 16. System angles of the flexible beam manipulator.

1 and 2, respectively, as shown in Fig. 16. Since the cantilevered-free beam mode shapes are used, the slopes at the link's origins are constrained to zero, thus making no contribution to the virtual work. Using the vector equation (74) for the local beam displacements, we get

$$
Y_{1E} = u'_{1E} = \frac{d}{dx}\left(\sum_j \Phi_{1j} q_{1j} \right)\Bigg|_{x=l_{-1}}
$$

$$
= \sum_j \Phi'_{1jE} q_{1j}, \tag{84}
$$

where the prime denotes spatial differentiation in the local coordinate system. The virtual work can then be expressed as:

$$\delta W = (\tau_1 - \tau_2)\, \delta Y_1 + \tau_2\, \delta Y_2 - \tau_2 \sum_j \Phi'_{1jE}\, \delta q_{1j}, \tag{85}$$

where δY_1 and δY_2 are the virtual changes in the time-dependent link coordinates. Generalized forces are found using

$$Q_{q_i} = -\frac{\partial(\delta W)}{\partial(\delta q_i)}, \tag{86}$$

where q_i is the i-th generalized coordinate. Thus the generalized forces due to the applied torques are:

$$Q_{Y_1} = \tau_1 - \tau_2 \tag{87}$$

$$Q_{Y_2} = \tau_2 - \tau_3 \tag{88}$$

$$Q_{Y_3} = \tau_3 \tag{89}$$

$$Q_{q_{1j}} = -\tau_2 \Phi'_{2JE} \tag{90}$$

$$Q_{q_{2j}} = -\tau_3 \Phi'_{2jE}. \tag{91}$$

H.   EQUATION OF MOTION

The Lagrange equation is used to develop the equation of motion for this system:

$$\frac{d}{dt}\left(\frac{\partial T}{\partial \dot{q_i}}\right) - \frac{\partial T}{\partial q_i} + \frac{\partial V_t}{\partial q_i} + F_i = Q_i, \tag{92}$$

where T and V_t are the total kinetic and potential energies of the system, respectively, while q_i and Q_i are the j-th generalized coordinate and its generalized force.

Substituting all these terms and damping forces into the above equation, we can get $3 + n_1 + n_2$ second-order ordinary differential equations. In vector notation, these equations may be written as

$$[M] \cdot \{\ddot{\psi}\} + [C] \cdot \{\dot{\psi} \cdot \dot{\psi}\} + [F] \cdot \{\psi\} + [G] \cdot \left\{ \begin{array}{c} \sin \psi \\ \\ \psi \end{array} \right\} = Q, \tag{93}$$

where ψ includes all joint angles and the generalized coordinates of vibration modes of both beams. The components of the M, C, F, and G matrices are presented in Appendix C in Ref. [14].

V.   CONTROL SCHEMES AND SIMULATION

A.   ADAPTIVE CONTROL ALGORITHM

From the manipulator dynamic system we have very complicated rigid body motion and flexible vibration nonlinear coupled equations which are shown in (93). Because the vibration states are difficult to measure or estimate in real time, handling the flexible effect on control-law design for rigid-body angle motion is not an easy job. Generally the elastic vibration of industrial robots is high-frequency dependent and time varying due to the changing of working conditions; so the elastic vibration is very difficult to control in a real-time situation. Here the robot system control-law design is based on joint angle-control considerations, and no extra actuators are designed to control the deflection in order to simplify and reduce the cost of the manipulator structure, but the beam's deflection effect is included in the joint angle control-law design. In our nonlinear model, the elastic vibration effect can be considered as a bounded random noise which can be compensated for by adding a biased term in the control law. Then one uses the adaptive control parameter identification scheme to identify it. From the dynamic model we have the equations

$$[M] \cdot \{A(k)\} + [C] \cdot \{V_i(k)V_j(k)\} + [F] \cdot \{V(k)\}$$

$$+ [G] \cdot \left\{ \begin{array}{c} \sin[Y(k)] \\ \\ q \end{array} \right\} = Q'(k), \tag{94}$$

where A is the acceleration vector of the joint angle and elastic vibration mode generalized coordinates; V is the angle velocity vector; q is the elastic mode generalized coordinates; and Y is the joint angle vector. Assuming that $\zeta_i(k)$ represents the elastic vibration effect on each angle degree of freedom, then the control model of angle motion of the manipulator can be written as

$$[\tilde{M}] \cdot \{A(k)\} + [\tilde{C}] \cdot \{V_i(k)V_j(k)\} + [\tilde{F}] \cdot \{V(k)\}$$

$$+ [\tilde{G}] \cdot \{\sin[Y(k)]\} + \{\tilde{W}_m\} = U(k), \tag{95}$$

where

$$\varepsilon\left\{\zeta(k) \mid \mathscr{L}(k-1)\right\} = w_m \tag{96}$$

$$\varepsilon\left\{\left[\zeta(k) - w_m\right]\left[\zeta(k) - w_m\right]^T \mid \mathscr{L}(k-1)\right\} = Q, \tag{97}$$

where Q is assumed to be a small positive semidefinite matrix, and $\mathscr{L}(k-1)$ is the information set which includes all the output and output product values until time step k:

$$\tilde{A}(k) = \frac{\tilde{Y}(k+1) - 2Y(k) + Y(k-1)}{T^2}.$$

From (10) we have

$$\tilde{Y}(k+1) = -E_1 \cdot Y(k) - E_2 \cdot Y(k-1) + H_1 \cdot Y^*(k) + H_2 \cdot Y^*(k-1).$$

Let us define the control law as

$$U(k) = \left[\tilde{M}, \tilde{C}, \tilde{F}, \tilde{G}, \tilde{W}_m\right] \cdot \begin{bmatrix} \tilde{A}(k) \\ V_i V_j(k) \\ V(k) \\ \sin\left[Y(k)\right] \\ 1 \end{bmatrix} \tag{98}$$

$$\equiv \tilde{\theta}_{k-1}\tilde{\varphi}_k, \tag{99}$$

where

$$\tilde{\theta}_{k-1} = \left[\tilde{M}(k-1), \tilde{C}(k-1), \tilde{F}(k-1), \tilde{G}(k-1), \tilde{W}_m(k-1)\right] \tag{100}$$

are the estimated parameter vectors and

$$\tilde{\varphi}_k = \left[\tilde{A}(k), V_i V_j(k), V(k), \sin\left[Y(k)\right], 1\right] \tag{101}$$

are the estimated or measured state products. The true functions of the components of M, C, F, G, and ζ matrices are time varying, which is described in the appendices of [14].

Similarly to the rigid arm adaptive control algorithm, the cost function is chosen as

$$J_0(\theta) = (\theta - \tilde{\theta}_0)P_0^{-1}(\theta - \tilde{\theta}_0)^T \tag{102}$$

$$J_n(\theta) = \alpha J_{n-1}(\theta) + \left(U_n - \theta\varphi_n\right)^2. \tag{103}$$

The error of the initial parameter θ_0 guess was accumulated for in $J_0(\theta)$. The forgetting factor α was chosen in order to obtain an exponential forgetting profile in the accumulated system output error signal criterion J. Minimizing J with respect to θ, we can derive the sequential least-squares with the exponential data weighting parameter identification formula as:

$$\tilde{\theta}^T(\kappa) = \tilde{\theta}^T(k-1) + \frac{P(k-1)\varphi(k)\left[U9K0 - \tilde{\theta}(k-1)\varphi(k)\right]}{\alpha + \varphi^T(k)p(k-1)\varphi(k)} \quad (104)$$

$$P(k) = \frac{1}{2}\left[P(k-1) - \frac{P(k-1)\varphi(k)\varphi^T(k)P(k-1)}{\alpha + \varphi^T(k)P(k-1)\varphi(k)}\right]. \quad (105)$$

Combining all these control-law and parameter estimators together with the dynamic model, we get a direct adaptive control algorithm. Figure 2 shows the control system block diagram. The adaptive control procedure is the same as the rigid arms control system, which is described in Section III,D.

B.   NUMERICAL SIMULATIONS

1.   Planar Manipulator System

The physical numerical data of this planar manipulator with two flexible beams used are as follows: the length of the two arms is $l_1 = 3.0$ ft and $l_2 = 2.0$ ft; the mass of these two arms is $m_1 = 2.328$ lb m/ft and $m_2 = 1.746$ lb m/ft; the mass of the actuator at joint 2 and end effector is $m = 2.0$ lb m, $m_3 = 1.0$ lb m; the friction damping at the joints is 0.75 lb f ft/sec. The stiffnesses of these two beams are $EI_1 = 7.5 \cdot 10^6$ and $EI_2 = 2.8125 \cdot 10^6$ lb f in^2. The cross section of both flexible beams is 1×2 in. for link 1 and 1×1.5 in. for link 2.

In Fig. 2, the model which is set between reference input Y* and estimated desired output $\tilde{Y}$ to be matched was

$$\tilde{Y}(k+1) = Y(k) - 0.29Y(k-1) + Y^*(k) - 0.71Y^*(k-1). \quad (106)$$

In this path tracking control we consider the tracking speed of the end effector to be constant, and the reference trajectory to be a quarter-circle in a Cartesian coordinate system:

$$X(k) = 4.5 \sin\left(\frac{P(62-k)}{120}\right) \quad (107)$$

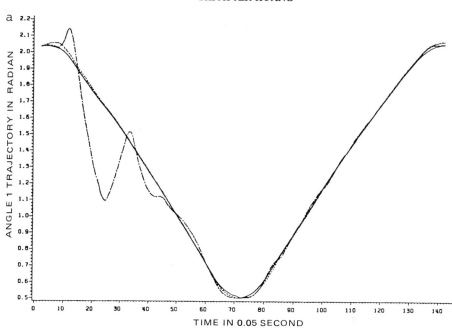

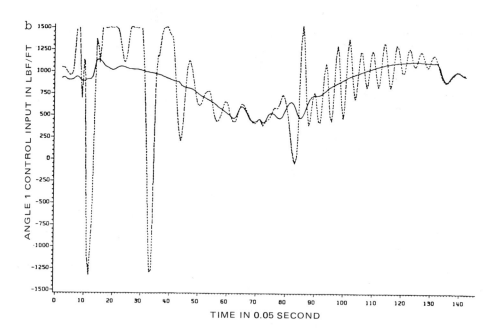

Fig. 17.   Angle 1 input and output response trajectories with cantilevered-free
beam mode shapes, $U_{1\ max}| = 1500$ lb f ft.   (a) Angle 1 trajectory: (–), reference;
(---), fixed control;(--), adaptive control.   (b) Angle 1 control input: (–), fixed control;
(---), adaptive control.

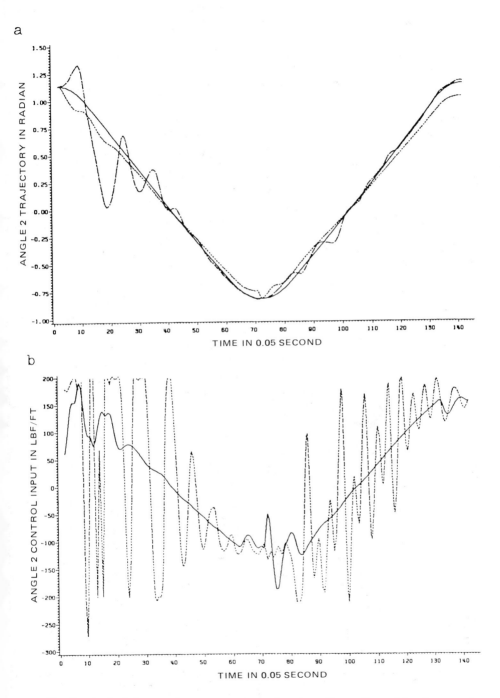

Fig. 18. Angle 2 input and output response trajectories with cantilevered-free beam mode shapes, $U_{2\ max} = 200$ lb f ft. (a) and (b) and legend as in Fig. 17.

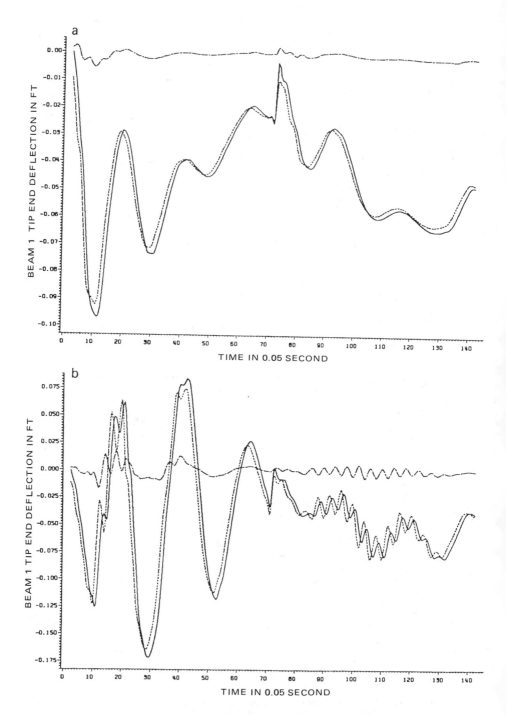

Fig. 19. The tip-end deflection trajectories of the first beam with cantilevered-free mode shapes. (a) Fixed control; (b) adaptive control. (–), net displacement; (– – –), due to first mode; (– • –), due to second mode.

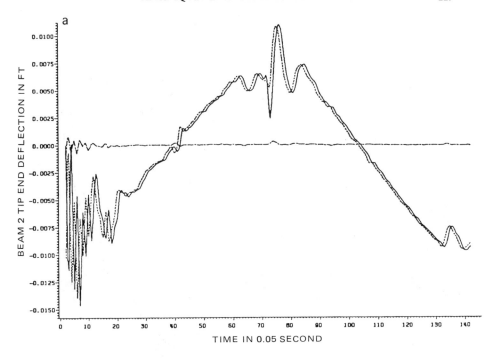

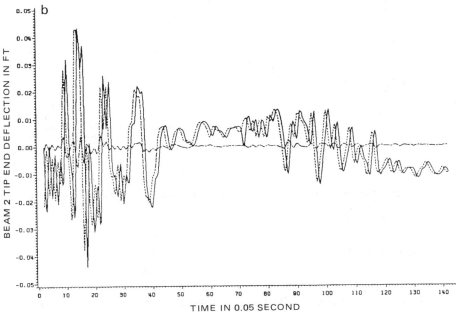

Fig. 20. The tip-end deflection trajectories of second beam with cantilivered-free mode shapes. (a), (b), and legend as in Fig. 19.

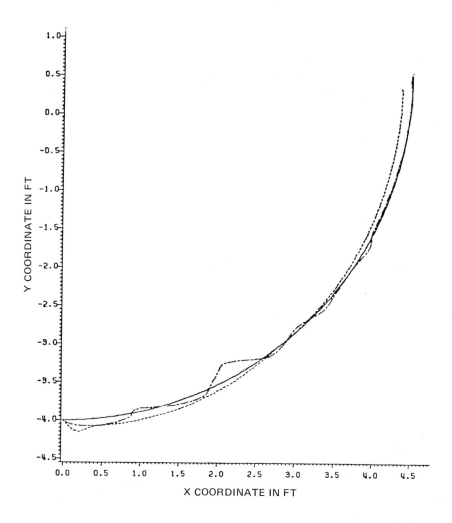

Fig. 21. The end-effector Cartesian position trajectories. (–) reference; (– – –), fixed control; (–•–), adaptive control.

$$Y(k) = 0.5 - 4.5 \sin\left(\frac{P(62 - k)}{120}\right).$$

(108)

The sampling period T is 0.05 sec. The initial parameters used for adaptive control parameter estimators are chosen within 20% of the parameters' true values. The motion path of the robot is that the end effector starts to move down with constant speed from the up position (3-o'clock direction) and stops at the bottom

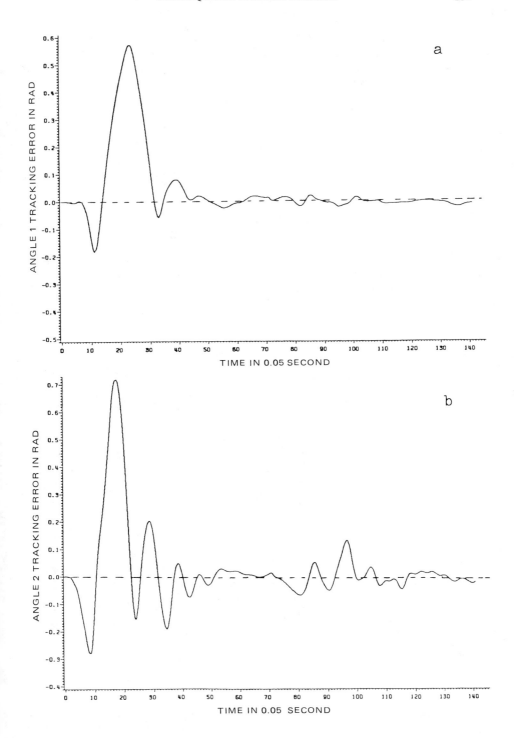

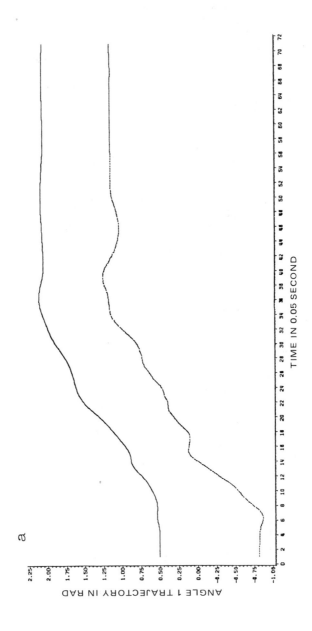

Fig. 23. Angle output paths and end-effector Cartesian coordinate trajectories of a robot moving between two points. (a) Angle trajectory: (–), angle 1; (– – –), angle 2. (b) (–), x coordinate; (– – –), y coordinate.

232

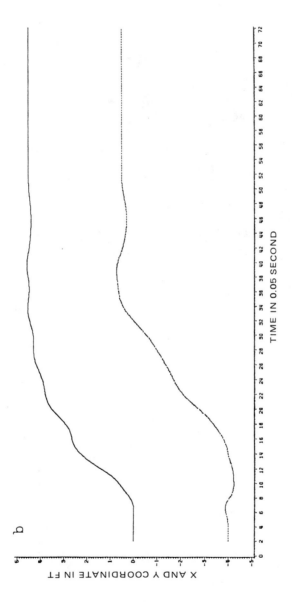

Fig. 23 b.

233

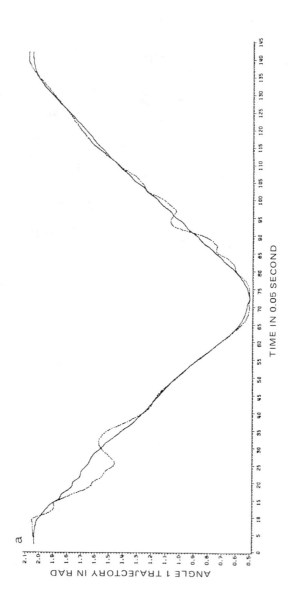

Fig. 24. Output trajectories for adaptive control angles 1 (a) and 2 (b) with three modes. (–), reference; (---), adaptive control.

234

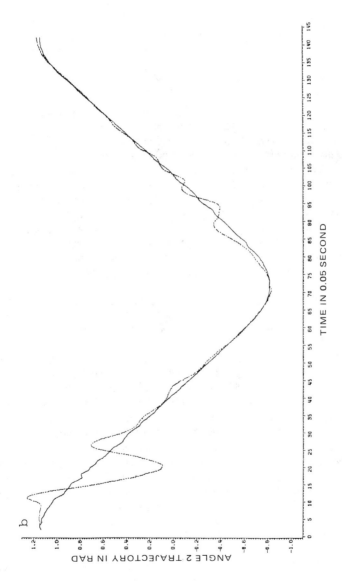

Fig. 24 b.

235

position (6-o'clock direction). After the end effector picks up an object of mass 0.5 lb m, the system moves up to the original position with constant speed.

2.   When Cantilevered-Free Beam Mode Shapes are Used

$$\Phi(x) = \cosh \lambda x - \cos \lambda x - \sigma\left(\sinh \lambda x - \sin \lambda x\right)$$

Figures 17a and 18a present the angle trajectories of reference desired values and plant output with respect to the fixed control and adaptive control. The control torque inputs of fixed control and adaptive control are compared in Figs. 17b and 18b. These figures show that the tracking trajectories are closed to the desired pathline and that the converged speed is faster than the result of the last section, which indicates that the cantilevered-free beam mode shape is better than the simple mode shape in representing the elastic deflection of beams. Figures 19 and 20 plot the deflection trajectory at the tip end of first and second flexible beams. Each contains the deflection due to the first and second vibration modes, respectively, and their combination. By inspecting results we know the first mode is always larger than other modes, and the second mode vibration amplitude is damped out very rapidly. The end-effector Cartesian position trajectories of both methods are shown in Fig. 21.

From these results we can see that adaptive control is more robust than fixed control when the system has an unknown payload added to the end effector, but the trajectory output tracking converged at a slower rate than in a rigid-arm robot system because of the flexible vibration effect. The trajectory tracking error history is shown in Fig. 22a, b. Inspecting this figure, we observe that the convergence speed of this adaptive control algorithm is acceptable.

The adaptive flexible manipulator control has difficulty in short-time position-tracking applications because of the large tracking deviation before the vibration effect set-down and the system parameters converge. If the control objective is to move an end effector from one point to another without any constraint of the trajectory between these two points, then this nonlinear adaptive control algorithm can work very well. The conclusion can be observed from angle trajectories and Cartesian coordinate trajectories in Fig. 23a, b. Thus the flexible manipulators are more useful in high-speed motion between two points and can handle the long-time system control better than the short-time trajectory tracking.

C.   TRUNCATED MODE PROBLEM

The conventional control laws which were designed based on truncated finite modes have the problem of unmodeled dynamics and the truncated mode spillover phenomenon. The nonlinear adaptive controller which was developed in this re-

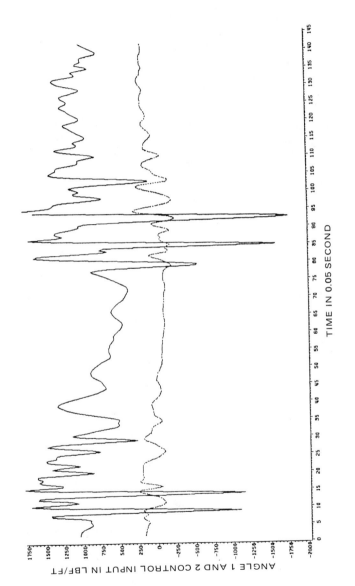

Fig. 25. Adaptive control angles' control torque input trajectories. (−), angle 1; (−−), angle 2.

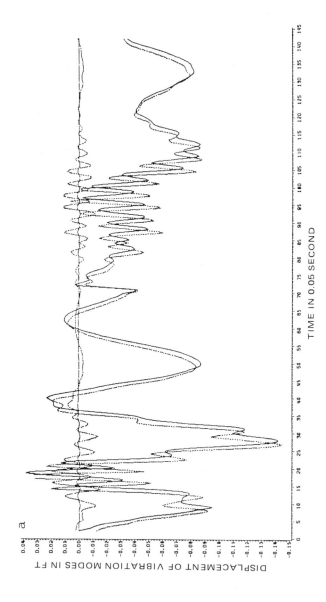

Fig. 26. The first (a) and second (b) beams tip-end elastic deflection trajectories. (–), total deflection; (– – –), first and second mode deflection; (-•-), third mode deflection.

238

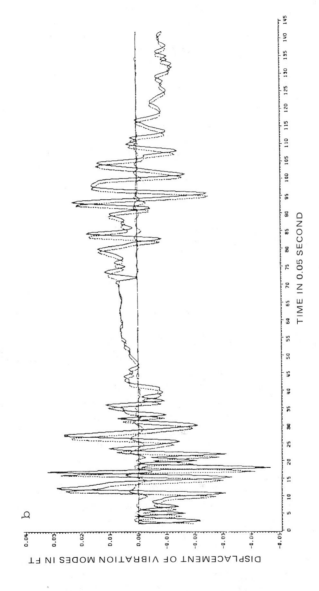

Fig. 26b.

239

search is not designed based on truncated finite modes. Therefore, theoretically we can avoid this kind of control-law spillover problem. Here we chose the planar manipulator, Fig. 11, with the first three cantilevered-free beam vibration modes in the dynamic model as a simulation example to investigate this problem by comparing the results with the two-mode model, which was shown in the last section. Figure 24a, b presents the angle trajectories. By inspecting these results, we know the tracking performance worked as well as those illustrated in Section V, B, 2. The control torque inputs of both angles are shown in Fig. 25. The tip-end deflections of both flexible beams are plotted in Fig. 26a, b, which illustrates that the displacement due to the first vibration mode dominated the beam's total deflection. Other modes have only a very small component. From these results we know that this nonlinear adaptive control scheme's performance is not dependent on the number of modes (2 or 3) chosen in the dynamic model.

VI. DISCUSSION AND CONCLUSION

In this research we have discussed a nonlinear adaptive control method with a time-varying parameter identification scheme. This method can be used not only for rigid-arm robot systems but also for flexible-beam manipulator systems. As in the case of rigid arm, it has four advantages:

1) The nonlinear model can compensate the Coriolis and trigonometric nonlinear effects.

2) System parameter time-varying changes due to the drifting of configuration or the changing of payload can be compensated for by using the time-varying system parameter identification scheme.

3) This nonlinear adaptive control does not need a detailed complicated mathematical model and physical information.

4) this simple adaptive control strategy requires less memory and computing time; therefore, it is easy to apply in a real-time manipulator control system.

A further advantage of using this nonlinear adaptive control in flexible-beam manipulator systems is that unmodeled dynamics problems or truncated mode spillover phenomena can be avoided. The traditional control-law design of a distributed infinite mode system is based on the finite truncated modes method; so the system controllability and stability cannot be guaranteed, since they depend on the truncated unmodeled dynamics. But in our algorithm we have the parameter identification scheme to estimate the effect of those infinite distributed beam modes, and the control-law design is based on system performance that includes all dynamic modes. Thus, theoretically, we do not have the unmodeled dynamics problem.

Similarly, in the design of a stochastic control law, we can regard the noise as a biased term and estimate it using a time-varying parameter identification scheme; therefore, the nonlinear adaptive control algorithm proposed in this research not only can be used in a deterministic system but also in stochastic systems.

Flexible-beam manipulator deflection control is a very difficult job. The first reason is that the performance of industrial robot manipulators is dependent on high elastic vibration frequencies; thus it is not easy to compensate for the deflection of each beam on a real-time basis in order to achieve precise position control. Even with an extra actuator or special device added on flexible beams, the performance still cannot be improved much. Yet we have to take the penalty of making the manipulator system more complicated and expensive.

The second reason is that the real-time deflection compensation in precise position tracking control can make the control inputs not smooth or even discontinuous. This will deteriorate the system performance in industrial applications. We have observed such a problem in the computer simulation of planar manipulator cases. One of the better ways to solve this problem is to compensate only for the static deflection and neglect the dynamic deflection part. This means that we accept the amplitude of dynamic deflection as the position accuracy tolerance. This will smooth the control inputs and make the control system useful. In spatial manipulator simulation cases we can see that, when flexible deflection is not compensated, the control inputs are smoother and all flexible deflections converge to some small values. If we compensate for the static deflection, then the position tolerance of the robot end effector is so controlled that it falls within the magnitude of the dynamic deflection amplitude.

To decide the constraint of maximum torque output for an actuator at each joint of a spatial flexible manipulator, careful design has to be done, since the performance, convergence speed, and stability of the whole system can be influenced. To make the problem more complicated, the coupling effect between all joints also has to be taken into consideration. We need not only to decide the constraint of the maximum for each joint actuator, but also devise a set of good combinations of such constraints for each case. According to my study, the combination is not unique. In some range of constraint values the system output can track the desired trajectory with different convergence speeds. To find the optimal combination that has the fastest convergence speed and good system performance needs further investigation.

REFERENCES

1. N. G. CHALHOUB and A. G. ULSOY, Dynamic simulation of a flexible robot arm and controller. *Proc. Am. Control Conf.*, pp. 631–637 (1984).
2. A. TRUCKENBRODT, Modeling and control of flexible manipulator structures. *Proc. CISM-IFTOMM Symp., 4th*, pp. 110–120 (1981).
3. O. MAIZZA NETO, Modal analysis and control of flexible manipulators. Ph.D. Thesis, Dept. of Mechanical Engineering, Massachusetts Institute of Technology, Cambridge, 1974.

4.   C. S. G. LEE and M. H. CHEN, A suboptimal control design for mechanical manipulators. *Proc. Am. Control Conf.*, pp. 1056–1060 (1984).
5.   W. H. SUNADA and S. DUBOWSKY, On the dynamic analysis and behavior of industrial robotic manipulators with elastic members. *Trans. ASME Mech. Transm. Autom. Design* 105, 42–51 (1983).
6.   A. TRUCKENBRODT, Truncation problems in the dynamics and control of flexible mechanical systems. *IFAC* 14, 60–65.
7.   D. W. CLARKE and J. P. GAWTHROP, Self-tuning controller. *Proc. Inst. Electr. Eng.* 122a, 929–924 (1975).
8.   J. Y. S. LUH, M. W. WALKER, and R. P. C. PAUL, On-line computational scheme for mechanical manipulators. *J. Dyn. Syst., Meas., Control* 102, 69–76 (1981).
9.   G. N. SARIDIS, Intelligent robotic control. *Proc. Jt. Autom. Control Conf., 1981.*
10.   R. P. PAUL, "Robot Manipulators: Mathematics, Programming, and Control." MIT Press, Cambridge, Massachusetts, 1982.
11.   BRADY, HOLLERBACK, JOHNSON, and LOZANO-PEREY, "Robot Motion: Planning and Control." MIT Press, Cambridge, Massachusetts, 1982.
12.   R. CANNON and E. SCHMITZ, Initial experiments on the endpoint control of a one-link flexible experimental manipulator. *Int. J. Robot. Res.* 3(3) (1984).
13.   J. Y. S LUH, M. W. WALKER, and R. P. C. PAUL, Resolved acceleration control of mechanical manipulators. *IEEE Trans. Autom. Control* AC-25(3), 468–474 (1980).
14.   S. J. HUANG, Position control of mechanical manipulators by using nonlinear adaptive control algorithms. Ph.D. Thesis, Dept. of Mechanical Engineering, University of California at Los Angeles (1986).
15.   M. E. KAHN and B. ROTH, Near minimum time control of open-loop articulated kinematics chains. *J. Dyn. Syst., Meas., Control* SMC-93, 164–172 (1971).
16.   M. A. TOWNSEND and T. L. TSAI, An optimal control law for a class of constrained dynamical systems. *J. Dyn. Syst., Meas., Control* 99 (1978).
17.   G. C. GOODWIN and K. S. SIN, "Adaptive Filtering Prediction and Control." Prentice-Hall, Englewood Cliffs, New Jersey, 1984.
18.   S. DUBOWSKY and D. T. DESFORGES, The application of model reference adaptive control to robotic manipulators. *J. Dyn. Syst., Meas., Control* 101, 193–200 (1979).
19.   A. J. KOIVO and T. H. GUO, Adaptive linear controller for robotic manipulators. *IEEE Trans. Autom. Control* AC-28(2), 162–171 (1983).
20.   C. H. CHUNG and G. C. LEININGER, Adaptive self-tuning control of manipulators in task coordinate system. *IEEE Int. Conf. Robot.*, 546–555 (1984).
21.   R. G. WALKERS and M. M. BAYOUMI, Application of a self-tuning pole-placement regulator to an industrial manipulator. *Proc. Conf. Decision Control, 1982.*
22.   H. ELLIOTT, T. DEPKOVICH, J. KELLY, and B. DRAPER, Nonlinear adaptive control of mechanical linkage systems with application to robotics. *Proc.Am. Control Conf.*, pp. 1050–1055 (1983).
23.   T. FUKUDA, Flexibility control of elastic robotic arms. *J. Robot. Syst.* 2, 73–88 (1985).
24.   W. J. BOOK, O. MAIZZA-NETO, and D. E. WHITNEY, Feedback control of two beams, two joints systems with distributed flexibility. *J. Dyn. Syst., Meas., Control* 97(4), 424–431 (1975).
25.   P. B. USORO, R. NADIRA, and S. S. MAHIL, Control of lightweight flexible manipulator: A feasibility study. *Proc. Am. Control Conf.*, pp. 1209–1216 (1984).
26.   D. E. WHITNEY, Resolved motion rate control of manipulators and human prostheses. *IEEE Trans. Man-Mach. Sys.* MMS-10 (2), 47–53 (1969).
27.   D. E. WHITNEY, Force feedback control of manipulator fine motions. *J. Dyn. Syst., Meas., Control.* (1977).
28.   R. C. PAUL, Modeling, trajectory calculation and servaing of a computer controlled arm. Ph.D. Thesis, Stanford University (1972).

29. R. E. KALMAN, Design of a self-optimizing control system. *Trans. ASME* **80**, 468–478 (1958).
30. P. C. YOUNG, Process parameter estimation and self-adaptive control. *In* "Theory of Self-Adapting Control System" (P. H. Hammound, ed.). Plenum, New York (1966).
31. A. CHANG and J. RISSANEN, Regulation of incompletely identified linear systems. *SIAM J. Control* **6** (3), 327–348 (1968).
32. K. J. ASTROM and B. WITTENMARK, On self-tuning regulators. *Automatica* **9**, 195–199 (1973).

A METHODOLOGY BASED ON REDUCED COMPLEXITY ALGORITHM FOR SYSTEM APPLICATIONS USING MICROPROCESSORS

T. Y. YAN

Communications System Research Section
Jet Propulsion Laboratory
California Institute of Technology
Pasadena, California 91109

K. YAO

Department of Electrical Engineering
University of California, Los Angeles
Los Angeles, California 90024

I.   INTRODUCTION

A large number of multiplications is often encountered in many signal-processing situations in modern communication, radar, and information-processing systems. The usage of specialized multiplication devices generally increases cost, volume, weight, design time, and possibly decreases reliability. However, designs using general-purpose low-cost microprocessors are flexible but yield a low throughput rate when many high-precision multiplications are required.

Most algorithms implemented on a digital computer are usually contaminated by various quantization effects. There are the usual analog-to-digital (A/D) quantization errors at the input as well as internal arithmetic roundoff errors. These errors are quite well understood [1, 2]. On the other hand, the quantization of the multiplication between the data and some basic system parameter intrinsic to the processing algorithm can be controlled to some extent by the system designer. This class of problems generally appeared not to have been studied in detail with respect to signal-processing situations with microprocessor implementations.

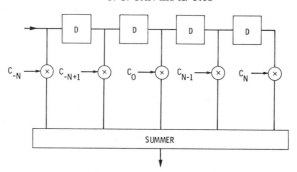

Fig. 1. A linear TDL model.

In Fig. 1 we consider a linear tapped delay line (TDL) structure which can be used to model a linear system having a finite impulse response (FIR) [1, p. 18]. This model is conceptually simple since it consists of $(2N + 1)$ multipliers, $2N$ delay units, and $2N$ summers. If the $(2N + 1)$ multiplier coefficients $\{c_n\}$ are fixed, then this TDL can model a linear time-invariant system, while if these coefficients are allowed to be time varying, it can model a linear time-variant system. By allowing these coefficients to vary as functions of the changing input under various manners, we can obtain adaptive TDL systems [3; 4, pp. 15–19].

The TDL model is basic and is used commonly in the design and analysis of digital data equalization [5, 6; 7, pp. 147–150]; array processing [4, p. 400; 8]; digital whitening filtering [7, pp. 272–275]; dynamical system identification and modeling [3, p. 7]; etc. Despite these seemingly different applications, if the analytically tractable minimum mean-square error (MMSE) criterion (which is also justifiable physically from the energy criterion point of view) is used, each of the resulting optimum subsystems uses a set of full-precision TDL coefficients $\{c_n\}$ to operate on the input. In practice, for a finite-precision implementation using microprocessors, we need to use finite precision and preferably some "simple" low-precision coefficients in the TDL.

In this article we shall consider a methodology on the analysis and design of an MMSE criterion linear system incorporating a TDL where all the full-precision multiplications in the TDL are constrained to be powers of two. The rationale for considering this class of problems is that, without using specialized multiplication hardware devices, the implementation of high-order finite-precision multiplications by software routines using a microprocessor generally involves numerous multiple-shift-and-add instructions, which can be quite time consuming. However, in using only powers of two multiplications, these operations can be implemented in a microprocessor as single-shift instructions with consequent higher throughput rate. Since the obvious operation of rounding the full-precision TDL coefficients to the nearest powers of two usually yields quite large system degradations, we need to find the optimum power of two TDL coefficients with respect to the MMSE criterion. As we shall see in Section III, this optimization is somewhat involved and needs considerable computational effort. However, now we have the possibility of trading a reduction in real-time on-line computational complexity in the microprocessor implemented system without significant loss of system performance against an increase in off-line computations in the design stage. Equivalently, if we do not want to incur the engineering design cost of off-line optimization, then we can either build a more costly and complicated system using specialized hardware multiplication devices or accept a simpler microprocessor system (performing finite-precision multiplications by software) with a lower throughput rate.

In order to demonstrate the philosophy and feasibility of the above-discussed methodology, we choose to consider the implementation of the simplest subsystem. Thus, among the various linear systems incorporating TDL devices mentioned above, we consider the well-known linear digital data equalizer. Our purpose is not to consider the most sophisticated (and thus complicated) data equalizer nor to use the latest microprocessor hardware. Our basic purpose is to demonstrate in a simple and direct manner the usefulness of the optimization methodology based on powers of two algorithms for system applications using microprocessors. In Section II we briefly present a linear equalizer based on the MMSE criterion for the detection and equalization of digital data over a linear dispersive and additive noise channel. In Section III some general concepts related to the MMSE criterion derived powers of two solutions formulated as constrained quadratic form minimization is first discussed. Then some details on the use of the branch-and-bound algorithm for the solution of this problem is given. In Section IV a hardware block diagram and software flowchart used in the implementation of this equalizer based on an 8080 microprocessor are summarized. In Section V some theoretical and experimental results and conclusions on the reduced multiplication complexity equalizer are given. Specifically, this simple microprocessor implementation with optimized power of two TDL coefficients achieves a system performance comparable to the optimum linear equalization with full-precision multiplications for an input data rate of 300 baud. It is interesting to note that if we use regular 8-bit multiplications (in software routines) instead of powers of two left or right shifts, the above equalizer definitely cannot support the 300-baud rate. Of course, a conventional full-precision implementation (using specialized multiplication hardware) with comparable system performance and input data rate would result in a more complicated and costly system.

II. LINEAR EQUALIZER

Consider a linear equalizer for the detection of binary digital data over the linear dispersive and additive noise channel given in Fig. 2. The input digits B_k are assumed to be independent and identically distributed, taking values ± 1 with equal probability, and the data duration is T. The combined transmitter and channel impulse response function is modeled by $s(t)$. The additive noise $n(t)$ is as-

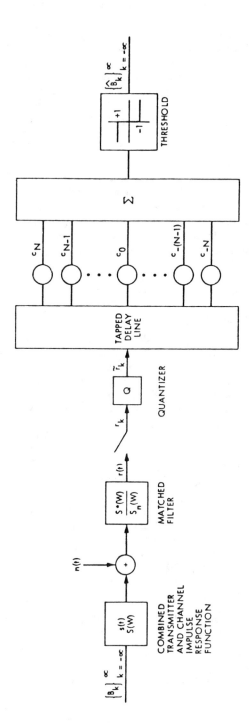

Fig. 2. Linear digital data equalizer.

sumed to be a Gaussian zero-mean wide-sense stationary random process of spectral density $S_n(\omega)$. It is well known that, if the data equalizer is constrained to be linear, the general structure of the equalizer is actually fixed [5, pp. 94–112; 6]. That is, the equalizer consists of a matched filter, matched to the combined transmitter and channel impulse response function $s(t)$ and the noise process $n(t)$, followed by a sampler with sampling rate $R = 1/T$, and a tapped delay line with a basic delay of T seconds between taps with coefficients $\{c_j, j = \pm N, ..., \pm 1, 0\}$. Different error criteria, however, affect only the tap coefficients $\{c_j\}$. For this article we use the mean-square error criterion. Furthermore, in order for the input and the tap coefficients of the TDL to take discrete values, we impose a quantizer Q between the sampler and the TDL in Fig. 2.

The output of the TDL is given by

$$y_k = \sum_{j=-N}^{N} \tilde{r}_{k-j} c_j, \tag{1}$$

where $\tilde{r}_j$ is the sampled response of the waveform $r(t)$ after quantization.

We make the usual assumption that the quantization error is uncorrelated with the data B_k and the noise $n(t)$. The mean-square error between B_k and the output of the TDL y_k at $k = 0$ can be written as

$$\varepsilon = E\left\{ (y_0 - B_0)^2 \right\} = 1 + Q(c), \tag{2}$$

where

$$Q(c) = c\Lambda_{cc}c' - 2cu', \tag{3}$$

$$u = (u_N, ..., u_0, ..., u_{-N}) \tag{4}$$

where u_j is the sampled impulse response of the matched filter. If the data are transmitted and the matched filter is sampled at the Nyquist rate, Λ_{cc} will be a positive-definite matrix. c and ε will have unique optimum solutions in the space of real numbers. The optimum infinite-precision real-valued TDL coefficient vector c is given uniquely by

$$\hat{c} = u \Lambda_{cc}^{-1}. \tag{5}$$

The optimum estimate $\hat{B}_k$ is $+1$ if y_k is positive or -1 if y_k is negative, where $\hat{y}_k$ is given by

$$\hat{y}_k = \sum_{j=-N}^{N} \hat{c}_j \tilde{r}_{k-j}. \tag{6}$$

III.   BRANCH-AND-BOUND ALGORITHM

In many practical systems, such as the linear equalizer presented in Section II, the high-precision multiplications needed in implementing the TDL equation in (6) may be objectionable. We propose the use of powers of two for each TDL coefficient c_j. A simple rounding of the optimum infinite-precision TDL coefficient vector $\hat{c}$ to the nearest powers of two usually yields quite poor system performance (i.e., large mean-square error and large equalizer error probability).

Thus, it is useful to consider the optimal solution of $c = (\tilde{c}_{-N}, ..., \tilde{c}_0, ..., \tilde{c}_N)$, where each $\tilde{c}_j$ is constrained to be in the space

$$Z = \left\{ z : z = \pm 2^{-t}, t \in \{0, 1, ..., b\} \right\}, \tag{7}$$

where b is a specified integer.

The infinite-precision solution of the TDL coefficient vector $\hat{c}$ is given by (5) and its direct implementation in (6) requires $(2N + 1)$ multiplications. However, the presence of the matched filter causes $\{\tilde{r}_k\}$ in Fig. 1 to be symmetric around the zeroth index. This means the TDL coefficients $\{\hat{c}_j\}$ in (5) are symmetric about the zeroth index. Since $\hat{c}_0$ is an arbitrary scaling constant, it can always be set to one. Thus, the solution in (5) has only N degrees of freedom. Now we can constrain $\{\tilde{c}_j\}$ to be symmetric about the zeroth index, and thus $\tilde{c}$ has $(N + 1)$ degrees of freedom. Unlike the infinite-precision case, where $\hat{c}_0$ is an arbitrary scaling constant, $\tilde{c}_0$ is a parameter that needs to be optimized. The optimal solution of $\tilde{c}$ under the power of two constraint becomes

$$\min_{c \in Z_{N+1}} Q(c) = Q(\tilde{c}), \tag{8}$$

where Z is defined in (7).

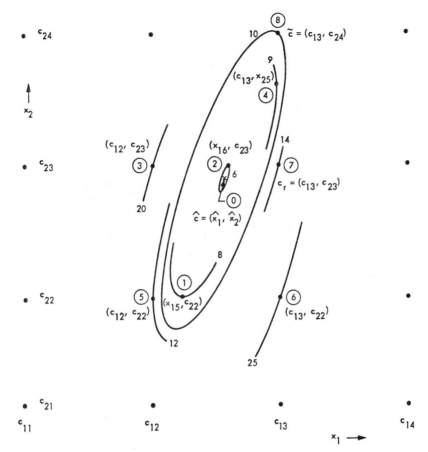

Fig. 3. Two-dimensional constant contour of concentric ellipses.

A direct brute-force search of all finite solutions for $\tilde{c}$ is possible in theory but not practical since the total number of points in Z^{N+1} is $[2(b + 1)]^{N+1}$. For example, even for a low-order TDL of $N = 5$ and $b = 8$, we have $18^6 = 3.4 \cdot 10^7$ number of feasible solutions.

There are various approaches for solving the constrained minimization problem in (8). One practical approach for finding the optimal solution of $\tilde{c}$ in (8) is based on the branch-and-bound algorithm. This algorithm is an efficient tree search procedure for constrained optimization problems in which the constraints need not be convex and some or all of the variables have discrete values. For our constrained minimization problem, the branch-and-bound recursive operation begins

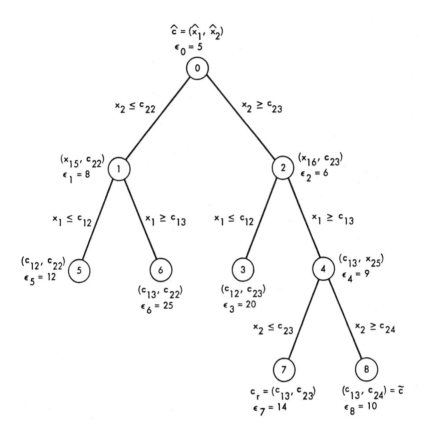

Fig. 4. Solution tree graph of Fig. 2.

by defining an extended solution space with a modified cost function. The solution space is repeatedly divided into smaller and smaller subsets and a bound is computed for the cost of the solutions within each subset. After each subdivision, those subsets with a bound that exceeds the cost of a known feasible solution are excluded from further consideration. This process continues until a feasible solution is found with a cost no greater than the bound for any subset. The precise statement of the branch-and-bound algorithm is quite complicated and lengthy. For details, see Refs. [9–12].

In this article we present the basic operations of the branch-and-bound algorithm by treating a specific two-dimensional example given in detailed graphical form in Fig. 3. Consider a generalized quadratic-form $Q(c)$ given by (3), where $c = (c_1, c_2)$. By constraining $Q(c)$ to be some specified real number, the set of c that yields this constant contour is known to be an ellipse in two dimensions. For different constraining values of $Q(c)$, we obtain different sets of concentric ellipses, as shown in Fig. 3.

The infinite-precision solution $\hat{c} = (\hat{x}_1, \hat{x}_2)$, given readily in analytical closed form by (5), yields the minimum of $Q(c)$ and is in the center of the family of ellipses in Fig. 3. This $\hat{c}$ solution is used as the initial solution (i.e., zeroth iteration) of the branch-and-bound algorithm. In Fig. 3, we assumed $\varepsilon_0 = Q(c) = 5$. The admissible constrained values of (c_1, c_2) are in the sets spanned by $\{c_{11}, c_{12}, c_{13}, c_{14}\}$ and $\{c_{21}, c_{22}, c_{23}, c_{24}\}$. Since $c_{12} < \hat{x}_1 < c_{13}$ and $c_{22} < \hat{x}_2 < c_{23}$, we can perform the branching operation on either variable. By constraining $x_2 \leq c_{22}$, we find the minimum occurs at (x_{15}, c_{22}) and has a cost of $\varepsilon_1 = 8$. In Fig. 3 and in the tree graph of Fig. 4, we label this node 1. Similarly, for $x_2 \geq c_{23}$, we obtain the node 2 at (x_{16}, c_{23}) with $\varepsilon_2 = 6$. Among these two nodes, we branch from the node with the lowest cost ε_2. Since $c_{12} < x_{16} < c_{13}$, by constraining $x_1 \leq c_{12}$ and $x_1 \geq c_{13}$, we obtain nodes 3 and 4 with $\varepsilon_3 = 20$ and $\varepsilon_4 = 9$. Among the present active nodes of 1, 3, and 4, the lowest cost is at ε_1. Branching at 1 yields nodes 5 and 6. Now, the active nodes are 3, 4, 5, and 6. Since ε_4 has the lowest cost, we branch from 4 to obtain 7 and 8. In general, the algorithm proceeds in this manner until the node with the lowest cost among all the active nodes at the instant is a valid admissible constrained solution. Then the algorithm terminates and that minimum-cost admissible solution is the desired solution of (8). In our example in Fig. 3, we note nodes 0, 1, 2, and 4 are not admissible solutions, while 5, 6, 7, and 8 are admissible solutions. In the last set of active nodes $\{5, 6, 7, 8\}$, we see $\varepsilon_8 = 10$ is lower than $\varepsilon_5 = 12$, $\varepsilon_6 = 25$, and $\varepsilon_7 = 14$. Thus, we can terminate the algorithm at node 8 with $\tilde{c} = (c_{13}, c_{24})$ and a mean-square error cost of 10. It is also interesting to observe that, from Fig. 3, if we had used simple round of $\hat{c}$ to the nearest admissible solution in the minimum Euclidean norm sense, then $c_r = (c_{13}, c_{23})$ is given by node 7 and has a cost of 14.

We note that the number of nodes needed to be considered in the branch-and-bound algorithm is highly dependent on the degree of eccentricity of the associated ellipse (or ellipsoid) in the generalized quadratic form. Indeed, if the generalized quadratic form is a circle (or sphere), then the rounded solution is the optimum constrained solution. Unfortunately, in most practical problems, when the dimension of the problem becomes large, the associated ellipsoids are almost always highly eccentric manifested in a ratio of largest to smallest eigenvalues that is quite large [13]. In such problems, direct enumeration of all admissible solutions in Z^{N+1} is clearly impossible. Even the use of the branch-and-bound algorithm can involve quite large computer storage space for the active nodes during the computation.

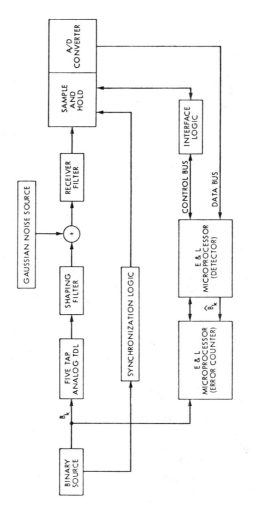

Fig. 5. Hardware subsection block diagram.

IV. HARDWARE AND
SOFTWARE DESCRIPTIONS

In Fig. 5 a block diagram of the hardware used in a 300 bits/sec (bps) binary data transmission system is given. The data source is a pseudorandom sequence of TTL level bit stream produced from a Wavetek 132 function generator. The equivalent transmitter and channel filter response is physically modeled by a five-tap analog TDL followed by a shaping filter. This subsection is realized by using an SN74164 eight-bit shift register with two LM339 quad comparators and two LM308 operational amplifiers. The resistor values in the TDL are adjusted to achieve the desired overall value of $\{\tilde{r}_k\}$ in Fig. 2. The noise source is produced from an HP3722A noise generator. The noise is band-limited white Gaussian with a bandwidth much larger than the data rate. The summer consists of two LM318 operational amplifiers, and the receiving filter approximating the theoretical matched filter uses an LM308 operational amplifier as a low-pass filter with an equivalent cutoff frequency of 135 Hz. The synchronization signal is obtained from the sync output of the Wavetek 132 generator. This additional sync signal path does not exist in a real data transmission system. However, for the purpose of verifying the reduced complexity equalization concept, this approach is quite acceptable. The sample and hold subsection uses two LM308 operational amplifiers, an SN74123 monostable multivibrator, and an LM311 comparator. The A/D converter uses a low-cost 12-bit AD574JD device, and the interface logic and control use two 74LS367 hex tri-state buffers and one each of 7476 JK flip-flop, 7474 D flip-flop, 7420 four-input NAND gate, 74LS04 hex inverter, and 7400 quad NAND gate. The data bus is then connected to a 8080 eight-bit microprocessor operating at 750 kHz clock rate.

The equalization TDL is completely implemented in software. It consists of two separate routines: a symbol detection routine and an error counting routine. Each of them is programmed separately using 8080 assembly language in two E&L Microprocessor Training Systems. For real-time application, both the detection and the error counting algorithms must finish all computations before a new data symbol arrives. In this experiment, if we count the number of states that each machine language executes, the detection algorithm involves much more computation than the error counting and display algorithm. The maximum allowable data rate for this software detector operating at 750 kHz clock rate is limited to 490 bps.

The software detector flow chart is shown in Fig. 6, where we have an initialization subroutine and detection subroutine. A handshaking control line interfaces the microprocessor and the A/D converter. When the data available flag is set in the sample and hold subsection, the microprocessor will enable the A/D converter into read mode and will input the sampled 12-bit data in a sequence of 8 bits and then 4 bits. The microprocessor will create a data array from these data and compute the weighted sum according to the TDL coefficients. After finishing

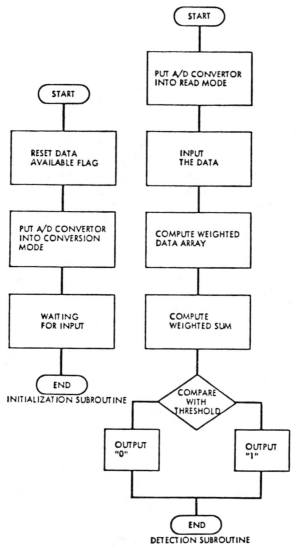

Fig. 6. Flow chart of detector implemented in software.

these computations, a threshold logic will determine the sign of the weighted average. The detected output is sent to another E&L microprocessor for error counting and display. The entire experiment will be run long enough to generate meaningful statistics.

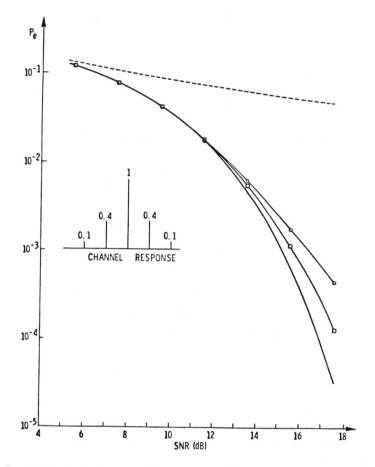

Fig. 7. Theoretical results of error probability versus SNR at the input of equalization TDL. (□), multiplication-free TDL; (o), infinite-precision rounded TDL; (- - - -), infinite-precision TDL; (——), no TDL.

V. NUMERICAL RESULTS AND CONCLUSIONS

In this section we consider two explicit examples to illustrate the usefulness of the multiplication-free equalization technique. In both examples, the equalization TDL is restricted to 9 taps, while the A/D converter, as well as the processing, are limited to 12 bits. In the first example, the sampled channel responses at the input of the TDL are given by (0.1, 0.4, 1, 0.4, 0.1). While the

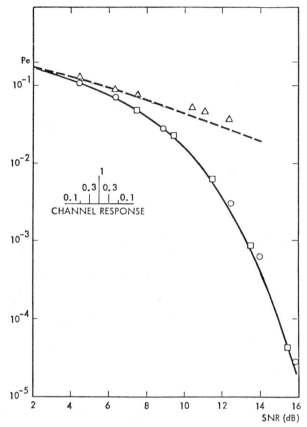

Fig. 8. Theoretical and experimental results on error probability versus SNR at the input of equalization TDL. (Δ), no TDL (expt.); (O), multiplication-free TDL (expt.); ( ), multiplication-free TDL (theor.); (——), no TDL (theor.); (–), infinite-precision TDL (theor.).

channel responses used in Fig. 7 only model a simplistic example (i.e., low number of impulse response terms) of a highly distorted linear channel, this type of channel response is adequate and commonly used [15, pp. 149–150] to compare the performances of various forms of equalizers. For this example, four sets of error probabilities as functions of signal-to-noise ratio (SNR) from 5.5 to 17.5 dB have been evaluated theoretically and plotted in Fig. 7. The solid curve represents the infinite-precision TDL performance results. The optimum 12-bit multiplication-free TDL results in the sense of Section III are given by the   points. The performances of the infinite-precision TDL with coefficients rounded to the nearest 12-bit multiplication-free values are given by the O points. The dashed curve represents the performances of the system with no TDL. For low to medium SNR values, there is a slight difference between the rounded multiplication-free solution and the optimum multiplication-free solution. However, at an SNR of 17.5 dB, the optimum result is almost four times lower in P_e as compared to the rounded result.

In the second example, the sampled channel responses are given by (0.1, 0.3, 1, 0.3, 0.1). These responses represent a fairly distorted channel with moderate intersymbol interference problems. In Fig. 8, the experimentally obtained error probabilities, using the procedure discussed in Section IV for the optimum multiplication-free case as well as for the no-TDL case, are presented along with the corresponding theoretical results. As can be seen, there is, in general, good agreement among the experimental and theoretical performances. The slight discrepancies at high SNR are due to the mismatch of the implemented low-pass detection filter to the theoretical matched filter. There is only a slight degradation of 0.3 dB between the reduced complexity and the infinite-precision performance curves. As expected, there is a significant difference between the reduced-complexity and the no-TDL results.

It is interesting to note that, if we use full multiplication procedure for the weighting of each data symbol, the software will not be able to keep up with the incoming data. (Software multiplication using 8080 assembly language requires at least 666 states for multiplying two unsigned 8-bit data [7]. At 1.33 μs clock period, it requires 0.88 ms for a full 8-bit multiplication.) This clearly demonstrates the advantage of this shift-only scheme for an efficient and low-cost data equalizer based on microprocessor implementation.

In conclusion, we have presented some analytical and practical results on the implementation of a linear data equalizer. We believe the replacement of high-precision multipliers by optimized binary shifts is a useful fast processing technique applicable to various practical signal-processing problems. The technique appears to be particularly attractive in conjunction with a low-cost microprocessor implementation.

ACKNOWLEDGMENTS

This work is supported in part by the Electronic Program of the Office of Naval Research. The authors are appreciative of the experimental work done by D. O. Anderton.

REFERENCES

1.   A. V. OPPENHEIM and R. W. SCHAFER, "Digital Signal Processing," Chapter 9. Prentice-Hall, Englewood Cliffs, New Jersey, 1975.
2.   L. R. RABINER and B. GOLD, "Theory and Application of Digital Signal Processing," Chapter 5. Prentice-Hall, Englewood Cliffs, New Jersey, 1975.
3.   S. HAYKIN, "Introduction to Adaptive Filters," Chapters 4–5. Macmillan, New York, 1984.

4. B. WIDROW and S. D. STEARNS, "Adaptive Signal Processing." Prentice-Hall, Engle-
    wood Cliffs, New Jersey, 1985.
5. R. W. LUCKY, J. SALZ, and E. J. WALTON, Jr., "Principles of Data Communication,
    Chapters 5–6. McGraw-Hill, New York, 1968.
6. J. G. PROAKIS, "Digital Communications," pp. 357–381. McGraw-Hill, New York,
    1983.
7. A. A. GIORDANO and F. M. HSU, "Least-Square Estimation." Wiley, New York, 1985.
8. R. A. MONZINGO and T. W. MILLER, "Introduction to Adaptive Arrays," pp. 60–64,
    433–439. Wiley, New York, 1980.
9. J. D. C. LITTLE, K. G. MURTY, D. W. SWEENEY, and C. KAREL, An algorithm for the
    traveling-salesman problem. *Oper. Res.*, 11, 972–989 (1963).
10. E. BALAS, A note on the branch-and-bound principle. *Oper. Res.* 16, 442–445
    (1968).
11. L. G. MITTEN, Branch-and-bound methods: General formulation and properties. *Oper.
    Res.* 18, 24–34 (1970).
12. T. Y. YAN and K. YAO, A multiplication-free solution for linear minimum mean-square
    estimation and equalization using the branch-and-bound principle. *IEEE Trans. Inf.
    Theory* IT-12, 26–34.
13. K. YAO and T. Y. YAN, On the statistical optimum design of a quantized coefficient re-
    cursive digital filter. *Proc. Eur. Signal Process. Conf., 1980*, pp. 753–757 (1980).
14. "8080/8085 Assembly Language Programming Manual." Intel. Corp., 1978.
15. J. G. PROAKIS, Advances in equalization for intersymbol interferences. *In* "Advances
    in Communication Systems: Theory and Applications" (A. J. Viterbi, ed.), Vol. 4.
    Academic Press, New York, 1975.

ALGORITHMS FOR IMAGE-BASED TRACKERS OF MANEUVERING TARGETS

D. D. SWORDER and R. G. HUTCHINS

Department of Applied Mechanics and Engineering Sciences
University of California, San Diego
La Jolla, California 92093

I.   INTRODUCTION

A "pointing-and-tracking" system utilizes noisy sensor data to make inferences regarding the dynamic state of a designated target. The motion clues thus deduced are then used to cause the line of sight of the tracker to follow the target with small error even in the presence of evasive maneuvers and clutter. In a fire-control application, the current estimate of the location of the target must be extrapolated forward in time, and another dynamic object (a gun) properly oriented with respect to the sensor platform.

In a generic encounter of this type, the global state consists of two parts: a controlled object with well-defined dynamics, e.g., the physical tracker and gun, and an external object with far less certain description. Figure 1 shows a functional block diagram of a general pointing-and-tracking system. The raw sensor data are first transformed by a preprocessor into a more convenient form. The sensor-preprocessor can be viewed as producing the "observation" of the encounter state that is utilized in traditional analyses of estimation and control. In an image-based system, the raw data may take the form of a sequence of pictures of a changing scene. In this event, the preprocessor serves to provide a frame-dependent stage of data reduction.

A specific example of sensor-preprocessor operation is provided by a conventional TV tracker. An optical sensor sequentially scans a rectangular window along horizontal lines. The resulting intensity profile forms a single frame of data. A preprocessing algorithm uses these data to locate the center of the target contour within the tracking window. The sensor-preprocessor can be thought of as providing a mapping of the dynamic state of the encounter into a (noisy) measure-

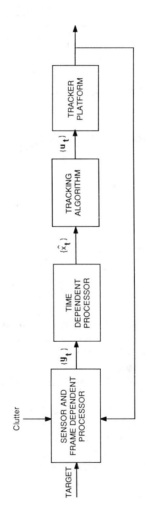

Fig. 1. Generic block diagram.

ment of this state. In this article, the word "measurement" refers to this derivative information rather than to the raw detector outputs.

A single observation gives an instantaneous picture of the encounter. A sequence of such observations can be used to provide a much more accurate estimate of the dynamic attributes of the target. To obtain this refined estimate, the measurements are transformed sequentially in the block labeled "time-dependent processor." The output of this block is then used in a tracking and/or prediction algorithm (TA) to generate an actuating signal which will direct the motion of the sensor platform and collateral objects in a suitable fashion.

There are a number of issues that influence the design of the algorithms which go in each of the blocks in the tracking system. For analytical design and simulation, a tractable mathematical model of the encounter dynamics is required. The dynamic model of the sensor platform and associated subsystems is typically well defined from test and observation. The relationship between the generalized tracker state and the endogenous variables can be phrased in terms of an ordinary differential equation with a wide-band additive disturbance used to quantify the influence of some unpredictable, parasitic effects.

A conventional observation model is a useful way of describing the measurements taken during the encounter, although, as the preprocessor becomes more sophisticated, some of the relevant peculiarities of the measurement subsystem may be lost or weakened thereby. For example, a precise description of structured clutter can complicate the observation equation considerably, but such topics will not be discussed here.

A more controversial submodel is that of the target. Not only is the physical object not available for a comprehensive test program but, further, the target is often under the direction of a human operator whose objective is antithetical to that of the tracker designer. The actions of the target's director create an exogenous acceleration, the fine structure of which displays certain anomalies.

The difficulties inherent in the quantification of target motion are illustrated quite well in the literature describing the evolution of the design of fire-control systems for engaging land vehicles. Until relatively recently, targets of this type were considered to be either stationary or slowly moving. For this reason, a constant velocity target became the "standard moving target representation to which weapons were designed and by which they were evaluated" [1]. The filtering and prediction problems have immediate solutions under the assumption the target speed is constant and the gunner tracks the target perfectly.[1]

In longer-range encounters involving mobile targets and considerable clutter, the dynamic hypotheses which delineate the scenario must be extensively modified. Indeed, as Gwinner points out in Ref. [1], even if the target moves with

---

[1]This was termed "Ye-olden-standard" in Ref. [1].

constant velocity in an earth-fixed coordinate system, the line-of-sight rate from a fixed sensor will not be constant.

A useful way to express the ever-present uncertainties with respect to target motion is to assume that the target acceleration is a random process. While many investigators have used discrete-time models, the basic notions can be expressed in terms of a continuous-time target model. Denote the conventional target state by x_T. Suppose that x_T satisfies a linear equation of the form

$$\dot{x}_T = A_T x_T + B_T a_T, \tag{1}$$

where a_T is an acceleration vector which accounts for both the target "dynamics neglected by the plant and the randomness of the (operator) commands" [2].

If a_T in (1) is thought to be a white-noise process, the target position can be expressed in terms of a "white-noise" integral [3]. Further, if the observation model is linear, Kalman filter/predictor methods find immediate application.[2] Indeed, these ideas have been utilized in novel ways to study the effectiveness of various prediction and estimation algorithms (e.g., see Ref. [5]).

The algorithms derived on the basis of a model like that given in (1) are simplified by the fact that, since a_T is white noise, it is inherently unpredictable. Hence, location predictions based upon such a model are solely contingent on the current estimates of position and velocity. If, alternatively, a_T is thought to be a smoother process, there is a performance advantage that accrues to its estimation.

To model the target acceleration more accurately, a detailed understanding of what a_T represents is essential. In Ref. [6] a useful distinction is made between different categories of target acceleration.

> "Whereas mobility describes the movement of the vehicle from one location to another in a given period of time, agility describes the vehicle's ability to alter its mean path during that time period .... A major component of agility of the vehicle arises from the driver's intent to maneuver. This is a product of training and the perception of threat. Any analytical approach to modeling of a maneuvering vehicle will inevitably encounter a requirement to represent this intentional motion. This phenomenon is so important that it deserves independent description and verification."

A natural trichotomy of target vehicle accelerations makes apparent certain of the difficulties that adhere to the synthesis of estimator/predictors in this type of problem. Reference [6] categorized accelerations as:

1) Intentional maneuver (agility): This represents evasive target motion. The "driver of the vehicle is expected to select levels of lateral and tangential

---

[2]See Ref. [4] for a complete development of this idea.

accelerations and their time durations. The selection is done from a set of possibilities constrained by vehicle capabilities."

2) Involuntary maneuver: This component captures that part of the motion which is not under the driver's direct control. It "may be modeled as the output of a linear dynamic system."

3) Goal-oriented motion (mobility): This component of acceleration describes the goals and objectives of the target; e.g., "go from point A to point B."

The indicated target accelerations lead to identifiable constituents of the total pointing error (TP). As pointed out by Burke [7, 8], the TP error consists of a system-induced error (SI) due to the failure of the tracker to identify the precise target location relative to the sensor, and a target-induced error (TI) due to target maneuvers during the prediction period. It was further observed that "current tactical vehicle mobility capabilities indicate that maneuvering targets require target acceleration estimates in addition to target velocity estimates to calculate effective" predictions of target position.

The indicated decomposition of target acceleration can be included in the model given in (1) in a natural way. Since the goal-oriented motion typically takes place on a relatively long time interval, it tends to act as a bias on the time scale of the tracker, and can be subsumed into the model as a constant forcing term.

At the other extreme, the involuntary maneuvers tend to have a wide bandwidth, and in many applications are well modeled as a white-noise disturbance. In what follows this will be done, although it should be acknowledged that more detailed models exist.

Of more concern here is the characterization of vehicle agility. At reasonable ranges, the evasive maneuvers will not only increase the errors in the target tracker (SI error), but they will make more difficult the prediction of future target position. A useful class of evasive maneuvers is discussed in Ref. [1]. A motion pattern is generated by assuming that the target follows a sequence of circular arcs joined to form a continuous path. This idea was introduced in Ref. [9] and is referred to as the Burke–Perkins (BP) model in Ref. [10]. In the BP model, the sequence of times spent on the individual arcs is a set of independent and identically distributed random variables. The locally circular motion of the target can be included in an explicit prediction algorithm [11].

A generic target model, motivated by the BP study, can be expressed as

$$dx_T = A_T x_T \, dt + F_T a_T \, dt + C_T \, dn_t. \tag{2}$$

Equation (2) warrants some discussion since it forms the basis for much of the analysis which follows. As in (1), x_T is the classical target state vector including as components the current position and velocity of the target. For reasons discussed earlier, target mobility has been neglected. The term $\{n_t\}$ is used to describe the wide-band accelerations of the target; i.e., the involuntary maneuvers. The term a_T is the BP acceleration, which is, in turn, related to the agility of the target.

Equation (2) is to be interpreted as a stochastic differential equation in the sense of Ref. [3]. Formally, division of both sides of (2) by (dt) would lead to an equation like that given in (1); i.e., $\dot{n}_t$ is white noise. More precisely, the forcing term $\{n_t\}$ in (2) is a vector Brownian motion with unit intensity:

$$n_0 = 0$$

$$E\{n_t n'_s\} = I \min(t, s). \tag{3}$$

The effect of interstate correlation and amplification is delineated by the matrix C_T.

The proper description of agility is more controversial. In Ref. [12], a_T is modeled as a generalized Poisson process. The resulting sample functions of a_T are piecewise constant with jumps at random times. Such an acceleration creates significant complications in the analytical treatment of (2). One way of obviating these difficulties is to assume that the "correlation time of the acceleration is long compared with the time of flight" [12], and to replace the jump acceleration process with a Brownian motion equivalent. While it has been asserted (see Ref. [12]) that "such a model is appropriate since the target of interest is a tank," the validity of the replacement is clearly dependent upon the specific character of the encounter.

The motivation for replacing the jump acceleration process by a Brownian motion stems from the fact that the complete encounter dynamics now have a linear-quadratic-Gaussian structure, and Kalman filter/predictor methods can be used to advantage. Unfortunately, even if the jumps in acceleration are infrequent, large and unpredicted tracking errors may occur soon after a jump in acceleration occurs. This phenomenon was examined in some detail in Ref. [13]. In this reference the time-dependent processor was made more responsive by assuming that the target model is formed by a concatenation of simpler submodels. Each of the various possible target accelerations was represented by an individual submodel. A jump change in the acceleration of the target was displayed as a change in the current submodel in this formulation. The time-dependent processor was then forced to adapt its own characteristics to those of the ostensible submodel. Of course, to the extent that the imputed submodel is incorrect, large errors in tracking and prediction may ensue.

In this article, some of the issues in tracking and prediction that have arisen in the indicated references will be addressed in the context of an image-based system. The target model will be that given in (2). The BP acceleration will be described by a random process with finite state space. Such a process avoids the tendency of a generalized Poisson process to grow without bound in magnitude.

The compound adjective "image-based" used in this paper will distinguish a sensor-preprocessor which makes more effective use of the fine structure of the scene than does its nonimaging counterpart. For example, the frame-dependent processor will not only provide the location of the target, but other attributes of the target that are germane to the tracking and prediction task will be estimated as well; e.g., the orientation of the target with respect to the image plane.

If properly designed, the image-based system is relatively insensitive to structured clutter. To illustrate the distinction between sensor-preprocessor types, suppose that a tank is being tracked with an EO sensor when suddenly the right half of the target is obscured by smoke. A conventional system (nonimaging) would observe that the measured center-of-area of the target had suddenly moved to the left, and infer from this that the target was strongly accelerating in this direction. If the tracking algorithm was such that it attempted to follow the path generated by this pseudoacceleration, it could easily lose the target completely. An image-based system, which recognizes the target shape, would correctly identify the sequence of events, and not ascribe an acceleration to the target due to the motion of an obscurant.

As this example shows, it is not the sensor alone that makes a system image-based, but instead the information extracted from the raw data. Of course, many sensors do not have the ability to generate the requisite structural information. Systems based upon such sensors are inherently nonimaging.

The image-based tracker has clear advantages, but these must be weighed against concomitant drawbacks. Of primary concern here are the dynamic penalties that are associated with the time delays in the frame-dependent processor. Not only is there a discrete sampling of the scene, but this processing may take a significant fraction of a frame time.[3] In a rapidly changing environment, there is a performance cost attributable to processing delays. Hence, to justify the choice of an image-based sensor, these delays must be compensated for by superior noise rejection.

In this article some elementary properties of an image-based tracker/predictor are explored. The next section reviews some aspects of image analysis that are relevant to the tracking problem. Sophisticated signal-processing algorithms are now available for the extraction of a large quantity of information from a scene. When an algorithm is recursive or is performed by multiple passes through the data, the system designer must make a judgment as to when further processing is no longer warranged. The decision must not be made solely on the basis of the quality of the target information, but rather it should be made to ensure that the system performance specifications are met.

To illustrate the fundamental design issues that arise when an imaging sensor is used, two general problems are discussed. In the first, the operational value of an image-based clutter suppression algorithm is quantified. In the second, the

---

[3]In some instances this fraction may be greater than one.

use of target orientation in prediction is considered. Both problems are discussed in a rather initiatory manner, but the analysis demonstrates the latent versatility of an image-based system. Because an image-based tracker makes use of an unconventional observation structure, novel methods of design are required in order to achieve enhanced performance. A simple modification of classical algorithms will not suffice to fully exploit the possibilities implicit in this new technology.

II.   CURRENT APPROACHES TO IMAGE-BASED TARGET TRACKING

A.   INTRODUCTION

The traditional model used in a target tracking problem consists of an equation of motion for the "center of mass" of the target, and a measurement or observation equation. These equations typically take the form:

$$dx_t = A(t)x_t \, dt + dn_t \tag{4}$$

$$dy_t = C(t)x_t \, dt + dw_t, \tag{5}$$

where x_t is the system state at time t, usually consisting of position, velocity, and perhaps acceleration of the center of mass of the target; y_t is the measurement at time t; and n_t and w_t are Brownian motion processes. The tracking problem is one of estimating elements of the system state at current and future times on the basis of the measurements. This formulation leads to the well-known Kalman filter algorithm for the state estimation (see, e.g., Ref. [14]). More generally, the dynamic and state equations may be nonlinear. In this event the nonlinear equations are linearized about a nominal trajectory, giving rise to the extended Kalman filter (EKF) solution [15].

Another situation that arises in applications is one in which the measurements are not continuous in time. This gives a discrete-time measurement equation [15]:

$$y(t_k) = C(t_k)x(t_k) + w(t_k), \tag{6}$$

where $w(t_k)$ is a discrete-time white noise process. Sequential measurements can also be handled with the traditional Kalman filtering technique [14, 15]. While the above equations do not explicitly contain the dynamics of the sensor platform or the control function required to sterr the platform so that the target remains within the field of view, this aspect of the problem is the same for traditional as well as image-based trackers. (A discussion can be found in Ref. [16].)

Image-based target trackers utilize discrete-time measurement subsystems. At each measurement time, an M × N array of numbers is produced. This is referred to as a frame of data. Each number represents the intensity of the electromagnetic radiation within a specific frequency band which reaches the corresponding receptor in the physical sensor array. Some receptors collect or "respond to" radiation in more than one frequency band simultaneously (e.g., red-green-blue receptors), producing multiple M × N arrays. Real-time trackers require both high sampling rates and high resolution (large M and N), thus creating raw data rates that are quite high. The image-specific portion of the tracker uses a single frame of data or a small number of such frames to detect and recognize the presence of a "target" within the field of view, and then to produce an estimate of its position, orientation, and other features that may be of interest. This is not an easy task, and sophisticated, image-specific algorithms tends to be computationally burdensome. The high data rates and concomitant computations incur processing time penalties that manifest themselves as time delays in the measurement equation. More will be said about this in Section III. The purpose of this section is to outline some of the approaches taken to image enhancement, target recognition, and target tracking that have appeared in the recent literature. In what follows it is important to note the image-specific aspects of the problem since it is their efficacy which must be judged.

B.   ELEMENTS OF IMAGE-BASED TARGET
      DETECTION AND RECOGNITION SYSTEMS

There are a number of steps involved in detecting and identifying the target from the data provided by an imaging sensor. In his survey of automatic target recognition systems [17], Bhanu provides a useful classification of these steps. This classification will be presented in some detail. The primary concern in [17] is that of locating and tracking targets over time using a forward-looking infrared (FLIR) imager. Bhanu focuses on the tactical military applications common to smart weapons and stand-off target designator platforms that must detect and track targets as well as prioritize and select aimpoints for effective attack. The relevant targets tend to be ground based, which means that the imager must deal with substantial background detail and foreground obscuration in addition to sensor noise. Bhanu divided current approaches to this problem into two categories: pattern-recognition procedures and knowledge-based (AI) approaches. Pattern recognition is further subdivided into a sequence of five overall processing tasks. These are preprocessing, target detection, segmentation, target classification, and everything else (which includes target prioritization, tracking, and aimpoint selection). All but portions of the last task are subsumed within the first block of Fig. 1. This partitioning illustrates the complexity involved in the image-specific processing portion of the system. Each of these five tasks will be discussed briefly.

Preprocessing includes all processing of pixel data designed to improve target contrast with the background, and to reduce noise and clutter in the image. This processing operates at the individual pixel level, and is done without any knowledge of actual target location in the image. Various image processing schemes have been proposed for this step, including median filters, thresholding filters, and transform techniques. (See Refs. [18, 19], as well as the references cited in Ref. [17].)

Target detection is "the process of localizing those areas in the image where a potential target is likely to be present" [17]. Many detection techniques rely on contrast between the target and background, and work as well for bright targets on dark backgrounds as for dark targets on bright backgrounds. "Windowing" is frequently useful. A rectangular window of pixels determined to be about the size of the expected target in the image plane (which is a function of range) is compared with a border area assumed to consist of background pixels only. If the contrast in pixel intensity between these two areas is large enough, then the inner window is declared a target area. Range in this detection algorithm often is approximated as the distance to the ground at a given slant angle (corresponding to the boresight angle of the imager) for airborne imaging platforms. Other detection methods include the use of edge identifiers, border following techniques, and histogram intensity profiles to isolate areas of the image likely to contain a target. Predictably, target detection rate is coupled with the false alarm rate; i.e., algorithms that find more targets also tend to produce more false alarms.

Segmentation refers to the extraction of a potential target from its background. This entails assigning each pixel in the area of a likely target either to the target or to the background (nontarget). Bhanu gives references to several algorithms designed to perform this function. Methods include various edge and boundary procedures as well as cluster detection and classification schemes.

Target classification involves three subtasks. The first is feature computation. This requires computing a set of features for each area of the image which has been identified as a target. A feature is some attribute of the target which can be quantified. Desirable properties of a feature are "invariance with respect to geometry (rotation, scale, and translation), computational efficiency, and extractability under adverse conditions" [17]. Most of the features used by current researchers are spectral, geometric, and/or topological.

The second subtask is feature selection, which entails selecting those features that "maximize the similarity of objects in the same class (as the expected target) while maximizing the dissimilarity of objects in different classes" [17]. This selection process also reduces the computation and memory requirements of the classifier.

The third subtask is the final target classification. Most techniques here assume that each feature vector is a random variable with a multivariable Gaussian distribution. Possible classification techniques include K-nearest-neighbor algorithms, projection techniques, linear and quadratic classifiers, structural classifiers, and tree-based techniques. Minter [20] presents an adaptive, nonparametric procedure based on a Bayesian discriminant function. This method is suitable when only one target class is of interest, and requires only *a priori* knowledge of that class.

The final task in this decomposition is a composite of target prioritization, target tracking, and aimpoint selection. Prioritization is required if more than one target is detected, and is simply "the process of assigning priorities to the targets in the field of view" [17]. This process depends on the results of the classification algorithm, and on prior knowledge. Aimpoint selection makes use of the imaging qualities of the sensor in ways a traditional tracking system cannot match. A traditional system utilizes only a point location for the target. An image-based tracker can supply silhouette or other information on target extent and orientation, thus giving the system many more options in aimpoint selection.

The target tracking problem itself has been approached in many different ways, a few of which are reviewed below. One recent trend is toward using two or more approaches in parallel. For example, a target lost by one algorithm may be maintained in the field of view by another. In the case of maneuvering targets, one algorithm might be tuned for precision estimation and prediction under the assumption of benign target dynamics, while another is tuned to detect maneuvers that could produce loss of the target by the first. One example of this is discussed later in this section.

Before leaving Bhanu's classification scheme, it is appropriate to comment on the knowledge-based approach. This includes the use of expert systems and other methods based on artificial intelligence techniques to increase the amount of prior knowledge and contextual cues available during the identification process. For example, the identification of a road in the scene would allow a "smart" processor to examine this area of the image for targets in more detail than an area identified as a lake. Similarly, the identification of a tank formation might aid in target prioritization if it is known that the command tank usually occupies a specific spot in the formation. This approach does indeed promise enhanced identification and aimpoint capabilities. However, it creates no fundamental changes in the overall target tracking problem. It merely changes the detail and quality of data available to the tracker.

An example of an algorithm designed to detect, characterize, and prioritize targets using infrared imagery data is one devised by McWilliams and Srinath [21]. They consider the problem faced by a fire-and-forget weapon which must detect only a single target during the automatic detection phase of its trajectory. The subsequent tracking and aimpoint selection issues are not considered. Their algorithm performs this task using only a single frame of image data. The algorithm is divided into two distinct parts, the screener and the ranker. The screener performs the tasks Bhanu has labeled preprocessing and target detection. The ranker provides segmentation, target classification, and target prioritization.

The screener uses a windowing approach to detect likely target areas in the image. Since the aspect ratio (width/height) depends on an unknown target orientation, there exists some uncertainty as to the proper window parameters. Once the inner window is determined, a border consisting of about the same number of pixels as the inner window is placed around it. This window-with-border configuration, referred to as the contrast box, is used to define a pixel operator. When the contrast box is placed over an area of the image, the intensities of the pixels in the inner window are averaged, the intensities of the border pixels are averaged, and the border average is subtracted from the inner window average. The magnitude of the difference is defined as the contrast value for this area: $C_{ij} = |\mu_{inner} - \mu_{border}|$. This pixel operator is then used to define the preprocessor algorithm: "The contrast box ... is convolved with the image, creating a new image by replacing each original pixel x_{ij} with its contrast value C_{ij} for every pixel for which the contrast box fits within the image" [21].

The resulting transformed image data are then examined for local peak intensities, and the first N of these peaks are declared the most likely target areas. Additional constraints prohibit a single target from producing more than one intensity region. The N regions thus selected are passed to the ranker, and the rest of the image data are discarded.

The ranker analyzes each of the N regions obtained from the screener by computing a feature vector for each region and a rank statistic based on this feature vector. The twelve elements of the feature vector were selected heuristically by the authors. The first three are the local peak contrast computed by the screener, the standard deviation of the intensities of the inner window pixels, and the standard deviation of the intensities of the border pixels. The next four are computed not from raw pixel data, but on the output of an edge-enhancement algorithm. These are the mean of the intensities of the transformed pixel data for both the inner window and border regions, and also the corresponding standard deviations. The final five are computed on the output of a segmentation algorithm, and include the ratio of height to width of the perceived target, the ratio of the square of the target perimeter to its area, the ratio of the density of target pixels in the inner window to the density of target pixels in the border, and two invariant moments computed on the transformed pixel data [21]. The ranking statistic is then given by:

$$\lambda = \ln\left[f_T(w^T f) / f_{NT}(w^T f) \right],$$

where f is the feature vector; w is the weighting vector; and f_T and f_{NT} are the probability density functions of $w^T f$ for targets and nontargets. Both are obtained as sample densities from an image data base. This is the log-likelihood ratio. The authors report that the likelihood function is generally estimated from training imagery and stored in a lookup table. The region with the maximum computed value of λ is chosen as the target.

The authors do not consider the tracking portion of the problem in Ref. [21]. The indicated algorithm computes enough structural detail to determine both a target center-of-area in the image plane and orientation information. Conceptually one can complete the tracking loop by incorporating a time-dependent processor, as shown in Fig. 1. The details of the above example illustrate both the overall complexity of the sensor-preprocessor and realistic approaches that have been implemented to overcome some of the difficulties.

C.   APPROACHES TO TARGET TRACKING USING IMAGE-BASED SYSTEMS

Early tracking algorithms attempted to minimize the computational burden by simplifying both the sensor-dependent processing and the time-dependent processing. Raw pixel data were compared directly from one frame to the next, and any shift in location between the two frames was used to produce velocity estimates. Three comparison techniques have been traditionally used to directly compare two-dimensional pixel arrays of the same size. These are correlation, sum of absolute differences, and sum of squared differences [22]. The first is a similarity measure, while the second two are difference measures. Correlation can be expressed as:

$$\left(\sum_{i,j} F_{ij} G_{ij}\right) \Big/ \left[\left(\sum_{i,j} F_{ij}^2\right)\left(\sum_{i,j} G_{ij}^2\right)\right]^{1/2}, \qquad (7)$$

where F and G are the two pixel data arrays of the same dimension. Similarly, the sum of absolute differences is given by

$$\sum_{i,j} |F_{ij} - G_{ij}|, \qquad (8)$$

and the sum of squared differences by

$$\sum_{i,j} (F_{ij} - G_{ij})^2. \qquad (9)$$

The correlation-based algorithm is a standard image-based tracking technique that uses (7) to compare subimages of consecutive data frames directly to determine target motion in the image. The subimage in the first frame is presumed to contain the target. Several portions of the second data frame are examined until a match (i.e., a high correlation) is found with this ostensible target. The translation of the second subimage relative to the first gives the target velocity.

Differencing techniques can be used in similar fashion. Subtracting one image from its successor using (8) produces a data frame in which all stationary elements have been set to zero. This method is used to locate moving elements in the field of view. Such a technique assumes that the background is unchanging and often neglects sensor jitter.

Recent approaches have sought to combine these techniques with more extensive image preprocessing and/or more elaborate time-dependent algorithms to improve tracking capability. Holben [23] uses a correlation-based preprocessing technique to remove relative background motion from the succeeding image before applying a differencing technique to detect the target and estimate its velocity. Legters and Young [24] have developed an elaborate operator-theoretic framework for estimating target translation and rotation in the image plane, and have coupled these models with a time-dependent Kalman filter to predict motion behavior when the target is obscured by foreground objects. They assume that image preprocessing and segmentation have reduced the image plane to a binary-valued gray scale designating black objects on a white background, and use scene differencing to eliminate nonmoving areas from the image.

A related approach by Schalkoff and McVey [25] proposes what they call a "Taylor series video image processor algorithm," which uses frame-to-frame difference measurements to estimate the coefficients in the Taylor series expansion of the motion equation. Specifically, they assume:

$$d(x, t_2) \approx [\partial f(x, t_1)/\partial x]^T [A(t_1, t_2)x + b(t_1, t_2)], \qquad (10)$$

where $x = [x_1, x_2]^T$ is the position vector on the image plane; $d(x, t_2)$ is the difference between the image at times t_2 and t_1; $f(x, t)$ is the pixel data for the target at time t, all background having been set to zero by a segmentation algorithm; $A(t_1, t_2)$ is a matrix that reflects the rotation and dilation of the target in the image plane from time t_1 to time t_2; and $b(t_1, t_2)$ is a vector reflecting the translation of the target in the image plane from time t_1 to t_2. The problem is to estimate the elements of A and b from the observations d and f. Two assumptions that are critical to this approach are first that the target dynamics can be adequately modeled by the affine transformation in (10), and second that the segmentation algorithm can provide an adequate measurement of the target "texture function" $f(x, t)$.

Other researchers have tended to focus more specifically on the issues involved in tracking maneuvering targets. Over the past several years a group headed by Dr. Peter Maybeck at the Air Force Institute of Technology (AFIT) has devised an extended Kalman filter approach to the image-based target tracking problem [26–30]. They have been able to structure the tracking task as a traditional discrete-time estimation problem in which the raw pixel data are used directly in the measurement equation. They consider the problem of tracking an air-to-air missile using a FLIR sensor. The sensor is assumed to be fixed and have no dynamic lags. A single frame of data consists of a set of 64 intensities at the pixels in an 8 × 8 array in a tracking window on the potentially larger FLIR image plane.

In Ref. [26] a single point target with benign dynamics was studied. This work assumes that the target produces a bivariate Gaussian intensity pattern in the image plane with circular equal intensity contours:

$$I_{target}(x, y, t) = I_{max} \exp\left(-(1/2\sigma^2)\left\{\left[x - x_{peak}(t)\right]^2 + \left[y - y_{peak}(t)\right]^2\right\}\right), \quad (11)$$

where $I_{target}(x, y, t)$ is the intensity at position x, y (relative to the center of the 8 × 8 array) and time t; I_{max} is the peak intensity (assumed known); σ is the variance in x and y (assumed known); and $x_{peak}(t)$ and $y_{peak}(t)$ locate the center of the pattern relative to the center of the 8 × 8 array. The point of maximum intensity ($x_{peak}(t)$, $y_{peak}(t)$) is given by a combination of target dynamics and atmospheric jitter; i.e.,

$$x_{peak}(t) = x_d(t) + x_a(t), \quad (12)$$

where $x_d(t)$ is the true target dynamics; and $x_a(t)$ is atmospheric jitter, with $y_{peak}(t)$ treated similarly. Target dynamics are modeled by first-order Gauss–Markov position processes x_d and y_d, with the same rms value σ_d and correlation time τ_d. The atmospheric jitter term is given by the output of a first-order shaping filter: $K\omega(s + \omega)^{-1}$, driven by white noise.

These assumptions lead to a four-dimensional state equation for the observed motion in the image plane:

$$dx_d(t) = -(1/\tau_d)x_d(t)\, dt + dn_d(t)$$

$$dx_a(t) = -\omega x_a(t)\, dt + K\omega\, dn_a(t), \quad (13)$$

where $n_d(t)$ is Gaussian with variance $Q_d(t) = \sigma_d^2 t$; and $n_a(t)$ is Gaussian with variance $Q_a(t) = t$, with a similar treatment for the vertical motion.

The measurements provided by the FLIR sensor are the complete set of 64 pixel intensity readings. The measurement equation is constructed as follows:

$$z_{jk}(t_i) = A_p^{-1} \left(\iint_{\{\text{region of jk-th pixel}\}} I_{target}(x, \ y, \ t) \ dx \ dy \right) + w_{jk}(t_i) + b_{jk}(t_i), \tag{14}$$

where A_p is the area of one pixel; $w_{jk}(t_i)$ models the FLIR noise effects on the jk-th pixel; and $b_{jk}(t_i)$ models the background effects on the jk-th pixel. Practical considerations led the researchers to simplify this equation to some degree. Arraying the 64 scalar equations of this form into a single vector provides the measurement model:

$$z(t_i) = h\left(x(t_i), \ t_i \right) + w(t_i) + b(t_i). \tag{15}$$

All of the exogenous disturbances are assumed to be independent, both spatially and temporally uncorrelated, and stationary random processes.

Equations (13) and (15) provide the framework for the standard extended Kalman filter solution of this tracking problem. Note that Eq. (15) uses the FLIR image data directly, and that no frame-dependent processing is employed.

The inverse covariance form of the extended Kalman filter was implemented with 4 states and 64 measurements. The investigators report simulation results indicating an order-of-magnitude decrease in rms errors over those achieved by correlation trackers [26, 28]. Robustness studies, on the other hand, indicated weaknesses [27, 28]. Severe performance degradation occurred when I_{max} was not set at the proper value, when the target size was incorrectly modeled, when target shape had highly elliptical contours instead of the assumed circular ones, or when nonzero mean velocities and accelerations, or varying degrees of maneuvering occurred.

In Ref. [28] various methods of circumventing these drawbacks were investigated. The state space model was enlarged to eight dimensions to include velocity and acceleration along with position. Target shape characteristics were made more robust by replacing (11) with a functional form permitting elliptical contours, and by implementing on-line estimation of the unknown equation parameters. Monte Carlo studies of these enhancements indicated that many of the sensitivity problems had been overcome. However, abrupt, high g maneuvers by the target would still break tracking lock.

Investigations of multiple hot-spot target images led, in Ref. [29], to algorithms for estimating the target's intensity pattern on the image sensor directly from the data, discarding functional forms such as (11) and its extensions. This reference examines two approaches to the use of image preprocessing techniques to estimate the function h(x, t) appearing in (15). The first approach performs a fast Fourier transform (FFT) on each frame of image data "to allow for both efficient data processing and possible spatial frequency filtering as well" [29]. Exponential smoothing is then used to produce an estimate of h. The derivative of h is computed using properties of the Fourier transform, both h and its derivative are put through an inverse transform, and these results are used in a standard EKF algorithm.

The second approach utilizes a correlation-based algorithm in conjunction with a standard Kalman filter. The intensity function h is estimated as above, and this is passed to a correlator which determines the offset between the new measurement and the center of the field of view. "The correlator in this design is enhanced in a number of ways. First, it uses the estimated function ... as its template instead of previous raw data as used by standard correlation trackers. Furthermore, a standard correlation algorithm does not exploit any knowledge of the target's dynamics, or of atmospheric disturbances which cause apparent translational offsets of intensity functions. This enhanced algorithm positions the template with the benefit of ... such knowledge. Moreover, to account for the correlator's errors, its position offset estimates are processed by the Kalman filter to produce better position estimates for actual tracking purposes, and the filter's internal dynamics model allows position predictions to be provided to the controller to compensate for delays due to computations, actuator dynamics, and inertia effects of the gimballed optics" [29].

These previous findings led the investigators in Ref. [30] to consider methods of tracking multiple hot-spot, highly maneuverable targets using a multiple model adaptive filtering approach. An eight-dimensional system state equation is used, as was suggested in Ref. [28]. Two models for the acceleration term are considered. The first treats acceleration as a first-order Gauss–Markov process:

$$da_t = -(1/T)a_t \, dt + dn_t, \tag{16}$$

where T is the correlation time, which is treated as a design tuning parameter; and n_t is Brownian motion, whose intensity is treated as a design tuning parameter. The second uses a "constant-turn-rate" model:

$$da_t = -\omega^2 v_t + dn_t, \tag{17}$$

where v is the target velocity; and ω is the turn rate: $\omega = |v_t \times a_t|/|v_t|^2$. Neither of these acceleration models provides for the abrupt changes in acceleration characteristics of the Burke–Perkins model discussed in Section I. The multiple model filtering approach compensates for this by providing a bank of filters, each tuned to a different set of target dynamic parameters. The filters are then run in parallel, and the state estimate at each measurement time is a weighted average of the estimates from the individual filters. The weights are determined by comparing the residuals from each filter and weighting small residuals highest.

In one respect the research by the AFIT group presented above does not meet the criterion of being "image-based" as defined in Section I. This is because the emphasis of that research is on locating the tracking the center-of-area ($x_{peak}(t)$, $y_{peak}(t)$), ignoring other aspects of an image-based system such as target orientation. Earlier work by Kendrick, Maybeck, and Reid [31] proposed a multiple sensor filter designed to take advantage of target orientation measurements. In Ref. [31] two-dimensional imagery data are used to augment a standard Kalman filter which uses radar data to estimate the target state. The image data are processed through a set of pattern-recognition techniques and a geometric conversion algorithm to produce an estimate of the aspect angle of the target. The target is assumed to be an aircraft, and its dynamics are strongly influenced by its orientation. In particular, acceleration is most likely to be in a direction perpendicular to the wings. Hence, knowledge of the wing orientation produces an acceleration model that is qualitatively different from an acceleration model based on center-of-mass dynamics only. The effect of orientation measurements is further discussed in Section IV.

The models and techniques presented in this section provide an introduction to the variety of approaches that have been proposed for using image-based sensors in target tracking. The next two sections examine some generic aspects of image-based systems, and present analytical studies that compare image-based approaches to their more traditional counterparts.

III. COMPARATIVE PERFORMANCE OF AN IMAGE-BASED SYSTEM

A. ENCOUNTER DYNAMICS

As indicated in the previous sections, an image-based tracker has capabilities that its nonimage-based counterparts do not share. Using sophisticated, multidimensional signal-processing algorithms, the frame-dependent processor can produce a relatively accurate estimate of the location of a maneuvering target. Unfortunately, the more comprehensive of these procedures require significant computation time. To illustrate how processing delays influence the choice of a sensor-preprocessor algorithm, it is good to contrast the performance attainable with an image-based sensor-preprocessor with that of a generic nonimage-based tracker which has negligible preprocessor delay but much more noise in the observation.

Suppose for simplicity that the target performs no intentional maneuvers; i.e., the BP acceleration $a_T = 0$. From (2)

$$dx_T = A_T x_T \, dt + C_T \, dn_t, \tag{18}$$

where $x_T(0)$ is $\mathrm{Nor}(x_T(0), P_T(0))$, and

$$C_T \, dn_t \, dn'_t \, C'_T = C_T C'_T \, dt. \tag{19}$$

To analyze the performance characteristics of the tracking system, it is convenient to combine the target and the tracker dynamics into a single encounter-state vector. In this introductory study, it will be assumed that the tracker is represented by a linear stochastic differential equation

$$dx_R = (A_R x_R + B_R u_t) \, dt + C_R \, dn_t, \tag{20}$$

where x_R is the tracker state. The endogenous process $\{u_t\}$ is chosen to direct the motion of the tracker and associated subsystems. The final term in (20), $C_R \, dn_t$, accounts for the usual broadband disturbances that impinge on the tracker.

The encounter model can be produced by combining (18) and (20). The encounter state satisfies a linear equation

$$dx_t = (Ax_t + Bu_t) \, dt + C \, dn_t, \tag{21}$$

where the matrices in (21) are composed of the matrices in (18)–(20) as subblocks.

Two types of tracking systems will be discussed here. The first is an image-based system (IMS) and the second a nonimage-based system (NMS). In the context of this development, an IMS will be distinguished by the fact that it employs a sensor that creates a discrete sequence of images of an evolving encounter, and that it has a non-negligible delay in the frame-dependent processor. Alternatively, the NMS provides target position measurements to the time-dependent processor continuously with inconsequential delay. These more expeditious observations do contain more clutter, however. Qualitatively, it is clear that the time-dependent processor carries more of the burden for accurate target location in the NMS than it does in the IMS.

The specific observation model depends upon the sensor category. Denote the sequence of target observations generated by the IMS by $\{y_t\}$, where

$$y_{n\Delta+\tau} = Dx_{n\Delta} + w_{n\Delta}; \quad n = 0, 1, \ldots. \tag{22}$$

The sensor sampling period is Δ, and the frame-dependent processing delay is τ. The observation noise $\{w_{n\Delta}\}$ is a sequence of independent Gaussian random vectors, independent of $\{x_t\}$ and $\{u_t\}$ and such that

$$E\{w_{n\Delta}\} = 0$$

$$E\{w_{n\Delta} w'_{n\Delta}\} = U > 0. \tag{23}$$

For the same encounter, the nonimaging sensor-preprocessor generates a continuous observation process denoted by $\{z_t\}$, where

$$dz_t = Dx_t \, dt + dw_t, \tag{24}$$

where $\{w_t\}$ is a Brownian motion independent of $\{x_t\}$ and $\{u_t\}$ with intensity[4]

$$(dw_t)(dw'_t) = W \, dt. \tag{25}$$

To quantify performance, suppose that, without regard to the sensor type, $\{u_t\}$ is to be selected to minimize a quadratic performance index. Denote the observation induced filtration by $\{Y_t\}$ for the IMS and $\{Z_t\}$ for the NMS, or nonspecifically $\{O_t\}$ to represent either as appropriate. The criterion used here has the form $\hat{J}_0$, where

---

[4]For notational convenience, the same symbol will be used for the observation noise in both sensors. The usage will be clear from the context.

$$\hat{J}_t = E\left\{ x_T'Sx_T + \int_t^T \left(x_s'Qx_s + u_sRu_s \right) ds \mid O_t \right\}; \quad Q, S > 0, R > 0, \tag{26}$$

with $O_t = Y_t$ for the IMS and $O_t = Z_t$ for the NMS.

B.   RELATIVE SENSOR PERFORMANCE

The problem as posed has a well-known solution, parts of which are independent of the sensor-preprocessor:

Tracking algorithm (TA). For any random variable x, let

$$E\{x \mid O_t\} = \hat{x}_t \tag{27}$$

or if $\{x_t\}$ is a random process, let

$$E\{x_t \mid O_t\} = \hat{x}_t. \tag{28}$$

It is shown in Ref. [32] that the tracking algorithm is independent of the sensor type, and is given by

$$u_t = -R^{-1}B\Pi_t\hat{x}_t, \tag{29}$$

where

$$\dot{\Pi}_t = -A'\Pi_t - \Pi_t A + \Pi_t BR^{-1}B'\Pi_t - Q$$
$$\Pi_T = S. \tag{30}$$

Time-dependent processor. By contrast to the TA block, the algorithm for the time-dependent processor is sensor-dependent. The IMS provides observations sequentially, and the time-dependent processor must both filter and extrapolate. The NMS provides a continuous observation process, and the time-dependent processor need only filter the input. Because of the linear-Gaussian structure of the encounter, the time-dependent processor is easily deduced from well-known Kalman filter formulas.

IMS. Let V be the set of times at which data from the frame-dependent processor are transmitted:

$$V = \{n\Delta + \tau; n = 0,1,\ldots\}. \tag{31}$$

The time-dependent processor has the form

$$d\hat{x}_t = (A\hat{x}_t + Bu_t)\,dt; \quad t \notin V \text{ (extrapolation)}$$

$$\Delta x_{n\Delta+\tau} = \Theta_A(\tau)K_{n\Delta}\,v_{n\Delta}; \quad n = 0,1,\ldots \text{ (filtering)} \tag{32}$$

where Θ_A is the transition matrix associated with A, $v_{n\Delta}$ the innovations process and $K_{n\Delta}$ a gain factor

$$K_{n\Delta} = P_{n\Delta}D'(DP_{n\Delta}D' + U)^{-1}$$

$$v_{n\Delta} = y_{n\Delta+\tau} - DE\{x_{n\Delta} \mid Y_{n\Delta+\tau-}\}. \tag{33}$$

The error covariance is piecewise continuous

$$\dot{P}_t = AP_t + P_tA' + N; \quad t \notin V$$

$$\Delta P_{n\Delta+\tau} = -\Theta_A(\tau)K_{n\Delta}DP_{n\Delta}\Theta'_A(\tau)$$

$$P_0 = \mathrm{Var}\{x_0 \mid Y_0\}$$

$$CC' = N. \tag{34}$$

NMS. The observation has the customary form in this case, and the time-dependent processor is given by the equations

$$d\hat{x}_t = (A\hat{x}_t + Bu_t)\,dt + K_t\,dv_t, \tag{35}$$

subject to

$$dv_t = dy_t - D\hat{x}_t\, dt$$

$$K_t = P_t D'W^{-1}$$

$$\dot{P}_t = AP_t + P_t A' + N - P_t D'W^{-1}DP_t. \tag{36}$$

The two sensors lead to time-dependent processors with readily identifiable peculiarities. The IMS produces a piecewise smooth estimate with isolated jumps. The resulting actuating signal [u_t in (29)] has this same character. For the NMS the actuating signal is continuous [see (35)], but locally volatile. This fundamental difference in structure has an anomalous effect on tracker performance.

Tracker performance. To contrast the performance properties of the two systems, the explicit expression for $\hat{J}_0$ must be deduced. This is again a routine calculation, but certain distinctive features warrant special attention.

IMS. It can be shown in a direct manner that

$$\hat{J}_0 = p_0 + \hat{x}'_0 \Pi_0 \hat{x}_0 \tag{37}$$

with Π_0 given in (30) and

$$p_t = \mathrm{Tr}\left(SP_T + \int_t^T QP_s\, ds \right) + \sum_{s \in [\tau, T] \cap V} \mathrm{Tr}(\Pi_s L_s). \tag{38}$$

The matrix $\{L_t\}$ is the quadratic variance of the $\{\hat{x}_t\}$ process

$$L_t = E\left\{ d\hat{x}_t\, d\hat{x}'_t \mid Z_{t-} \right\}$$

$$= \Theta_A(\tau) K_{n\Delta} \left(DP_{n\Delta}D' + U \right) K'_{n\Delta} \Theta'_A(\tau). \tag{39}$$

Since $\{\hat{x}_t\}$ is purely discontinuous, L_t is nonzero only on V.

In most cases of interest, the second term in (37) is bounded without regard to the terminal time T. This can be viewed as the "disturbance-free" cost of operation. The first term, however, tends to grow without bound as the time horizon increases. Since this term dominates performance over long time intervals, it is convenient to study its properties in some detail. Equation (38) has a natural decomposition:

$$p_t = p_{t1} + p_{t2} \tag{40}$$

with

$$p_{t1} = \mathrm{Tr}\left(SP_T + \int_t^T QP_s \, ds \right) \tag{41}$$

$$p_{t2} = \mathrm{Tr} \sum_{s \in [t,T] \cap V} \Pi_s L_s. \tag{42}$$

The "disturbance-dependent" cost, p_t, is the sum of two terms. The first, p_{t1}, is intimately associated with the accuracy of the output of the time-dependent processor. The second, p_{t2}, is more closely identified with the tracking algorithm. This partition is for evocative purposes only because it is certainly true that the system noise influences the evolution of both $\{P_t\}$ and $\{L_t\}$.

NMS. A performance decomposition like that presented above can be provided for the nonimage-based system. Indeed,

$$\hat{J}_0 = p_{01} + p_{02} + \hat{x}_0' \Pi_0 \hat{x}_0, \tag{43}$$

where

$$p_{t1} = \mathrm{Tr}\left(SP_T + \int_t^T QP_s \, ds \right) \tag{44}$$

$$p_{t2} = \mathrm{Tr} \int_t^T \Pi_s L_s \, ds \tag{45}$$

subject to

$$(d\hat{x}_t)(d\hat{x}_t') = L_t \, dt$$

$$= K_t W K_t' \, dt. \tag{46}$$

Equation (44) is identical to its IMS analog. The difference between (42) and (45) is more apparent than real. In both cases

$$P_{t2} = \mathrm{Tr} \int_t^T \Pi_s \, d\langle \hat{x}, \hat{x} \rangle_s, \tag{47}$$

where $\langle \hat{x}, \hat{x} \rangle_t$ is the quadratic variance of $\{\hat{x}_t\}$.

An encounter involving a tracker and a target will frequently last for many system time constants. In this event, a quasi-steady-state performance measure provides a straightforward indication of the relative merit of the sensor systems. Define

$$T^{-1} \lim \hat{J}_0 = H_I \text{ for the IMS system}$$

$$= H_N \text{ for the NMS system.} \tag{48}$$

With the indicated decomposition of costs as shown in (41) and (42) [or alternatively in (44) and (45)], and the subscript I (respectively, N) used to distinguish the IMS (respectively, the NMS)

$$H_I = H_{I1} + H_{I2} \tag{49}$$

with

$$H_{I1} = \mathrm{Tr} \, \Delta^{-1} \int_0^\Delta Q P_s \, ds \tag{50}$$

$$H_{I2} = \Delta^{-1} \, \mathrm{Tr} \, \Pi_\infty L_\infty \tag{51}$$

Respectively,

$$H_N = H_{N1} + H_{N2} \tag{52}$$

with

$$H_{N1} = \text{Tr } QP_\infty \tag{53}$$

$$H_{N2} = \text{Tr } \Pi_\infty P_\infty D'WDP_\infty \tag{54}$$

In (53) and (54), P_∞ and Π_∞ are the stationary, positive solutions to (36) and (30), respectively.[5] In (50), $\{P_t\}$ is the limiting periodic solution to (34).

As discussed earlier, H_{I1} and H_{N1} provide a measure of the performance of the sensor-signal-processor blocks of the tracker, i.e., the accuracy of the $x_t \rightarrow \hat{x}_t$ map. $H_{\cdot 1}$ is (weighted) time-average of the error variance. The IMS and the NMS will be said to be sensor equivalent (or H_1 equivalent) if $H_{N1} = H_{I1}$.

The ability of the tracking algorithm to effectively utilize the estimates of the encounter state developed by the signal processor is measured by $H_{\cdot 2}$. The two systems will be termed tracker equivalent (or H_2 equivalent) if $H_{N2} = H_{I2}$. Finally, the two systems are performance equivalent (or H equivalent) if $H_N = H_I$.

Under the dynamic hypotheses contained in the encounter model, the H. equivalences make it simple to compare sensor types. Indeed, the sensor-preprocessors need not be of different types to make the H.-based comparison. It would be noted that there are stronger equivalences [33], but this topic will not be pursued here.

C. AN EXAMPLE

To illustrate the preceding development, it is useful to consider a simple example in some detail. Suppose that the target moves in one dimension with equation of motion

$$d\theta_{T,i} = -a\theta_{T,t} \, dt + dn_{T,i}; \quad a > 0. \tag{55}$$

---

[5]The systems are assumed to satisfy the technical conditions that guarantee the existence and uniqueness of these matrices.

The target dynamics have a low pass character. The variance of the target motion depends upon a parameter, a, which is small in a sense made more precise later. For small a, the target has only a weak connection to the origin, and will tend to wander over long distances over time.

The tracker also operates in one dimension, and it is described by a first-order differential equation

$$d\theta_{R,t} = bu_t \, dt + dn_{R,t}. \tag{56}$$

The tracker has neutral open-loop stability and can be made as responsive as desired by choice of the tracking algorithm.

The two exogenous processes n_T and n_R are independent Brownian motions with intensities N_T and N_R, respectively. In most cases it will be true that

$$N_T \gg N_R;$$

i.e., the local volatility of the target motion is considerably greater than the local volatility of the tracker.

Equations (55) and (56) can be combined to form the encounter state

$$dx_t = (Fx_t + Gu_t) \, dt + dn_t, \tag{57}$$

where $x_t = (\theta_{T,t}, \theta_{R,t})'$ the matrices have their usual definitions.

There is a sensor on the tracking vehicle which provides a measurement of the status of the encounter. It will be supposed that, in each of the tracking systems, the sensor-preprocessor provides a measurement of the relative position of the tracker and the target; i.e.,

$$C = (1, -1). \tag{58}$$

Hence, depending on whether an imaging or a nonimaging sensor is used, the equation for the observation will be one of

$$y_{n\Delta+t_i} = \theta_{T,n\Delta} - \theta_{R,n\Delta} + w_{n\Delta} \tag{59}$$

$$dy_t = (\theta_{T,t} - \theta_{R,t}) \, dt + dw_t,$$

where the w's satisfy the usual assumptions.

The objective of the tracking system is to cause the tracker position to follow the target as closely as possible as measured by the performance index

$$\hat{J}_t = E\left\{\int_t^T\left[\left(\theta_{T,t} - \theta_{R,t}\right)^2 + ru_t^2\right] dt \mid O_t\right\}, \tag{60}$$

where r is a parameter used to shape the response characteristics of the tracking loop. Equation (60) can be written in the form of (26):

$$\hat{J}_t = E\left\{\int_t^T \left(x_t'Qx_t + ru_t^2\right) dt \mid O_t\right\} \tag{61}$$

with appropriate Q.

Although the analysis presented in the preceding sections considers a more general situation, it will be assumed here that the imager provides a perfect, albeit delayed, measurement of the target location;

$$U = 0. \tag{62}$$

In order that the imaging tracker be able to follow the target motion closely, it must be responsive to changes in target direction. For this reason, it is reasonable to assume that

$$a\Delta \ll 1. \tag{63}$$

To quantify the performance attainable with an imaging sensor, the covariance equation (34) must first be solved. For notational convenience, consider the steady-state solution with the sample time reinitialized to $t = 0$. Direct calculation yields

$$P_t = \begin{bmatrix} \sum\left(1 - 2a(\Delta + t)\right) + N_t(\Delta + t) & \cdots \\ \sum\left(1 - a(\Delta + t)\right) & \sum + N_R(\Delta + t) \end{bmatrix},$$

$$t \in [0, \tau_1]$$

$$= \begin{bmatrix} \sum (1 - 2at) + N_T t & \cdots \\ \sum (1 - at) & \sum + N_R t \end{bmatrix},$$

$$t \in [\tau_1, \Delta]$$

$$\Delta P_t = \Delta (N_T + N_R)^{-1} \begin{bmatrix} \left(N_T - a\sum \right)^2 & \cdots \\ -\left(a\sum + N_R \right)\left(N_T - a\sum \right) & \left(a\sum + N_R \right)^2 \end{bmatrix}, \tag{64}$$

where the conditional variance of x_0 is

$$\sum \begin{bmatrix} 1 & 1 \\ 1 & 1 \end{bmatrix} = \sum_0,$$

and

$$\sum = \frac{N_R}{a} \left(-1 + \sqrt{1 + N_T/N_R} \right).$$

Under the conditions given in (37), the equations for the H_i can be deduced simply. Direct calculation under the assumption the $N_T W^{-1} \gg a$ yields

$$H_1 = N_T \left(\tau + \frac{1}{2}\Delta \right); \text{ IMS}$$

$$= \sqrt{WN_T}; \text{ NMS.} \tag{65}$$

Under most conditions $\tau < \Delta$. Hence, as Δ approaches zero, the sensor cost of the imaging system approaches zero. This is not surprising since, in this event, there is neither delay nor noise in the sensor-preprocessor. Note, however, that this does not imply that $P_t \equiv 0$. In fact, $\lim_{\Delta \to 0} P_t = \Sigma_0$. Thus, while $P_t > 0$, its value is irrelevant to the tracking task; i.e., Tr $Q\Sigma_0 = 0$. For a given sample period, the sensor cost increases as a function of the noise intensities and the frame-dependent processing delay.

The nonimaging system has the behavior that would be expected. The system cost grows with the square root of the relevant noise intensities. Sensor equivalence can be expressed quite simply if the processor delay is a fixed fraction of the frame time

$$\tau = \zeta\Delta. \tag{66}$$

The two systems are estimation equivalent if

$$\Delta = \left(\zeta + \frac{1}{2}\right)^{-1} \left(WN_T^{-1}\right)^{1/2}. \tag{67}$$

Since $\zeta + \dfrac{1}{2} < \dfrac{3}{2}$, the IMS is H_1 superior to the NMS if

$$\Delta < \frac{3}{2}\left(WN_T^{-1}\right)^{1/2}. \tag{68}$$

Equation (68) displays a characteristic pattern in the comparison of the different sensor types. As the noise intensity in the nonimaging sensor increases, the performance of the NMS deteriorates. Similarly, as the frame time of the IMS decreases, performance is improved. What may be unforeseen is the dependence of the comparison on the volatility of the target. Not surprisingly, both systems have more difficulty following a more mobile target than they do a less mobile one. However, the rate at which performance deteriorates is not the same for the different sensors. The inherent sampling of the IMS produces a stronger dependence on the target volatility than exists in the NMS. Hence, as the target motion becomes less predictable, a continuous, albeit noisy, measurement of the scenario becomes more advantageous.

For the simple dynamic model selected for this example, the sensors are always tracker equivalent. The resulting performance comparison can be written

$$H = N_T\left(\tau + \frac{1}{2}\Delta + rb^{-1}\right); \quad NMS$$

$$= N_T\left(\sqrt{WN_T} + rb^{-1}\right); \quad NMS. \tag{69}$$

IV.   ORIENTATION INFORMATION
IN PREDICTION

A.   INTRODUCTION

Established techniques for the design of pointing-and-tracking systems are based upon the dynamic properties of a "point-mass" target. For example, a radar return signal locates the center of the reflecting area of a target. The target "position" is identified with this point.

If the target is a long distance away, there is little error involved in replacing a distributed quantity (the target location) with a single point. When the target is closer, and the sensor is more sophisticated, anomalous situations may arise. In the first section of this article a prototypical encounter was described. A TV sensor was used on board a self-directed missile. The sensor generated an image of the target. Even in the absence of target motion, the image would change in size as the range decreased.

In addition to scale changes, a variety of peculiar behaviors could be encountered as the missile approaches the target. For example, certain features of the target might be highlighted by the sun for a given approach angle of the missile, and at close ranges these features may be distinguishable at the sensor. If the target location logic is based upon an observed contrast with the background, the tracker might perceive these features to be more targetlike than the target itself. In this event the target would appear to be accelerating in the direction of the strongly sensed features. This putative acceleration could cause guidance errors to be introduced into the system. Such errors have a significant impact on performance because they are most pronounced during the terminal phase of the mission.

Although the TV sensor described above is an imaging sensor in a strict sense, it is a very primitive one. The output of the frame-dependent processor is a measurement of a "center-of-area" state of the target. None of the fine structure in the image of the target is used in the target location algorithm. In one sense, of course, this is an advantage. The tracker works equally well with any target. It is therefore not prone to target misclassification problems. Unfortunately, this insensitivity prevents the tracking system from using all of the information that is conveyed by the image.

Problems of the above type are accentuated in the design of predictors. It is obvious that the acceleration of the target has an important influence on the estimate of the future location of the target. A processor that is subject to phantom accelerations will, as a consequence, have poor prediction accuracy.

In an application involving prediction, the inherent capability of a truly image-based system manifests itself. In principle, such a system would contain a frame-dependent processor that utilizes knowledge of the fine structure of the target. If the target has a known shape, the tracker is not confused by a partial ob

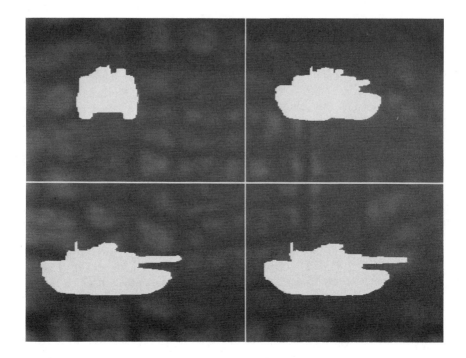

Fig. 2. A tank at several aspect angles.

scuring of the target. Indeed, the frame-dependent processor can infer the existence of structured clutter as well as estimate the encounter state.

To illustrate the potential superiority of an imaging system, consider how a measurement of target orientation can be used in predicting a future target position. Equation (2) gives the basic encounter model with a_T the evasive or BP acceleration. This acceleration is measured in an earth-fixed coordinate system, and is typically expressed in that way; i.e., the acceleration is expressed in terms of its tangential and radial components. Therefore, for example, a target under attack may turn alternately left and right. This would be described by a BP acceleration that switched back and forth between positive and negative values.

In the image plane of the tracker, the effect of this same sequence of accelerations will depend upon the orientation of the target with respect to the image plane. For example, if the target is moving at right angles to the line of sight, the initial effect of a radial acceleration is to slow the horizontal motion of the target vehicle in the image plane; i.e., a radial acceleration is perceived as a longitudinal acceleration.

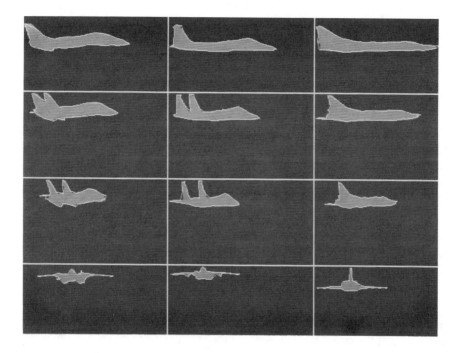

Fig. 3. Target images with edge detection.

To use the dynamic model of the encounter effectively in the prediction of the location of the target, there must be a mapping of the behavior of the earth-fixed model given in (2) into equivalent behavior in the image plane. To do this, a measurement of target orientation is quite valuable.

There currently exist imaging sensors which provide a highly detailed picture of the target.[6] Figure 2 displays an image of an M1 tank at different rotation angles with respect to the image plane. Figure 3 shows several different aircraft at different orientations with respect to the image plane. In this latter figure a frame-dependent processing algorithm has been used to determine the outline of the target image. This algorithm has been developed by the Hughes Aircraft Company as part of their work on the development of image-based tracking and targeting systems. Some of this work, including a more complete set of images, is presented in an unclassified report given as Ref. [34].

---

[6]The images shown in Figs. 2 and 3 are from a data base prepared by the Hughes Aircraft Company, Electro-Optical and Data Systems Group for the Center for Night Vision and Electro-Optics, Fort Belvoir, Virginia.

It is apparent from these figures that there is much more information contained in an image than is utilized by a center-of-area tracker. Figure 3 displays this clearly. The different aircraft have distinctly different silhouettes. Hence, the images could be used for automatic target recognition.

Additionally, the images provide orientation information. Careful analysis of the image of the tank in Fig. 2 makes it possible to estimate orientation directly from the image. Consequently, the frame-dependent processor can provide both the conventional measurement of target location, and also a (noisy) measurement of orientation as well.

The usefulness of such a measurement is explored in this section. It will be assumed that, at the current time, the image-based sensor-signal processor provides an estimate of the conventional target states (position, velocity, and acceleration) along with a correlated estimate of orientation. The algorithm for finding the best mean-square estimate of the target position T seconds in the future is then derived. For a simple target model the predictor is displayed explicitly.

B.   TARGET MODEL AND PREDICTION ALGORITHM

For this preliminary study it will be assumed that the target vehicle moves without damping on the horizontal axis. In contrast to the conventional methods of description, the vehicle will not be assumed to be a point mass, but rather it will be assumed to have the property of "orientation." For convenience it will be assumed that the target has, at any given time, one of J possible orientations. Let $\{\varphi_t\}$ be an indicator of orientation; i.e., φ_t is a J-dimensional unit vector with a one in the j-th position if the current target orientation is the j-th. All other elements of φ_t are zero.

The target vehicle accelerates in an earth-fixed coordinate system. For convenience it will be assumed that the acceleration is a scalar variable, although in truth both radial and tangential accelerations are possible. The state space of the evasive acceleration will be assumed to be finite, and let $\{\rho_t\}$ be a K-dimensional indicator of this acceleration.

The acceleration in the image plane depends upon both the orientation of the vehicle and the inertial acceleration. This can be described by saying that the BP acceleration in the image plane is given by

$$a_t = \varphi_t' A \rho_t, \tag{70}$$

where a_t is the BP acceleration and A is a J × K matrix of accelerations.

Suppose that the target moves with velocity $\{v_t\}$ along a horizontal line with dynamic equation

$$dv_t = a_t\, dt + \sigma\, dw_t, \tag{71}$$

where $\{w_t\}$ is an exogenous high-frequency residual. Equation (71) can be written in terms of the target position $\{y_t\}$ in the image plane as

$$dy_t = v_t\, dt \tag{72}$$

$$dv_t = \varphi'_t A\rho_t\, dt + \sigma\, dw_t.$$

Equation (72) is to be interpreted as a martingale differential equation.

To complete the development of the target model, the dynamics of $\{\varphi_t\}$ and $\{\rho_t\}$ must be specified. It will be assumed that $\{\rho_t\}$ is a Markov process with transition rate matrix Q^ρ

$$\Pr\left(\rho_{t+dt,j} = 1 \mid \rho_{t,i} = 1\right) = \begin{cases} 1 + q^\rho_{ii}\, dt + o(dt); & i = j \\ q^\rho_{ij}\, dt + o(dt); & i \neq j \end{cases} \tag{73}$$

This leads to a dynamic model of $\{\rho_t\}$ given by

$$d\rho_t = Q^{\rho'}\rho_{t^-}\, dt + dM^\rho_t, \tag{74}$$

where $\{M_t^\rho\}$ is a $\{\Xi_t^\rho\}$ martingale and $\{\Xi_t^\rho\}$ is the filtration generated by $\{\rho_t\}$.

The structure of the orientation process is more complex. Denote the filtration generated by $\{\varphi_t, \rho_t\}$ by $\{\Xi_t^{\rho,\varphi}\}$. It will be assumed that

$$\Pr\left(\varphi_{t+dt,j} = 1 \mid \varphi_{t,i} = 1, \rho_{t,k} = 1, \Xi_t^{\rho,\varphi}\right) = \begin{cases} 1 + q^k_{ii}\, dt + o(dt); & i = j \\ q^k_{ij}\, dt + o(dt); & i \neq j. \end{cases} \tag{75}$$

A few words of interpretation makes the behavioral character of the orientation process easier to understand. The evasive acceleration is assumed to be independent of the relationship of the target and the image plane. Such dependence as exists would more properly be in the category of "goal-oriented motion" anyway. Consequently, the BP model of acceleration is used *in toto*.

An acceleration produces a change in orientation in the image plane. The null acceleration produces change slowly, while a strong radial acceleration will produce orientation change more rapidly. Hence, the realized change in orientation is dependent on the sample function of acceleration. This effect is delineated by (75). This is a primitive description insofar as the dependence on the past of the acceleration process is neglected. Still it does give a preliminary indication of the dependence of image plane aspect on the target acceleration.

While not independent, the acceleration and orientation processes will be assumed to be orthogonal, i.e., they do not have simultaneous jumps:

$$E\left(d\rho_t (d\varphi_t)' \mid \Xi_t^{\rho,\varphi}\right) = 0. \tag{76}$$

The dynamic equation for orientation becomes the nonlinear differential equation

$$d\varphi_t = \sum_{k=1}^{J} Q^{k'} \varphi_t \rho_{t^-k} \, dt + dM_t^{\varphi}, \tag{77}$$

where $\{M_t^{\varphi}\}$ is a $\{\Xi_t^{\rho,\varphi}\}$ discontinuous martingale.

Define the target state by $x_t = (y_t, v_t)'$. Then the target dynamics can be written as

$$dx_t = Fx_t \, dt + G \, dw_t + \left(0, \varphi'_{t^-} A\rho_{t^-}\right)' dt, \tag{78}$$

where F and G have obvious definitions.

Let $\{Y_t\}$ be the observation-induced filtration. The prediction problem is that of finding the best Y_t measurable estimate of y_{T+t}. The notion of "best" in this context is controversial. Wolff points out in Ref. [10] that estimation of the current state of the target is a necessary part of a pointing-and-tracking system. This estimation is carried out in a closed-loop fashion, and modest model deficiencies are compensated for thereby. But prediction is intrinsically open loop, thus magnifying any deficiencies in the model.

Furthermore, since the criterion of choice for such a system is something akin to "probability of hit," the proper selection of the predicted position of the target is nearer the conditional mode than it is the conditional mean. It is further observed in Ref. [10] that the "Burke–Perkins model belongs to a class which produces distributions which are strikingly skew.... (Nevertheless it has been) shown that under very restrictive assumptions the degradation of the hitting probability resulting from aiming at the conditional mean instead of the optimal mode is small."

Since the time origin is arbitrary, the prediction problem can be phrased as finding $E\{y_t|Y_0\} = \hat{y}_{T,0}$. From (78) it follows immediately that

$$
d\hat{x}_{t,0} = F\hat{x}_{t,0} \; dt + \left(0, \; (\widehat{\varphi_t' A \rho_t})_0\right)' dt \tag{79}
$$

subject to appropriate initial conditions.

To solve this problem, $(\widehat{\rho_t \varphi_t})_0$ must first be determined. Since the time origin is fixed, the final subscript in the conditional expectation will be dropped. Define

$$
S_t = \rho_t \varphi_t'. \tag{80}
$$

Then direct calculation yields [35]

$$
dS_{ijt} = \left(\varphi_{t^-,j} \sum_l Q^{\rho}_{li} \rho_{t^-,l} + \rho_{t^-,i} \sum_l \sum_k Q^k_{lj} \varphi_{t^-,l} \rho_{t^-,k}\right) dt + dM_{ijt}, \tag{81}
$$

where $\{M_{ijt}\}$ is another $\{\Xi_t^{\rho,\varphi}\}$ martingale.

Equation (81) can be simplified by observing that

$$
\begin{aligned}
\rho_{t^-,i} \rho_{t^-,k} &= \rho_{t^-,i}, \quad \text{if } k = i \\
&= 0, \text{ otherwise.}
\end{aligned} \tag{82}
$$

Consequently,

$$
dS_{ijt} = \left(\sum_l Q^{\rho}_{li} S_{ljt^-} + \sum_l Q^l_{ij} S_{ilt^-}\right) dt + dM_{ijt}. \tag{83}
$$

Equation (83) is a linear stochastic differential equation. The solution to the prediction problem is immediate:

$$d\hat{S}_{ijt} = \left(\sum_l Q^{\rho}_{li} \hat{S}_{ljt} + \sum_l Q^l_{li} \hat{S}_{ilt} \right) dt. \tag{84}$$

Equation (84) is a linear, matrix, ordinary differential equation. Denote the solution by $\hat{S}(t; \hat{S}_0)$. From (79) then the predicted position of the target can be written as

$$\hat{y}_T = \hat{y}_0 + \hat{v}_0 T + \int_0^T (t - \tau) \, Tr\left[A\hat{S}(\tau, \hat{S}_0) \right] d\tau. \tag{85}$$

C.   AN EXAMPLE

To illustrate the results of this section, consider the simple situation in which $\{\varphi_t\}$ and $\{\rho_t\}$ are $\{\Xi_t^{\rho,\varphi}\}$ independent, and the wide-band disturbance is zero. To be specific, suppose further that both acceleration and orientation are symmetric two-state chains:

$$Q' = \frac{\lambda_i}{2} \begin{bmatrix} -1 & 1 \\ 1 & -1 \end{bmatrix}; \quad i = \rho, \, \varphi. \tag{86}$$

The equation for $\hat{S}_t$ is easily produced:

$$\hat{S}_t = e^{Q^{\rho'}} \Sigma_0 e^{Q^{\varphi}} + \hat{\rho}_{t,0} \hat{\varphi}'_{t,0}, \tag{87}$$

where

$$\Sigma_0 = E\left\{ S_0 \mid Y_0 \right\} - \hat{\rho}_{0,0} \hat{\varphi}'_{0,0}. \tag{88}$$

Equation (87) has an interesting interpretation. If orientation and acceleration were conditionally uncorrelated, then their predicted values would remain so over time. If an initial correlation exists, the effect of this correlation decreases exponentially fast in the predictor. The first term in (87) gives this decaying term explicitly.

To carry out a numerical example, suppose that the sensor and signal processor are so poor that the filtered estimates of both acceleration and orientation have a very low confidence rating. Indeed, assume that $\hat{\varphi}_{t,0} \equiv \hat{\rho}_{t,0} \equiv (0.5, 0.5)'$, the stationary distributions associated with (86). Suppose further that the estimates are correlated; $\Pr(\rho_0 = \varphi_0) = 0.8$.

Direct calculation yields

$$\hat{y}_{T,0} = y_0 + v_0 T + 0.25 \frac{T^2}{2} \sum_{i,j} A_{ij}$$

$$+ 0.15 Z(\varphi, \rho, T)(A_{11} - A_{22} - A_{12} - A_{21}),$$

where

$$Z(\varphi, \rho, t) = \frac{t}{\lambda} + \frac{1}{\lambda^2}\left(\varepsilon^{-\lambda t} - 1\right). \tag{89}$$

Equation (89) has an interesting interpretation. The first two terms in the equation for $\hat{y}_T$ are the usual constant velocity predictor ("ye olden standard"). The third term is a correction due to the estimate of acceleration. Since the sensor and signal processor are so deficient, the best estimate of acceleration, both now and in the future, is given by the average over all possible accelerations.

The fourth term in (89) quantifies the influence of the sensor assessed correlation between orientation and acceleration. It has a similar form to that derived by Wolff [10] in his study of predictions based upon the BP acceleration model. Specifically, the exponential decay to a certainty-equivalent estimate is also found in the referenced work.

If the prediction time is small, the final term in the predictor takes an even simpler form:

$$\hat{y}_{T,0} = y_0 + v_0 T + \frac{T^2}{2}\sum_{i,j}\frac{A_{ij}}{4} + 0.15T\left(\frac{A_{11} + A_{22}}{2} - \frac{A_{12} + A_{21}}{2}\right) \tag{90}$$

It is apparent that the correlation in the filtered estimate of the features of the encounter influences the prediction algorithm to the degree that the average diagonal element of A differs from the average off-diagonal element. Note that the diagonal elements of A are the most likely ones to be realized by the target vehicle.

V.   CONCLUSIONS

In this article, some of the salient features of an image-based pointing-and-tracking system have been discussed. An imaging sensor provides design flexibility that a conventional sensor cannot match. Still, the full utilization of the inherent capability of the image-specific aspects of the system remains to be done. Much has been accomplished in image interpretation, but the implications with respect to global system performance remain vague.

Two aspects of this problem were discussed in the preceding sections. To keep the presentation as simple as possible, the elementary models of both the target and the sensor platform were used. Many of the important issues were not introduced: e.g., automatic target recognition. Nevertheless, it is evident that proper system design requires analytical models that differ from those used in conventional design practice if the peculiarities of an imager are to be exploited. Specifically, the notation of "feature" behavior assumes significance.

The performance indices developed here are simple to compute, and have a natural meaning in the context of the encounters examined. Confirmation of the performance attributes in a realistic situation is required to substantiate the validity of the analytical procedures. This is a task of current effort.

REFERENCES

1.   H. G. GWINNER, "The Maneuvering Target," AMSAA TR 268(AD B045229L). 1979.
2.   R. A. SCHEDER, "Adaptive Estimation," AMSAA TR 166(AD B016228L). 1976.
3.   E. WONG and B. HAJEK, "Stochastic Processes in Engineering Systems." Springer Verlag, Berlin and New York, 1985.
4.   H. H. BURKE, T. R. PERKINS, and J. F. LEATHRUM, "State Estimation of Maneuvering Targets via Kalman Filtering," AMSAA TR 186(AD B016206L). 1976.
5.   J. F. LEATHRUM, "A Design Methodology for Estimators and Predictors in Fire Control Systems," AMSAA TR 315(AD B054331). 1980.
6.   T. R. PERKINS, H. H. BURKE, and J. F. LEATHRUM, "Maneuvering Vehicle Path Simulator," AMSAA TR 331. 1982.
7.   H. H. BURKE, "A Discussion About Fire Control System Configurations," AMSAA IN C-82. 1979.
8.   H. H. BURKE, Concepts for improved gun fire control systems. *Proc. 19th Annu. Allerton Conf. Commun., Control, Comput., 1981.*
9.   H. H. BURKE, Fire control system performance degradation when a tank engages a maneuvering threat. *Proc. 17th Annu. Army Oper. Res. Symp., 1978.*

10. S. S. WOLFF, "Lead Prediction for a Class of Maneuvering Targets," Ballist. Missile Lab. Int. Rep. No. 648. 1979.
11. H. H. BURKE, A Circular arc aimed munition (CAAM). Private communication.
12. N. R. SANDELL, Jr., *et al.*, "Research of Fire Control Concepts for Maneuvering Targets; Phase I and Phase II," TARADCOM TR 12511. 1980 and 1982.
13. J. KORN and L. BEEAN, "Application of Multiple Model Adaptive Estimation Algorithms to Maneuver Detection and Estimation," Alphatech TR 152 (AD B075921). 1983.
14. P. S. MAYBECK, "Stochastic Models, Estimation and Control," Vol. 1. Academic Press, New York, 1979.
15. P. S. MAYBECK, "Stochastic Models, Estimation and Control," Vol. 2. Academic Press, New York, 1982.
16. P. S. MAYBECK, "Stochastic Models, Estimation and Control, Vol. 3. Academic Press, New York, 1982.
17. B. BHANU, Automatic target recognition: State-of-the-art survey. *IEEE Trans. Aerosp. Electron. Syst.* **AES-22**, 364–379 (1986).
18. R. M. MERSEREAU and D. E. DUDGEON, Two-dimensional digital filtering. *Proc. IEEE* **63**, 610–623 (1975).
19. A. K. JAIN, Advances in mathematical models for image processing. *Proc. IEEE* **69**, 502–528 (1981).
20. T. C. MINTER, Jr., A discriminant procedure for target recognition in imagery data. *Proc. IEEE NAECON*, pp. 822–828 (1980).
21. J. E. McWILLIAMS and M. D. SRINATH, Performance analysis of a target detection system using infrared imagery. *IEEE Trans. Aerosp. Electron. Syst.* **AES-20**, 38–48 (1984).
22. J. K. AGGARWAL, L. S. DAVIS, and W. N. MARTIN, Correspondence processes in dynamic scene analysis. *Proc. IEEE* **69**, 562–572 (1981).
23. R. D. HOLBEN, An MTI (moving target identification) algorithm for passive sensors. *Proc. IEEE NAECON*, pp. 114–121 (1980).
24. G. R. LEGTERS, Jr. and T. Y. YOUNG, A mathematical model for computer image tracking. *IEEE Trans. Pattern Analy. Mach. Intell.* **PAMI-4**, 583–594 (1982).
25. R. J. SCHALKOFF and E. S. McVEY, A model and tracking algorithm for a class of video targets. *IEEE Trans. Pattern Anal. Mach. Intell.* **PAMI-4**, 2–10 (1982).
26. P. S. MAYBECK and D. E. MERCIER, A target tracker using spatially distributed infrared measurements. *IEEE Trans. Autom. Control* **AC-25**, 222–225 (1980).
27. P. S. MAYBECK, D. A. HARNLY, and R. L. JENSEN, Robustness of a new infrared target tracker. *Proc. Nat. Aerosp. Electron. Conf., 1980.*
28. P. S. MAYBECK, R. L. JENSEN, and D. A. HARNLY, An adaptive extended Kalman filter for target image tracking. *IEEE Trans. Aerosp. Electron. Syst.* **AES-17**, 173–180 (1981).
29. P. S. MAYBECK and S. K. ROGERS, Adaptive tracking of multiple hot-spot target IR images. *IEEE Trans. Autom. Control* **AC-28**, 937–943 (1983).
30. P. S. MAYBECK and R. I. SUIZU, Adaptive tracker field-of-view variation via multiple model filtering. *IEEE Trans. Aerosp. Electron. Syst.* **AES-21**, 529–539 (1985).
31. J. D. KENDRICK, P. S. MAYBECK, and J. G. REID, Estimation of aircraft target motion using orientation measurements. *IEEE Trans. Aerosp. Electron. Syst.* **AES-17**, 254–260 (1981).
32. E. TSE, On the optimal control of stochastic systems. *IEEE Trans. Autom. Control* **AC-16**, 776–785 (1971).
33. D. D. SWORDER, On the relative advantage of image vs. continuous trackers. *Proc. Asilomar Conf. Circuits, Syst. Comput., 20th*, 585–589, 1986.

34.   W. G. HANLEY and M. A. LEPLEY, "Performance Modeling of Autonomous Electro-Optical Sensors," Semi-Annu. Rep., Contract No. DAAB10-86-0534. Hughes Aircraft Company, 1986.
35.   D. D. SWORDER, Improved target prediction using an IR imager. *Proc. SPIE Infrared Sys. and Compon.* **750**, 105–108, 1987.

MODELING AND SIMPLIFICATION OF LINEAR AND NONLINEAR SYSTEMS

ALAN A. DESROCHERS

Electrical, Computer, and Systems Engineering Department
Rensselaer Polytechnic Institute
School of Engineering
Troy, New York 12180

I.   INTRODUCTION

To utilize modern control theory, it is necessary to construct difference equations that model the input–output relationship of the system. For a linear plant, such identification techniques are fairly well developed. The purpose of this article is to present methods for obtaining the structure of a nonlinear plant. Model simplification techniques occur as a byproduct of these methods.

Even if we restrict our attention to the approximation of a polynomial, difficulty arises rapidly as the number of terms gets large. To find an accurate approximant that uses only a few terms, it is necessary to design and test all possible approximants to find the optimal one. The requirement of using only a few terms is important in order to determine the underlying structural characteristics of the plant. Similar reasoning applies to the modeling of nonlinear dynamic systems where we are forced to an exhaustive, somewhat trial-and-error approach to obtain, say, a good least-squares error fit of a simple model.

One method of circumventing this problem is the group method of data handling (GMDH) [1]. GMDH uses polynomial models and the perceptron concept as a basis for its structure. A large amount of clever heuristic reasoning is used, and so a theoretical justification of its performance has not been possible. The success of the method can only be judged from its applications.

Basically, GMDH is a multilayer decision scheme for fitting a function with a polynomial. Each layer of GMDH consists of a bank of quadratic polynomial functions with inputs from the previous layer having been passed through a selection layer. Although this is a suboptimal scheme, GMDH has experienced a lot of success.

In this work, a layered approach is also taken. We start with some simple projection methods and then proceed to derive an algorithm for selecting the optimal combination of terms from a larger set of basis functions. Nonlinear dynamic systems are also treated.

In Section II we discuss the problem to be solved. It is formulated for the polynomial case, which is also shown to cover linear and nonlinear dynamic systems. In Section III projection methods are introduced as a first approach to the modeling problem. These algorithms are also applied to the reduced-order modeling problem for linear systems. Next, Section IV presents an optimal modeling algorithm that is based on the projection methods of Section III. These techniques are then extended to nonlinear dynamic systems in Sections V and VI. The latter section deviates from the projection-method approach and presents a new approach for modeling nonlinear dynamic systems from input–output data. Several examples are presented throughout the article, many of which are based on actual system data.

II. PROBLEM STATEMENT

System modeling first involves the choice of a set of basis functions. In the case of GMDH, polynomials are used. Such polynomials find their way into models for process control problems, socioeconomic problems, and as decision surfaces in a pattern-recognition device. In most cases, the order and structure of the polynomial are poorly known. Typically, inputs (features) are selected and a Kolmogorov–Gabor-type polynomial is chosen to model the unknown system (decision surface). This quickly leads to a complicated identification problem. For example, with four inputs X_1, X_2, X_3, and X_4 the complete fourth-order polynomial, including terms of all powers and covariations of arguments, has 70 terms. To determine the coefficients by solving normal equations would require the inversion of 70×70 matrices and the use of input or training sequences having no fewer than 70 distinct data points. Furthermore, to build a model that reveals the input–output structure of the system, all one-term models, two-term models, three-term models, etc., should really be designed and tested. This is clearly an enormous computational problem, but it is, in fact, the basic problem being considered here.

Specifically, the problem is concerned with nonlinear systems that can be modeled by

$$z(i) = b^T Y\big(u(i)\big), \quad i = 1, 2, \ldots, \tag{1}$$

where $z(i)$ is the scalar output at the i-th instant of time, b is an $m \times 1$ vector of constant coefficients, $u(i)$ is a vector input of dimension r in the Euclidean r-dimensional space E^r, and $Y(u(i))$ is an $m \times 1$ vector of nonlinear continuous functions $\varphi_k(u(i))$, $k = 1, 2, \ldots, m$, which are linearly independent and differentiable.

Let E^m be the Euclidean m-dimensional space spanned by the elements of G, where

$$G = \left\{ \varphi_k\big(u(i)\big); \; u(i) \in E^r; \; k = 1, 2, ..., m \right\}. \tag{2}$$

The problem is to find a subset of G called G_n, in an n-dimensional space E^n, $n < m$, whose elements approximate z(i) in the sense of least-squared error. Define

$$G_n = \left\{ \varphi_{pj}\big(u(i)\big); \; j = 1, 2, ..., n \right\}, \tag{3}$$

where $1 \leq p1, p2, ..., pn \leq m$ are n distinct integer subscripts used to indicate which of the subsets of G results in the optimal n-term model in E^n. Then the model being sought is

$$z_n(i) = a^T Y_n\big(u(i)\big), \; i = 1, 2, ..., \tag{4}$$

where a is an $n \times 1$ vector of constant coefficients and $Y_n(u(i))$ is an $n \times 1$ vector containing the elements of G_n.

The basic idea is to build a model by selecting terms from the set G. This set could be a standard set of basis functions and/or it might include functions which are suspected *a priori* to be candidate terms for the model; e.g., for a robot manipulator we expect to see trigonometric functions of the joint angles.

Equation (1) covers a wide range of systems. Consider the following non-linear dynamic system

$$z(i + 1) = A\Phi\big(z(i), u(i)\big), \tag{5}$$

where z(i) is the $p \times 1$ state vector, Φ is an $m \times 1$ vector of nonlinear functions of the state and control, and A is the $p \times m$ matrix of constant coefficients. This can be put into the form of (1) by rewriting it as:

$$z(i + 1) = \sum_{k=1}^{m} A_k \varphi_k\big(z(i), u(i)\big), \tag{6}$$

where A_k denotes the columns of A and $\varphi_k(z(i), u(i))$ are the elements of $\Phi(z(i), u(i))$. Systems that can be modeled in this manner will be considered in Section V.

Equation (1) can also be used to represent a linear system. Consider a stable transfer function H(s)

$$H(s) = \frac{a_0 + a_1 s + ... + a_{n-1} s^{n-1}}{b_0 + b_1 s + ... + b_n s^n}, \tag{7}$$

where s represents the complex frequency, $s = \sigma + jw$.

The transfer function H(s) can be expanded as a sum of partial fractions

$$H(s) = \sum_{k=1}^{n'} \frac{b_k}{s + a_k} + \sum_{k=1}^{n''} \frac{d_k(s + e_k)}{s^2 + 2r_k s + (r_k^2 + v_k^2)}, \tag{8}$$

where $n = n' + 2n''$ and the first sum represents the real eigenvalues and the second represents the complex conjugate poles of the form $r_k \pm jv_k$.

H(s) is now in the form of a linear combination of nonlinear functions in the complex frequency s, or

$$H\big(s(i)\big) = \sum_{k=1}^{n'+n''} c_k \varphi_k\big(s(i)\big), \tag{9}$$

which is in the form suitable for the algorithm. In this formulation, s(i) is a sequence of frequencies that serves as the "input" to the modeling algorithm. The user selects this frequency range of interest based on the intended use of the model. Also, the $\varphi_k(\bullet)$'s become the elements of the basis set G. Note that this has taken the dynamic problem and converted it into a static optimization problem with respect to s. Furthermore, we shall see that the c_k's do not have to be calculated, which avoids the large amount of work associated with partial fraction expansions. Problems of this type are discussed in Sections III and IV.

A.   MODELING AND MODEL REDUCTION

The problem formulation also resembles a model reduction problem. If we already have a complex model, each term can be put into G, and a simpler n-term model can be obtained. This is true for both the linear (9) and the nonlinear case, (1) and (6). On the other hand, in the modeling problem our initial set G repre-

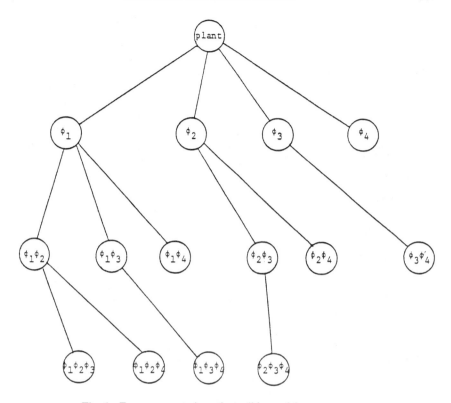

Fig. 1. Tree representation of possible model structures.

sents terms that are candidates for possible inclusion in the model we are building. Thus, both problems require efficient algorithms for obtaining the subset G_n.

B. TREES IN THE MODELING PROBLEM

The idea is to retain n terms without significantly sacrificing accuracy in the ability to approximate $z(i)$ after projecting E^m onto E^n. This projection involves the consideration of many models. In fact, there are $m!/[n!(m-n)!]$ models with n terms. One approach is to design and test all possible models using, say, a least-squares approach. This exhaustive approach is not very practical.

With the aim of avoiding this brute-force method, we propose [2, 3] to represent the modeling problem as a tree structured problem, where each node in the tree represents a possible model structure.

The basic idea is to let the admissible set of models be those which are formed from linear combinations of any and all of the elements in G. Furthermore, let each model structure be represented as a node in a tree, as shown in Fig.

1, for the case m = 4. To avoid designing and testing all possible models, a scalar cost is assigned, based on a least-squared error criterion, as a measure of the reduction in error that results when a term is added to a particular model. Basically, this assigns a weight to the relative importance of each component of the model. These costs appear on the branches of the tree.

In Section IV we will show that these costs can be derived such that the optimal n-term model is the maximum cost path from the root to a node at depth n. In addition, the sum of the costs from the root to any node can be shown to be related to the squared error for that model so that the algorithm stops when some acceptable modeling error is achieved. This avoids an arbitrary choice of n and also avoids generating costs for all possible model structures. Thus, in practice, the tree is not really expanded to include a node for every possible structure. If it must be completely expanded, then no simple model exists for the system at hand.

For a tree with the above properties, the maximum cost path search (which corresponds to minimum squared error) becomes a dynamic programming problem. Again, if a simple model of the system exists, then $n \ll m$ and the search is quite simple. Details of the cost-assignment algorithm will be presented in the next section.

The purpose of this discussion has been to show that the proposed algorithm retains the layered or the treelike structure similar to GMDH, but it results in the optimal n term structure.

To summarize, there are at least three reasons why the treelike structure of these algorithms is superior to single-layered structures like least squares, which try to determine all of the parameters for the full m-term model:

1) The complete polynomial model is rarely needed to accurately model the system. This is true in the dynamic counterpart also.

2) The coefficient matrix of the equations for a complete polynomial is nearly always ill-conditioned. It is much easier to find well-conditioned matrices of systems of low dimension.

3) Short input–output sequences are available more often than lengthy ones. Only sequences of length n are needed here as opposed to length m.

In addition, there are at least three reasons why these algorithms are superior to brute-force approaches like designing and testing all possible models with least squares:

1) Selection of the optimal model in E^n is done by comparing structural properties of the models, which eliminates the need to explicitly find the parameters for every possible model.

2) The error of the approximant can be calculated at each level of the tree, which removes the arbitrary choice of n. Calculating this error does not require any parameter identification.

3) The tree-structure approach requires one matrix inversion to identify the n parameters of the final optimal n-term model, while least squares would require $m!/[n!(m-n)!]$ matrix inversions to identify $m!/[(n-1)(m-n)!]$ parameters.

The next three sections will develop and apply these tree-structured algorithms for modeling and model-reduction problems.

III.   PROJECTION METHODS

The basic ideas for all of the modeling methods are presented in this section. We use these basics to develop an algorithm which finds a suboptimal subset of G. Our experience with the method indicates that the algorithm is easy to program, is computationally efficient, and generally succeeds in finding the optimal subset, G_n. A simple modification is made in Section IV, which is shown to always yield the optimal model.

Here we summarize the essential features of the technique. Proofs and details of mathematical manipulations can be found in Ref. [3].

Definitions. Let $\{u(i)\}$ be an input sequence of length L. Then each element of G will provide a vector function $\Phi_k(u(i))$, k = 1, 2, ..., m, of dimension L × 1. Similarly, let $Z(u(i))$ represent the L × 1 vector of outputs.

For the sake of clarity, Φ_k will be used instead of $\Phi_k(u(i))$ and $Z(i)$ will denote $Z(u(i))$. Next, we define

$$P_k = \frac{\Phi_k \Phi_k^T}{\Phi_k^T \Phi_k}, \quad k = 1, 2, ..., m. \tag{10}$$

Note that P_k is a projection matrix since $P_k^T = P_k$ and $P_k^2 = P_k$. Also define

$$M^{(j)} = I - \sum_{s=1}^{j} P_s = M^{(j-1)} - P_j. \tag{11}$$

The properties of these matrices will now be investigated before incorporating them into the proposed algorithm.

Theorem 1. If

$$P_k P_h = D_{kh} P_k, \tag{12}$$

where the Dirac delta matrix $D_{kh} = I$ if k = h and 0 if k ≠ h, then the matrix $M^{(j)}$ is a projection matrix.

Lemma. The projection matrices $M^{(j)}$, j = 1, 2, ..., m, have the following property:

$$M^{(j)}M^{(j-1)} = M^{(j-1)}M^{(j)}$$

$$= M^{(j)}; \ j = 1, 2, \ldots, m. \tag{13}$$

A.   PROPOSED MODELING ALGORITHM

To select the nonlinearities for the n-term model, the following method can be used:

Algorithm 1.

Step 1. Set $j = 1$, and the integer subscripts $p_e = 0$ for $e = 1, 2, \ldots, m$. Assume an input sequence $\{u(i)\}$ of length L. Let $\Phi_k^{(1)} = \Phi_k$ for $k = 1, 2, \ldots, m$. Set $z_r^{(0)} = Z(i)$, $\varepsilon^{(0)} = Z(i)^T Z(i)$, and $M^{(0)} = I$.

Step 2. For $k = 1, 2, \ldots, m$, $k \neq p_e$, $e = 1, 2, \ldots, j$, compute

$$P_k^{(j)} = \frac{\Phi_k^{(j)}\Phi_k^{(j)T}}{\Phi_k^{(j)T}\Phi_k^{(j)}} \tag{14}$$

$$z_k^{(j)} = P_k^{(j)}z_r^{(j-1)} \tag{15}$$

$$R_k^{(j)} = z_k^{(j)T}z_k^{(j)}$$

$$= z_r^{(j-1)}P_k^{(j)}z_r^{(j-1)}. \tag{16}$$

Now determine $\max_k\{R_k^{(j)}\}$ and call it $R_{pj}^{(j)}$ so that $\varphi_{pj}^{(j)}(u(i))$ and $P_{pj}^{(j)}$ are the function and the projection matrix associated with the maximum, respectively.

Step 3. Compute

$$M^{(j)} = M^{(j-1)} - P_{pj}^{(j)} \tag{17}$$

If the elements of G are mutually orthogonal, set

$$\Phi_k^{(j+1)} = \Phi_k^{(j)}; \ k = 1, 2, \ldots, m,$$

$$k \neq p_e, e = 1, 2, ..., j$$

and go to Step 5; otherwise proceed.
Step 4. Set

$$\Phi_k^{(j+1)} = M^{(j)} \Phi_k^{(j)} \tag{18}$$

for $k = 1, 2, ..., m, k \neq p_e, e = 1, 2, ..., j$.
Step 5. Compute the squared error of the model:

$$z_T^{(j)} = M^{(j)} Z(i) \tag{19}$$

$$\varepsilon^{(j)} = z_T^{(j)T} z_T^{(j)}$$

$$= Z(i)^T M^{(j)} Z(i)$$

$$= Z(i)^T Z(i) - R_{p1}^{(1)} - R_{p2}^{(2)} - ... - R_{pj}^{(j)}$$

$$\varepsilon^{(j)} = \varepsilon^{(j-1)} - R_{pj}^{(j)}. \tag{20}$$

If

$$|\varepsilon^{(j)} - \varepsilon^{(j-1)}| = |R_{pj}^{(j)}| \leq \delta, \tag{21}$$

then the model contains the terms

$$\left\{ \varphi_{p1}(u(i)), \varphi_{p2}(u(i)), ..., \varphi_{pj}(u(i)) \right\}. \tag{22}$$

Otherwise, set $j = j + 1$ and go to Step 2.

Remark. In (21), δ is a preselected small positive number to stop the algorithm when some acceptable error of the approximant has been achieved. The algorithm could just as easily be stopped when j reaches n, the number of desired terms in the model. Also, note that Steps 3 and 4 ensure that (12) holds. Further, by utilizing the projection matrix $M^{(j)}$ in (19), it becomes clear that the error calculation requires no parameter identification.

A Geometric Interpretation of the Algorithm. We now provide some insight into what is actually taking place at each step of this least-squares projection algorithm [4].

In Step 1, the algorithm is at the root of the model tree shown earlier in Fig. 1. At this point there is no model and the squared error of approximation is equal to the squared magnitude of the output vector, i.e., $\varepsilon^{(0)}$.

The main purpose of Step 2 is to calculate R_k for each of the functions not already included in the model, which in this first pass is all of them. R_k represents the reduction in squared error that would occur if the k-th term were added to the current model. These are the costs that appear along the branches of the tree. The function which maximizes this reduction is then included in the model. Effectively, this maximum R_k has just chosen a path to one of the nodes at the first level of the tree.

Before returning to Step 1 to determine which of the remaining functions should be added next, it is first necessary to modify the output vector and the function vectors. This is the purpose of Steps 3 and 4. First, the projection matrix, P_{pj}, corresponding to the function just included in the model, is used to determine the matrix $M^{(j)}$.

In Step 4, each of the function vectors not already included in the model is now multiplied by $M^{(j)}$, which has the effect of removing the projection of each of these vectors in the direction of all the function vectors included in the current j-term model. This leaves a new set of function vectors that are orthogonal to each of the functions currently in the model. There are two important reasons for this step. The first is to satisfy (12). The second reason will be seen later, when it will be shown that this process leads to a simple method for determining the coefficients in the final selected model.

Finally, in Step 5, the original output vector is multiplied by $M^{(j)}$. This has the effect of removing the projection of the output vector in the direction of each term currently included in the model. Thus, the residual error vector represents the unmodeled portion of the system; i.e., it is orthogonal to the error vector corresponding to the model selected so far.

Therefore, the role of R_k is to select the term that causes the maximum reduction in this residual error as seen from (20). The orthogonalization and selection procedure is repeated and the algorithm continues to move down the tree structure until a satisfactory approximant is found.

In summary, the algorithm is basically a repeated Gram–Schmidt orthogonalization procedure where the role of R_k is analogous to column pivoting.

Determining the Model Coefficients. Once a model structure has been determined, the vector a^T in (4) must be determined. A simple addition to the projection algorithm of the previous section will now be presented for calculating the coefficients of the final n-term model. It will be seen that identifying these n coefficients can be reduced to the trivial problem of finding the vector **a** that satisfies a triangular set of algebraic equations.

Let

$$\left\{ \Phi_{pj}, j = 1, 2, ..., n \right\}$$

be the set of original function vectors which correspond to the functions that were selected at each stage of the projection algorithm. Let $M^{(j)}, j = 0, 1, ..., n - 1$ be the resulting sequence of projection matrices generated by the algorithm. Then for any choice of integers i and k from 1 to n, if $i > k$,

$$\Phi_{pi}^T M^{(i-1)} \Phi_{pk} = 0. \tag{23}$$

This property may be proved by induction [3] and is essential for arriving at the final method for identifying the model parameters. The parameters that minimize the squared error of approximation may be found by solving the system of linear equations

$$Z(i) = \sum_{j=1}^n a_j \Phi_{pj}. \tag{24}$$

Premultiplying both sides of (24) by the matrices $M^{(j)}, j = 0, 1, ..., n - 1$, the system of equations becomes

$$M^{(0)} Z(i) = a_1 M^{(0)} \Phi_{p1} + a_2 M^{(0)} \Phi_{p2} + ... + a_n M^{(0)} \Phi_{pn}$$

$$M^{(1)} Z(i) = a_1 M^{(1)} \Phi_{p1} + a_2 M^{(1)} \Phi_{p2} + ... + a_n M^{(1)} \Phi_{pn}$$

$$\vdots$$

$$M^{(n-1)} Z(i) = a_1 M^{(n-1)} \Phi_{p1} + a_2 M^{(n-1)} \Phi_{p2} + ... + a_n M^{(n-1)} \Phi_{pn}. \tag{25}$$

Premultiplying the i-th equation by Φ_{pi}^T, $i = 1, 2, ..., n$, respectively, the system is reduced to a set of n linear equations. Using the property in (23), the following triangularized set of equations results:

$$\Phi_{p1}^{T} M^{(0)} Z(i) = a_1 \Phi_{p1}^{T} M^{(0)} \Phi_{p1} + \ldots + a_n \Phi_{p1}^{T} M^{(0)} \Phi_{pn}$$

$$\Phi_{p2}^{T} M^{(1)} Z(i) = 0 + \ldots + a_n \Phi_{p2}^{T} M^{(1)} \Phi_{pn}$$

$$\vdots$$

$$\Phi_{pn}^{T} M^{(n-1)} Z(i) = 0 + 0 + \ldots + a_n \Phi_{pn}^{T} M^{(n-1)} \Phi_{pn}. \tag{26}$$

The scalars on the left side of (26) may be easily computed during the execution of the algorithm and stored as entries in a column vector $\mathbf{y}$, while the scalar factors after the model parameters on the right-hand side of (26) may be similarly computed and stored in an upper triangular matrix T. Identifying the parameter vector $\mathbf{a}$ thus reduces to the trivial problem of solving the triangular system of equations $\mathbf{y} = T\mathbf{a}$.

B.   APPLICATION TO PROCESS MODELING

The projection algorithm has been applied to building a model which will predict roll forces in a hot steel rolling mill [5, 6]. Specifically, a model is needed which will predict the individual stand forces required to achieve a certain exit gauge of the steel strip before the strip enters the hot mill finishing stands. Results have been obtained from two sets of actual rolling mill data [5, 6].

The modeling of rolling processes usually involves assuming a structure for the model and then identifying the coefficients via regression analysis. However, the choice of a model structure here is a difficult one because the process does not lend itself to accurate physical modeling. Instead, models are often developed by empirical methods [7, 8].

The mathematical structures of the models obtained from physical modeling are as diverse as the assumptions used to derive them. For example, some models are derived assuming that the steel rolls with slipping; others assume sticking. Some assume that the steel strip is infinitely wide, while others derive their models assuming finite width. This results in a catalog [9] or library of possible models, depending upon which assumptions are valid for a particular rolling mill. In Ref. [5], we compiled a library of possible models and let each model be an element of the set G in (2). Eight model candidates comprised the elements of G.

The projection algorithm was used to find the subset G_n that produced an accurate approximation to the roll force data. Initially, n was unknown, but soon it became evident that only a few elements of G were needed for the model. Table I shows the two-term models that were selected by the algorithm. These are compared with the full eight-term models obtained by the traditional method of least squares. In Table I, the average percent difference refers to

TABLE I. Modeling Results for Roll Force Prediction

Finishing stand	Average difference (%)	
	Two-term models	Eight-term models
1	4.7	5.6
2	3.6	4.2
3	7.7	8.1
4	8.3	6.0
5	9.7	11.4
6	8.1	8.6

$$\frac{1}{N} \sum_{i=1}^{N} \frac{|F_a(i) - F_m(i)|}{F_a(i)} (100\%) \tag{27}$$

where $F_a(i)$ is the actual measured force; $F_m(i)$, the predicted model force; and N, the number of steel runs.

If one examines the model parameters for the eight-term models [5], it is clear that there is no way of telling which terms are significant. On the other hand, the sequential selection procedure of the projection algorithm sorts these terms automatically because of the orthogonalization process that is built into the method.

The two-term models selected by the algorithm appear to be more effective than the full eight-term models in their ability to model the system. The effectiveness of the eight-term models has probably been eroded by the matrix inversion operations used to find the eight coefficients. Rolling mills tend to be operated under similar conditions, which makes the coefficient matrix of the equations ill-conditioned.

Polynomial models were also used on another set of data [6]. This time the set G contained 35 terms, corresponding to all covariations of a third-order polynomial model with four inputs. Again the algorithm selected simple two- and three-term models that were effective predictors of roll force.

C.   A PROJECTION METHOD FOR REDUCED-ORDER MODELING OF LINEAR SYSTEMS

We now return to the problem originally described by (7)–(9). This is the model reduction problem where now the set G consists of all linear combinations of the partial fractions of the original transfer function. Each subset of G represents a model structure. Then each structure is represented as a node in the tree of Fig. 1, where nodes at depth n are reserved for n-th-order models and then first-order terms are selected to generate the (n + 1)-th nodes, and so forth.

The "input" for this problem is a sequence of frequencies s(i). This sequence is selected by the user and should be chosen so that it sweeps across those frequencies at which it is most important (or desired) for the reduced-order model (ROM) to approximate the original system. The tree-structured approach has several advantages. It gives a measure of how well a ROM approximates the original transfer function without requiring that the entire model be solved for and tested. The sequential nature of the tree-structured approach also eliminates the need to arbitrarily choose the order of the ROM being computed, since n-th-order ROMs are generated from (n − 1)-th-order ROMs until an acceptable modeling error is achieved. Only a few stages of the algorithm should be necessary; if not, then reduced-order modeling has little to offer to the transfer function at hand.

Essential Features of the Algorithm. The reduction algorithm attempts to choose a ROM from a set of admissible models of the form

$$H(s) = \sum_{j=1}^{n} a_j \varphi_{pj}(s), \tag{28}$$

where $\varphi_{pj}(s)$ are elements of a subset of the partial fractions of the original transfer function as described in (7)–(9). As before, these functions will be selected to minimize the sum of the squared error between the original transfer function and the ROM over a selected set of frequencies. This effectively measures the similarity of the Bode plots of the two transfer functions.

The key to the algorithm is the derivation of the factor R_k which determines what φ_k is added to the model. Let the selected frequencies of interest be represented as

$$\left\{ s = jw_i; \quad i = 1, 2, \ldots, L \right\}. \tag{29}$$

Also, for the original H(s) and for each mode function $\varphi_k(s)$, we define a set of column vectors

$$\mathbf{h} = \left[H(jw_1), H(jw_2), \ldots, H(jw_L) \right]^T$$

$$\Phi_k = \left[\varphi_k(jw_1), \varphi_k(jw_2), \ldots, \varphi_k(jw_L) \right]^T,$$

$$k = 1, 2, \ldots, m. \tag{30}$$

With these definitions we can define a squared error for an n-th-order ROM as

$$\varepsilon = \left[h - \sum_{j=1}^{n} a_j \Phi_{pj} \right]^T \left[h - \sum_{j=1}^{n} a_j \Phi_{pj} \right]^*$$

$$= h_r^{(n)T} h_r^{(n)*} , \tag{31}$$

where * denotes the complex conjugate. Now the next φ_k which is added to the model should cause a maximum (over all k) reduction in this error. This term should be selected [4] by maximizing the new selection factor:

$$R_k = \frac{\left(\left[h_r^{(n)} \right]^T \left[\Phi_k^* \right] + \left[\Phi_k \right]^T \left[h_r^{(n)*} \right] \right)^2}{4 [\Phi_k]^T [\Phi_k^*]} . \tag{32}$$

Before presenting the final projection algorithm, we define a new set of column vectors as

$$H = \begin{bmatrix} h \\ h^* \end{bmatrix}; \quad \Phi_k = \begin{bmatrix} \Phi_k \\ \Phi_k^* \end{bmatrix}; \quad H_r^{(n)} = \begin{bmatrix} h_r^{(n)} \\ h_r^{(n)*} \end{bmatrix}$$

for k = 1, 2, ..., m. $\tag{33}$

This makes it possible to rewrite R_k as

$$R_k = \frac{\left(\left[H_r^{(n)} \right]^T \left[\Phi_k^* \right] \right)^2}{2 [\Phi_k]^T [\Phi_k^*]} .$$

Finally, we define our new projection matrix to be

$$P_k = \frac{[\Phi_k][\Phi_k^*]^T}{[\Phi_k]^T [\Phi_k^*]} .$$

TABLE II. Method of Determining the Mode Functions of a System from the System's Poles

Type of pole	Mode function
Distinct real pole at s = p	$\varphi(s) = \dfrac{1}{s-p}$
Real pole of order r at s = p	$\varphi_i(s) = \left(\dfrac{1}{s-p}\right)^i, \quad i = 1, \ldots, r$
Distinct complex poles at s = p and s = p*	$\varphi_1(s) = \dfrac{s}{s^2 - (p + p^*)s + pp^*}$
	$\varphi_2(s) = \dfrac{1}{s^2 + (p + p^*)s + pp^*}$
Complex poles of order r at s = p and s = p*	$\varphi_{ij}(s) = \dfrac{s^j}{\left[s^2 - (p + p^*)s + pp^*\right]^i}, \quad \begin{array}{l} i = 1, \ldots, r. \\ j = 0, \ldots, i \end{array}$

Additional details and derivatives can be found in Ref. [4].

   The Projection Algorithm for Reduced-Order Modeling. The first thing that must be done is to classify the forms of the partial fractions that are present in the original transfer function according to the categories listed in Table II. Note that the coefficients of the partial fractions are never calculated. The algorithm then proceeds as follows:

   Algorithm II.

   Step 1. Set j = 1 and $p_e = 0$, e = 1, 2, ..., m. From (33) define **H** and set $\Phi_k^{(1)} = \Phi_k$. Let $H_r^{(0)} = \mathbf{H}$, $M^{(0)} = \mathbf{I}$. Calculate $\varepsilon^{(0)} = \tfrac{1}{2}\mathbf{H}^T\mathbf{H}^*$.

   Step 2. For k = 1, 2, ..., m, k ≠ p_e, e = 1, 2, ..., j, find

$$R_k^{(j)} = \frac{\left([H_r^{(j-1)}]^T[\Phi_k^{(j)*}]\right)^2}{[\Phi_k^{(j)}]^T[\Phi_k^{(j)*}]}. \tag{34}$$

Set $R_{pj} = \max_k\{R_k^{(j)}\}$, letting p_j take the value of the index k at which the maximum value of R_k was found.

   Step 3. Calculate the modeling error

$$\varepsilon^{(j)} = \varepsilon^{(j-1)} - \frac{1}{2} R_{pj}. \tag{35}$$

If $\varepsilon^{(j)}$ is less than the maximum desired squared error of approximation, or if $j = m$, go to Step 7; otherwise proceed.

Step 4. Compute

$$P_{pj}^{(j)} = \frac{[\Phi_{pj}^{(j)}][\Phi_{pj}^{(j)*}]^T}{[\Phi_{pj}^{(j)}]^T [\Phi_{pj}^{(j)*}]} \tag{36}$$

$$M^{(j)} = M^{(j-1)} - P_{pj}^{(j)}. \tag{37}$$

Step 5. For $k = 1, 2, \ldots, m$, $k \neq p_e$, $e = 1, 2, \ldots, j$, set

$$\Phi_k^{(j+1)} = M^{(j)} \Phi_k^{(j)}. \tag{38}$$

Step 6. Compute

$$H_r^{(j)} = M^{(j)} H, \tag{39}$$

then set $j = j + 1$ and go back to Step 2.

Step 7. Stop. The j-th-order model contains the set of functions

$$\left\{ \varphi_{pi}(s); \ i = 1, 2, \ldots, j \right\} \tag{40}$$

with the squared error of approximation given by (35).

After the algorithm selects the partial fractions to retain for the ROM, the coefficients of these terms must be calculated. This is done using (26), where $Z(i)$ is replaced by H.

Examples and Comparisons. Consider the system

$$H(s) = \frac{13.5s^8 + 655.5s^7 + 12174s^6 + 116341s^5 + 632440.5s^4}{s^9 + 51s^8 + 1086s^7 + 12726s^6 + 90489s^5 + 404019s^4}$$

$$\frac{+ 1989651s^3 + 3447600s^2 + 2805840s + 604800}{+ 1127384s^3 + 1881444s^2 + 1684080s + 604800}, \qquad (41)$$

which has poles at s = –1, –2, –3, –4, –5, –6, –7, –8, and –15. Comparisons will be made with the ROMs obtained by the following methods:

	ROM denoted by
Dominant pole [10]	$H_D(s)$
Continued fraction [11]	$H_C(s)$
Time moment fitting [12]	$H_S(s)$
Dominant pole time moment fitting [13]	$H_S(s)*$
Routh approximation [14]	$H_{HF}(s)$
Schwarz approximation [15]	$H_{LD}(s)$
Frequency response approximation [16]	$H_H(s)$
Dynamic programming approach [2]	$H_{DA}(s)$

The mode functions were determined by using Table II, and a set of 75 frequencies distributed nonuniformly over the interval w = 0 to 100 rad/sec was chosen. From the frequency response of (41), it is seen that there is a peak in the magnitude of the response over the range w = 0.1 to 10 rad/sec. Thus, 36 of the 75 frequencies were chosen in this range, at intervals of 0.05 rad/sec from w = 0.1 to 1 rad/sec and of 0.5 rad/sec between w = 1.5 and 10 rad/sec. In an attempt to also achieve good steady-state performance, 21 frequencies were chosen uniformly spaced from w = 0 to 0.1 rad/sec, while to ensure acceptable high-frequency approximation, the remaining 18 frequencies were selected uniformly distributed between w = 15 and 100 rad/sec. The mode functions and system transfer functions were then sampled at these frequencies.

The reduced-order models are listed in Table III. Based upon the values of the squared error measure, it is possible to obtain a very good approximation to the original ninth-order system using only a third-order model. This choice is further justified by looking at the Bode plots of the first three models produced by the least-squares projection algorithm in Figs. 2 and 3.

One problem in comparing reduced-order modeling methods is that authors are tempted to choose examples which favor their method. With that in mind, the proposed algorithm was compared to the example from the paper in which that particular method was originally presented. These results [17] demonstrate that the projection approach is a strong competitor. Table IV summarizes the results.

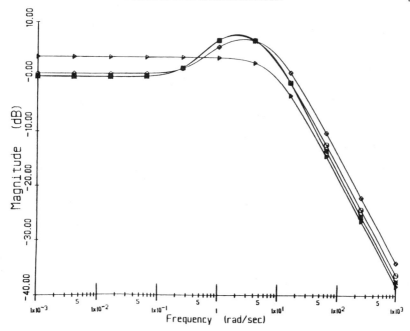

Fig. 2. Frequency response of original ninth-order system and first three reduced models: magnitude. (*), Original; (Δ), $H_1(s)$; ($\Diamond$), $H_2(s)$; and (o), $H_3(s)$.

The projection algorithm and the Routh method use a multistage approach in computing a ROM. Successively higher-order models are generated at each stage using the calculations from the model of the previous stage. In addition, each of these methods has some measure of how well a ROM will approximate the original system without fully computing or testing the model. The least-squares projection algorithm uses the sum of the squared error of approximation over a discrete set of frequencies, while the Routh approximation method uses the model's impulse energy. In contrast, when using the other methods it is necessary to fully compute, test, and recompute a sequence of models of different orders in order to find a satisfactory ROM, while for these two methods it is necessary only to proceed stage by stage until the associated measure reaches some desired value.

IV. AN OPTIMAL MODELING ALGORITHM

The previous algorithms may not always select the optimal subset G_n. This can be seen by studying (20). Clearly the goal is to minimize the error represented by (20). At present, this optimization is attempted one stage at a time through the selection of $R_{p1}^{(1)}$, $R_{p2}^{(2)}$, ... Since the sum of the $R_{pi}^{(i)}$ contributes

TABLE III. Reduced Models Calculated for the Ninth-Order System

Stage	Function added	Model	Squared error	Computer time (min)	Impulse energy[a]
1	$\dfrac{1}{s+8}$	$H_1(s) = \dfrac{12.22}{s+8}$	26.5027	1.32	3.0550
2	$\dfrac{1}{s+1}$	$H_2(s) = \dfrac{19.99s+8.61}{s^2+9s+8}$	3.8448	2.47	4.7660
3	$\dfrac{1}{s+4}$	$H_3(s) = \dfrac{15.53s^2+101.70s+32.38}{s^3+13s^2+44s+32}$	0.0932	3.47	4.3435
4	$\dfrac{1}{s+15}$	$H_4(s) = \dfrac{14.38s^3+338.40s^2+1543.72s+486.75}{s^4+28s^3+239s^2+692s+480}$	0.0621	4.37	4.3120
5	$\dfrac{1}{s+2}$	$H_5(s) = \dfrac{13.42s^4+373.80s^3+2161.65s^2+3641.26s+960.93}{s^5+30s^4+259s^3+1170s^2+1864s+960}$	0.00016	5.08	4.2789

6	$\dfrac{1}{s+3}$	$H_6(s) = \dfrac{13.47s^5 + 413.48s^4 + 3286.88s^3 + 10113.33s^2 + 11891.26s + 2880.22}{s^6 + 33s^5 + 385s^4 + 2055s^3 + 5374s^2 + 6552s + 2880}$	0.000017	5.75	4.2785
7	$\dfrac{1}{s+7}$	$H_7(s) = \dfrac{13.48s^6 + 507.89s^5 + 6183.01s^4 + 33129.29s^3 + 82710.83s^2 + 86149.41s + 20175.32}{s^7 + 40s^6 + 616s^5 + 4750s^4 + 19759s^3 + 44170s^2 + 48744s + 20160}$	0.000017	6.38	4.2796
8	$\dfrac{1}{s+6}$ 4.2788	$H_8(s) = \dfrac{13.48s^7 + 588.49s^6 + 9229.79s^5 + 70206.48s^4 + 281456.4s^3 + 582248.6s^2 + 536930.1s + 120960.7}{s^8 + 46s^7 + 856s^6 + 8446s^5 + 48259s^4 + 162724s^3 + 313764s^2 + 312624s + 120960}$	0.0	6.82	4.2788

[a]Original system impulse energy = 4.2785.

323

TABLE IV. Comparison with Examples of Other Authors

Ref. example	System H(s)	Impulse energy of H(s)	Original method/projection algorithm		
			Reduced-order model	Squared error	Impulse energy
Davison, 1966	$\dfrac{s^3 + 7s^2 + 24s + 24}{s^4 + 10s^3 + 35s^2 + 50s + 24}$	0.6655	$H_D(s) = \dfrac{0.8055s + 1.4166}{s^2 + 3s + 2}$	1.7507	0.5248
			$H_L(s) = \dfrac{0.7447s + 2.0052}{s^2 + 3s + 2}$	0.0188	0.6538
Chen and Shieh, 1968	$\dfrac{s^2 + 15s + 50}{s^4 + 5s^3 + 33s^2 + 79s + 50}$	0.6718	$H_C(s) = \dfrac{0.035s + 3.73}{s^2 + 4.811s + 3.73}$	0.1592	0.6227
			$H_L(s) = \dfrac{0.9664\, s^2 + 1.286\, s + 23.5228}{s^3 + 3s^2 + 27.01s + 25.01}$	0.2294	0.6531
Shamash, 1974	$-^a$	0.4451	$H_S(s) = \quad -^b$	0.0696	0.3795
			$H_L(s) = \dfrac{0.1452s^2 - 1.1052s + 10.5068}{s^3 + 21s^2 + 120s + 100}$	0.0613	0.0702
Shamash, 1975	Same as Davison, 1966	0.6655	$H_S(s) = \dfrac{0.834s + 2}{s^2 + 3s + 2}$	0.0461	0.6703
			$H_L(s) = \dfrac{0.7447s + 2.0052}{s^2 + 3s + 2}$	0.0188	0.6538

Reference	Reduced model			
Hutton and Friedland, 1975	$\dfrac{12s^3 + 528s^2 + 1440s + 4320}{2s^4 + 36s^3 + 204s^2 + 360s + 240}$	11.1770		
	$H_{HF}(s) = \dfrac{24s + 72}{3s^2 + 6s + 4}$		17.232	11.1355
	$H_L(s) = \dfrac{33.793}{s^2 + 2.394s + 1.913}$		100.489	11.1659
Lucas and Davidson, 1983	$-^c$	6.5614		
	$H_{LD}(s) = \dfrac{12.48s + 38.71}{s^2 + 5.14s + 6.52}$		4.8031	6.1243
	$H_L(s) = \dfrac{14.158s + 55.184}{s^2 + 6.55s + 8.4}$		0.0031	6.5556
Hsia	Same as Davison, 1966	0.6655		
	$H_H(s) = \dfrac{0.2917s + 1}{0.399s^2 + 1.375s + 1}$		0.0290	0.6642
	$H_L(s) = \dfrac{0.7447s + 2.0052}{s^2 + 3s + 2}$		0.0188	0.6538
Desroches and Al - Jaar, 1985	$\dfrac{4s^3 + 30s^2 + 70s + 50}{s^4 + 10s^3 + 35s^2 + 50s + 24}$	1.9046		
	$H_{DA} = \dfrac{3.9785s + 6.2865}{s^2 + 4s + 3}$		0.0032	1.9040

(continued)

TABLE IV. (*continued*)

Ref. example	System H(s)	Impulse energy of H(s)	Original method/projection algorithm		
			Reduced-order model	Squared error	Impulse energy
			$H_L(s) = \dfrac{3.5742s + 4.0210}{s^2 + 3s + 2}$	0.1823	1.8645

a
$$\frac{s^5 + 1014s^4 + 1469s^3 + 6914s^2 + 140100s + 100000}{s^6 + 222s^5 + 14541s^4 + 248420s^3 + 1454100s^2 + 2220000s + 1000000}.$$

b
$$\frac{5.3673s^2 + 15.28212s + 19.68001}{s^3 + 103.12032s^2 + 314.0005s + 196.8001}.$$

c
$$\frac{14.7s^3 + 1363.38s^2 + 28566.8s + 92024.7}{s^4 + 97s^3 + 2268s^2 + 11680s + 14000}$$

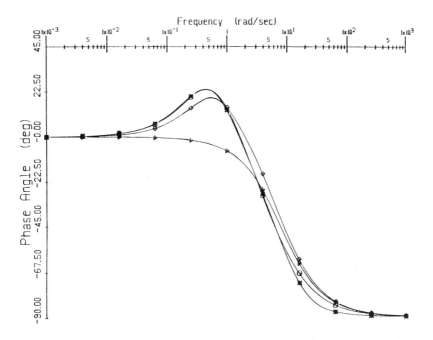

Fig. 3. Frequency response of original ninth-order system and first three reduced models: phase angle. Legend as for Fig. 2.

to the error, we wish to maximize this sum. Now, the value of $R_{p2}^{(2)}$ depends on the function that was chosen by $R_{p1}^{(1)}$. Their sum is not necessarily maximized by first maximizing $R_{p1}^{(1)}$ and then finding the function with maximum $R_k^{(2)}$ *given* that p1 was chosen. That is

$$\max_{p1}\left\{R_{p1}^{(1)}\right\} + \max_{p2}\left\{R_{p2}^{(2)}\right\}\bigg|_{p1} \neq \text{(necessarily)}$$

$$\max_{p1,p2}\left\{R_{p1}^{(1)} + R_{p2}^{(2)}\right\}.$$

This combinatorial problem has a dynamic programming solution [2, 18]. The $R_k^{(j)}$ are viewed as costs in a dynamic programming problem. These costs must be assigned along every branch of the tree in Fig. 1. Then the optimal n-term model corresponds to the maximum cost path from the root to the nodes at depth n. This maximizes the sum of the $R_{pi}^{(i)}$ which in turn minimizes the error in (20).

The optimal modeling algorithm consists of repeated applications of the previous algorithms until all nodes have a cost assigned to all of their branches.

AN OPTIMAL METHOD FOR
LINEAR SYSTEM REDUCTION

Utilizing the dynamic programming approach, an algorithm has been developed for linear system model reduction [2]. It is basically the method of Section III with the simple addition that R_k is computed for all branches of the tree and the optimal model is found using dynamic programming. An example of the method was already included as the last entry in Table IV.

Additional examples and comparisons with other methods have also been done [2]. Again, the impulse energy of the models obtained from this method are high and very close to that of the original system.

From a programming point of view, the dynamic programming requirement for optimality introduces some overhead. Our experience with these algorithms leads us to conclude that the one-stage-at-a-time approach of algorithms I and II provides models which are nearly indistinguishable from the optimal ones. However, this tradeoff must be made with full consideration for the intended use of the model.

V.   MODELING OF NONLINEAR SYSTEMS
FROM STATE INFORMATION

We now turn our attention to nonlinear dynamical systems. First we address the problem of reducing the complexity and/or dimensionality of the system. Then we show how the same approach can be used to obtain the nonlinear model for a robot manipulator. In both cases, we require state information and retain the basic projection approach.

The key ingredient in these projection algorithms is the factor R_k which must be derived for each new class of problems. First, consider the nonlinear dynamic system represented by (5) and (6). The goal is to develop a projection-type algorithm which retains the n most dominant nonlinearities in (6). If no $\varphi_k(z(i), u(i))$ is a function of more than one state, then eliminating certain $\varphi_k(z(i), u(i))$ will eliminate certain states, and a model reduction will occur. Otherwise, eliminating terms in (6) will lead to a model simplification.

For example, the dynamics of an aircraft can be sufficiently modeled using three states only (angle of attack, angular displacement, and velocity). However, the states are a linear combination of many linear and nonlinear terms. Here model reduction is not possible since three states is the minimum number required for a meaningful description of the system. Yet, model simplification is possible and will be illustrated later with an example.

To derive the criterion necessary to select the optimal model, let the original system be approximated by one function, say $\varphi_k(i)$. Then define the equation error as

$$e(i + 1) = z(i + 1) - A_k' \varphi_k(i), \tag{42}$$

where A_k does not necessarily equal A_k', and define

$$\varepsilon_k = \min_{A_k'} \sum_{i=1}^{L} e^T(i + 1)e(i + 1). \tag{43}$$

For ease of presentation, let $n = 2$ and $A_k' = [a_{1k}', a_{2k}']^T$ and summations are understood to be from 1 to L. Then (43) becomes

$$\varepsilon_k = \min_{A_k'} \sum \left\{ \left[z_1(i + 1) - a_{1k}' \varphi_k(i) \right]^2 \right.$$

$$\left. + \left[z_2(i + 1) - a_{2k}' \varphi_k(i) \right]^2 \right\} \tag{44}$$

with $k = 1, 2, \ldots, m$.

We now take the following steps: differentiate (44) with respect to a_{1k}' and a_{2k}', set these derivatives equal to zero, and then solve for a_{1k}' and a_{2k}'. Next, substitute these back into (43). This will represent the error when the original system is approximated by one function $\varphi_k(i)$ and we denote it by ε_k. For a different function, say $\varphi_j(i)$, we will have an error ε_j. If we assume that the k-th function represents the optimal one-term model (*), then it is required that

$$\varepsilon^* = \varepsilon_k < \varepsilon_j. \tag{45}$$

Manipulating the equations for the errors in (45) yields

$$\frac{\left(\langle z_1(i + 1), \varphi_k(i) \rangle \right)^2 + \left(\langle z_2(i + 1), \varphi_k(i) \rangle \right)^2}{\langle \varphi_k(i), \varphi_k(i) \rangle} >$$

$$\frac{\left(\langle z_1(i+1), \varphi_j(i)\rangle\right)^2 + \left(\langle z_2(i+1), \varphi_j(i)\rangle\right)^2}{\langle \varphi_j(i), \varphi_j(i)\rangle},$$

where

$$\langle \varphi_a(i), \varphi_b(i)\rangle = \sum_{i=1}^{L} \varphi_a(i)\varphi_b(i).$$

Equation (46) provides a criterion for selecting the optimal one-term model. Define R_k as

$$R_k = \sum_{s=1}^{2} \frac{\left[\langle z_s(i+1), \varphi_k(i)\rangle\right]^2}{\langle \varphi_k(i), \varphi_k(i)\rangle},$$

$$k = 1, 2, ..., m. \tag{47}$$

Then the optimal one-term model is the one that yields the maximum value of R_k. Also, the modeling error will be

$$\varepsilon_k = \sum_{s=1}^{2} \langle z_s(i+1), z_s(i+1)\rangle - R_k. \tag{48}$$

As for the selection of the second function in the optimal two-term model, the orthogonalization process must be used to take into account the choice of $\varphi_k(i)$. Therefore, the remaining functions are orthogonalized with respect to $\varphi_k(i)$ and will be denoted by $\varphi_j^{(2)}(i)$, $j = 1, 2, ..., m$; $j \neq k$. Then the second term is selected according to

$$R_j^{(2)} = \max\left\{\sum_{s=1}^{2} \frac{\left[\langle z_s(i+1), \varphi_j^{(2)}(i)\rangle\right]^2}{\langle \varphi_j^{(2)}(i), \varphi_j^{(2)}(i)\rangle}\right\}, \tag{49}$$

for $j = 1, 2, ..., m$; $j \neq k$.

Similarly, the error at this stage is

$$\varepsilon_{kj} = \sum_{s=1}^{2} \langle z_s(i + 1), z_s(i + 1) \rangle - R_k^{(1)} - R_j^{(2)}$$

$$= \varepsilon_k - R_j^{(2)}. \tag{50}$$

These results can be used to modify Algorithm I in order to handle nonlinear dynamic systems.

Algorithm III. Algorithm I is used with the following modifications.

Step 1. Rewrite the system in the form of (6).

Step 2. Solve the difference equations to establish the vector

$$Z_s = \begin{bmatrix} z_s(1) \\ z_s(2) \\ \vdots \\ z_s(L + 1) \end{bmatrix}$$

and the function vectors $\Phi_k(z(i), u(i))$ abbreviated as Φ_k, $k = 1, 2, \ldots, m$.

Step 3. Define $z_{rs}^{(0)} = Z_s$, $s = 1, 2, \ldots, p$. In Algorithm I, replace (15) and (16) with

$$z_{ks}^{(j)} = P_k^{(j)} z_{rs}^{(j-1)}, \qquad s = 1, 2, \ldots, p$$

and

$$R_k^{(j)} = \sum_{s=1}^{p} \left[z_{ks}^{(j)} \right]^T \left[z_{ks}^{(j)} \right]$$

$$= \sum_{s=1}^{p} \left[z_{rs}^{(j-1)} \right]^T P_k^{(j)} z_{rs}^{(j-1)}.$$

Step 4. Replace (19) and (20) with

$$z_{rs}^{(j)} = M^{(j)} Z_s, \quad s = 1, 2, \ldots, p$$

and

$$\varepsilon^{(j)} = \sum_{s=1}^{p} \left[Z_{rs}^{(j)} \right]^T \left[Z_{rs}^{(j)} \right]$$

$$= \sum_{s=1}^{p} Z_s^T M^{(j)} Z_s$$

$$= \sum_{s=1}^{p} Z_s^T Z_s - R_{p1}^{(1)} - R_{p2}^{(2)} - \ldots - R_{pj}^{(j)}$$

$$= \varepsilon^{(j-1)} - R_{pj}^{(j)}.$$

An alternate version of this method can be found in Ref. [2].

A.   APPLICATION TO FLIGHT CONTROL
      SYSTEM DESIGN

Consider the state equations describing the dynamics of an F-8 aircraft [19]. The nonlinear equations of motion in the form of (6) are

$$
\begin{bmatrix} \dot{x}_1 \\ \dot{x}_2 \\ \dot{x}_3 \end{bmatrix} = \begin{bmatrix} -0.877 \\ 0 \\ -4.208 \end{bmatrix} x_1 + \begin{bmatrix} 1 \\ 1 \\ -0.396 \end{bmatrix} x_3 + \begin{bmatrix} -0.215 \\ 0 \\ -20.967 \end{bmatrix} u
$$

$$
+ \begin{bmatrix} -0.088 \\ 0 \\ 0 \end{bmatrix} x_1 x_3 + \begin{bmatrix} 0.47 \\ 0 \\ -0.47 \end{bmatrix} x_1^2
$$

$$
+ \begin{bmatrix} -0.019 \\ 0 \\ 0 \end{bmatrix} x_2^2 + \begin{bmatrix} -1.0 \\ 0 \\ 0 \end{bmatrix} x_1^2 x_3
$$

$$+ \begin{bmatrix} 3.846 \\ 0 \\ -3.564 \end{bmatrix} x_1^3 + \begin{bmatrix} 0.280 \\ 0 \\ 6.265 \end{bmatrix} ux_1^2$$

$$+ \begin{bmatrix} 0.47 \\ 0 \\ 46.0 \end{bmatrix} u^2 x_1 + \begin{bmatrix} 0.63 \\ 0 \\ 61.40 \end{bmatrix} u^3,$$

where x_1 is the angle of attack in radians, x_2 is the pitch angle, x_3 is the pitch rate, and u is the control.

Algorithm III, in conjunction with the dynamic programming approach, was used to generate the optimal n-term models. Table V gives a summary of all the simplified models and their corresponding squared error. These results justify neglecting the nonlinear terms in u, which was done by previous researchers [22]. The results also reveal that the most dominant nonlinearity is the x_1^3 term; therefore, the optimal four-term model was chosen and later used [20] to design a linear controller for the original full-term model whose performance was indistinguishable from the second- and third-order controllers of Garrard and Jordan [19]. Note that it is the simplification algorithm which makes this all possible and readily apparent.

Simulation was done on an IBM 370 system. Execution time for searching through all 2046 possible model structures was 20 sec. This includes the identification of the parameters for the optimal four-term model, which is given by

$$\dot{X} = \begin{bmatrix} -0.891 & 0 & 0.954 \\ 0 & 0 & 1.0 \\ -4.230 & 0 & -0.400 \end{bmatrix} X$$

$$+ \begin{bmatrix} -0.424 \\ 0 \\ -20.895 \end{bmatrix} u + \begin{bmatrix} 5.550 \\ 0 \\ -4.552 \end{bmatrix} x_1^3.$$

TABLE V. Model Simplification Results for the F-8 Aircraft Fighter

Term model	Model basis	Squared error[a]	Ratio of reduction error
i			$(i - 1)/i$
3	(x_1, x_2, u)	5.01	–
4	(x_1, x_3, u, x_1^3)	$1.14{\times}10^{-1}$	44
5	$(x_1, x_3, u, x_1^2 x_3, x_1^3)$	$4.76{\times}10^{-2}$	2
6	$(x_1, x_3, u, x_1^3, ux_1^2, u^2 x_1)$	$1.16{\times}10^{-2}$	4
7	$(x_1, x_3, u, x_1^2, x_1^3, ux_1^2, u^2 x_1)$	$4.44{\times}10^{-3}$	3
8	$(x_1, x_3, u, x_1^2, x_1^2 x_3, x_1^3, ux_1^2, u^2 x_1)$	$8.82{\times}10^{-4}$	5
9	$(x_1, x_3, u, x_1^2, x_1^2 x_3, x_1^3, ux_1^2, u^2 x_1, u^3)$	$1.51{\times}10^{-5}$	58
10	$(x_1, x_2, u, x_1 x_3, x_1^2, x_1^2 x_3, x_1^3, ux_1^2, u^2 x_1, u^3)$	$2.74{\times}10^{-6}$	6

[a]Error accumulated from input–output data points.

Algorithm III without dynamic programming was also used on this same problem [3]. Model terms were selected stage by stage, as done earlier. The same four-term model would have been selected with this method. From experience, it appears that the issue of optimality is overstated.

The major purpose of this example is to illustrate that such a simplification (and subsequent controller design) would not be possible without a projection-type algorithm. The brute-force approach of designing and testing all possible models is prohibitive. In fact, it was found that the computer time required to generate all of Table V was about the same as generating the eleven one-term models by ordinary least squares. This is a distinct advantage, which opens up the possibility of reducing and simplifying complicated nonlinear systems. This also applies to the modeling problem as illustrated in the next section.

B.   MODELING OF ROBOTIC MANIPULATORS

The equations of motion for a robotic manipulator are a very lengthy and complicated set of nonlinear, highly coupled differential equations. For an n-joint manipulator the number of acceleration terms is of the order of n^3 [21]. The num-

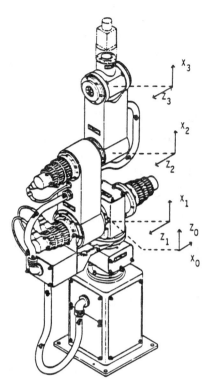

Fig. 4. The GCA robot.

ber of terms due to the centrifugal and Coriolis forces are on the order of n^4. For a new manipulator, these equations of motion are quite tedious to derive, and model parameters must be computed from mass and motor data, which are often unreliable. We would like to be able to identify the mathematical structure of the model as well as the model parameters.

This modeling problem is ideally suited for Algorithm III because we have joint angle position and velocity (the states) information available, and from Lagrangian dynamics we know that the set G will consist of trigonometric functions of these states. Thus, we can create a general library of robot model terms and apply the projection algorithm to a new robot, like the one shown in Fig. 4.

The general form of the manipulator equations for an n-degree-of-freedom manipulator [21] is

$$T(t) = H(q(t))\ddot{q}(t) + C(q(t), \dot{q}(t))\dot{q}(t) + G(q(t)), \tag{51}$$

where T(t) is the n × 1 input torque vector, q(t) is an n × 1 joint angle vector, H(q(t)) is n × n and represents the inertia loading of the manipulator, C(•, •) is the n × n matrix of Coriolis and centrifugal force loading terms, and G(q(t)) is the n × 1 gravity loading vector. Equation (51) describes the effects of numerous dynamic terms that tend to be highly interactive and highly nonlinear. It also indicates that a robot manipulator can be represented by a linear combination of nonlinear functions representing inertia, Coriolis, centrifugal, and gravity terms. We shall illustrate this, along with our basic approach to the modeling problem, for a two-degree-of-freedom manipulator operating in a horizontal workspace. The model for this arm is

$$T_2 = h_{22}\ddot{\varphi}_2(t) + h_{23}\ddot{\varphi}_3(t) + 2C_{223}\dot{\varphi}_2(t)\dot{\varphi}_3(t) + C_{233}\dot{\varphi}_3^2(t) \tag{52}$$

$$T_3 = h_{23}\ddot{\varphi}_2(t) + h_{33}\ddot{\varphi}_3(t) + C_{322}\dot{\varphi}_2^2(t), \tag{53}$$

where the notation for joints 2 and 3 is used for consistency with the 3-degree-of-freedom robots, and

$$h_{22} = \text{joint 2 inertia} = 6.821 + 1.500 \cos\varphi_3(t) \tag{54a}$$

$$h_{23} = \text{joints 2 and 3 inertial coupling} = 1.156 + 1.500 \cos \varphi_3(t) \tag{54b}$$

$$h_{33} = \text{joint 3 inertia} = 2.156 \tag{54c}$$

$$C_{223} = \text{Coriolis force at joint 2 produced by joint 3} = -1.500 \sin \varphi_3(t) \tag{54d}$$

$$C_{233} = \text{centrifugal force at joint 2 produced from joint 3} = -1.500 \sin \varphi_3(t) \tag{54e}$$

$$C_{322} = -C_{223}. \tag{54f}$$

Equations (52)–(54) show that the torques in (51) can be written as a linear combination of a set of nonlinear basis terms given by

$$B = \left\{ \ddot{\varphi}_2(t), \ddot{\varphi}_3(t), \cos[\varphi_3(t)]\ddot{\varphi}_2(t), \right.$$

$$\cos[\varphi_3(t)]\ddot{\varphi}_3(t), \sin[\varphi_3(t)]\ddot{\varphi}_2(t),$$

TABLE VI. Basis Functions for the Robot Modeling Problem

$f_1 = \ddot{\varphi}_1$ $\qquad\qquad$ $f_{15} = \sin(2\varphi_2)\dot{\varphi}_1\dot{\varphi}_1$

$f_2 = \ddot{\varphi}_2$ $\qquad\qquad$ $f_{16} = \sin(\varphi_2)\dot{\varphi}_2\dot{\varphi}_1$

$f_3 = \ddot{\varphi}_3$ $\qquad\qquad$ $f_{17} = \cos(\varphi_2+\varphi_3)\sin(\varphi_2)\dot{\varphi}_1\dot{\varphi}_1$

$f_4 = \sin(\varphi_2+\varphi_3)^2\ddot{\varphi}_1$ $\qquad\qquad$ $f_{18} = \cos(\varphi_3)\ddot{\varphi}_2$

$f_5 = \sin(\varphi_2+\varphi_3)\sin(\varphi_2)\ddot{\varphi}_1$ $\qquad\qquad$ $f_{19} = \cos(\varphi_3)\ddot{\varphi}_3$

$f_6 = \cos(\varphi_2)\ddot{\varphi}_2$ $\qquad\qquad$ $f_{20} = \sin(\varphi_3)\dot{\varphi}_2\dot{\varphi}_3$

$f_7 = \sin(\varphi_2)^2\ddot{\varphi}_1$ $\qquad\qquad$ $f_{21} = \sin(\varphi_3)\dot{\varphi}_3\dot{\varphi}_3$

$f_8 = \sin(2\varphi_2+2\varphi_3)\dot{\varphi}_1\dot{\varphi}_2$ $\qquad\qquad$ $f_{22} = \sin(\varphi_3)\dot{\varphi}_2\dot{\varphi}_2$

$f_9 = \sin(2\varphi_2)\dot{\varphi}_1\dot{\varphi}_2$ $\qquad\qquad$ $f_{23} = \sin(\varphi_2)$

$f_{10} = \sin(2\varphi_2+2\varphi_3)\dot{\varphi}_1\dot{\varphi}_3$ $\qquad\qquad$ $f_{24} = \sin(\varphi_2+\varphi_3)$

$f_{11} = \cos(\varphi_2+\varphi_3)\sin(\varphi_2)\dot{\varphi}_1\dot{\varphi}_3$ $\qquad\qquad$ $f_{25} = \sin(\varphi_2)\dot{\varphi}_3\dot{\varphi}_3$

$f_{12} = \sin(\varphi_2)\dot{\varphi}_2\dot{\varphi}_2$ $\qquad\qquad$ $f_{26} = \cos(\varphi_2\varphi_3)\sin(\varphi_2)\dot{\varphi}_1\dot{\varphi}_1$

$f_{13} = \cos(\varphi_2)\ddot{\varphi}_1$ $\qquad\qquad$ $f_{27} = \sin(\varphi_2)\dot{\varphi}_2\dot{\varphi}_3$

$f_{14} = \sin(2\varphi_2+2\varphi_3)\dot{\varphi}_1\dot{\varphi}_1$

TABLE VII. Modeling Results for the GCA Robot

Model basis	Normalized error, %
f_{23}	83.0
f_{23}, f_1	9.6
f_{23}, f_1, f_{15}	4.3
$f_{23}, f_1, f_{15}, f_{12}$	1.5
$f_{23}, f_1, f_{15}, f_{12}, f_6$	1.0
$f_{23}, f_1, f_{15}, f_{12}, f_6, f_{24}$	0.29
$f_{23}, f_1, f_{15}, f_{12}, f_6, f_{24}, f_4$	0.058
$f_{23}, f_1, f_{15}, f_{12}, f_6, f_{24}, f_4, f_{19}$	0.016
$f_{23}, f_1, f_{15}, f_{12}, f_6, f_{24}, f_4, f_{19}, f_{18}$	0.004
$f_{23}, f_1, f_{15}, f_{12}, f_6, f_{24}, f_4, f_{19}, f_{18}, f_9$	1.2×10^{-10}

$$\sin[\varphi_3(t)]\dot{\varphi}_2(t)\dot{\varphi}_3(t),\ \sin[\varphi_3(t)]\dot{\varphi}_3^2(t) \Big\} . \tag{55}$$

We can use this simple case to illustrate the basic approach to the modeling problem. The algorithm assumes that a set of input torques, $T(i)$, $i = 1, 2, \ldots, L$, have been selected to drive the manipulator. These can be obtained from a stabilizing controller. The torques play the role of $Z(i)$ in Algorithm III. So the error which we seek to minimize is given by (42) and (43), where the torques are assumed proportional to the joint currents. The joint angle information is used to sample the basis functions in B in order to generate the necessary projection matrices. The success of the method for the general robot modeling problem is linked to the establishment of a general basis set, B.

A basis set for a three-degree-of-freedom robot can be obtained from Lagrangian dynamics. The elements of the set are shown in Table VI. This set was used with the projection algorithm to identify models for two-degree-of-freedom arms in both the horizontal and vertical configurations. In each case, the proper subset was selected and the corresponding model parameters were obtained by solving the triangularized linear equations.

Next, the same library was used on the outer three degrees of freedom of the GCA/DK P300V arm shown in Fig. 4. Table VII shows the models and the corresponding normalized error. It can be seen that the error declines very rapidly as the number of terms included in the model increases. Therefore, we can select a simplified model for this complex nonlinear system as well.

It has been known for quite some time that not all of the terms in the manipulator model are significant (from a magnitude point of view). Some terms dominate during fast motions of the manipulator and then are insignificant during slow motions. The projection algorithm approach has been used to sort out the important terms in a study of the dominant dynamics of robot manipulators [22].

VI. MODELING OF NONLINEAR DISCRETE-TIME SYSTEMS FROM INPUT–OUTPUT DATA

In this section we remove the luxury of having state information available and restrict future algorithms to use only data from the input and output. Now the modeling problem requires us to find a state-space model using exclusively the input and output data of the nonlinear system. This appears to hit the limitations of the projection methods and forces us to consider a new approach [23] to this important modeling problem.

A.   RECENT TRENDS AND FUTURE DIRECTIONS

In the usual description of the input–output characteristics of a nonlinear system is the discrete Volterra series [24]. The main disadvantage of the Volterra series is the large number of parameters in the Volterra kernel.

In our approach, we fit a polynomial difference equation to the input–output data. It has the form

$$z(i) = p\big(z(i-1), \ldots, z(i-s), u(i-1), \ldots, u(i-s)\big). \tag{56}$$

The rationale behind the choice of this model is the fact that the output contains a great deal of information about the state of the system. It turns out that a simpler model can be obtained by using this description, rather than a full Volterra series. Models of this type are called NARMA (nonlinear autoregressive moving average).

It has been shown that the coefficients in (56) can be used to generate a behavior matrix [23]. This matrix is then used in a state affine realization algorithm that produces the desired state-space model directly from the difference equation without the intermediate step of determining a complete Volterra series description. As a byproduct, we obtain a new method for the determination of the

Volterra kernels of the system. This method requires the estimation of very few parameters, which allows the use of smaller data sets.

B.   DESCRIPTION OF THE MODELING ALGORITHM

Let the input/output (I/O) map of the system be designated as f. The algorithm proceeds as follows:

Step 1. Identify a polynomial regression-type difference equation that approximates the given I/O data. The response map corresponding to this description is denoted by h.

Step 2. The behavior matrix, B(f), of the system is approximated by B(h), the behavior matrix of h. The elements of B(h) are obtained from the coefficients of the difference equation [23].

Step 3. In this step we construct a state affine realization [25]. Since the rank of B(h) is unknown, this algorithm starts with a submatrix Φ_n of rank n = 1, and produces an approximate partial realization of dimension 1. The I/O behavior of this realization is compared to the original data. Then we search for a submatrix Φ_{n+1} with rank n + 1. The process is iterated until the I/O data are well approximated, or until a maximum dimension is obtained.

The algorithm generates a sequence of state affine models of increasing dimension.

The problem of determining the rank of B(f) is very sensitive to numerical inaccuracies. Therefore, a very stable algorithm has to be used. We used a recursive algorithm developed by de Jong [26].

C.   APPLICATIONS

The proposed method has been used to obtain a state-space model of a reheater of a thermal power plant [23].

In a second application, a biological system was modeled. Specifically, a dog was subjected to a treatment in which a drug (Nitropruside) was infused into the dog's blood to control the dog's blood pressure.

The input function in this set of input–output data is the drug infusion rate in ml/h. The output is the mean arterial pressure of the dog measured in mm Hg.

We used the resulting set of input–output data pairs to obtain a state-space model of this system.

First, a polynomial difference equation was obtained from the input–output data:

$$z(i) = 0.712z(i-1) + 0.084z(i-2) + 0.055z(i-3)$$
$$+ 0.019u(i-1) - 0.118u(i-2) - 0.0003u(i-3)$$

$+ 0.014z(i - 1)^2 + 0.018z(i - 1)z(i - 2)$
$- 0.066z(i - 1)z(i - 3) + 0.011z(i - 2)^2$
$+ 0.007z(i - 2)z(i - 3) - 0.003z(i - 3)^2$
$- 0.014u(i - 1)z(i - 1) + 0.007u(i - 1)z(i - 2)$
$- 0.022u(i - 1)z(i - 3) - 0.009u(i - 2)z(i - 1)$
$- 0.002u(i - 2)z(i - 3) + 0.018u(i - 3)z(i - 1)$
$- 0.021u(i - 3)z(i - 2) - 0.001u(i - 3)z(i - 3)$
$+ 0.001u(i - 1)^2 - 0.002u(i - 1)u(i - 3)$
$- 0.003u(i - 2)^2 + 0.002u(i - 2)u(i - 3).$

From this difference equation, the modeling algorithm computed the following state-space model:

$$x(i + 1) = \left[F_0 + u(i)F_1 + u(i)^2 F_2 \right] x(i)$$

$$+ u(i)G_1 + u(i)^2 G_2$$

$$y(i) = \left[H_0 + u(i)H_1 \right] x(i),$$

where

$$F_0 = \begin{bmatrix} 0.8088 & 1.0 & 0.3614 \\ 0.0857 & 0.0 & -0.296 \\ -0.1692 & 0.0 & 0.0898 \end{bmatrix}$$

$$F_1 = \begin{bmatrix} 0.0247 & -0.0241 & 0.0049 \\ 0.0105 & 0.0053 & 0.004 \\ -0.0055 & -0.0025 & -0.0012 \end{bmatrix}$$

$$F_2 = \begin{bmatrix} 0.0002 & 0.0001 & 0.0 \\ -0.0002 & 0.0002 & 0.0 \\ -0.0002 & 0.0001 & 0.0 \end{bmatrix}$$

$$G_1 = \begin{bmatrix} 0 & 1 & 0 \end{bmatrix}^T$$

$$G_2 = \begin{bmatrix} 0.0151 & -0.0289 & 0.0085 \end{bmatrix}^T$$

$$H_0 = \begin{bmatrix} -0.1024 & 0.019 & -0.0539 \end{bmatrix}^T$$

$$H_1 = \begin{bmatrix} -0.0031 & -0.002 & -0.0004 \end{bmatrix}^T$$

The simulated response of this model was in very good agreement for the input sequence given [27].

ACKNOWLEDGMENTS

The author wishes to thank Robert Al-Jaar, Hernando Diaz, Soleyman Mohseni, Michael Pavol, Attila Sakarcan, and Christopher Seaman for their many contributions to the theory and applications contained in this article. Portions of this work were supported by the National Aeronautics and Space Administration and the National Science Foundation.

REFERENCES

1. J. S. FARLOW, "Self-Organizing Methods in Modeling, GMDH-Type Algorithms." Dekker, New York, 1984.
2. A. A. DESROCHERS and R. Y. AL-JAAR, A method for high-order linear system reduction and nonlinear system simplification. *Automatica* **21**, 93–100 (1985).
3. A. A. DESROCHERS and S. MOHSENI, On determining the structure of a nonlinear system. *Int. J. Control* **40**(5), 923–938 (1984).
4. A. A. DESROCHERS and M. J. PAVOL, A projection algorithm for model reduction. *Proc. Am. Control Conf., 1986*, 1578–1583 (1986).
5. A. A. DESROCHERS and G. N. SARIDIS, A model reduction technique for nonlinear systems. *Automatica* **16**, 323–329 (1980).
6. A. A. DESROCHERS, A general technique for process modeling. *J. Manuf. Syst.* **4**(2), 195–196 (1985).
7. G. F. BRYANT, I. G. CUMMING, W. J. EDWARDS, and J. H. WESTCOTT, Research in tandem mill automation. *J. Iron Steel Inst.* **209**, 869–875 (1971).
8. D. J. ROY, Present and future trends in hot strip mill computer control. *J. Iron Steel Inst.* **207**, 907–915 (1969).
9. SANDMARK, Comparison of different formulae for the calculation of force in hot rolling mills. *Scand. J. Metall.* **1**, 313–318 (1972).
10. E. J. DAVISON, A method for simplifying linear dynamic systems. *IEEE Trans. Autom. Control* **AC-11**, 93–101 (1966).
11. C. F. CHEN and L. S. SHIEH, A novel approach to linear model simplification. *Int. J. Control* **8**, 561–570 (1968).

12. Y. SHAMASH, Stable reduced-order models using Pade-type approximations. *IEEE Trans. Autom. Control* **AC-19**, 615–616 (1974).

13. Y. SHAMASH, Linear system reduction using Pade approximation to allow retention of dominant modes. *Int. J. Control* **21**, 257–272.

14. M. F. HUTTON and B. FRIEDLAND, Routh approximations for reducing order of linear time-invariant systems. *IEEE Trans. Autom. Control* **AC-20**, 329–337 (1975).

15. T. N. LUCAS and A. M. DAVIDSON, Frequency domain reduction of linear systems using Schwarz approximation. *Int. J. Control* **37**, 1167–1178 (1983).

16. T. C. HSIA, On the simplification of linear systems. *IEEE Trans. Autom. Control* **AC-17**, 272–274 (1972).

17. M. J. PAVOL, A projection algorithm for reduced-order modeling. M.S. Thesis, Rensselaer Polytechnic Institute, Troy, New York (1985).

18. A. A. DESROCHERS, On an improved model reduction technique for nonlinear systems. *Automatica* **17**(2), 407–409 (1981).

19. W. L. GARRARD and J. M. JORDAN, Design of nonlinear automatic flight control systems. *Automatica* **13**, 497–505 (1977).

20. A. A. DESROCHERS and R. Y. AL-JAAR, Nonlinear model simplification in flight control system design. *J. Guidance, Control, Dyn.* **7**(6), 684–689 (1984).

21. J. Y. S. LUH, An anatomy of industrial robots and their controls. *IEEE Trans. Autom. Control*, pp. 133–153 (1983).

22. A. A. DESROCHERS and C. S. SEAMAN, A projection algorithm for simplifying robot manipulator models. *Proc. IEEE Conf. Robot. Autom., 1986*, pp. 504–509 (1986).

23. H. DIAZ and A. A. DESROCHERS, Modeling of nonlinear discrete-time systems from input–output data. *Proc. World Congr. Int. Fed. Autom. Control, 10th, 1987.*

24. A. SCHETZEN, "The Volterra and Wiener Theories of Nonlinear Systems." Wiley, New York, 1980.

25. E. SONTAG, Realization theory of discrete-time nonlinear systems: The bounded case. *IEEE Trans. Circuits Syst.* **CAS-26**, 342–356 (1979).

26. L. S. DE JONG, Numerical aspects of recursive realization algorithms. *SIAM J. Control Optim.* **16**, 646–659 (1978).

27. H. DIAZ, Modeling of nonlinear systems from input–output data. Ph.D. Thesis, Rensselaer Polytechnic Institute, Troy, New York (1986).

INDEX

of maneuvering targets, algorithms for, 261–300
performance, 283–284
proper design, 267
time-dependent processor, 282
use of term, 267
nonimage-based, 279–281
performance, 284–286
time-dependent processor, 282–283
orientation information in prediction, 291–294
example, 298–300
target model and prediction algorithm, 294–298
target tracking problem, 271
Two-point boundary-value problem, 80

U

Unbiasedness property, 33
Uncertainties
control design under stochastic indeterminacy and, 21

in eigenvalues and eigenvectors, 15
management in modeling and control of large-space structures, 19
in modeling and control, 2
modeling of, in linear quadratic Gaussian systems, 5–6
occurrence and management in LFSS, 19–21
stochastic nature of modeling under, 4

V

Vector Lagrangian function, 160, 165
Vector Lagrangian problem, 161
Vector optimization problem, constrained, conversion to unconstrained problem, 160
Vibrational modes, of LFSS, 21–22

W

Whitening procedures, 80